C0-AZU-212

SCHIZOPHRENIA

This is a volume in
PERSONALITY, PSYCHOPATHOLOGY, AND PSYCHOTHERAPY
A Series of Monographs, Texts, and Treatises

Under the Editorship of David T. Lykken and Philip C. Kendall

SCHIZOPHRENIA

A Life-Course Developmental Perspective

Edited by

Elaine F. Walker

Department of Psychology
Emory University
Atlanta, Georgia

ACADEMIC PRESS, INC.
Harcourt Brace Jovanovich, Publishers
San Diego   New York   Boston   London   Sydney   Tokyo   Toronto

This book is printed on acid-free paper. ∞

Copyright © 1991 by ACADEMIC PRESS, INC.
All Rights Reserved.
No part of this publication may be reproduced or transmitted in any
form or by any means, electronic or mechanical, including photo-
copy, recording, or any information storage and retrieval system,
without permission in writing from the publisher.

Academic Press, Inc.
San Diego, California 92101

United Kingdom Edition published by
Academic Press Limited
24–28 Oval Road, London NW1 7DX

Library of Congress Cataloging-in-Publication Data

Schizophrenia : a life-course developmental perspective / [edited by]
    Elaine F. Walker.
        p.   cm. -- (Personality, psychopathology, and psychotherapy
    series)
    Includes index.
    ISBN 0-12-732080-6
    1. Schizophrenia--Etiology..   2. Developmental psychology.
    I. Walker, Elaine F.   II. Series: Personality, psychopathology, and
    psychotherapy.
    [DNLM: 1. Schizophrenia--etiology.   WM 203 S337234]
    RC514.S3342   1991
    616.89'82071--dc20
    DNLM/DLC
    for Library of Congress   91-4588
                                                              CIP

PRINTED IN THE UNITED STATES OF AMERICA
91 92 93 94   9 8 7 6 5 4 3 2 1

Contents

Part II CHILDHOOD AND ADOLESCENCE

Part III ADULTHOOD: THE ONSET AND COURSE OF CLINICAL SYMPTOMS

Part IV   DEVELOPMENTAL CONCEPTUALIZATIONS OF SCHIZOPHRENIA

14 Developmental Trajectories in Schizophrenia: Elucidating the
    Divergent Pathways
    Elaine F. Walker, Dana M. Davis, Lisa A. Gottlieb, and Jay A. Weinstein

Contributors

Numbers in parentheses indicate the pages on which the authors' contributions begin.

Joan Rosenbaum Asarnow (95), Department of Psychiatry, Neuropsychiatric Institute, School of Medicine, University of California, Los Angeles, Los Angeles, California 90024

Robert F. Asarnow (95), Department of Psychiatry, Neuropsychiatric Institute, School of Medicine, University of California, Los Angeles, Los Angeles, California 90024

Christopher E. Barr (9), Social Science Research Institute, University of Southern California, Los Angeles, California 90089

Tyrone D. Cannon (9), Social Science Research Institute, University of Southern California, Los Angeles, California 90089

Barbara A. Cornblatt (123), Elmhurst General Hospital, and Mount Sinai School of Medicine, New York, New York 10032

Dana M. Davis (299), Department of Psychology, Emory University, Atlanta, Georgia 30322

Jeri A. Doane (213), Yale University School of Medicine, New Haven, Connecticut 06520

L. Erlenmeyer-Kimling (123), New York State Psychiatric Institute, and Columbia University College of Physicians and Surgeons, New York, New York 10032

Sherryl H. Goodman (59), Department of Psychology, Emory University, Atlanta, Georgia 30322

Lisa A. Gottlieb (299), Department of Psychology, Emory University, Atlanta, Georgia 30322

Sydney L. Hans (33), Department of Psychiatry, University of Chicago, Chicago, Illinois 60637

Courtenay M. Harding (257), University of Colorado School of Medicine, University of Colorado Health Sciences Center, Denver, Colorado 80262

Philip D. Harvey (139), Department of Psychiatry, Mount Sinai School of Medicine, New York, New York 10029

Nancy Hornstein (95), Department of Psychiatry, Neuropsychiatric Institute, School of Medicine, University of California, Los Angeles, Los Angeles, California 90024

Richard R. J. Lewine (195), Department of Psychiatry, Emory University School of Medicine, Atlanta, Georgia 30322

Joseph Marcus (33), Deparment of Psychiatry, University of Chicago, Chicago, Illinois 60637

Sarnoff A. Mednick (9), Social Science Research Institute, University of Southern California, Los Angles, California 90089

Michael F. Pogue-Geile (277), Department of Psychology and Department of Psychiatry, University of Pittsburgh, Pittsburgh, Pennsylvania 15260

Andrew Russell (95), Department of Psychiatry, Neuropsychiatric Institute, School of Medicine, University of California, Los Angeles, Los Angeles, California 90024

Christopher Saiz (157), Department of Psychology, University of Denver, Englewood, Colorado 80111

Elaine F. Walker (1, 299), Department of Psychology, Emory University, Atlanta, Georgia 30322

Norman F. Watt (157), Department of Psychology, University of Denver, Englewood, Colorado 80111

Jay A. Weinstein (299), Department of Psychology, Emory University, Atlanta, Georgia 30322

Lynn Winters (123), State University of New York at Purchase, and New York State Psychiatric Institute, New York, New York 10032

R. Yassa (243), Department of Psychiatry, McGill University, and Douglas Hospital, Verdun, Quebec, Canada H4H 1R3

Preface

The chief aim of this volume is to draw together research findings and ideas concerning the entire life course of schizophrenia. The developmental focus represented by this volume has expanded in recent years and now constitutes a significant force in psychopathology research. The chapters discuss data spanning from infancy to old age, and some of the authors report links between characterstics and/or events separated by decades in the individual's life span. Clearly, we have made progress in our efforts to elucidate the developmental course of schizophrenia, although many tasks lie ahead of us.

It is not uncommon to hear disparaging comments regarding the lack of progress in research on schizophrenia. Many believe that an enormous amount of effort has been expended and that a voluminous literature has evolved with relatively little payoff in the way of reliable findings. Although it may be true that no one finding has constituted a "major breakthrough," investigators have been slowly, but steadily, fitting together the myriad of pieces that comprise the puzzle of schizophrenia. Each replicable finding that is added represents a small step toward the identification of etiologic mechanisms.

Significant progress has also been achieved in the areas of conceptualization and methodology. Researchers have become increasingly sensitive to the likely etiologic complexity of the schizophrenic syndrome. The accumulated data base suggests that there are multiple contributing factors to vulnerability, and this compels us to reject all previous theories and models that posited a unitary etiologic agent, be it genetic or environmental, and to eliminate from consideration the notion that there is a uniform premorbid or postmorbid course. For the sake of linguistic convenience, many writers in the field, including myself, often use the singular term "schizophrenia"; however, most assume the existence of multiple schizophrenias with differing etiologic determinants.

As our conceptualizations have become more complex, the sophistication of our methodologies has concomitantly grown. A perusal of the literature indicates that multivariate, multimodal studies are more common now than in the past. Many studies simultaneously examine biological, cognitive, and phenomenological aspects of patients. Moreover, longitudinal designs are more apparent. Researchers are relating antecedent variables to various aspects of clinical outcome, as well as exploring the longitudinal features of the clinical symptoms.

Schizophrenia undoubtedly is a disorder that presents formidable challenges to researchers; however, it is not unique in this respect. Tremendous investigative resources have been devoted to many physical illnesses (e.g., cancer) with relatively modest progress. Given that the resources devoted to research on schizophrenia pale in comparison to those allocated for many other debilitating illnesses, we should not be disheartened by the modest advances we have made in understanding the nature and origins of this disorder. Instead, we should acknowledge the likely complexity of the investigative tasks ahead, and confront these tasks with the awareness that we must be prepared to gain gratification from the modest incremental gains in knowledge we are likely to achieve.

This volume features the work of a talented group of researchers. They are distinguished by a broad base of knowledge in the biological and psychological mechanisms that subserve behavioral development. All of them have devoted their careers to the study of psychopathology, in part because they possess the determination and tolerance for ambiguity that this endeavor requires. I have no doubt that the work featured in this volume will be followed by further creative research from these investigators.

Special appreciation is extended to the contributors to this volume. They are excellent colleagues who make participation in this research enterprise more fulfilling. The completion of this volume is also due to the efforts of the research assistants and graduate students who work in my laboratory. Dana Davis, Lisa Gottlieb, Kathleen Grimes, Lauren Hill, and Jay Weinstein contributed substantively to the completion of this project. In particular, Dana Davis devoted many hours to the editing and preparation of the manuscripts for publication.

Elaine F. Walker

Research on Life-Span Development in Schizophrenia

Elaine F. Walker

Schizophrenia is a disorder that has posed a tremendous challenge to investigators. The clinical symptoms of the disorder are often so pervasive and debilitating that the patient is unable to function occupationally and interpersonally. Yet the symptoms, which typically have their onset in early adulthood, are often preceded by a developmental history that was perceived as unremarkable by the parents. The emergence of such pervasive impairment, against a background of apparent normalcy, baffles family members and challenges the conceptual abilities of investigators.

But the unremarkable developmental course preceding the onset of schizophrenic symptoms may be more apparent than real. Gradually accumulating evidence indicates that behavioral abnormalities are present long before psychiatric symptoms are manifested. Moreover, it is becoming increasingly apparent that the course of schizophrenia is highly variable and that a chronic, deteriorating course represents only one of several pathways. This volume documents our expanding knowledge of the life-span developmental course of schizophrenia, from signs of vulnerability in infancy to geriatric outcomes.

Most would agree that the literature abounds with comparative, cross-sectional studies of the cognitive, affective, interpersonal, neurological,

1

Copyright © 1991 by Academic Press, Inc.
All rights of reproduction in any form reserved.

and biochemical aspects of schizophrenic disorders. Also, within the past two decades, intensive effort has been directed at reliably specifying the clinical symptoms and diagnostic boundaries of schizophrenia. But commensurate effort has not been directed at elucidating the developmental features of the illness. Compared with cross-sectional studies, systematic longitudinal investigations of schizophrenia have been relatively rare. Consequently, although we can speak with some degree of precision about the phenotypic adult outcome labeled "schizophrenia," we are just beginning to build a data base on the precursors and long-term outcome.

The importance of expanding our data base on the life span of patients with schizophrenia is becoming increasingly apparent. First, as illustrated by the chapters in this volume, the results of research on genetic factors, obstetrical complications, and morphological brain abnormalities indicate that constitutional vulnerability is congenital for many patients. Because the emergence of clinical symptoms probably *does not* mark the onset of the neuropathological process, documenting the developmental trajectories leading to schizophrenia takes on greater importance.

Second, as part of the evolution of neuroscience, investigators have shed new light on neurodevelopment (e.g., Goldman-Rakic, 1987; Nowakowski, 1987). Research findings in this field have altered conceptual frameworks for understanding the interplay between neural and behavioral development. For example, we now have animal models of neuroanatomical impairments that are relatively age-specific in their effects on behavior. Lesions in some structures have relatively little impact on the behavior of the immature animal but dramatically alter adult behavior. Other neuroanatomical lesions disrupt early behavior but are "silent" in adulthood. Furthermore, a singular lesion or biochemical challenge can influence different functional domains, depending on the organism's developmental stage. Clearly, neurodevelopment is a complex process that involves simultaneous anatomical and physiological changes that have implications for the behavioral capacities of the organism. The elucidation of the behavioral sequelae of specific neural lesions or pathology requires a developmental approach. And, conversely, attempts to elucidate a neuropathological process are likely to benefit from a developmental approach to the study of manifest behavior.

Finally, the results of numerous investigations force us to contend with the probability that schizophrenia is heterogeneous in etiology. Most notably, recent applications of sophisticated molecular genetic techniques fail to yield replicable findings, indicating that there is *not* a unitary genetic liability for schizophrenia (Owen *et al.*, 1990). In current usage, then, the term "schizophrenia" refers to a syndrome, not to a specific disease.

As Dalen and Hays (1990) point out, the assumption of heterogeneity dictates our approach to research. Cross-sectional comparisons of schizophrenic patients with control groups of normals, or other patients, implies the assumption that schizophrenia is a single disease. In contrast, the elucidation of heterogeneous etiologies requires the careful study of differences *among* schizophrenic patients. This includes differences in putative etiologic factors, premorbid course, and postmorbid course, as well as current status. In other words, cross-sectional studies focusing on within-group differences in symptoms, brain morphology, biochemistry, or cognitive performance are necessary but unlikely to be sufficient. In addition, we must extend our study of heterogeneity backward and forward in time. This will enable us to describe heterogeneity from a longitudinal standpoint, thus increasing our opportunities for identifying etiologic subtypes.

The application of developmental approaches to the study of psychopathology is receiving greater attention from investigators in the field (Cicchetti, 1984). By charting the developmental courses associated with schizophrenia, we will be in a better position to speculate on the neuropathology subserving the disorder. The temporal characteristics of the cognitive, interpersonal, and motor abnormalities shown by patients across the life span are especially important. From a biological standpoint, temporal factors are important because the development of the central nervous system is characterized by changes in the functional ascendance of various structures and systems that subserve behavior. For example, motor dysfunction with an onset in infancy suggests a different neuropathological process from motor dysfunction that first appears in adulthood. Temporal aspects are also of critical relevance to the elucidation of interactional process. The dominant etiologic models of schizophrenia, such as the diathesis-stress and vulnerability models, posit an interactional process in which exogenous stressors trigger behavioral dysfunction in constitutionally vulnerable individuals. By examining the convergence between environmental events and the developmental course, we can better understand the nature of such interactions.

IMPEDIMENTS TO THE STUDY OF THE LIFE COURSE OF SCHIZOPHRENIA

Given the many potential benefits of a developmental approach to research on schizophrenia, we are left with the question of why there has been a relative dearth of investigations of this type. Specifically, why has so much of the literature on schizophrenia concerned itself with various behavioral and biological aspects of samples of young and middle-aged adult patients, while relatively little attention has been focused on earlier and later points in the life span of patients? Undoubtedly, methodological problems are a major part of the answer.

Because schizophrenia has a population base rate of about 1% and is typically diagnosed in early adulthood, the collection of premorbid data, particularly data on early childhood, is procedurally difficult. Furthermore, the collection and analysis of such data requires a great deal of time as well as methodological and statistical sophistication. Those who possess the greatest expertise with longitudinal methodology, namely, developmental psychologists, have traditionally focused their attention on normal development. Only recently has the field of developmental psychopathology gained broad recognition as a subdiscipline. Researchers in this field view psychopathology as the manifestation of a deviant developmental process, and some argue for a reconceptualization of certain mental illnesses as "disorders of development" (Sroufe and Rutter, 1984).

A somewhat different set of problems is associated with the study of development after the onset of clinical symptoms. Because most patients experience a variety of treatments, the illness rarely runs its "natural" developmental course. Differentiating the longitudinal features of the illness from epiphenomena produced by treatment is a difficult task. Further complicating the study of illness progression is the fact that many of the disorders associated with aging, particularly the dementias, involve cognitive and motoric symptoms that could be easily confused with symptoms of schizophrenia. The problems of epiphenomena and geriatric disorders have undoubtedly contributed to the preference for cross-sectional studies of young, recently diagnosed patients.

Despite the methodological problems inherent in research on the precursors and progression of schizophrenic illnesses, some investigators have persevered in their efforts to chart the longitudinal course of the disorder. As a result, the data base upon which we can begin to build a developmental framework is now substantive. This volume is testimony to the progress that has been achieved in illuminating important relations among events and characteristics that are separated in time.

METHODOLOGICAL APPROACHES TO LONGITUDINAL RESEARCH ON SCHIZOPHRENIA

The research findings presented in this volume emanate from a variety of methodological approaches, including prospective, follow-back, and follow-up methods. When applied to the study of precursors of schizophrenia, these approaches differ with respect to the populations they sample. Consequently, each offers a unique perspective on the development of schizophrenia. By identifying convergent and divergent findings across methods, a clearer picture may emerge.

Prospective high-risk research, for example, has typically focused on offspring of schizophrenic parents (Watt et al., 1984). The high-risk subjects who eventually manifest schizophrenia constitute a unique subgroup of patients for two reasons. First, unlike the majority of patients, they have a biological parent with the disorder. They may, therefore, constitute a subgroup with a particularly virulent or distinct genetic predisposition. Second, they experience a caretaker with a severe psychiatric illness that undoubtedly has implications for the quality of the child-rearing environment. Consequently, high-risk subjects are likely to experience a high degree of psychosocial stress. In sum, there is reason to expect that the patients who emerge from high-risk samples will be unique with respect to both genetic and environmental factors.

The prospective nature of high-risk research makes it possible for investigators to collect extensive data on subjects, and these data can span a broad period, sometimes beginning in infancy. On the other hand, the lengthy period of time between the initiation of most high-risk studies and the ascertainment of adult psychiatric outcome can pose the problem of subject attrition. But despite this problem, high-risk research has already contributed substantively to our knowledge of developmental precursors of schizophrenia.

Follow-up studies of precursors of schizophrenia typically focus on a subgroup of patients with the poorest premorbid histories. Many follow-up studies examine the adult psychiatric outcomes of clinic-referred children. Thus, these investigations will inform us about the nature of the childhood clinical syndromes or behavior problems most likely to be manifested by preschizophrenics. As is the case with high-risk subjects, these patients constitute a unique subgroup in that the majority of adult schizophrenic patients have no history of childhood clinical disorder.

Follow-back studies begin by identifying a sample based on adult psychiatric outcome. Precursors are then examined by using medical or academic records. Of all the approaches used to study precursors, the follow-back method is the one most likely to sample a representative cross-section of patients. This method will, therefore, yield information on the full spectrum of premorbid courses, from above-average functioning to severe impairment.

When applied to research on the course of schizophrenia, the above methods do not necessarily yield different subgroups of patients. However, subject attrition can alter sample characteristics in prospective studies of illness outcome. This problem is especially salient in studies aimed at determining long-term prognosis. Patients who are not located for follow-up may be characterized by higher rates of remission or by the poorest outcomes. Investigators who have conducted such research have devoted considerable energy to the ascertainment of outcome for all subjects in their samples. As Courtenay Harding illustrates in Chapter 12 of this volume, many have been successful. Their findings have clearly demonstrated that outcomes are highly variable, with a substantial number of patients showing remission.

Some investigators, including several whose work is featured in this volume, combine the above approaches in their research. For example, the Danish high-risk project, discussed by Cannon, Barr, and Mednick in Chapter 2, combines follow-back and prospective methods in the study of high-risk subjects. Ultimately, such multimethod studies may hold the greatest promise for research progress.

SUMMARY

There is reason to anticipate a paradigm shift in research on schizophrenia. As the complexities of both normal human development and schizophrenia have become more apparent, so has the need for a developmental approach in our research. We must embark on the task of systematically documenting the developmental pathways manifested by patients and then relate these with potential etiologic agents.

At the same time, we would be well advised to explore the role of moderating factors that may serve to alter the trajectories manifested by vulnerable individuals. As Richard Lewine points out in Chapter 9 of this volume, gender is a particularly salient correlate of the course of schizophrenia, and sex differences may hold important clues to etiology. Similarly, the moderating influences of contextual factors, including the family milieu, must be examined.

REFERENCES

Cicchetti, D. (1984). The emergence of developmental psychopathology. *Child Development, 55,* 1–7.

Dalen, P., and Hays, P. (1990). Aetiological heterogeneity of schizophrenia: The problem and evidence. *British Journal of Psychiatry, 157,* 119–122.

Goldman-Rakic, P. S. (1987). Development of cortical circuitry and cognitive function. *Child Development, 58,* 601–622.

Nowakowski, R. S. (1987). Basic concepts of CNS development. *Child Development, 58,* 568–595.

Owen, M., Craufurd, D., and St. Clair, D. (1990). Localization of a susceptibility locus for schizophrenia on chromosome 5. *British Journal of Psychiatry, 157,* 123–127.

Sroufe, A. L., and Rutter, M. (1984). The domain of developmental psychopathology. *Child Development, 55,* 17–29.

Watt, N., Anthony, E. J., Wynne, L., and Rolf, R. (Eds.), (1984). *Children at risk for schizophrenia.* New York: Cambridge.

PART I

Perinatal Factors and Infancy

OVERVIEW

Despite the fact that the disordered behavior we label "schizophrenia" does not typically emerge until young adulthood, our search for its origins apparently must extend back to the very beginnings of life. The first chapter in this section, by Cannon, Barr, and Mednick, indicates that prenatal and perinatal events are linked with symptom characteristics in adulthood. In the second chapter, Hans and Marcus present strong evidence for neuromotor deficits in high-risk children, suggesting that the neuropathology subserving schizophrenia can be functionally manifested in the infant's motor behaviors. The data presented in the chapter by Goodman indicate that socioemotional signs of dysfunction in infancy may also predate the emergence of schizophrenia later in life.

Together, the chapters in this section provide strong support for the notion that, at least for some patients, vulnerability to schizophrenia is manifested as early as the first year of life. Moreover, Cannon, Barr, and Mednick demonstrate that variability among adult patients in clinical symptomatology is associated with variability in exposure to perinatal insult to the central nervous system. Clearly, investigative efforts aimed at elucidating the pathways leading to schizophrenia must encompass the individual's entry into the life course.

7

Copyright © 1991 by Academic Press, Inc.
All rights of reproduction in any form reserved.

Genetic and Perinatal Factors in the Etiology of Schizophrenia

Tyrone D. Cannon
Christopher E. Barr
Sarnoff A. Mednick

INTRODUCTION

In our research in Scandinavia, we have been concerned with isolating genetic and environmental contributions to the etiology of schizophrenia. This research has been primarily of two types: (1) prospective, longitudinal investigations of the offspring of schizophrenic mothers [high-risk (HR) studies] and (2) studies of the incidence of schizophrenia in populations exposed to severe teratogenic agents during gestation. Based on this work and other evidence, we have developed a framework for research in schizophrenia that suggests that an important part of the genetic predisposition to schizophrenia is expressed as disruptions of fetal neural development, probably centered in the second trimester of gestation. The framework also suggests that the quality of the perinatal and early family–social environments determines the risk for overt schizophrenia and the predominant symptom pattern.

First, we outline the rationale for HR research and describe the study upon which most of the chapter is based. We then present a set of hypotheses concerning the roles of genetic and environmental factors in the

Copyright © 1991 by Academic Press, Inc.
All rights of reproduction in any form reserved.

etiology and developmental course of two clinical subtypes of schizophrenia: schizophrenia with predominantly negative symptoms and schizophrenia with predominantly positive symptoms. In the final section, we present evidence testing these hypotheses.

THE COPENHAGEN HIGH-RISK STUDY

High-Risk Design

In the 1950s, research into the etiology of schizophrenia was typically conduced by comparing schizophrenic patients with nonschizophrenic controls (Mednick and Higgins, 1960). A major difficulty of this approach is that differences between schizophrenics and controls could either be related to the causes of the disorder or be the result of the unique life experiences of the schizophrenic. It became clear that schizophrenics should be examined premorbidly, in a prospective framework, before the lifelong concomitants of their illness could obscure potential etiological agents.

The HR, prospective design is attractive for several reasons. First, the outcome yield of psychopathology is increased by selecting children of severely schizophrenic mothers. The empirical risk of schizophrenia among such individuals is 10–16%, as compared with 1% among the general population (Gottesman and Shields, 1982). Second, data on the premorbid experiences and functioning of these subjects are obtained systematically, uniformly, and prospectively and are, therefore, free of the biases of retrospective reporting or knowledge of the subjects' eventual diagnostic status. In addition, by including a low-risk (LR) control group in the design, it is possible to examine the effects of environmental etiological agents at two levels of genetic vulnerability, encouraging study of gene–environment interaction effects. A detailed statement of the rationale for HR research can be found in Mednick and McNeil (1968).

Initial Assessment (1962)

In 1962, Mednick and Schulsinger initiated a prospective, longitudinal investigation of 207 Danish children of severe, process schizophrenic mothers and 104 matched controls without a family history of mental illness (Mednick and Schulsinger, 1965, 1968). Demographic characteristics of the HR and LR groups appear in Table 2.1. The initial assessment included a skin conductance, heart rate conditioning procedure, and teacher reports on the school behavior of the subjects. In addition, the original midwife reports on the pregnancy and birth experiences of the subjects

TABLE 2.1. Sociodemographic Characteristics of the High-Risk and Low-Risk Groups

	Group	
Characteristics	High-risk	Low-risk
Number of cases	207	104
Males	121	59
Females	86	45
Mean age (in 1962)	15.1 years	15.1 years
Mean social class[a]	2.2	2.3
Mean years education	7.0	7.3
Percentage of group in children's homes (5 years or more)[b]	16	14
Mean number of years in children's homes (5 years or more)[b]	9.4	8.5
Percentage of group with rural residence[c]	26	22

[a]On a scale of 0 (low) to 6 (high).
[b]In matching the samples for amount of institutional rearing, we only considered experience in children's homes of 5 years or greater duration.
[c]Population of 2500 persons or fewer.

were located and transcribed. At the time of the initial assessment in 1962, the mean age of the subjects was 15.1 years and none were psychiatrically ill.

Five-Year Follow-Up Assessment (1967)

By 1967, 20 HR subjects had suffered some form of psychiatric breakdown (not necessarily schizophrenia). This "sick" group was matched on a variety of characteristics (including level of adjustment in 1962) to 20 well-functioning HR subjects ("well" group) and 20 well-functioning LR subjects ("control" group). Factors that differentiated the sick group from the well and control groups included a high incidence of pregnancy and delivery complications, loss of mother early in life to psychiatric hospitalization, psychophysiological lability in adolescence, and poorly controlled and disruptive school behavior (Mednick and Schulsinger, 1968).

Ten-Year Follow Up Assessment (1972)

In 1972–1974, 85% of the subjects were recontacted for diagnostic evaluations (Schulsinger, 1976). The procedure included two structured psychiatric interviews: the Present State Examination (PSE) (Wing *et al.*, 1974) and the Current and Past Psychopathology Scales (CAPPS) (Endicott and

TABLE 2.2 Frequencies of Psychiatric Diagnoses in the High-Risk Group and Low-Risk Group (in parentheses) at 10-Year Follow-Up

	Criteria					
Diagnoses	Interviewer (ICD—8)		CAPPS-DIAGNO II		CATEGO (PSE + SCL +AS)	
Schizophrenia	13[a]	(1)	30	(6)	10	(1)
Borderline states	71[b]	(5)	20	(1)	35	(3)
Psychopathy	5	(4)	2	(1)	4	(4)
Other personality disorders	26	(10)	3	(2)	22	(9)
Neuroses (symptoms and character	34	(44)	31	(16)	43	(38)
Nonspecific conditions	0	(0)	43	(17)	24	(17)
No mental illness	23	(27)	44	(47)	15	(17)
Other conditions[c]	1	(0)	0	(0)	20	(2)
Total	173	(91)	173	(91)	173	(91)

AS, Associated Symptoms; CAPPS, Current and Past Psychopathology Scales; PSE, Present State Examination; SCL, Syndrome Checklist; SPD, Schizotypal Personality Disorder.

[a]Two additional schizophrenics committed suicide before the interview period, but hospital charts clearly indicated the presence of schizophrenia (with predominantly positive symptoms).

[b]These 71 individuals include 29 borderline schizophrenics (SPD), 29 SPDs, and 13 paranoid personality disorders. Neither the CAPPS nor the PSE diagnostic systems included a category for SPD.

[c]Including affective and paranoid psychoses.

Spitzer, 1972), each of which arrived at a psychiatric diagnosis. In addition, the interviewer formed an ICD-8 (World Health Organization, 1967) clinical diagnosis on the basis of the structured interviews and a set of additional items. Table 2.2 lists the frequencies of the various psychiatric diagnoses assigned to the HR and LR groups under each set of diagnostic criteria. Thirteen HR subjects received clinical diagnoses of schizophrenia (all of these also received schizophrenia diagnoses by CAPPS and/or PSE criteria). An additional two HR subjects who had committed suicide prior to the interview period were diagnosed schizophrenic on the basis of psychiatric hospital records (for further details of the diagnostic assessment, see Schulsinger, 1976).

Computed Tomography Scan Examination (1980)

A subsample of HR subjects were examined by computed tomography (CT) scan in 1980 (Schulsinger *et al.*, 1984). The subsample included 10 subjects diagnosed (in 1972) as schizophrenic, 10 subjects with schizotypal personality disorder (SPD), and 14 subjects with no mental illness (NMI). CT scan measures of the area of the lateral ventricles; widths of the cortical sulci, interhemispheric fissure, sylvian fissures, and third ventricle; and ratings of dysgenesis of the cerebellar vermis were obtained. Some relations between the CT scan measures and other variables are described in following sections.

A RESEARCH FRAMEWORK:
GENE–ENVIRONMENT INTERACTION

By relating the premorbid data bank to the adult diagnoses and CT scan measures, we identified several precursors of schizophrenia. We summarize this work and other relevant research in the form of a research framework integrating both genetic and environmental hypotheses.

Genetic Hypothesis: Fetal Neural Development

Several lines of evidence suggested to us that disturbances of fetal neural development may be part of the genetic predisposition to schizophrenia. First, a series of neuropathology studies have demonstrated cellular abnormalities in the brains of many schizophrenics consistent with disruptions of fetal neural development (Benes and Bird, 1987; Bogerts et al., 1985; Jakob and Beckmann, 1986; Kovelman and Scheibel, 1984). In two of these studies, the abnormalities were said to be attributable to genetic or teratogenic disturbances in the second trimester of gestation (Jakob and Beckmann, 1986; Kovelman and Scheibel, 1984).

Second, in the context of a Helsinki birth cohort exposed to a severe Type A2 influenza epidemic, we examined the hypothesis that disturbances of fetal neural development are related to later schizophrenia. Individuals who were exposed to the epidemic in their second trimester of gestation evidenced a significantly elevated rate of adult schizophrenia diagnoses compared with individuals born during the 4 years preceding the epidemic. Individuals exposed to the epidemic in their first or third trimesters did not evidence an increased risk for schizophrenia. The finding seems reliable; it held for both males and females and for each of several hospitals in the greater Helsinki area (Mednick et al., 1988). Barr et al. (1990) have recently replicated these findings in Denmark.

These results suggest that disturbances of fetal brain development during critical periods of gestation are capable of increasing the risk for adult schizophrenia. We have suggested that it may be the timing of the stress, rather than the nature of the stressor itself, that is critical in determining the risk for schizophrenia (Mednick et al., 1988). Thus, teratogenic agents such as viruses may be responsible for the fetal neural disturbances leading to schizophrenia in some cases. In view of the relatively stable incidence of schizophrenia across national and generational boundaries however, genetic factors may be responsible for the fetal neural disturbances leading to schizophrenia in many or most cases. Rakic and Sidman (1978) and Nowakowski (1987) have found that genetic factors are capable of disrupting fetal neural development in laboratory animals.

To determine if the genetic predisposition to schizophrenia is related to abnormal brain development, we examined the adult CT scan records of a subsample of HR subjects in relation to their degree of genetic risk. The CT scan measures were found to form two separate factors: (1) multisite neural developmental deficits (as reflected in cerebellar dysgenesis and widening of the Sylvian and interhemispheric fissures and cortical sulci) and (2) periventricular damage (as reflected in enlargement of the third and lateral ventricles). In a stepwise multiple regression analysis it was found that the multisite developmental deficits factor was related to an elevated genetic risk for schizophrenia (i.e., schizophrenia in the mother *and* schizophrenia spectrum illness in the father), but it was not significantly related to several potential obstetric factors that we examined (Cannon *et al.*, 1989). Other work indicates that HR children evidence elevated levels of neuromotor impairments suggestive of subtle neurological insult, perhaps originating during pregnancy (Marcus *et al.*, 1985).

Based on this work, we hypothesize that the basic genetic disorder in schizophrenia is expressed as a disruption of fetal brain development. The fetal neural developmental disturbances are held to be common to all schizophrenics and schizophrenia spectrum disorders. As such, the fetal neural developmental disturbances may be responsible for some of the fundamental symptoms of schizotypy, such as eccentricity, cognitive slippage, neuromotor impairments, and poorly controlled emotional responses to stress. We should emphasize that teratogenic agents occurring during critical gestational periods may be partially capable of mimicking the action of the genetic factors.

Environmental Stress

We discuss two types of environmental etiological agents: (1) pregnancy and delivery complications and (2) instability of the early family rearing environment. Serious perinatal difficulties are more frequent in the histories of adult schizophrenics than they are in individuals with other psychiatric disorders and normal controls (for a review, see McNeil, 1988). In the Copenhagen HR project, the HR children who became schizophrenic had suffered significantly more pregnancy and delivery complications than individuals with SPD or NMI (Parnas *et al.*, 1982). The evidence of birth difficulties suggested the possibility that the HR children who became schizophrenic were those who suffered perinatal brain damage.

We tested this hypothesis by examining the ventriculomegaly scores of a subsample of HR subjects selected to include 10 schizophrenics, 10 SPDs, and 14 NMIs. As a group, the schizophrenics evidenced significantly larger third and lateral ventricles than the SPDs and NMIs (Schulsinger *et al.*, 1984). In addition, third and lateral ventricular sizes were strongly related to prospectively assessed complications of *delivery* ($r = 0.71$), but only among individuals with an elevated genetic risk for schizophrenia (i.e., schizophrenia in the mother and schizophrenia spectrum illness in the father) (Cannon *et al.*, 1989); i.e., those at especially high genetic risk evidenced greater ventricular enlargement if they suffered delivery complications. Studies using intrafamilial designs [i.e., comparisons among discordant monozygotic (MZ) twins or siblings] have found evidence supporting a joint genetic–perinatal determination of ventriculomegaly in schizophrenia (DeLisi *et al.*, 1986; Reveley *et al.*, 1982; Weinberger *et al.*, 1981); less methodologically adequate studies (i.e., those using retrospective designs and unselected patient samples) have obtained conflicting results (for a review, see Cannon, 1991).

Instability of the early family rearing environment represents the other type of environmental etiological agent associated with the development of schizophrenia in HR children. While poor parenting behaviors such as negative affective style and communication deviance appear to be predictive of schizophrenia spectrum disorders in general (Goldstein, 1987), more severe forms of family instability are uniquely predictive of schizophrenia (Beuhring *et al.*, 1982; Mednick and Schulsinger, 1968; Parnas *et al.*, 1985; Walker *et al.*, 1981; Watt and Nichols, 1979). In the Copenhagen study, the HR children who became schizophrenic had experienced significantly more separation from parents and institutional rearing than any other diagnostic subgroup (Walker *et al.*, 1981). Better outcomes were obtained by children fortunate enough to find foster placements (Parnas *et al.*, 1985). It is also important to note that there was not an increase in schizophrenic outcomes among LR subjects matched for amount of separation and institutionalization, suggesting that the level or quality of stress associated with parental absence and institutional rearing was only pathogenic among those who possess a genetic predisposition to schizophrenia.

Etiological and Phenomenological Variability

Despite the large and significant differences between schizophrenics and other HR subjects in terms of delivery complications, ventricular enlargement, and family instability, it is important to note that variance in the schizophrenic group on each of these measures is high (Cannon *et al.*,

1990). The large variance indicates that not all of the etiological factors were equally important for all schizophrenic outcomes. Our recent work has been concerned with relating specific etiological predictors to different clinical *subtypes* of schizophrenia. Such specificity is desirable because (1) the clinical manifestations of schizophrenia are commonly recognized as heterogeneous, (2) diverse clinical presentations are unlikely to have identical etiologies, and (3) treatment implications may vary according to the specific pathologic processes underlying each symptom complex. The subtypes we propose below are based on certain assumptions regarding the central nervous system abnormalities underlying schizophrenia.

Several important excitatory centers of the autonomic nervous system (ANS), including the anterior hypothalamus, are situated on or near the third ventricle (Darrow, 1937; Larsen *et al.*, 1986; Venables and Christie, 1973; Wang, 1964). In view of this, we examined the hypothesis that enlargement of the third ventricle (i.e., perhaps involving damage to these excitatory autonomic centers) is related to reduced autonomic responsiveness. We found that in a subsample of HR subjects, enlargement of the third ventricle (assessed in 1980) was associated with a marked reduction in electrodermal responses measured when the subjects were adolescents in 1962 (Cannon *et al.*, 1988). [We have also recently found a relationship between third ventricle enlargement and reduced premorbid heart rate levels in the same subjects, suggesting that third ventricle enlargement is related to a generalized deficit in excitatory autonomic activity (Cannon, Raine, Herman, Mednick, and Schulsinger, in press).] These findings are of interest particularly in light of evidence linking decreased autonomic responsiveness and ventricular enlargement to the negative symptom complex (Bernstein, *et al.*, 1981; Besson *et al.*, 1987; Cazullo *et al.*, 1989; Gruzelier, 1976; Kemali *et al.*, 1985; Owens *et al.*, 1985; Pearlson *et al.*, 1985; Seidman *et al.*, 1987; Straube, 1979; Williams *et al.*, 1985). It is important to note that not all studies have found significantly more negative symptoms in schizophrenics who are electrodermal nonresponders or who have enlarged ventricles (Andreasen *et al.*, 1982; DeLisi *et al.*, 1986; Johnstone *et al.*, 1976; Losonczy *et al.*, 1986; Luchins *et al.*, 1984; Mathew *et al.*, 1985; Nasrallah *et al.*, 1983; Ota *et al.*, 1987; Pandurangi *et al.*, 1986); however, several of the studies with negative findings found significantly fewer positive symptoms in the nonresponder or enlarged ventricle subgroups (Andreasen *et al.*, 1982; Luchins *et al.*, 1984; Ota *et al.*, 1987), supporting a distinction between *predominantly* negative and positive forms of illness.

Together, these findings suggest that in individuals at elevated genetic risk for schizophrenia (1) delivery complications may lead to enlargement of the third and lateral ventricles; (2) widened third ventricles may involve damage to diencephalic and limbic structures invovled in excitatory autonomic functioning; and (3) enlarged third ventricles and reduced autonomic responsiveness may contribute to the pathogenesis of a form of schizophrenia characterized by predominantly *negative* symptoms.

The large variance birth history in the schizophrenic group indicates that some of the HR subjects who became schizophrenic had normal births (Parnas *et al.*, 1982). These individuals tended to evidence narrow ventricles on CT scan (Cannon *et al.*, 1989). HR individuals with narrow ventricles were relatively autonomically responsive during adolescence (Cannon *et al.*, 1988, in press). These findings suggest that HR individuals who escape periventricular damage are characterized by a relatively high level of ANS responsiveness.

Several lines of evidence suggest that excessive autonomic activation and/or disinhibition may constitute a vulnerability to a particular subtype of schizophrenia. First, some studies have found that the offspring of schizophrenics evidence a higher average level of autonomic excitability than LR controls (Mednick and Schulsinger, 1968; Prentky *et al.*, 1981; Van Dyke *et al.*, 1974), suggesting that heightened ANS responsiveness to stress may be associated with the genetic predisposition to schizophrenia (Zahn, 1977). The failure of some HR studies to replicate these findings (Erlenmeyer-Kimling and Cornblatt, 1987; Janes *et al.*, 1977) could be due to the use of HR samples with relatively lower genetic loadings, an excessive number of delivery complications, or both. Second, some studies have found evidence of ANS hyperarousal in a subgroup of adult schizophrenics (Bartfai *et al.*, 1983, 1987; Frith *et al.*, 1979; Gruzelier and Venables, 1975; Rubens and Lapidus, 1978). However, whether excessive arousal in these patients reflects a stable underlying vulnerability to psychosis or merely a fluxuation of physiological arousal with clinical state (Dawson and Neuchterlein, 1984) is not known. Third, schizophrenics with these autonomic characteristics tend to evidence more active, positive symptomatology than schizophrenics with low levels of ANS responsiveness (Bartfair *et al.*, 1983, 1987; Bernstein *et al.*, 1981; Frith *et al.*, 1979; Gruzelier, 1976; Gruzelier and Venables, 1975; Rubens and Lapidus, 1978; Straube, 1979). Again, however, the evidence supports of subgroup distinction based on relative degrees of symptoms rather than a clear division into positive and negative subtypes.

It is important to note that only about one-tenth of the individuals with a schizophrenic parent eventually develop the disorder themselves (Gottesman and Shields, 1982). This result suggests that genetic predisposition to schizophrenia may constitute a vulnerability but that environmental stressors are required for overt schizophrenia. As noted previously, one postnatal source of environmental stress that predicted adult schizophrenia in the HR sample was severe instability in parental contact and early rearing environment in the first 5 years of life (Parnas *et al.*, 1985; Walker *et al.*, 1981). Severe instability in early rearing environment might be expected to produce pathological effects on emotional development and behavioral functioning, especially in those individuals who tend to evidence large autonomic responses to stressful stimulation.

Together, these considerations suggest that high ANS responsiveness (and other predispositional genetic factors), in interaction with stress resulting from severe instability of the early family rearing environment, may contribute to the pathogenesis of a form of schizophrenia characterized by predominantly *positive* symptoms.

The findings reviewed above suggest that the pathological processes underlying schizophrenic negative and positive symptomatology are present early in life. Thus, signs of the underlying disturbances may exist in the premorbid state. It is important to note, however, that if predominantly negative and predominantly positive forms of schizophrenia result from partially *independent* etiological processes, they would be expected to be preceded by *different* forms of premorbid behavior disturbance. If these premorbid disturbances are analogous to the adult negative and positive-symptom complexes, it would support the view that predominantly negative and predominantly positive forms of schizophrenia represent *discrete longitudinal syndromes.* Preliminary support for this hypothesis was found by examining the clinical records of the mothers of the Copenhagen HR subjects. Those mothers whose symptomatology was predominantly of the positive type evidenced greater degrees of active premorbid behavior disturbance. Those mothers with predominantly negative symptoms as adults evidenced greater degrees of passive premorbid behavior problems (Jorgensen *et al.*, 1987).

Hypotheses

Based on the above research framework, we posit the following hypotheses:

1. Individuals at elevated genetic risk for schizophrenia who suffer severe delivery complications and who evidence an ANS response deficit in adolescence will be at elevated risk for schizophrenia with predominantly negative symptoms.

2. Individuals at genetic risk who escape delivery complications, who evidence a relatively high degree of autonomic responsiveness in adolescence, and who experience a severely disrupted early family rearing environment will be at elevated risk for schizophrenia with predominantly positive symptoms.

3. Predominantly negative symptom schizophrenics will be characterized by social isolation and behavioral passivity in the premorbid state; predominantly positive symptom schizophrenics will be characterized by active, disruptive behavior disturbance in the premorbid state.

AN EMPIRICAL TEST

We tested the above hypotheses in the context of the Copenhagen HR sample (Cannon *et al.*, 1990). Negative- and positive-symptom scales were constructed by combining items from the PSE, CAPPS, and clinical interviews conducted in 1972, following Andreasen's criteria (Andreasen, 1982; Andreasen and Olsen, 1982). This yielded four negative-symptom scales (ALOGIA, ASOCIALITY-ANHEDONIA, ANERGIA-RETARDA-TION, and FLAT AFFECT) and three positive-symptom scales (HAL-LUCINATIONS, DELUSIONS, and THOUGHT DISORDER). Composite scales of NEGATIVE SYMPTOMS and POSITIVE SYMPTOMS were also formed. The mean Cronbach's α for these scales was 0.85 (range = 0.78–0.92). The items used in the negative- and positive-symptom scales have been previously published (Cannon *et al.*, 1990). The scales were standardized in the HR sample to have a mean of 50 and a standard deviation of 10.

Schizophrenia with Predominantly Negative Symptoms

The composite NEGATIVE SYMPTOMS scale was used to form an outcome classification code dividing the sample into schizophrenics with predominantly negative symptoms versus individuals with all other outcomes (including predominantly positive-symptom schizophrenics). To be classified as predominantly negative-symptom schizophrenic, the subject must have had (1) a 1972 diagnosis of schizophrenia, (2) an elevation of 1 standard deviation or more on the composite NEGATIVE SYMPTOMS scale, and (3) a higher NEGATIVE SYMPTOMS score than POSITIVE SYMPTOMS score.

We used three variables as predictors for this outcome classification: degree of genetic risk (i.e., father spectrum diagnosis), delivery complications score, and a score reflecting the level of ANS responsiveness (i.e., responder versus nonresponder) in the 1962 skin conductance assessment. There was a total of 138 HR subjects with all of the relevant measures available.

A decision-tree model was used to analyze the precursor pattern associated with outcomes of predominantly negative-symptom schizophrenia.

This model is shown in Fig. 2.1. As can be seen from Fig. 2.1, the base rate of schizophrenia with predominantly negative symptoms in the HR sample is 5%. Among HR individuals with schizophrenia spectrum fathers, the rate of schizophrenia with predominantly negative symptoms is 14%; if these individuals also experienced two or more delivery complications, then the rate of schizophrenia with predominantly negative symptoms is 35%; if these individuals were also ANS nonresponders, then the rate of schizophrenia with predominantly negative symptoms is 86%. Only one subject in the other outcome group evidenced this same etiological pattern. Analyses of variance and log-linear regressions confirmed that all three predictor variables were significantly associated with predominantly negative-symptom schizophrenia outcomes (Cannon *et al.*, 1990).

If schizophrenia with predominantly negative symptoms results from early developmental processes, we might expect some signs of the underlying processes to exist in the premorbid state. To test this hypothesis, we formed scales of the adolescent school behavior of the subjects (as rated by their teachers) using items that we considered analogous to the adult negative- and positive-symptom complexes. Items in the premorbid NEG-

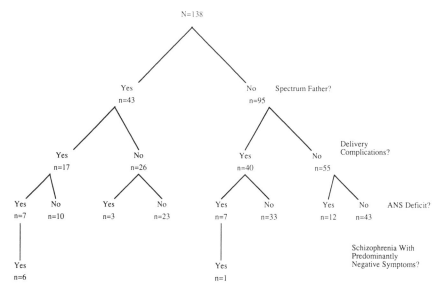

Figure 2.1 Decision-tree model of the etiology of schizophrenia with predominantly negative symptoms. There was a total of 138 subjects with all of the relevant measures available. [Reprinted with permission from the AMA, Cannon *et al.* (1990).]

ATIVE BEHAVIOR scale included passivity, lack of spontaneity, social unresponsiveness, and isolation. Cronbach's α for the scale was 0.76.

Table 2.3 shows the premorbid behavior pattern of the three subgroups of HR subjects. Bonferroni t-tests revealed that schizophrenics with predominantly negative symptoms evidenced significantly more negative-type premorbid school behavior disturbance than the schizophrenics with predominantly positive symptoms and the remaining HR subjects. The latter two subgroups did not differ significantly from each other on the NEGATIVE BEHAVIOR scale. It is also important to note that schizophrenics with predominantly negative symptoms did *not* evidence elevated levels on the *premorbid* POSITIVE BEHAVIOR scale.

We were also interested in determining the adult symptom pattern of schizophrenics with predominantly negative symptoms. As can be seen from Table 2.4, predominantly negative-symptom schizophrenics evidenced significant elevations on each of the adult NEGATIVE SYMPTOMS scales (i.e., 1–2 standard deviations above the HR sample mean). Predominantly negative-symptom schizophrenics also evidenced mild elevations on the POSITIVE SYMPTOMS scales (i.e., one-half to three-fourths of a standard deviation above the HR sample mean). Examination of the individual scale items indicated that their positive symptoms took the form of mild auditory hallucinations, somatic delusions, and simple ideas of reference.

It should be noted that predominantly negative- and predominantly positive-symptom schizophrenics exhibited a comparable degree of certain negative symptoms (i.e., FLAT AFFECT, ASOCIALITY-ANHEDO-

TABLE 2.3. Mean Standard Scores[a] of the Three Subgroups on Scales of Negative- and Positive-Type School Behavior.

	Subgroup[b]		
School behavior scale	Predominantly negative-symptom schizophrenics ($n = 7$)	Predominantly positive-symptom schizophrenics ($n = 8$)	Other high-risk ($n = 152$)
NEGATIVE BEHAVIOR	61.6[1]	45.5[2]	49.7[2]
POSITIVE BEHAVIOR	50.5[2]	62.5[1]	49.8[2]

[a]The high-risk sample's distribution of scores on each behavior scale was standardized to mean 50 and standard deviation 10.

[b]Means with common superscripts in each scale row do not differ significantly at a comparisonwise α level of 0.05 (Bonferroni t-tests).

[Reprinted with permission from the AMA, Cannon *et al.* (1990).]

NIA, and ALOGIA). Predominantly negative-symptom schizophrenics, however, scored significantly higher than predominantly positive-symptom schizophrenics on ANERGIA-RETARDATION. In addition, predominantly negative-symptom schizophrenics were found to score significantly lower than the predominantly positive-symptom schizophrenics on each of the POSITIVE SYMPTOMS scales (HALLUCINATIONS, DELUSIONS, THOUGHT DISORDER, and composite POSITIVE SYMPTOMS).

On the basis of previous work linking genetic and perinatal factors and autonomic nonresponding to ventriculomegaly and the negative-symptom complex, we have suggested that perinatal damage to diencephalic and/or limbic structures involved in excitatory autonomic functioning may be part of the basis of predominantly negative-symptom schizophrenia. The findings presented above provide initial support for this hypothesis. Both the sources (i.e., genetic and perinatal factors) and premorbid correlates (i.e., ANS nonresponding) of ventriculomegaly were significantly associated with outcomes of schizophrenia with predominantly negative symptoms. We could not examine the role of ventriculomegaly directly because CT scans were available only for a subsample.

In view of the probable (partial) perinatal origins of ventriculomegaly in schizophrenia, we hypothesized that signs of the underlying pathological process(es) may be present early in the premorbid state. We found that in late childhood and early adolescence, predominantly negative-symptom schizophrenics were rated by their teachers as showing school behavior disturbances analogous to adult negative symptoms (i.e., isolation, passivity, lack of affect, social unresponsiveness). These findings suggest that in a subgroup of schizophrenics there is continuity between premorbid "negative" characteristics and adult negative symptoms. This continuity implies an insidious, slow-developing process.

It is important to emphasize that despite the overlap between the two subtypes in certain adult negative symptoms, the predominantly negative-symptom schizophrenics did not show signs of active, positive-type school behavior disturbance premorbidly, nor were the antecedents of negative schizophrenia associated with predominantly positive-symptom schizophrenic outcomes. Together with evidence of continuity between premorbid "negative" traits and adult negative symptoms, these findings suggest that the pathological processes underlying predominantly negative-symptom schizophrenia are to some extent distinct from those involved in predominantly positive-symptom schizophrenia.

Finally, we considered the possibility that the genetic contribution to predominantly negative-symptom schizophrenia (i.e., schizophrenia or schizophrenia spectrum illness in both parents) is possibly confounded with a poorer early family rearing environment because having two mentally ill parents could lead to unstable rearing conditions. This interpretation seems unlikely, however, because predominantly negative-symptom schizophrenics did not evidence an elevated level of parental separation or family instability.

Schizophrenia with Predominantly Positive Symptoms

To analyze the precursor pattern associated with predominantly positive-symptom schizophrenia, we formed an outcome classification code dividing the sample into schizophrenics with predominantly positive symptoms versus individuals with all other outcomes (including predominantly negative-symptom schizophrenics). Criteria for the classification of predominantly positive-symptom schizophrenia were (1) a 1972 diagnosis of schizophrenia, (2) an elevation of 1 standard deviation or more on the composite POSITIVE SYMPTOMS scale, and (3) a higher POSITIVE SYMPTOMS score than NEGATIVE SYMPTOMS score. Examination of the psychiatric hospital records of the two schizophrenics who committed suicide before the 1972 assessment indicated a preponderance of positive symptoms; therefore, they were assigned to the predominantly positive-symptom schizophrenia subgroup.

Predictor variables for this analysis were (1) degree of genetic risk (i.e., father spectrum diagnosis), (2) a score reflecting the amount of separation from parents and institutional rearing in the first 5 years of life (family instability score), and (3) degree of ANS responsiveness in the 1962 skin conductance assessment. Relevant measures were available for a total of 160 subjects.

Figure 2.2 shows a decision-tree model of the etiology of predominantly positive-symptom schizophrenia in the HR group. As can be seen from Fig. 2.2, the base rate of schizophrenia with predominantly positive symptoms in the HR sample is 5%. Among individuals with severely unstable early rearing environments (i.e., scores of three or above on the family instability index), the rate of schizophrenia with predominantly positive symptoms is 24%; if these individuals also evidenced ANS response frequencies in the upper half of the HR sample distribution then the rate of 1972 diagnoses of schizophrenia with predominantly positive symptoms is 40%. Nine subjects with other outcomes (including eight with spectrum personality disorders) also evidenced this etiological pattern. Analyses of variance and log-linear regressions performed on these variables indicated that the interaction of ANS responsiveness and family instability was the best and only significant predictor of predominantly positive-symptom schizophrenia outcomes (Cannon et al., 1990).

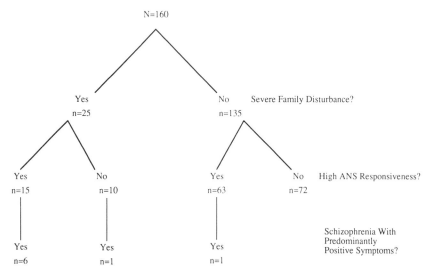

Figure 2.2 Decision-tree model of the etiology of schizophrenia with predominantly positive symptoms. There was a total of 160 subjects with all of the relevant measures available. [Reprinted with permission from the AMA, Cannon *et al.* (1990).]

As noted previously, a scale of the positive-type premorbid behavior of the subjects was formed from the school reports. Items in the premorbid POSITIVE BEHAVIOR scale included overactivity, irritability, distractibility, and aggression. The scale has a Cronbach's α of 0.84. Table 2.3 shows the premorbid behavior pattern of predominantly positive-symptom schizophrenics. Schizophrenics with predominantly positive symptoms were found to show significantly more positive-type premorbid school behavior disturbance than the schizophrenics with predominantly negative symptoms and the remaining HR subjects. The latter two subgroups did not differ significantly from each other on the POSITIVE BEHAVIOR scale. It is also important to note that predominantly positive-symptom schizophrenics did *not* show an elevated level of negative-type behavior disturbance in the premorbid state.

The symptom pattern of the three subgroups is shown in Table 2.4. Predominantly positive-symptom schizophrenics evidenced extremely elevated scores on each of the POSITIVE SYMPTOMS scales (i.e., 4 standard deviations greater than the HR sample mean). Predominantly positive-symptom schizophrenics also evidenced elevated levels of some negative symptoms (i.e., FLAT AFFECT, ASOCIALITY-ANHEDONIA, and composite NEGATIVE SYMPTOMS). Their negative-symptom scores, however, were on average 3 standard deviations lower than their positive-symptom scores.

We have suggested that the development of schizophrenia with predominantly positive symptoms in HR individuals may be a function of a vulnerable ANS and stressful rearing experiences in childhood. The findings presented above indicate that HR individuals who experienced severe disruption of the early family rearing environment and who exhibited a high degree of autonomic responsiveness in adolescence were at elevated risk for 1972 diagnostic outcomes of schizophrenia with predominantly positive symptoms. The *interaction* of ANS responsiveness and family rearing stress provided the most successful prediction of this outcome. Unfortunately, we cannot specify the nature of this effect further. It is conceivable that high ANS responsiveness is associated with the genetic predisposition to schizophrenia and may have been expressed in some of our subjects at birth (Mednick and Schulsinger, 1968; Prentky *et al.*, 1981; Van Dyke *et al.*, 1974; Zahn, 1977). In this case, high ANS responsiveness may constitute a specific vulnerability to the stress associated with severe

TABLE 2.4. Mean Standard Scores[a] of the Three Subgroups on Scales of Negative and Positive Symptoms

Symptom scale	Subgroup[b]		
	Predominantly negative-symptom schizophrenics ($n = 7$)	Predominantly positive-symptom schizophrenics ($n = 6$)[c]	Other high-risk ($n = 158$)
FLAT AFFECT	68.8[1]	64.1[1]	48.7[2]
ANERGIA-RETARDATION	68.8[1]	50.9[2]	49.2[2]
ASOCIALITY-ANHEDONIA	71.6[1]	73.4[1]	48.2[2]
ALOGIA	60.1[1]	53.6[1]	49.4[1]
NEGATIVE SYMPTOMS	72.1[1]	65.3[1]	48.5[2]
HALLUCINATIONS	58.2[2]	86.4[1]	48.3[3]
DELUSIONS	58.-6[2]	90.3[1]	48.1[3]
THOUGHT DISORDER	54.5[2]	90.7[1]	48.3[2]
POSITIVE SYMPTOMS	57.8[2]	94.2[1]	48.0[3]

[a]The high-risk sample's distribution of scores on each symptom scale was standardized to mean 50 and standard deviation 10.

[b]Means with common superscripts in each symptom row do not differ significantly at a comparison-wise α level of 0.05 (Bonferroni *t*-tests).

[c]Two of the eight predominantly positive-symptom schizophrenics were diagnosed from hospital records and, therefore, do not have scorable interview data available.

[Reprinted with permission from the AMA, Cannon *et al.*, 1990.]

disruption of the early family rearing environment. Alternatively, it is possible that severe family disturbance produced the relatively high levels of ANS responsiveness evidenced by the HR individuals who later developed predominantly positive-symptom schizophrenia. However, because a systematic relationship between autonomic response level and severity of family disturbance did not exist in the HR group, this interpretation would only be viable if the early family stress produced high levels of ANS responsiveness in some subjects and not in others, implying some sort of prior susceptibility of vulnerability. It is also possible that the most highly autonomically responsive infants in our sample were the most difficult to manage and that this characteristic contributed directly to the instability of their rearing conditions.

Another potentially useful (and not necessarily mutually exclusive) explanation focuses on the observation that many schizophrenics and their relatives are indiscriminately "open" to environmental stimulation (Carlsson, 1987; Crosson and Hughes, 1987; Oke and Adams, 1987; Rubens and Lapidus, 1978). This condition has been attributed to a possible disturbance of sensory-integrative centers such as the thalamus or entorhinal cortex. Both of these structures experience rapid growth in the second trimester (Gilles, 1983), when genetic mechanisms may be most likely to disrupt neural development and increase the risk for schizophrenia (Jacob and Beckmann, 1986; Kovelman and Scheibel, 1984; Mednick *et al.*, 1988). A defective thalamic gate might be unable to screen complex and insistent stimuli adequately. The consequent flooding of stimulation might, in association with other precursors, contribute to a state of confusion, ANS hyperarousal, and other symptoms of acute psychotic turmoil.

The finding that adult positive-symptom schizophrenia was preceded by analogous forms of behavior disturbance in the premorbid state suggests that schizophrenia with predominantly positive symptoms is a discrete longitudinal syndrome. It is also worth noting that predominantly positive-symptom schizophrenics did not evidence premorbid behavioral signs analogous to adult negative symptoms, nor were the antecedents of predominantly positive-symptom schizophrenia associated with predominantly negative-symptom schizophrenic outcomes. These findings suggest an underlying etiological process that is somewhat distinct from that involved in predominantly negative-symptom schizophrenia.

Predominantly positive-symptom schizophrenics also evidenced some negative symptoms as adults. While their negative symptoms probably were not related to the factors involved in predominantly negative-symptom schizophrenia (i.e., they did not evidence an elevated level of delivery complications or an autonomic response deficit), narrowing the list of potential contributing factors any further is difficult. The timing of appearance of negative symptoms in schizophrenics with predominantly positive symptoms may provide an important clue concerning their pathogenesis. The fact that predominantly positive-symptom schizophrenics did not show behavior analogous to negative symptoms in school (as did predominantly negative-symptom schizophrenics) suggests that their negative symptoms developed later. This pattern is consistent with a learned avoidance theory (Mednick, 1958), which predicts that negative avoidant symptoms may develop secondary to the onset of active psychosis. According to this theory, individuals who poorly modulate their autonomic reactions to stressful stimulation will on occasion experience excessive levels of arousal. These individuals learn to avoid stressful stimulation by directing their attention away from the stress to irrelevant or remote associations and behaviors. This avoidance produces momentary relief from aroused states, which reinforces and stamps in the avoidance response. Avoidance of social contact and emotional stimulation serves to reduce the likelihood of challenge to the fragile ANS controls. Thus, Mednick (1958) would predict that successful learned avoidance in predominantly positive-symptom schizophrenics results in lower levels of arousal leading to the appearance of (secondary) negative symptoms (see also Carpenter *et al.*, 1985; Heilbrun *et al.*, 1986; Venables and Wing, 1962).

CONCLUSIONS

We recognize that negative and positive symptoms are complex behavior patterns involving multiple sources of causation. Our models of predominantly negative- and predominantly positive-symptom schizophrenia are greatly oversimplified. We believe that some symptoms may be "fundamental" to schizophrenia, reflecting aspects of the genetic predisposition, whereas other (both negative and positive) symptoms may require environmental stressors to be activated. Our future work will attempt to specify these possible relationships further.

ACKNOWLEDGMENTS

This research was supported by a Research Scientist Award (1 K05 MH 006 19–01) from the ADAMHA awarding institution (NIMH) and Grant 5 R01 MH 37692–02 to S. A. Mednick, and a National Research Service Award from the NIMH to T. D. Cannon.

REFERENCES

Andreasen, N. C. (1982). Negative symptoms in schizophrenia: Definition and reliability. *Archives of General Psychiatry, 39*, 784–788.
Andreasen, N. C., and Olsen, S. (1982). Negative v. positive schizophrenia: Definition and validation. *Archives of General Psychiatry, 39*, 789–794.

Andreasen, N. C., Olsen, S. A., Dennert, J. W., and Smith, M. R. (1982). Ventricular enlargement in schizophrenia: Relationship to positive and negative symptoms. *American Journal of Psychiatry, 139,* 297–302.

Barr, C. E., Mednick, S. A., and Munk-Jorgensen, P. (1990). Exposure to influenza epidemics during gestation and adult schizophrenia: A 40 year study. *Archives of General Psychiatry, 47,* 869–874.

Bartfair, A., Lavender, S., Edman, G., Schalling, D., and Sedvall, G. (1983). Skin conductance orienting responses in unmedicated recently admitted schizophrenic patients. *Psychophysiology, 20,* 180–187.

Bartfai, A., Lavender, S. E., Nyback, H., and Schalling, D. (1987). Skin conductance nonresponding and nonhabituation in schizophrenic patients. *Acta Psychiatrica Scandinavica, 75,* 321–329.

Benes, F. M., and Bird, E. D. (1987). An analysis of the arrangement of neurons in the cingulate cortex of schizophrenic patients. *Archives of General Psychiatry, 44,* 608–616.

Bernstein, A. S., Taylor, K. W., Starkey, P., Juni, S., Lubowsky, J., and Paley, H. (1981). Bilateral skin conductance, finger pulse volume, and EEG orienting response to tones of differing intensities in chronic schizophrenics and controls. *Journal of Nervous and Mental Disease, 169,* 513–528.

Besson, J. A. O., Corrigan, F. M., Cherryman, G. R., and Smith, F. W. (1987). Nuclear magnetic resonance brain imaging in chronic schizophrenia. *British Journal of Psychiatry, 150.* 161–163.

Beuhring, T., Cudeck, R., Mednick, S. A., Walker, E. F., and Schulsinger, F. (1982). Vulnerability and environmental stress: High-risk research on the development of schizophrenia. In R. W. J. Neufeld (Ed.), *Psychological stress and psychopathology* (pp. 69–90). New York: McGraw-Hill.

Bogerts, B., Meertz, E., and Schonfeldt-Bausch, R. (1985). Basal ganglia and limbic system pathology in schizophrenia: A morphometric study of brain volume and shrinkage. *Archives of General Psychiatry, 42,* 784–791.

Cannon, T. D. (1991). Genetic and perinatal sources of structural brain abnormalities in schizophrenia. In S. A. Mednick, T. D. Cannon, C. E. Barr, and M. Lyon (Eds.), *Fetal neural development and adult schizophrenia.* (pp. 174–198). Cambridge: Cambridge University Press.

Cannon, T. D., Fuhrmann, M., Mednick, S. A., Machon, R. A., Parnas, J., and Schulsinger, F. (1988). Third ventricle enlargement and reduced electrodermal responsiveness. *Psychophysiology, 25,* 153–156.

Cannon, T. D., Mednick, S. A., and Parnas, J. (1989). Genetic and perinatal determinants of structural brain deficits in schizophrenia. *Archives of General Psychiatry, 46,* 883–889.

Cannon, T. D., Mednick, S. A., and Parnas, J. (1990). Antecedents of predominantly negative and predominantly positive symptom schizophrenia in a high-risk population. *Archives of General Psychiatry, 47,* 622–632.

Cannon, T. D., Raine, A., Herman, T. M., Mednick, S. A., Parnas, J., and Schulsinger, F. (1990). Third ventricle enlargement and reduced heart rate levels. *Psychophysiology.*

Carlsson, A. (1987). The role of dopamine in normal and abnormal behavior. Paper presented at the International Congress on Schizophrenia Research (March–April 1987), Clearwater, FL.

Carpenter, W. T., Heinrichs, D. W., and Alphs, L. D. (1985). Treatment of negative symptoms. *Schizophrenia Bulletin, 11,* 440–452.

Cazullo, C. L., Vita, A., and Sacchetti, E. (1989). Cerebral ventricular enlargement in schizophrenia: Prevalence and correlates. In S. C. Schulz and C. A. Tamminga (Eds.), *Schizophrenia: Scientific progress* (pp. 195–206). New York: Oxford University Press.

Crosson, B., and Hughes, C. W. (1987). Role of the thalamus in language: Is it related to schizophrenic thought disorder. *Schizophrenia Bulletin, 13,* 605–619.

Darrow, C. W. (1937). Neural mechanisms controlling the palmar galvanic skin reflex and palmar sweating. *Archives of Neurological Psychiatry, 37*, 641–663.

Dawson, M. E., and Neuchterlein, K. H. (1984). Psychophysiological dysfunctions in the developmental course of schizophrenic disorders. *Schizophrenia Bulletin, 10*, 204–232.

DeLisi, L. E., Goldin, L. R., Hamovit, J. R., Maxwell, E., Kurtz, D., and Gershon, E. S. (1986). A family study of the association of increased ventricular size with schizophrenia. *Archives of General Psychiatry, 43*, 148–153.

Endicott, J., and Spitzer, R. (1972). Current and past psychopathology scales (CAPPS). *Archives of General Psychiatry, 27*, 678–687.

Erlenmeyer-Kimling, L., and Cornblatt, B. (1987). The New-York high-risk project: A follow-up report. *Schizophrenia Bulletin, 13*, 451–461.

Frith, C. D., Stevens, M., Johnstone, E. C., and Crow, T. J. (1979). Skin conductance responsivity during acute episodes of schizophrenia as a predictor of symptomatic improvement. *Psychological Medicine, 9*, 101–106.

Gilles, F. H. (1983). Changes in growth and vulnerability at the end of the second trimester. In F. H. Gilles, A. Leviton, and E. C. Dooling (Eds.), *The developing human brain: Growth and epidemiologic neuropathology* (pp. 316–326). Boston: John Wright PSG.

Goldstein, M. J. (1987). The UCLA high-risk project. *Schizophrenia Bulletin, 13*, 505–514.

Gottesman, I. I., and Shields, J. (1982). *Schizophrenia: The epigenetic puzzle.* Cambridge: Cambridge University Press.

Gruzelier, J. H. (1976). Clinical attributes of schizophrenic skin conductance responders and nonresponders. *Psychological Medicine, 6*, 245–249.

Gruzelier, J. H., and Venables, P. H. (1975). Evidence of high and low levels of physiological arousal in schizophrenics. *Psychophysiology, 12*, 66–73.

Heilbrun, A. B., Diller, R., Fleming, R., and Slate, L. (1986). Strategies of disattention and auditory hallucinations in schizophrenics. *Journal of Nervous and Mental Disease, 174*, 265–273.

Jakob, H., and Beckmann, H. (1986). Prenatal-developmental disturbances in the limbic allocortex in schizophrenia. *Biological Psychiatry, 21*, 1181–1183.

Janes, C. L., Hesselbrock, V., and Stern, J. A. (1977). Parental psychopathology, age, and race as related to electrodermal activity of children. *Psychophysiology, 15*, 24–34.

Johnstone, E. C., Crow, T. J., Frith, C. D., Husband, J., and Kreel, L. (1976). Cerebral ventricular size and cognitive impairment in chronic schizophrenia. *Lancet.* (1) 924–926.

Jorgensen, A., Teasdale, T. W., Parnas, J., Schulsinger, F., and Mednick, S. A. (1987). The Copenhagen high-risk project: The diagnosis of maternal schizophrenia and its relation to offspring diagnosis. *British Journal of Psychiatry, 151*, 753–757.

Kemali, D., Maj, M., Galderisi, S., Ariano, M. G., Cesarelli, M., Milici, N., Salvati, A., Valente, A., and Volpe, M. (1985). Clinical and neuropsychological correlates of cerebral ventricular enlargement in schizophrenia. *Journal of Psychiatric Research, 19*, 587–596.

Kovelman, J. A., and Scheibel, A. B. (1984). A neurohistological correlate of schizophrenia. *Biological Psychiatry, 19*, 1601–1621.

Larsen, P. B., Schneiderman, N., and Pasin, R. D. (1986). Physiological bases of cardiovascular psychophysiology. In M. G. H. Coles, E. Donchin, and S. W. Porges (Eds.), *Psychophysiology: Systems, processes, and applications.* New York: Guilford Press.

Losonczy, M. F., Song, I. S., Mohs, R. C., Small, N. A., Davidson, M., Johns, C. A., and Davis, K. L. (1986). Correlates of lateral ventricular size in chronic schizophrenia, I: Behavioral and treatment response measures. *American Journal of Psychiatry, 143*, 976–981.

Luchins, D. J., Lewine, R. R. J., and Meltzer, H. Y. (1984). Lateral ventricular size, psychopathology, and medication response in the psychoses. *Biological Psychiatry, 19*, 29–44.

Marcus, J., Hans, S. L., Mednick, S. A., Schulsinger, F., and Michelsen, N. (1985). Neurological dysfunctioning in offspring of schizophrenics in Israel and Denmark: A replication analysis. *Archives of General Psychiatry, 42*, 753–761.

Mathew, R. J., Partain, C. L., Rakash, R., Kulkarni, M. V., Logan, T. P., and Wilson, W. H. (1985). A study of the septum pellucidum and corpus callosum in schizophrenia with MR imaging. *Acta Psychiatrica Scandinavica, 72,* 414–421.

McNeil, T. F. (1988). Obstetric factors and perinatal injuries. In M. T. Tsuang and J. C. Simpson (eds.), *Handbook of schizophrenia (Vol. 3. Nosology, epidemiology and genetics)* (pp. 319–344). New York: Elsevier.

Mednick, S. A. (1958). A learning theory approach to research in schizophrenia. *Psychological Bulletin, 55,* 316–327.

Mednick, S. A., and Higgins, S. (1960). *Current research in schizophrenia.* Ann Arbor, MI: Edwards Brothers.

Mednick, S. A., Machon, R. A., Huttunen, M. O., and Bonett, D. (1988). Adult schizophrenia following prenatal exposure to an influenza epidemic. *Archives of General Psychiatry, 45,* 189–192.

Mednick, S. A., and McNeil, T. (1968). Current methodology in research on the etiology of schizophrenia: Serious difficulties which suggest the use of the high-risk group method. *Psychological Bulletin, 70,* 681–693.

Mednick, S. A., and Schulsinger, F. (1965). A longitudinal study of children with a high risk for schizophrenia: A preliminary report. In S. Vandenberg (Ed.), *Methods and goals in human behavior genetics* (pp. 255–296). New York: Academic Press.

Mednick, S. A., and Schulsinger, F. (1968). Some premorbid characteristics related to breakdown in children with schizophrenic mothers. *Journal of Psychiatric Research, 6,* 267–291.

Nasrallah, H. A., Kuperman, S., Hamra, B. J., and McCallay-Whitters, M. (1983). Clinical differences between schizophrenic patients with and without large cerebral ventricles. *Journal of Clinical Psychiatry, 44,* 407–209.

Nowakowski, R. S. (1987). Basic concepts of CNS development. *Child Development, 58,* 568–595.

Oke, A. F., and Adams, R. N. (1987). Elevated thalamic dopamine: Possible link to sensory dysfunctions in schizophrenia. *Schizophrenia Bulletin, 13,* 589–604.

Ota, T., Maeshiro, H., Ishido, H., Shimizu, Y., Uchida, R., Toyoshima, R., Ohshima, H., Takazawa, T., Motomura, H., and Noguchi, T. (1987). Treatment resistant chronic psychopathology and CT scans in schizophrenia. *Acta Psychiatrica Scandinavica, 75,* 415–427.

Owens, D. G., Johnstone, E. C., Crow, T. j., Frith, C. D., Jagoe, J. R., and Kreel, L. (1985). Lateral ventricular size in schizophrenia: Relationship to the disease process and its clinical manifestations. *Psychological Medicine, 15,* 27–41.

Pandurangi, A. K., Dewan, M. J., Boucher, M., Levy, B., Ramachandran, T., Bartell, K., Bick, P. A., Phelps, B. H., and Major, L. (1986). A comprehensive study of chronic schizophrenic patients: II. Biological, neuropsychological, and clinical correlates. *Acta Psychiatrica Scandinavica, 73,* 161–171.

Parnas, J., Schulsinger, F., Teasdale, T. W., Schulsinger, H., Feldman, P. M., and Mednick, S. A. (1982). Perinatal complications and clinical outcome within the schizophrenia spectrum. *British Journal of Psychiatry, 140,* 416–d420.

Parnas, J., Teasdale, T. W., and Schulsinger, H. (1985). Institutional rearing and diagnostic outcome in children of schizophrenic mothers: A prospective high-risk study. *Archives of General Psychiatry, 42,* 762–679.

Pearlson, G. D., Garbacz, D. J., Moberg, P. J., Ahn, H. S., and DePaulo, J. R. (1985). Symptomatic, familial, perinatal, and social correlates of computerised axial tomography (CAT) changes in schizophrenics and bipolars. *Journal of Nervous and Mental Disease, 173,* 42–50.

Prentky, R. A., Salzman, L. F., and Klein, R. H. (1981). Habituation and conditioning of skin conductance responses in children at risk. *Schizophrenia Bulletin, 7,* 281–291.

Rakic, P., and Sidman, R. L. (1978). Sequence of developmental abnormalities leading to granule cell deficit in cerebellar cortex of weaver mutant mice. *Journal of Comparative Neurology, 152,* 103–132.

Reveley, A. M., Reveley, M.A., Clifford, C. A., and Murray, R. M. (1982). Cerebral ventricular size in twins discordant for schizophrenia. *Lancet.* (1) 540–541.

Rubens, R. L., and Lapidus, L. B. (1978). Schizophrenic patterns of arousal and stimulus barrier functioning. *Journal of Abnormal Psychology, 87,* 199–211.

Schulsinger, F., Parnas, J., Petersen, E. T., Schulsinger, H., Teasdale, T. W., Mednick, S. A., Moller, L., and Silverton, L. (1984). Cerebral ventricular size in the offspring of schizophrenic mothers. *Archives of General Psychiatry, 41,* 602–606.

Schulsinger, H. (1976). A ten year follow-up of children of schizophrenic mothers: Clinical assessment. *Acta Psychiatrica Scandinavica, 53,* 371–386.

Seidman, L. J., Sokolove, R. L., McElroy, C., Knapp, P. H., and Sabin, T. (1987). Lateral ventricular size and social network differentiation in young, nonchronic schizophrenic patients. *American Journal of Psychiatry, 144,* 512–514.

Straube, E. R. (1979). On the meaning of electrodermal nonresponding in schizophrenia. *Journal of Nervous and Mental Disease, 167,* 601–611.

Van Dyke, J. L., Rosenthal, D., and Rasmussen, P. V. (1974). Electrodermal functioning in adopted-away offpsring of schizophrenics. *Journal of Psychiatric Research, 10,* 199–215.

Venables, P. H., and Christie, M. J. (1973). Mechanisms, instrumentation, recording techniques, and quantification of responses. In W. F. Prokasy and D. C. Raskin (Eds.), *Electrodermal activity in psychological research* (pp. 2–124). New York: Academic Press.

Venables, P. H., and Wing, J. K. (1962). Level of arousal and the subclassification of schizophrenia. *Archives of General Psychiatry, 7,* 114–119.

Walker, E. F., Cudeck, R., Mednick, S. A., and Schulsinger, F. (1981). Effects of parental absence and institutionalization on the development of clinical symptoms in high-risk children. *Acta Psychiatrica Scandinavica, 63,* 95–109.

Wang, G. H. (1964). *Neural control of sweating.* Madison: University of Wisconsin Press.

Watt, N. F., and Nichols, A., Jr. (1979). Early death of parent as an etiological factor in schizophrenia. *American Journal of Orthopsychiatry, 49,* 465–00.

Weinberger, D. R., DeLisi, L. E., Neophytides, A. N., and Wyatt, R. J. (1981). Familial aspects of CT scan abnormalities in chronic schizophrenic patients. *Psychiatry Research, 4,* 65–71.

Williams, A. O., Reveley, M. A., Kolakowska, T., Ardern, M., and Mandelbrote, B. M. (1985). Schizophrenia with good and poor outcome: II: Cerebral ventricular size and its clinical significance. *British Journal ofPsychiatry, 146,* 239–246.

Wing, J. K., Cooper, J. E., and Sartorious, N. (1974). *The measurement and classification of psychiatric symptoms.* London: Cambridge University Press.

World Health Organization (1967). *Manual of the international classification of diseases, injuries and causes of death* (8th ed.). Geneva: Author.

Zahn, T. P. (1977). Autonomic nervous system characteristics possibly related to a genetic predisposition to schizophrenia. *Schizophrenia Bulletin, 3,* 49–60.

Neurobehavioral Development of Infants at Risk for Schizophrenia: A Review

Sydney L. Hans
Joseph Marcus

Prior to 1960, most knowledge about the early antecedents of schizophrenic illness came from the retrospective reports of patients and families, although family members are generally not trained observers of child development and may have only limited awareness of important aspects of early neurobehavioral functioning. Furthermore, through the years their observations may be lost to memory or distorted by subsequent events including the signs of the offspring's illness (cf. Garmezy and Streitman, 1974). While prospective longitudinal studies are the ideal source of information about the early development of mental illness, samples drawn from the general population contain too few children who eventually become schizophrenic to warrant the great expense of such research. Sampling strategies in which children at risk for schizophrenia are followed—either offspring of schizophrenic parents or children showing early behavior problems—allow researchers to prospectively study groups that contain larger numbers of children who will eventually become schizophrenic.

Copyright © 1991 by Academic Press, Inc.
All rights of reproduction in any form reserved.

While the importance of high-risk studies in the field of schizophrenia became recognized during the 1970s, the number of such studies actually conducted has been limited by the difficulties of recruiting and maintaining such samples; however, findings from this small group of studies have begun to show an impressive congruence of findings. Specifically, high-risk studies indicate that school-age and adolescent offspring of schizophrenic parents show subtle deficits in information processing and attentional functioning. These deficits are evident both in mean differences, relative to comparison samples, and in the presence of a disproportionately large subgroup of children with poor information-processing skills among children born to schizophrenic parents. Deficits are most consistently observed in vigilance tasks, such as the continuous performance task, and particularly when such tasks are administered under demanding conditions (Rutschmann *et al.*, 1977, 1986; Nuechterlein and Dawson, 1984; Nuechterlein, 1983).

Signs of motor dysfunction have also been found consistently in studies of school-age and adolescent offspring of schizophrenic parents (Marcus, 1974; Marcus *et al.*, 1985a,b; Hanson *et al.*, 1976; Rieder and Nichols, 1979; Erlenmeyer-Kimling *et al.*, 1982). Current data suggest that such motoric signs at school age, if combined with attentional performance, may help to predict later psychiatric disorder within samples of children born to schizophrenic parents (Erlenmeyer-Kimling *et al.*, 1982; Hans and Marcus, 1987; Marcus *et al.*, 1987).

These high-risk studies of school-age children and adolescents do little to elucidate the origin of neurobehavioral deficits in individuals at risk for schizophrenia. Are neurobehavioral deficits early signs of schizophrenic illness or markers for genetic vulnerability? Are they developmental or degenerative? Are they related to genetic, perinatal, or environmental factors? Such questions require exploration of development from before middle childhood. However, the number of studies examining the infant offspring of schizophrenic parents is very limited, as is the number of infants examined in each study. Previous reviews of these studies on infant offspring of schizophrenic parents have reported that findings across these studies only moderately converge (Walker and Emory, 1983; Erlenmeyer-Kimling, 1987; Asarnow, 1988). However, these reviews paid little attention to differences in infant ages at which abnormalities were observed, the types of assessments made, and the methods used for analyzing data. The purpose of the present chapter is to review again the state of the knowledge on neurobehavioral development of infants at risk for schizophrenia and perhaps to offer greater clarity on the points of agreement across studies.

OVERVIEW OF EXISTING STUDIES

Most information about the development of infants at risk for schizo-phrenia comes from six prospective investigations designed specifically to study infants at risk for schizophrenia. All of these studies (1) recruited samples during gestation or soon after birth of the target child, (2) have at least one nonschizophrenic comparison group, (3) made assessments at multiple infant ages, and (4) made assessments that were tightly linked to specific infant ages. These six studies are Fish's New York Infant Study, the Pittsburgh Study, the Rochester Longitudinal Study (RLS), the Jerusalem Infant Development Study (JIDS), the Swedish High-Risk Study, and the Boston High-Risk Study.

The earliest reports on the behavior of infant offspring of schizophrenic women came from the New York Infant Study of Fish (1957, 1960). This research grew out of the investigator's clinical work at Bellevue Hospital in New York City. In 1952, she began to study the infants of 14 mothers from very disadvantaged backgrounds. Two of these mothers were later chronically hospitalized and diagnosed as schizophrenic (Fish, 1957). Data from the two infants with schizophrenic mothers—particularly the now well-known "Peter"—suggested disruption of the integrated aspects of visual–motor performance (Fish and Hagin, 1972) and prompted Fish to recruit during the years 1959 and 1960 an additional 10 infants with schizo-phrenic mothers for the sample. All schizophrenic mothers were recruited from two major New York State hospitals, and maternal diagnoses were based on the clinical judgment of senior staff at these institutions. The full sample of 24 children was followed regularly during infancy (with assess-ments at birth, 3 days, and 1, 2, 3, 4, 6, 9, 13, 18, and 24 months) and at 10 years, 15–16 years, and 20–22 years of age. Due to the perseverance of the investigator, the entire sample remains intact at the present day.

Fish's first reports were followed a decade later by data from Pittsburgh on the development of a small sample of high-risk infants (Ragins *et al.,* 1975). These infants were identified through psychiatric screening of vir-tually all pregnant women who came for prenatal care to a large uni-versity-affiliated obstetric hospital. Schizophrenic diagnoses were based on responses to the Current and Past Psychopathology Scales (Endicott and Spitzer, 1972). Comparison-group mothers were those judged clearly not schizophrenic, although over one-third of them had other psychiatric diagnoses identified as personality disorders or adjustment reactions to adult life. The full sample included 14 schizophrenic mothers and 18 nonschizophrenic mothers. A subgroup of 6 schizophrenic and nonschizo-phrenic group infants received neurobehavioral assessments once between the ages of 4 and 8 months; a subgroup of 10 schizophrenic and 10 nonschizophrenic group infants received neurobehavioral assessments once between the ages of 12 and 19 months. The children were not assessed at ages beyond infancy.

The next generation of high-risk studies went beyond previous research in their methodology by recruiting slightly larger initial samples, providing greater controls in terms of examiner blindness, and including comparison groups of infants whose parents had other psychiatric disorders. Sameroff and colleagues initiated the RLS (Sameroff et al., 1982, 1987) by comparing psychiatric registers in an upstate New York county with lists of women enrolled for prenatal care. A group of 29 infants whose mothers were schizophrenic was identified and enrolled in the study in a 3-year period beginning in 1970. Comparison groups consisted of 57 infants whose mothers had no history of mental illness, 58 infants whose mothers had diagnoses of depression, and 40 infants whose mothers had personality disorders. The groups were matched for age of mother, race, socioeconomic status (SES), marital status, and number of previous children. The final sample was a mixed race sample with a wide range of socioeconomic groups, although many children were from very low SES families. During infancy, the children were assessed neonatally and at 4 and 12 months of age. Follow-up assessments were conducted at 30 months, 7 years, and most recently at 13 years. The adolescent follow-up sample included 11 offspring of schizophrenics and 88 children from the other comparison groups.

The JIDS (Marcus et al., 1981) was initiated in 1973 by Joseph Marcus, who had previously been involved with the NIMH Israeli City-Kibbutz High-Risk Study of school-age offspring of schizophrenic parents (Marcus, 1974; Marcus et al., 1985a). The original sample consisted of 19 infants with schizophrenic parents, 6 infants whose parents had affective disorders, 14 infants whose parents had personality disorders or neuroses, and 19 infants from families with no mental illness (NMI). This study differed from the previous studies by including infants whose fathers were the mentally ill parent. The parents were primarily from working class families of both Asian and European Jewish backgrounds. All families were recruited before the birth of the child through well-baby clinics and psychiatric clinics in Jerusalem, Israel. The early neurobehavioral development of the infants was assessed at 3 and 14 days of age and at 4, 8, and 12 months of age. Recently the neurobehavioral development of 15 offspring of schizophrenics and 30 comparison-group children has been assessed at school age, and data collection on an adolescent follow-up will begin in 1990.

The Swedish High-Risk Study (McNeil and Kaij, 1984, 1987) recruited a sample of 88 infants with mentally ill index mothers in Lund, Sweden, during the period from 1973 through 1977. To identify the sample, they cross-checked the names of women registered in prenatal clinics against a list of women who had been admitted to eight different psychiatric hospitals and six inpatient psychiatric clinics. The mentally ill mothers were further subdivided into types: schizophrenics, cycloids, affectives, psychogenics, postpartum psychotics, and other psychotics. For each index subject, a control subject was selected who was the next consecutive admission from the same prenatal clinic, who was of Scandinavian ethnicity, and who was matched for parity, maternal age, and social class. Children were assessed on multiple measures neonatally and at intermediate ages through 1 year. The most recent follow-up was when the children were 6 years of age.

D'Angelo et al. (1983) assessed 30 Boston infants whose mothers received diagnoses of schizophrenia, comparing them with 25 infants whose mothers had recurrent major depression and 17 infants in an unaffected control group. Both clinical groups were recruited from private practice referrals, aftercare clinics, and community-based programs for previously hospitalized psychiatric patients. The unaffected women were selected from three obstetric and family medical practices. These comparison women were of similar SES. Comparison and mentally ill groups were recruited during the first trimester of pregnancy. Sixteen of the schizophrenic group infants were placed in foster care. The sample was assessed at 2 days of age and at 2, 4, 6, 8, 10, and 12 months of age. No follow-up after infancy has been conducted.

In addition to these prospective longitudinal studies, data on the development of infants with schizophrenic parents also come from several large data banks that were generated to explore scientific questions unrelated to schizophrenia. In these studies, subsamples in which parents could be identified as schizophrenic were retrospectively selected from previously collected large perinatal data sets.

In the Danish Obstetrical Study (Mednick et al., 1971), a total of 9006 pregnant women who delivered at the University Hospital in Copenhagen between September 21, 1959, and December 21, 1961, were observed as part of a perinatal study. Years after the initial assessments of mothers and infants, the parents' names were cross-checked through the Danish Central Psychiatric Registry of all admissions to psychiatric hospitals in the kingdom of Denmark. This procedure yielded 83 parents with a clear diagnosis of schizophrenia. Comparison groups were selected in which parents had character disorders or in which parents had no record of mental illness. Comparison groups were matched to the ill groups (in order of importance) based on sex of ill parents, sex of child, race, multiple-birth status, pregnancy number, social class, mother's age, mother's height, and father's age. The primary data on early behavioral development came from neurological examination during the neonatal period and a comprehensive follow-up at school age administered to the selected sample (Orvaschel et al., 1979; Marcus et al., 1985b).

The Collaborative Perinatal Project (CPP) on Cerebral Palsy, Mental Retardation, and other Neurological and Sensory Disorders of Infancy and Childhood was conducted between 1959 and 1973 under the auspices of the National Institute of Neurological and Communicative Disorders and Stroke (Berendes, 1966; Niswander and Gordon, 1972). A standard set of measures was collected on infants born to 55,000 mothers at 12 different hospitals across the United States. Children were followed longitudinally through the age of 7 years. Data from the CPP have been analyzed retrospectively with respect to risk for schizophrenia.

Marcuse and Cornblatt (1986) reviewed the CPP data from the state of New York: 5,800 pregnancies from three hospitals. Through cross-referencing with a variety of psychiatric facilities in New York State, they identified a sample of 22 children with schizophrenic parents, 17 of whom had behavioral data during the first year of life. A comparison group of 68 low-risk children with no family history of mental illness was also selected from the total pool of cases, matching for hospital of birth, race, sex, mother's age, and SES.

At the 7-year follow-up of the CPP conducted at the University of Minnesota Hospitals, Hanson et al. (1976) administered the Minnesota Multiphasic Personality Inventory (MMPI) to parents and identified 29 parents who could be diagnosed schizophrenic by a consensus of three raters. These parents had 33 children in the project. Thirty-six comparison children whose parents had other psychiatric disorders were selected as well as 66 children whose parents had no history of psychiatric problems. Table 3.1 summarizes the characteristics of the major studies of infants at risk for schizophrenia as described above.

While several other investigators have reported data on the infant offspring of schizophrenics, aspects of their research design often make interpretation of data with respect to schizophrenia difficult. For example, some studies combine schizophrenic and other psychotic (particularly affective) diagnoses in their analyses, and others pool data from children who were assessed at widely disparate ages (e.g., Stott et al., 1983; Goodman, 1987; Grunebaum et al., 1974). These studies will not be reported here.

NEONATAL BEHAVIOR

The earliest reports on the behavior of neonatal offspring of schizophrenic women came from the New York Infant Study (Fish, 1957, 1960).

TABLE 3.1.   Characteristics of Studies of Infants with Schizophrenic Parents

Study	Initial sample	Infant assessment ages	Primary neuro-behavioral measures	Follow-up assessment ages	Most recent follow-up sample size
			Characteristics		
New York Infant Study	Schizophrenia (12) No illness(12)	3 days and 1, 2, 3, 4, 6, 9, 13, 18, and 24 months	Gesell vestibular	10, 15, and 22 years	Schizophrenia (12) No illness (12)
Pittsburgh	Schizophrenia (10) No illness (10)	4–8 months and 12–19 months	Bayley neurological	None	
Rochester Longitudinal Study	Schizophrenia (29) No illness (57) Affective (58) Personality disorders (40)	Neonatal and 4 and 12 months	NBAS Bayley	4 and 13 years	Schizophrenia (11) No illness (41) Other illness (47)
Jerusalem Infant Development Study	Schizophrenia (19) No illness (19) Affective (6) Personality disorders/ neuroses (14)	3 and 14 days and 4, 8, and 12 months	NBAS Bayley	10 years	Schizophrenia (15) No illness (15) Other illness (15)
Swedish High-Risk Study	Schizophrenia (17) No illness (104) Cycloid (15) Affective (15) Psychogenic (6) Postpartum (18) Other psychotic (17)	3 days, 3 and 6 weeks, and 3, 6, and 12 months	Neonatal neurological examination	6 years	Schizophrenia (11) No illness (97) Other illness (53)
Boston High-Risk Study	Schizophrenia (30) No illness (17) Affective (25)	2 days and 2, 4, 5, 8, 10, and 12 months	NBAS Bayley	None	
Danish Obstetrical Study	Schizophrenia (83) No illness (83) Character disorder (83)	Neonatal	Neonatal neurological examination	10 years	
CPP–New York	Schizophrenia (17) No illness (68)	Neonatal	Neonatal neurological examination	7 years	
CPP–Minnesota	Schizophrenia (33) No illness (66) Other illness (36)	Birth and 4 and 12 months	Neonatal neurological Bayley	7 years	

CPP, Collaborative Perinatal Project; NBAS, Neonatal Behavioral Assessment Scale.

Four offspring of schizophrenic mothers were described as having an "abnormally quiet state." They differed from other neonates in their ability to maintain a prolonged, unbroken state of quiet visual alertness for 15–80 minutes, without a pacifier, as early as 18 hours of age (Fish, 1963; Fish and Alpert, 1962, 1963). Normally active neonates cried spontaneously when awake and remained alert for only 2–5 minutes without a pacifier during the first month of life. The abnormally quiet infants did not cry during the first month, even with vigorous postural manipulation. The infants were lethargic with hypotonia and spontaneous activity level that was decreased in amount, speed, and vigor. Despite this lethargy, their responses to visual, auditory, and tactile stimuli were normal or even increased.

In addition, Fish and Dixon (1978) also reported reduced vestibular responsiveness in some infants with schizophrenic parents. Vestibular stimulation was generated by administering puffs of cold air to each ear separately, and eye movements were recorded for 3 minutes following stimulation. Ten of the 12 high-risk infants were assessed with this procedure. Six of them showed strong nystagmus during crying and weaker nystagmus while asleep that was comparable with the responses reported for normal infants. One of the 10 infants had tonic deviation and brief nystagmus during crying that was similar to her responses when asleep. Three infants—all also characterized as abnormally quiet—showed absent or brief nystagmus, often with tonic deviation, when they were quietly alert. Two of these also showed absent or brief nystagmus when crying.

Since the work of Fish, three prospective studies have conducted comprehensive assessments of the neonatal behavior of infants at risk for schizophrenia. These studies employed Brazelton's (1973) Neonatal Behavioral Assessment Scale (NBAS)—an examination that emphasizes the assessment of individual differences in newborn infants, particularly in self-organizational skills and style of interaction with the environment.

In the RLS, Sameroff et al. (1982) administered the NBAS when the infants were between 48 and 72 hours old. The NBAS items were reduced into seven clusters (Sameroff et al., 1978): orientation, arousal, tonus, quieting, motor maturity, cuddliness, and response decrement. Comparing the groups on these cluster scores, infants of depressed mothers had poorer tonus and less self-quieting ability than those of the NMI group. The personality disorder group also had lower self-quieting ability. The investigators report no statistically significant group effects involving the group of children at risk for schizophrenia. Looking at nonsignificant group trends, the schizophrenic group was the poorest functioning of the four groups on three of the seven factors: orientation, motor maturity, and cuddliness. No analyses were conducted to identify subgroups of poor-functioning offspring of schizophrenics.

The JIDS infants were assessed on the NBAS at 3 and 14 days of age. Comparison of the group of infants at risk for schizophrenia with the other infants on individual NBAS items yielded few statistically significant group differences (Hans *et al.*, 1987). Specifically, at 3 days of age, offspring of schizophrenics showed poorer motor maturity than infants from all the other groups combined. At 14 days of age, offspring of schizophrenics showed poorer motor maturity, easier consolability, and lower activity level than infants from all the other groups combined. The authors also reported their NBAS data in terms of two dimensions of functioning: motor functioning (tonus, motor maturity, pull-to sit, defensive movements, activity, and tremulous) and sensorimotor functioning (orientation items and alertness). Visual inspection of scatterplots of these two dimensions showed that a subgroup of neonates with schizophrenic parents performed more poorly jointly on motoric and sensorimotor items than did the neonates with healthy parents or parents with other illnesses. This subgroup was clearer at 14 days than at 3 days.

D'Angelo *et al.* (1983) assessed their Boston sample 2 days after birth on the NBAS. Behaviorally, infants with a schizophrenic mother were more irritable than other infants; displayed significantly less alertness, consolability, cuddliness, and capacity to self-quiet than other infants; and exhibited inferior defensive movements, hand-to-mouth movements, general tonus, motor maturity, and pull-to sit than did those of either depressed or unaffected mothers. Table 3.2 summarizes the neonatal behavioral findings from the above studies.

While the NBAS is not primarily an assessment of neurological functioning, it does include a brief assessment of infant reflexes and tone. No data on reflex items were reported for the RLS. In the JIDS, offspring of schizophrenics on average displayed weaker Moro reflexes at 3 days and stronger nystagmus when compared with infants of nonschizophrenic

TABLE 3.2. Summary of Data on Neonatal Behavior in Offspring of Schizophrenics

	Study			
Neonatal behavior	New York	Rochester	Jerusalem (age)	Boston
Orientation/alertness	Good	Poor (trend)	Poor (trend) (14 days)	Poor
Arousal	Low	—	—	High
Tonus	Low	—	—	Low
Quieting/consolability	Good	Good	Good (14 days)	Poor
Motor maturity	—	Poor (trend)	Poor (3 and 14 days)	Poor
Cuddliness	—	Poor (trend)	Poor (14 days)	Poor
Activity level	Low	—	Low (14 days)	—

parents. In the Boston sample, infants born to schizophrenic mothers had, on average, significantly weaker performance in sucking and crawling reflexes at 2 days of age.

Several other high-risk studies have done more complete neonatal neurological assessments (McNeil and Kaij, 1984; Mednick *et al.*, 1971; Hanson *et al.*, 1976; Marcuse and Cornblatt, 1986). Compared with the data collected using the NBAS, these assessments place greater emphasis on the detection of abnormal behavioral signs and report their data in terms of, not average performance, but proportion of individuals with abnormal functioning.

McNeil and Kaij (1984) administered a neurological examination to their Swedish sample on the third or fourth day of life. This examination included items such as reflexes, response patterns, and neurological syndromes, but it also devoted special attention to "softer" signs such as muscle tone, changes in arousal and wakefulness, sensitivity to touch and stimulation, and activity level. The authors report that clear neurological abnormality was very rare in the entire sample. Sixty-nine percent of the neonates were judged to have no neurological abnormality, 21% had suspicious but not certain neurological signs, and 10% were clearly neurologically abnormal. The total group with mentally ill mothers showed slightly more neurological abnormalities than the control group. A gross summary score of neurological status indicated that 13% of the infants with ill mothers were abnormal; only 6% of the control infants were abnormal. The most deviant subgroup of infants included those who had mothers diagnosed as "cycloid" (a diagnosis similar to schizoaffective). One-third of the infants with cycloid mothers had a clear neurological syndrome. The greatest abnormalities were observed in the offspring of the cycloids, followed by offspring of schizophrenics, and then the other psychotics.

Neonatal neurological assessments were also made in the Danish Obstetrical Study of Mednick *et al.* (1971). A neurological examination was given to neonates at birth and at 5 days of age. Tallies were made of non-normal findings. In general, both the character-disorder and schizophrenic-group infants had more abnormalities than those of the normal group. Abnormalities present at birth were likely to have disappeared by 5 days in the normal and character-disorder group but not in the schizophrenic group. The schizophrenic and character-disorder groups also differed in the types of abnormalities they exhibited. The abnormalities for the children of schizophrenics tended to come in the absence or weakness of their motor reflexes.

Finally, Hanson *et al.* (1976) also reported neonatal neurological data from the subsample of infants assessed at the University of Minnesota Hospital as part of the CPP. The investigators reported that the offspring of schizophrenics were in no way different from the other groups in neurological functioning at birth. However, the authors did not provide mean scores or percentages of abnormal findings by group to allow evaluation of trends in the data that might be comparable with other samples.

Marcuse and Cornblatt (1986), in analyzing the neonatal data from the New York CPP data base, combined neonatal neurological findings with all other neonatal medical complications. They reported a nonsignificant trend for offspring of schizophrenics to have more neonatal complications. A significant difference existed between black infants with schizophrenic parents and other infants in the sample, in that the former showed a higher degree of neonatal medical complications.

In summary, virtually all of the studies of neonatal offspring of schizophrenic parents that made neurological assessment have reported either a subgroup of offspring of schizophrenics with definite abnormalities or trends for offspring of schizophrenics to display a higher mean number of abnormalities—trends that are likely accounted for by a subgroup with clear dysfunctioning. No particular type of neurological sign has been consistently implicated by these studies as related to risk for schizophrenia.

The three prospective studies that used the NBAS—Rochester, Jerusalem, and Boston—also suggested that the infants of schizophrenic parents showed more problems neonatally than comparison infants. While the nature of these problems was different across studies, all three studies reported at least trends for the offspring of schizophrenics to be poorer in orientation, motor maturity, and cuddliness.

While the studies reviewed above almost all point to the presence of abnormal neonatal behavior in infants at risk for schizophrenia, discrepancies and even contradictions exist among some of the studies. The Boston sample in particular describes the infant offspring of schizophrenics as hypertonic, irritable, and difficult to console. This is in striking contrast to Fish's description of her high-risk infants as abnormally quiet. While these reports would seem to be contradictory, it is important to note that the Fish study was done during an earlier era than the others—a time that predated antipsychotic medication. Auerbach *et al.* (unpublished data) have presented data to suggest that infants exposed to antipsychotic medication were more likely to be hypertonic, tremulous, and have poor motor maturity than high-risk infants not exposed to medication *in utero*. Thus, neonatal withdrawal from these powerful drugs, if it causes hypertonicity, could mask the underlying pattern of an abnormally inactive state.

Finally, interesting patterns have emerged in the samples that had multiple assessments of neonatal behavior. The Danish Obstetrical Study found an increasing incidence of neurological abnormalities in offspring of schizophrenics over the first weeks of life. Similarly, the Jerusalem data showed increasing differences between offspring of schizophrenics and other infants during the first 2 weeks of life. As Fish (1971b) has suggested, such a pattern in the neonatal period suggests that abnormalities are not merely the aftermath of difficult deliveries but, instead, may have a more developmental origin.

POSTNEONATAL BEHAVIOR

Again, the earliest data available on the development of infants at risk for schizophrenia after the neonatal period come from Fish's New York Infant Study. The absent or decreased vestibular responses observed during the neonatal period remained a characteristic of a subgroup of infants with schizophrenic parents (Fish and Dixon, 1978).

The bulk of the infancy data from the New York Infant Study was derived from observations made during repeated administrations of the Gesell (1947) test. The Gesell is a developmental assessment that evaluates whether or not infants are acquiring key motor and sensorimotor milestones at a normal rate of development. On these tests, infants with schizophrenic parents showed visual–motor disorders during infancy, in particular, failures of integrated bimanual skills (Fish, 1957, 1960, 1971a, 1976; Fish and Hagin, 1973). Depending on the age of the infant, differing aspects of visual–motor performance appeared to be delayed, including fixation on objects held in the infant's own hand, mutual fingering of one hand by the other, reaching, manipulation, transferring objects from one hand to the other, and simultaneous grasp of one object in each hand.

Finally, in eight of the infants, analysis of developmental curves revealed "a major disorganization of neurological maturation" that involved postural–motor, visual–motor, and physical development. Fish calls this phenomenon *pandysmaturation* (PDM) and describes it as a disorder of the timing and integration of neurological maturation. It is characterized by fluctuation in rate of development with marked retardation followed by acceleration, not by uniformly slow development. Development sometimes follows a peculiar trajectory. For example, a child might show a temporary loss of a previously acquired ability or a reversal of the normal cephalocaudal gradient of postural development. An additional aspect of developmental disorganization included infants who would fail items normally passed at a much younger age and simultaneously pass more advanced items (Fish *et al.*, 1965).

While no other high-risk study administered the Gesell, four of the prospective longitudinal studies administered the Bayley Scales of Infant

Development (Bayley, 1969) at multiple ages during the first year and a half of life: the Pittsburgh study, the RLS, the JIDS, and the Boston sample. Like the Gesell, the Bayley Scales measure the rate of acquisition of motor and sensorimotor behaviors. It produces two primary subscales: the Mental Development Index (MDI) and the Psychomotor Development Index (PDI).

In the Pittsburgh study (Ragins *et al.*, 1975), the Bayley Scales were administered during the middle of the first year of life and again after the first birthday. The investigators reported that no statistically significant differences existed between experimental and control groups on the MDI or PDI, although offspring of schizophrenics showed trends for poorer performance. In particular, during the first year of life, these children tended to lag in prehension skill. In addition to the Bayley Scales, the examiners administered a neurological examination to the group assessed between the ages of 12 and 19 months. None of the nonschizophrenic and four of the schizophrenic group infants showed delayed reflex maturation.

In the RLS (Sameroff *et al.*, 1982), the Bayley Scales were administered at 4 and 12 months of age. On the 4-month assessment, the schizophrenic group performed the poorest of the four groups on both the MDI and PDI. Diagnostic group differences even remained statistically significant after entering covariates of SES and severity. On the 12-month assessment, the schizophrenic group was significantly lower than the depression group on both the MDI and PDI, but neither was different from the NMI control group, which fell in between.

In the JIDS (Marcus *et al.*, 1981), the Bayley Scales were administered at 4, 8, and 12 months of age to the offspring of schizophrenics, the other illness comparison groups, and the NMI comparison group. At each of the three ages, the offspring of schizophrenics had the lowest mean score of the four groups, and the schizophrenic group infants were significantly poorer than the NMI groups on the MDI. The primary analyses conducted by the JIDS investigators were examinations of individual differences in two dimensions of functioning: motor functioning and sensorimotor functioning. A subset of the Bayley Scales items was selected through confirmatory multidimensional scaling for use with these analyses. On the motor and sensorimotor dimensions combined, the offspring of schizophrenics as a group were significantly poorer than the other groups at each of the three ages. Visual inspection of scatterplots of these two dimensions at 4, 8, and 12 months shows a clear *subgroup* of neonates with schizophrenic parents who performed more poorly jointly on motoric and sensorimotor items than did neonates with healthy parents or parents with other illnesses. At 4 months of age this subgroup did not exhibit visually guided reaching or age-level hand coordination; at 8 months they could not raise themselves to sitting or standing, pick up small objects, combine objects at midline, or search for disappearing objects; and at 12 months many could not stand alone or walk with help, and most had difficulties in retrieving objects after elapsed time and in imitating complex behavior.

The Boston study (D'Angelo *et al.*, 1983) administered the Bayley Scales at 2, 4, 6, 8, 10, and 12 months of age to offspring of schizophrenics and their comparison groups. There were significant MDI and PDI differences between the offspring of schizophrenic and NMI group mothers at each of the ages, with the offspring of schizophrenics performing the most poorly. The infants of schizophrenic mothers had lower psychomotor developmental scores than the infants of depressed mothers at each of the ages, but differences on the MDI disappeared after 8 months.

Several investigators have also given brief reports of the development of infants at risk for schizophrenia from single time periods. Marcuse and Cornblatt (1986) reported that the New York CPP offspring of schizophrenics did not perform more poorly on the Bayley Scales (Bayley, 1969) administered at 8 months of age. Similarly, in the Minnesota CPP sample (Hanson *et al.*, 1976), no differences existed between offspring of schizophrenics and other infants on 8-month Bayley Scales assessments. These authors report no data on trends in group differences. Table 3.3 summarizes mean developmental scores for each of the studies that reported specific data.

In summary, the four prospective longitudinal studies using the Bayley Scales and the one using the Gesell Scales reported that offspring of schizophrenics consistently lag in acquisition of motor and sensory motor milestones when compared with offspring of mentally healthy parents and with offspring of parents with other mental illnesses. Fish also reported that delays in acquisition of motor and sensory motor milestones were accompanied by lags in physical growth. None of the other studies collected data on physical growth.

The only data thus far that have not shown lags in offspring of schizophrenics come from the two cohorts of the CPP. Ways in which these samples differ from those in the other studies designed specifically to investigate issues in schizophrenia may need further consideration. One obvious such difference is that the perinatal studies are the only ones to include parents whose onset of illness may come after the birth of the target child. Other differences might well be related to means of making psychiatric diagnoses, reliability of such diagnoses, and heterogeneity of individuals within the schizophrenic group.

TABLE 3.3. Summary of Mean Developmental Scores Based on the Bayley Scales of Infant Development

Study	Age					
	2 Months	4 Months	6 Months	8 Months	10 Months	12 Months
Bayley Mental Development Index						
Pittsburgh						
Schizophrenia	—	—	112	—	—	108
Nonschizophrenia	—	—	117	—	—	111
Rochester Longitudinal Study						
Schizophrenia	—	104	—	—	—	107
Depression	—	112	—	—	—	116
Personality disorder	—	110	—	—	—	115
No mental illness	—	115	—	—	—	113
Jerusalem Infant						
Development Study						
Schizophrenia	—	95	—	97	—	95
Affective disorders	—	97	—	98	—	96
Personality disorders neuroses	—	101	—	108	—	99
No mental illness	—	103	—	106	—	106
Boston High-Risk Study						
Schizophrenia	97	94	96	98	98	97
Other illness	101	104	109	103	104	103
No mental illness	103	108	107	108	107	109
Bayley Psychometer Development Index						
Pittsburgh						
Schizophrenia	—	—	113	—	—	106
Nonschizophrenia	—	—	103	—	—	106
Rochester Longitudinal Study						
Schizophrenia	—	107	—	—	—	96
Depression	—	117	—	—	—	106
Personality disorder	—	115	—	—	—	101
No mental illness	—	118	—	—	—	100
Jerusalem Infant						
Development Study						
Schizophrenia	—	103	—	94	—	87
Affective disorders	—	104	—	82	—	92
Personality disorder/ neurosis	—	103	—	92	—	93
No mental illness	—	104	—	103	—	93
Boston						
Schizophrenia	89	88	89	89	91	90
Other illness	104	104	104	105	104	104
No mental illness	105	106	106	109	111	110

RELATION OF OTHER BIOLOGICAL AND
SOCIAL FACTORS TO INFANT BEHAVIOR

Investigators finding neurobehavioral dysfunctioning in offspring of schizophrenics have suggested that such dysfunctioning is a behavioral marker for schizophrenic genotype (Fish, 1977; Marcus *et al.*, 1981); however, acceptance of such an explanation for neurobehavioral deficits requires ruling out other causal explanations for the deficits—particularly the effects of a poor early rearing environment and the influence of pregnancy and birth complications.

The effects of early rearing environments have not been the focus of high-risk studies beginning during the infancy period. Considerable exploration of this issue apparently remains to be done; however, rearing environment is not a plausible explanation for neonatal deficits in offspring of schizophrenics, and none of the high-risk studies to date have presented evidence suggesting that developmental lags in older infant offspring of schizophrenics are related to rearing environment. The Boston study (D'Angelo *et al.*, 1983) found that infants who were placed in foster care environments away from their mentally ill mother actually did more poorly developmentally than those remaining in the care of their natural mother—although they also reported that children with developmental problems were much more likely to be placed in foster care. Fish found evidence of PDM in children being reared by their ill mothers and children reared in other, more stable environments. In the Jerusalem sample, while evidence indicated that children placed in orphanage environments often showed developmental lags during infancy, there were also signs of such lags in offspring of schizophrenics living in good adoptive homes.

Although much attention has been given to the question of whether or not pregnancy and birth complications contribute to the development of schizophrenia, little evidence suggests a simple causal linkage between such complications and schizophrenic illness (Goodman, 1988; McNeil and Kaij, 1978; Jacobsen and Kinney, 1980; Parnas *et al.*, 1982). Evidence from epidemiological studies of schizophrenia has suggested that genetically based neural developmental disruptions may result in a heightened vulnerability to complications of delivery, but not that the delivery complications themselves cause schizophrenia (Cannon *et al.*, 1989). While some data suggest that schizophrenic patients suffer an increased number of pregnancy and birth complications compared with matched controls, this has not generally been the case in the high-risk studies of infancy, and no linkage has been reported between complications and early neurobehavioral development. Several of the high-risk studies—the RLS, the JIDS, and the Danish Obstetrical Study—have reported lower birthweights in

the offspring of schizophrenics. It has been suggested that the most parsimonious explanation for these low birthweights is that intrauterine
growth retardation is a fetal manifestation of the effects of a schizophrenic
genotype, just as is poor extrauterine growth and development (Marcus *et
al.*, 1981; Fish, 1977; Goodman, 1988).

PREDICTION FROM INFANCY TO LATER BEHAVIOR

If lags in development during infancy are evidence of a neurointegrative defect that is central to a genotype for schizophrenia, then there
should be a stable subgroup of children who also have problems at later
ages and who eventually become schizophrenic. Data bearing on this issue
are rather sparse because of the long time period that elapses between
infancy and adult breakdown.

Fish's sample is the only one, so far, to report longitudinal data spanning from infancy through the young adult ages at which actual schizophrenic breakdown is likely to occur. She rank-ordered the infants on the
severity of PDM, i.e., lags and disorganization in gross motor and/or
visual–motor development associated with a lag in physical growth during the first two years of life. At the 10-year follow-up, children were
independently evaluated on the severity of their psychopathology (Fish,
1987). Ratings of severe to moderately severe disorder occurred in all
seven high-risk subjects with PDM. PDM during infancy did not predict
hard neurological signs at school age but did show a modest association
with other aspects of neurobehavioral functioning—specifically, Bender
Gestalt results described as "schizophrenic" (Fish, 1987). PDM during
infancy also related to mental illness at age 23 years. Seven of the 12
high-risk subjects showed PDM, and 6 of the 7 were the sickest adolescents
and adults in the sample.

The JIDS is the only other sample that analyzed continuity between
infancy and older ages. At approximately age 10 years, the children from
the original Jerusalem sample were assessed on a battery of neurobehavioral measures that included a neurological examination, intelligence test,
and other cognitive and attentional tasks (Auerbach *et al.*, 1991). In both
infancy and middle childhood, they identified subgroups of children of
schizophrenic parents who were performing poorly on these neurobehavioral measures. Fifteen of the children in the schizophrenic group were
assessed at both infancy and middle childhood. The pattern of continuity
for the majority of children in the comparison groups (i.e., with parents
suffering from a mental illness other than schizophrenia or with mentally
healthy parents) is one of continuity in development for well-functioning

infants or of improvement for the poorly functioning infants. In contrast to the children in these groups, the developmental trend in the schizophrenic offspring group is more variable. Only 50% of the well-functioning infants continued to perform well in childhood. Two-thirds of the poor-functioning infants in the schizophrenic group continued to have difficulties in both motor and cognitive functioning in childhood (Auerbach *et al.*, 1990). The profiles of dysfunctional behavior shown by the offspring of schizophrenics in the Jerusalem sample are quite similar to the profiles that were predictive of later schizophrenic breakdown in the earlier Israeli High-Risk Study sample (Marcus *et al.*, 1985a). Common to the poor-functioning children in both samples were perceptual–motor dysfunctioning as measured on the Bender-Gestalt, fine motor dyscoordination, and attentional problems.

The Jerusalem finding of a greater percentage of childhood neurointegrative problems in poor-functioning infants of schizophrenics, together with similar findings in Fish's work, suggest that such deficits in middle childhood may be an important behavioral marker of vulnerability to schizophrenia.

SUMMARY

In attempting to draw conclusions about the nature of infant development in individuals who will later become schizophrenic, one is limited by several features of the available data. First, the total number of studies of infants with schizophrenic parents is quite small—barely half a dozen. Second, the difficulty of high-risk research has limited the sample sizes in any given investigation. The population of pregnant schizophrenic women in any one geographic area is likely to be small, making recruitment slow; without a very high degree of cooperation from multiple obstetric and psychiatric institutions, pregnant schizophrenic women are difficult to identify; and the women themselves, because of the nature of their illness, are difficult to enlist in the research process and to keep engaged over time. None of the studies reported above had samples of more than 20 infants with schizophrenic parents. Groups of that size are only large enough to detect very strong group-difference effects.

Third, even among the infants with schizophrenic parents, only a small subgroup will ultimately develop a schizophrenic illness. This fact has important implications for data analysis, which have often been overlooked by researchers. The data available for review in this paper were generally summarized by the authors in terms of differences between group means. Such group-difference analyses may work to obscure findings in samples of this sort and can distort interpretations (see Marcus *et al.*, 1985a). Because only a subgroup of children with a schizophrenic parent will carry a genetic predisposition to schizophrenia or eventually become schizophrenic, the high-risk group is heterogeneous, containing many children who are presumably not at genetic risk for schizophrenia. The necessary inclusion of these children in analyses of group differences reduces the likelihood of achieving statistically significant effects; the strongest findings reported by researchers studying infant offspring of schizophrenics have generally come from those investigators who have looked for dysfunctional subgroups rather than those who have looked at group means. The exclusive use of data analytic methods relying on mean differences in many of the studies reported here, and elsewhere in the high-risk literature, is a serious problem because it may obscure the existence of a dysfunctional subgroup.

Finally, with respect to the instruments used, the Gesell and the Bayley scales were designed to measure infant milestones that emerge in a relatively fixed pattern. Such milestones are quite resistant to perturbations in development and, thus, are not especially sensitive to risk factors (Horowitz, 1989). In addition, the items included in these tests measure a wide variety of functions and obviously were not selected because of their relevance to a theory of schizophrenia. Because summary developmental scores are global measures, they are probably not optimal for detecting effects that are specific to schizophrenia.

Despite these methodological limitations, the studies of infant offspring of schizophrenics do provide evidence indicating the presence of neurodevelopmental irregularities during the first year of life in children at risk for schizophrenia. These neurodevelopmental findings are as follows.

1. Weak evidence indicates that neonates at risk for schizophrenia show more neurological abnormalities than do offspring of mentally healthy parents, although not necessarily more than infants whose parents have other illnesses. These neurological abnormalities do not seem to be specific to any particular sign. Also, some evidence from studies that conducted repeated neonatal assessments indicates that the differences in neurological functioning between offspring of schizophrenics and other infants become greater later in the neonatal period—presumably after the transitory effects of obstetric medication and delivery trauma on neurological functioning have begun to disappear and no longer obscure deficits related to the schizophrenic genotype.

2. Clear evidence indicates less optimal patterns of behavior in at least a subgroup of neonates of schizophrenic parents. There are several reports of low activity level, poor alertness and orientation, poor motor maturity, low muscle tonus, and poor cuddliness. Overall, these behaviors suggest

that the neonate at risk for schizophrenia is an underaroused and unresponsive infant who relates poorly to the outside world. Available studies, however, do not completely replicate one another. At least one study reports that the offspring of schizophrenic parents are highly irritable, difficult to console, and hypertonic. While discrepancies may be related to differences in maternal medication, or other unexplored differences between the populations of schizophrenics included in the samples, at this point it is impossible to fully reconcile the cross-study results.

3. Clear evidence from five samples indicates lags in the acquisition of developmental milestones in high-risk infants after the neonatal period. Fish, who to date has done the most careful study of developmental patterns, has further observed that lags in high-risk infants are not necessarily present at all assessment ages in an individual child, that lags in behavioral development are accompanied by delays in physical growth, and that not only the timing but also the pattern of the acquisition of milestone skills may be disordered. The limited follow-up data past infancy—from the New York Infant Study and the JIDS—suggest that developmental lags during infancy may be related to later neurobehavioral dysfunctioning and even to schizophrenic breakdown.

Thus, the findings from neonatal and older infant offspring of schizophrenic parents are consistent with a hypothesis that children who will later become schizophrenics show neurodevelopmental abnormalities from the earliest days of life. These findings, combined with those observed during school-age and adolescence, suggest that schizophrenia is a developmental disease. Schizophrenia may be a disease of the entire life span with different manifestations at different ages—growth retardation and neural dysplasia during gestation and possibly later during infancy; abnormal state and motoric functioning during the neonatal period; delays in motor and sensorimotor development during infancy; motor, attentional, and social dysfunctioning during school-age and adolescence; and eventually the traditional signs of schizophrenic illness emerging during young adulthood.

The findings of the high-risk studies converge with and are given strength by a growing body of brain science research suggesting that schizophrenia may be a neuodevelopmental rather than a neurodegenerative disease. Numerous investigators have now suggested that the types of cytoarchitectural and neuroimagery variations in brain structure that have been observed in schizophrenic patients are likely to have their origins during gestation and early life (Kovelman and Scheibel, 1984; Jakob and Beckmann, 1986; Benes *et al.*, 1986; Falkai *et al.*, 1988; Crow *et al.*, 1989; Reveley *et al.*, 1987; Weinberger, 1987; Cannon *et al.*, 1989).

There obviously remains a great deal that is unknown about the infant development of individuals who will later become schizophrenic. Future research needs to adopt two priorities. The first of these is the continued following of existing high-risk samples through the age period of schizophrenic breakdown. The role of early neurobehavioral abnormalities in the development of schizophrenia hinges on demonstrating that such abnormalities can be observed at various periods of the life cycle in the same individuals, and that individuals with these abnormalities are those who ultimately develop schizophrenic illness. Existing samples have not all matured to the point of being able to explore this issue. A second priority should be the initiation of new infancy studies of shorter duration. The purpose of such studies would be to attempt to replicate previous findings that have not yet been investigated by more than one research group and to explore key areas of behavior not yet studied. To date there have been no attempts to replicate at least two of the key findings in Fish's original study: (1) patterns of slowed physical growth during infancy and (2) the abnormal nature of vestibular functioning. The field is clearly ready for the collection of new data. The data in most of the high-risk studies reported here were collected during the 1970s. During the 20 years since the initiation of these previous high-risk studies, the sophistication of research tools available for the assessment of infants has greatly increased. In particular, future investigators should consider employing sophisticated procedures for assessment of sensory processing, measures of electrophysiological functioning, and noninvasive brain-imaging techniques. Future research needs to be more developmental, more multidisciplinary, and more "schizophrenia-based." Although the existing data strongly suggest that a subgroup of children born to schizophrenic parents exhibit early and continuous signs of neurobehavioral deficits, the future work in this area needs to clarify the nature of these deficits, the specific patterns of continuities between developmental stages, and the role of these behavioral deficits in brain-based theories of schizophrenia.

REFERENCES

Asarnow, J. R. (1988). Children at risk for schizophrenia: Converging lines of evidence. *Schizophrenia Bulletin, 14,* 613–631.

Auerbach, J. G., Hans, S. L., Marcus, J., and Auerbach, A. G. (1991). Neurobehavioral functioning from infancy to middle childhood in children at risk for schizophrenia. In C. W. Greenbaum and J. G. Auerbach (Eds.), *Longitudinal Studies of Children at Risk: Cross-National Perspectives.* Norwood, New Jersey: Ablex Press.

Auerbach, J. G., Hans, S. L., Marcus, J., and Maier, S. (1990). Maternal psychotropic medication and neonatal behavior. Unpublished manuscript.

Bayley, N. (1969). *The Bayley Scales of Infant Development.* New York: Psychological Corporation.

Benes, F. M., Davidson, J., and Bird, E. D. (1986). Quantitative cytoarchitectural studies of the cerebral cortex of schizophrenics. *Archives of General Psychiatry, 43,* 31–35.

Berendes, H. W. (1966). The structure and scope of the collaborative project on cerebral palsy, mental retardation, and other neurological and sensory disorders of infancy and childhood. In S. S. Chipman, A. M. Lilienfeld, B. G. Greenberg, and J. F. Donnelly (Eds.), *Research methodology and needs in perinatal studies* (pp. 118–138). Springfield, IL: Charles C Thomas.

Brazelton, T. B. (1973). *Neonatal Behavioral Assessment Scale.* London: William Heinemann Medical Books.

Cannon, T. D., Mednick, S. A., and Parnas, J. (1989). Genetic and perinatal determinants of structural brain deficits in schizophrenia. *Archives of General Psychiatry, 46,* 883–889.

Crow, T. J., Joanna, B., Bloom, S. R., Brown, R., Bruton, C. J., Colter, N., Frith, C. D., Johnstone, E. C., Owens, D. G., and Roberts, G. W. (1989). Schizophrenia as an anomaly of development of cerebral asymmetry: A postmortem study and a proposal concerning the genetic basis of the disease. *Archives of General Psychiatry, 46,* 1145–1150.

D'Angelo, E. J., Krock, L. A., O'Neill, L. D., and Boyle, M. P. (1983). Developmental and temperamental characteristics of infants at risk for serious psychopathology. In J. D. Call, E. Galenson, and R. L. Tyson (Eds.), *Frontiers of infant psychiatry* (Vol. 2, pp. 190–200). New York: Basic Books.

Endicott, J., and Spitzer, R. L. (1972). Current and Past Psychopathology Scales (CAPPS): Rationale, reliability, and validity. *Archives of General Psychiatry, 27,* 678–687.

Erlenmeyer-Kimling, L. (1987). High-risk research in schizophrenia: A summary of what has been learned. *Journal of Psychiatric Research, 21,* 401–411.

Erlenmeyer-Kimling, L., Cornblatt, B., Friedman, D., Marcuse, Y., Rutschmann, J., Simmens, S., and Devi, S. (1982). *Neurological, Electrophysiological and Attentional Deviations in Children at Risk for Schizophrenia.* In F. A. Henn and Nasrallah (Eds.), *Schizophrenia as a brain disease* (pp. 61–98). New York: Oxford University Press.

Falkai, P., Bogerts, B., and Rozumek, M. (1988). Limbic pathology in schizophrenia: The entorhinal region—A morphometric study. *Biological Psychiatry, 24,* 515–521.

Fish, B. (1957). The detection of schizophrenia in infancy. *Journal of Nervous and Mental Disease, 125,* 1–24.

Fish, B. (1960). Involvement of the central nervous system in infants with schizophrenia. *Archives of Neurology, 2,* 115–121.

Fish, B. (1963). The maturation of arousal and attention in the first months of life: A study of variations in ego development. *Journal of the American Academy of Child Psychiatry, 2,* 253–270.

Fish, B. (1971a). Contributions of developmental research to a theory of schizophrenia. In J. Hellmuth (Ed.), *Exceptional infant, Vol. 2: Studies in abnormalities* (pp. 473–482). New York: Brunner/Mazel.

Fish, B. (1971b). Genetic or traumatic deviation? *Social Biology, 18,* S117–S119.

Fish, B. (1976). An approach to prevention in infants at risk for schizophrenia: Developmental deviations from birth to 10 years. *Journal of the American Academy of Child Psychiatry, 15,* 62–82.

Fish, B. (1977). Neurobiologic antecedents of schizophrenia in children. *Archives of General Psychiatry, 34,* 1297–1313.

Fish, B. (1987). Pandysmaturation as an infant predictor of schizotypal development. Paper presented at a meeting of the High-Risk Consortium (May 1987), Newport, RI.

Fish, B., and Alpert, M. (1962). Abnormal states of consciousness and muscle tone in infants born to schizophrenic mothers. *American Journal of Psychiatry, 119,* 439–445.

Fish, B., and Alpert, M. (1963). Patterns of neurological development in infants born to schizophrenic mothers. In J. Wortis (Ed.) *Recent advances in biological psychiatry* (Vol. 5, pp. 24–37). New York: Plenum.

Fish, B., and Dixon, W. J. (1978). Vestibular hyporeactivity in infants at risk for schizophrenia: Association with critical developmental disorders. *Archives of General Psychiatry, 35,* 963–971.

Fish, B., and Hagin, R. (1973). Visual–motor disorders in infants at risk for schizophrenia. *Archives of General Psychiatry, 28,* 900–904.

Fish, B., Shapiro, T., Halpern, F., and Wile, R. (1965). The prediction of schizophrenia in infancy: 3. A ten-year follow-up report of neurological and psychological development. *American Journal of Psychiatry, 121,* 768–775.

Garmezy, N., and Streitman, S. (1974). Children at risk: The search for the antecedents of schizophrenia. Part 1. Conceptual models and research methods. *Schizophrenia Bulletin, 1,* 14–90.

Gesell, A. (1947). *Developmental diagnosis* (2nd ed.). New York: Hoeber.

Goodman, R. (1988). Are complications of pregnancy and birth causes of schizophrenia? *Developmental Medicine and Child Neurology, 30,* 391–406.

Goodman, S. H. (1987). Emory University Project on children of disturbed parents. *Schizophrenia Bulletin, 13,* 411–424.

Grunebaum, H., Weiss, J. L., Gallant, D., and Cohler, B. J. (1974). Attention in young children of psychotic mothers. *American Journal of Psychiatry, 131,* 887–891.

Hans, S. L., and Marcus, J. (1987). A process model for the development of schizophrenia. *Psychiatry, 50,* 361–370.

Hanson, D. R., Gottesman, I. I., and Heston, L. L. (1976). Some possible childhood indicators of adult schizophrenia from children of schizophrenics. *British Journal of Psychiatry, 129,* 142–154.

Horowitz, F. D. (1989). The concept of risk: A re-evaluation. Paper presented at the meeting of the Society for Research in Child Development (April 1989), Kansas City, MO.

Jacobsen, B., and Kinney, D. K. (1980). Perinatal complications in adopted and non-adopted schizophrenics and their controls: Preliminary results. *Acta Psychiatrica Scandinavica, Suppl., 285,* 337–346.

Jakob, H., and Beckmann, H. (1986). Prenatal developmental disturbances in the limbic allocortex of schizophrenics. *Journal of Neural Transmission, 65,* 303–326.

Kovelman, J. A., and Scheibel, A. B. (1984). A neurohistological correlate of schizophrenia. *Biological Psychiatry, 19,* 1601–1621.

Marcus, J. (1974). Cerebral functioning in offspring of schizophrenics: A possible genetic factor. *International Journal of Mental Health, 3,* 57–73.

Marcus, J., Auerbach, J., Wilkinson, L., and Burack, C. M. (1981). Infants at risk for schizophrenia: The Jerusalem Infant Development Study. *Archives of General Psychiatry, 38,* 703–713.

Marcus, J., Hans, S. L., Lewow, E., Wilkinson, L., and Burack, C. M. (1985a). Neurological findings in high-risk children: Childhood assessment and five year followup. *Schizophrenia Bulletin, 11,* 85–100.

Marcus, J., Hans, S. L., Mednick, S., Schulsinger, F., and Michelsen, N. (1985b). Neurological dysfunction in offspring of schizophrenics in Israel and Denmark: A replication analysis. *Archives of General Psychiatry, 42,* 753–761.

Marcus, J., Hans, S. L., Nagler, S., Auerbach, J. G., Mirsky, A. F., and Aubrey, A. (1987). Review of the NIMH Israeli Kibbutz-City Study and the Jerusalem Infant Development Study. *Schizophrenia Bulletin, 13,* 425–438.

Marcuse, Y., and Cornblatt, B. (1986). Children at high risk for schizophrenia: Predictions from infancy to childhood functioning. In L. Erlenmeyer-Kimling and N. E. Miller (Eds.), *Life-span research on the prediction of psychopathology* (pp. 81–100). Hillsdale, NJ: Erlbaum.

McNeil, T. F., and Kaij, L. (1978). Obstetric factors in the development of schizophrenia: Complications in the births of preschizophrenics and in reproduction by schizophrenic parents. In L. C. Wynne, R. L. Cromwell, and S. Matthysse (Eds.), *The nature of schizophrenia. New approaches to research and treatment.* New York: Wiley.

McNeil, T. F., and Kaij, L. (1984). Offspring of women with nonorganic psychoses. In N. F. Watt, E. J. Anthony, L. C. Wynne, and J. E. Rolf (Eds.), *Children at risk for schizophrenia: A longitudinal perspective* (pp. 465–481). Cambridge: Cambridge University Press.

McNeil, T. F., and Kaij, L. (1987). Swedish High-Risk Study: Sample characteristics at age 6. *Schizophrenia Bulletin, 13,* 373–382.

Mednick, S. A., Mura, E., Schulsinger, F., and Mednick, B. (1971). Perinatal conditions and infant development in children with schizophrenic parents. *Social Biology (Suppl.), 18,* S103–S113.

Niswander, K. R., and Gordon, M. (1972). *The Collaborative Perinatal Study of the National Institute of Neurological Diseases and Stroke: The women and their pregnancies.* Washington, DC: U.S. Government Printing Office.

Nuechterlein, K. H. (1983). Signal detection in vigilance tasks and behavioral attributes among offspring of schizophrenic mothers and among hyperactive children. *Journal of Abnormal Psychology, 92,* 4–28.

Nuechterlein, K. H., and Dawson, M. E. (1984). Information processing and attentional functioning in the developmental course of schizophrenic disorders. *Schizophrenia Bulletin, 10,* 160–203.

Orvaschel, H., Mednick, S., Schulsinger, F., and Rock, D. (1979). The children of psychiatrically disturbed parents. *Archives of General Psychiatry, 36,* 691–695.

Parnas, J., Schulsinger, F., Teasdale, T. W., Schulsinger, H., Feldman, P. M., and Mednick, S. A. (1982). Perinatal complications and clinical outcome within the schizophrenic spectrum. *British Journal of Psychiatry, 140,* 416–420.

Ragins, N., Schachter, J., Elmer, E., Preisman, R., Bowes, A., and Harway, V. (1975). Infants and children at risk for schizophrenia. *Journal of the American Academy of Child Psychiatry, 14,* 150–177.

Reveley, M. A., Reveley, A. M., and Baldy, R. (1987). Left cerebral hemisphere hypodensity in discordant schizophrenic twins. *Archives of General Psychiatry, 44,* 625–632.

Rieder, R. O., and Nichols, P. L. (1979). The offspring of schizophrenics. 3. Hyperactivity and neurological soft signs. *Archives of General Psychiatry, 36,* 665–674.

Rutschmann, J., Cornblatt, B., and Erlenmeyer-Kimling, L. (1977). Sustained attention in children at risk for schizophrenia. *Archives of General Psychiatry, 34,* 571–575.

Rutschmann, J., Cornblatt, B., and Erlenmeyer-Kimling, L. (1986). Sustained attention in children at risk for schizophrenia: Findings with two visual continuous performance tests in a new sample. *Journal of Abnormal Child Psychiatry, 14,* 365–385.

Sameroff, A. J., Krafchuk, E. E., and Bakow, H. A. (1978). Issues in grouping items from the Brazelton Neonatal Behavior Assessment Scale. In A. J. Sameroff (Ed.), *Organization and stability of newborn behavior: A commentary on the Brazelton Neonatal Behavior Assessment Scale. Monographs of the Society for Research in Child Development, 43*(5–6, Serial No. 177).

Sameroff, A. J., Seifer, R., and Zax, M. (1982). Early development of children at risk for emotional disorder. *Monographs of the Society for Research in Child Development, 47*(7, Serial No. 199).

Sameroff, A. J., Seifer, R., Zax, M., and Barocas, R. (1987). Early indicators of developmental risk: Rochester Longitudinal Study. *Schizophrenia Bulletin, 13,* 383–394.

Stott, F., Musick, F., Clark, R., and Cohler, B. J. (1983). Developmental patterns in the infants and young children of mentally ill mothers. *Infant Mental Health, 4,* 217–235.

Walker, E., and Emory, E. (1983). Infants at risk for psychopathology: Offspring of schizophrenic parents. *Child Development, 54,* 1269–1285.

Weinberger, D. R. (1987). Implications of normal brain development for the pathogenesis of schizophrenia. *Archives of General Psychiatry, 44,* 660–669.

Early Social and Affective Development in Schizophrenic Offspring

Sherryl H. Goodman

Social and affective development in young offspring of schizophrenic parents has been of interest to researchers studying high-risk children for three reasons. First, hypotheses can be tested about possible developmental pathways in the etiology of schizophrenia. For example, it has been speculated that passive, socially withdrawn children may behave in ways that begin the pathway toward the development of schizophrenia. This course may be set by early failure experiences due to lower social competence (Ricks and Berry, 1970) or early withdrawal due to heightened autonomic arousal to stress (Mednick, 1967). In either case, such children may be seen as odd and, thus, neglected by peers and adults. Although children may protest the rejection with some aggressiveness, they are likely to become socially isolated by adolescence.

Second, difficulties or delays in social and affective competence may be indications of a broader range of developmental outcomes for which children of schizophrenic parents are at risk. That is, most high-risk children (i.e., 85–90%) will not develop schizophrenia or even spectrum disorders; many, however, may have significant problems in the development of competence in the social and affective domains.

Copyright © 1991 by Academic Press, Inc.
All rights of reproduction in any form reserved.

Third, unique characteristics of the development of high-risk children may indicate early signs of disorder. For example, measures of social competence, such as poor premorbid social adjustment, have been shown to be predictive of both course and outcome in adult schizophrenics (Garmezy *et al.*, 1978; Goldstein, 1980). Although not yet demonstrated, earlier detection holds the promise of intervening early in pathological development and, ideally, reducing the severity or impact of the disorder. Preventive interventions could be aimed at enhancing social competence, emotional communication, and so forth (Goodman, 1984b).

Despite the cogent arguments for the study of early social and affective development in high-risk children, many risk researchers have steered clear of such work and remain skeptical of the value of its findings. The reaction is justified in terms of the impracticality of studying children at risk for schizophrenia from infancy or preschool age, given the number of years that would be required to follow the subjects into the risk period for onset of schizophrenia in adulthood. This argument, of course, applies generally to studies of such young children, including Fish's (1987a,b) and Marcus *et al.*'s (1987) work on neurological and cognitive-intellectual factors, McNeil and Kaij's (1987) research on pregnancy and birth complications, and Sameroff *et al.*'s (1987) longitudinal study of high-risk children from birth. More specific to social and affective development, the reaction is also justified in terms of the possibility/probability of identifying characteristics of early social and affective development, which would be unique to offspring of schizophrenic parents. Instead, children's social and affective development may be more broadly associated with general characteristics of inadequate parenting. While the uniqueness of a deficit to an offspring group does not guarantee its genetic origin, researchers must still interpret findings in terms of a model (genetic, environmental, or interactive) for the development of schizophrenia and other disorders.

Children of schizophrenic parents are presumed to be at risk for problems in social and affective development not only because they may have inherited vulnerability to the disorder, but also because of the nature of their experiences interacting with presumably less competent parents. Symptoms of schizophrenia, expressed in the context of mother–child[a] interaction, may interfere with the mother's ability to be appropriately and contingently responsive, to interpret qualities of the environment adequately for the child, and so forth. Parental psychopathology may also adversely affect child development because of the often-associated physical separations due to psychiatric hospitalizations and the consequences of other adverse life events. Researchers studying the effects of schizophrenia on children's social and affective development need to demon-

---

[a]The word "mother" is used to refer to the primary caregiver. Most high-risk studies are of children of schizophrenic mothers. Exceptions are noted in the text.

strate the means by which the parent's disorder might impact on the child's development.

This chapter provides a review of the current status of knowledge of early social and affective development in offspring of schizophrenic parents. The reviewed research encompasses early social interaction, social–emotional competence, and the role of parenting in the development of children's social–emotional competence. The review is presented and summarized in such a way as to allow conclusions to be drawn about the value of this area of study. What questions have been answered? Have any etiological models been elucidated? Are certain aspects of early social and affective development specific to the offspring of schizophrenic parents? What indications exist of a connection between such early development and the course of unfolding psychopathology? What methodological problems remain to be solved? What direction should future work take?

The majority of data on young children's social and emotional functioning discussed in this review comes from five prospective studies of children at high risk for schizophrenia due to the presence of the disorder in one of their biological parents. These studies all began with children at birth or early infancy. The five studies are (1) the Rochester Longitudinal Study of Sameroff and his colleagues (Sameroff et al., 1982, 1984, 1987; Seifer and Sameroff, 1982; Seifer et al., 1981), (2) the Swedish High-Risk Study of McNeil and his colleagues (McNeil, 1986; McNeil and Kaij, 1984; McNeil et al., 1983), (3) the Thresholds Mothers' Project of Cohler and his colleagues (Cohler et al., 1987; Cohler and Musick, 1984; Musick et al., 1985; Stott et al., 1984), (4) the author's Emory University Project Parents and Children Together (PACT) (Goodman, 1984a,b, 1987a,b; Goodman and Brumley, 1990), and (5) the Jerusalem Infant Development Study of Marcus and his colleagues (Hans et al., 1987; Marcus et al., 1981, 1987).

Sample and design features of these four studies are summarized in Tables 4.1 and 4.2. To avoid redundancy, these features will only be mentioned in the review when particularly relevant; the reader is invited to refer back to the tables as necessary in the context of each of the ensuing sections. Material for the review of the quality of caregiving by disturbed parents and its role in children's social and emotional functioning comes from a somewhat broader array of sources. Sample and design features of studies that are not included in the tables will be described when first mentioned.

EVIDENCE FOR SOCIAL AND EMOTIONAL COMPETENCE: SOCIAL INTERACTION

Increasing sophistication in research methodologies and theories of infant development have allowed investigators to examine the capacities

TABLE 4.1. Social and Emotional Functioning in High-Risk Children: Major Studies Reviewed

	Subjects			
Study/location	Child's age at entry	Child's age(s) at follow-up	Risk group	Comparison group(s)
Rochester Longitudinal Study/Rochester, NY	birth	4, 12, 30, and 48 months	S[a]	D, PD, NMI
Swedish High-Risk Study/Malmo, Sweden	birth	multiple first year, 24 months, and 6 years	S	cycloid psychosis, psychogenic psychosis, post-partum psychosis, other psychosis, D, NMI
Thresholds Mothers' Project/Chicago	2 months to 5 years	4–10 years	S, D, PD, schizoafffective	NMI
Emory University Project PACT/Atlanta, GA	birth to 5 years	1–6 years, 2–7 years	S	D, NMI
Jerusalem Infant Development Study/Jerusalem	birth	3 and 14 days, 4, 8, 12 months, and 7–12 years	S	D, PD, N, NMI
Infants at Risk Study/Boston	birth	2 days and 2, 4, 6, 8, 10, and 12 months	S, D	NMI

D, depressed; N, neurotic; NMI, no mental illness; PD, personality disordered; S, schizophrenia.
[a]Disturbed parents were all mothers except in the Jerusalem study where some schizophrenic parents were fathers, unless otherwise noted in text.

TABLE 4.2. Sociodemographic Characteristics of Major Studies Reviewed

	Subjects		
Study	SES	Race[a] (% White)	% Married
Rochester Longitudinal Study	middle–low	63	74
Swedish High-Risk Study	mixed	100	NA[b]
Thresholds Mothers' Project	low	50	50
Emory University's Project PACT	low	2	10
Jerusalem Infant Development Study	middle–low	100	100
Boston Infants at Risk Study	middle	unspecified	75

[a]The nonwhite subjects in the Rochester and Emory studies were black; in the Thresholds Mothers' Project they were black, Asian, or Hispanic.
[b]The precise figure is not available, but the authors report that "most" of the mothers were married when first studied.

of high-risk infants in early interactions with their mothers and others. Child development researchers have demonstrated the primary endowment with which infants are born, including the capacities to attract and engage in social interactions (Tronick and Adamson, 1980). Infants vary in their response to stimuli (over- or under-responding), in the clarity and consistency with which they convey their needs, and in attentiveness. Infants also strongly differ in temperament factors such as irritability, soothability, sociability, and regularity. Any such aspects of infant responding that could be considered unique to offspring of schizophrenic parents could be early signs or markers of vulnerability for later developmental problems.

Infants, of course, exist in the context of their relationships with their mothers. Thus, the developing capacities of the infant carry strong implications for the quality of the mother–infant relationship. From an interpersonal, transactional point of view, the infant's individuality contributes to the mother–infant relationship as does the mother's parenting capacity. Qualities of the infant such as alertness, readability, and responsiveness can powerfully alter the mother's experience of and response to her infant. An alert, responsive baby can serve as a powerful stimulus to a mother, who then would be inclined to respond contingently with the infant's state (Brazelton *et al.*, 1974; Stern, 1985; Stern *et al.*, 1985). In contrast, an irritable, unpredictable, difficult-to-soothe baby could create severe strain even in a healthy mother (Field and Sostek, 1983).

Reason to be concerned about the relationships between schizophrenic mothers and their babies comes partly from evidence that many offspring of schizophrenic parents are born with characteristics that could affect the relationship with the mother. For example, as Hans and Marcus point out in this volume (Chapter 3), infants of schizophrenic mothers have been shown to have abnormal muscle tone, motor reflexes, and sensory–motor functioning. Furthermore, they have been described as more irritable, less sensitive, and more often wakeful (Fish and Alpert, 1962; Marcus *et al.*, 1981; Mednick *et al.*, 1971). The evidence for unique qualities of the attachment relationship and other social interactions are reviewed next.

Mother–Child Interaction: Attachment

A few researchers of high-risk children have asked the specific question of whether or not the infants are at risk of developing maladaptive attachment patterns. Attachment refers to the relatively enduring emotional ties of one individual to another. Infants or young children demonstrate attachment in several ways. Behaviors that are typically examined include seeking proximity or physical contact with the caregiver, protesting separations from the caregiver, showing pleasure or relief on reunion, and orienting behaviors toward the caregiver (e.g., attending to the person's voice and actions and directing actions toward the caregiver). The prototypical Ainsworth procedure conceptualizes and measures attachment as the critical balance between dependence and independence (Ainsworth 1973; Ainsworth *et al.*, 1978). Specifically, by 12 months of age, the child who feels securely attached to the primary caregiver should also feel free to separate enough to explore an attractive environment. Securely attached infants have been demonstrated to have mothers who are more psychologically accessible to the infant during the first year of life (Ainsworth *et al.*, 1978).

Only two of the longitudinal studies of children at risk for schizophrenia have included measures of attachment. McNeil and his colleagues (Naslund *et al.*, 1984a,b,c) studied infants' attachments to their mothers at 1 year of age using three different procedures. Their first measure of attachment was a modified Ainsworth Strange Situation procedure (Naslund *et al.*, 1984a). The procedure was modified in three ways. First, infants were observed in the home, rather than in a lab. Second, the infants were exposed to only one episode of separation from and reunion with the mother, rather than the usual two such episodes. The stranger was present in both episodes. Third, the stranger had already spent 1 hour in the home with the infant. Thus, the procedure was probably less stressful for infants than the original Ainsworth procedure.

No significant differences were found between high-risk (the mixed group of infants whose mothers had nonorganic psychosis [n = 46]) versus matched control infants (n = 80) on rates of anxious versus secure attachment patterns. However, differences emerged when the groups of infants with psychotic mothers were separately compared with controls. Specifically, a significantly higher rate of anxious attachment was found for the offspring of schizophrenic parents versus controls. Anxious attachment (both avoidant and ambivalent) was found in 50% of the offspring of schizophrenic parents (5 of the 10) relative to only 17% of the controls. In contrast, anxious attachment was no more likely in infants of affectively ill mothers than in well controls.

The second measure of attachment used by McNeil and his colleagues was fear of strangers (Naslund *et al.*, 1984b). Fear of strangers, or stranger anxiety, indicates the development of the ability to discriminate between familiar and unfamiliar people. Fear of strangers appears first around 8 months of age and then is present through the rest of the first year. Infants who are either extremely fearful or show an absence of fear may be manifesting early signs in the development of psychopathology (Sroufe and Waters, 1977). Naslund *et al.* (1984b) used the standard Schaffer and Emerson Fear of Strangers procedure when the infants were 12 months old. A phone call from the observer to the mother prior to the visit instructed the mother to have the child standing or sitting on the floor several feet inside the entry door with the mother not holding or interacting with the infant at that time. The observer, upon arrival, noted any sign of fear shown by the infant at each of six consecutive steps of approach. The extreme absence of fear of strangers was more often found for the total group of offspring of mothers with nonorganic psychosis and the subgroups of offspring of mothers with schizophrenia and cycloid psychosis compared with demographically matched well controls. A total absence of fear of strangers was found in 7 out of the 10 (70%) offspring of schizophrenic parents compared with 21 out of the 80 (26%) of the controls.

The third index of attachment was measured during the modified Ainsworth procedure (Naslund et al., 1984c). With both the mother and observer present, a colorful rubber ball was presented by the stranger and placed on the floor a few feet from the mother and the infant. The observer noted the length of time the infant delayed approaching the ball and the amount of time spent exploring the ball. No diagnostic group differences were found on exploratory behavior. However, children who showed deviations on two of the three attachment measures were significantly more likely to be high-risk infants and most likely to be offspring of schizophrenic mothers.

Sameroff and his colleagues in the Rochester Longitudinal Study (Sameroff et al., 1982) also measured attachment in high-risk infants. They used a different modification of the Ainsworth Strange Situation procedure when the children were 12 months of age. The children were observed in the lab, with standard criteria for classifying children as secure, avoidant, or resistant. However, only five of the usual seven episodes were observed: The episode of the child alone with the stranger and one of the reunions with the mother were omitted. [Naslund et al. (1984a) also had only one reunion with the mother but included the child alone with the stranger.] Infants of schizophrenic mothers were found to be no less securely attached to their mothers than the infants of mothers with neurotic depression, personality disorder, or no psychiatric disorder.

Thus, of the two longitudinal high-risk projects that included measures of attachment, the results are contradictory. Evidence for less secure attachment of schizophrenic mother–child pairs was found by NcNeil and his colleagues but not by Sameroff and his colleagues.

Both procedural and sample differences may help to explain the discrepant results. Procedurally, neither group of researchers used the standard Ainsworth procedure, making direct comparisons impossible. Furthermore, each had their own variation. Both may have been less stressful than the standard procedures in their own ways. The situation in the Swedish study may have been less stressful in that the procedure occurred in the home after the stranger had already spent 1 hour in the home with the mother and infant. Both mother and infant were likely to have felt more comfortable. Furthermore, the infant was only left by the mother once, in the presence of the "stranger," and was never left alone. In contrast, in the Rochester study the procedure occurred in the lab and the child was left alone, but never with the less familiar stranger, and only once was separated from the mother. One can only speculate as to which procedure was more stressful and which was more valid. Of particular concern in attempts to compare either set of findings to studies that used standard Ainsworth procedures was the use of only one reunion episode. Ainsworth et al. (1978) found that of all eight episodes in the procedure, the ratings of the two reunion episodes contributed most to the classification of the child. Furthermore, Waters (1981) and others have argued that brief separations in the home are likely to be less stressful (Tracy et al., 1976; Vaughn et al., 1980). Therefore, behavior that is classified as avoidant in the lab (e.g., turning away from the mother to greet a stranger or to explore a toy) would be more accurately interpreted as independent gestures by a comfortable baby in the home. This conclusion would fit with Naslund et al.'s (1984b) finding of absence of fear of strangers in offspring of schizophrenic parents; i.e., these offspring may appear to be nonreactive to a variety of situations that are stressful to other babies (e.g., mother absence, stranger presence).

Characteristics of the sample may also have contributed to the discrepant findings. According to attachment researchers, sociodemographic variables and separation histories may influence the findings on quality of attachment. The Swedish sample was European Caucasian, and both rural and urban, with predominantly middle socioeconomic status (SES), intact families; the Rochester sample was urban, low and middle SES, approximately 40% Black, and approximately 30% unmarried. Grossman et al. (1981) found a cultural difference in the rates of attachment classifications. Middle SES German children showed secure attachment relationships to their mothers less often than did comparable U.S. samples. Patterns of attachment behavior observed in the Strange Situation procedure may also be less stable in urban, low SES samples (Vaughn et al., 1979).

Furthermore, the samples may have varied on the separation histories of the offspring of schizophrenic parents in their first year of life. Naslund et al. (1984a) noted that 12 out of the 34 psychotic mothers had been hospitalized during the child's first year. The figure for schizophrenic mothers, specifically, was not reported. No comparable data were reported by Sameroff and his colleagues. Evidence for the role of separation histories in quality of attachment was found by Vaughn et al. (1980). They found that significantly more of the infants who were placed in "out-of-home" care before 12 months of age were classified in the anxious-avoidant group. This is in contrast to infants who were between 12 and 18 months before being placed in out-of-home care or those who were still at home with their mothers at 18 months. Furthermore, it was also noted that the children with more anxious attachments were more likely to have mothers who were single parents and who experienced greater life stress. Attachment is related to both the mother's psychological and physical availability to her infant; therefore, the attachment relationship between schizophrenic mothers and their infants is probably of lower quality. Unfortunately, because of nonstandard procedures and different sample characteristics, the data do not allow for conclusions about the quality of attachment relationships between schizophrenic mothers and their babies.

Mother–Child Interaction: Unstructured and Structured Observations

Offspring of schizophrenic mothers have also been observed during unstructured (free play) and structured (feeding or teaching) interactions with their mothers. As part of the Thresholds Mothers' Project, Clark developed The Mothers' Project Rating Scales of Mother–Child Interaction (Clark et al., 1980). Children's interactions with their mothers were videotaped and observed. The tapes were rated on a 53-item, 5-point Likert scale, with 5 as the most positive score. Among the 53 items are ratings of the mother, the child, and the dyad. In this section of the chapter, results on the child ratings will be reported; findings on the quality of the mothers' interactions with their children will be reported in a later section of this chapter.

Clark (1983) reported the results of comparisons across maternal diagnostic groups (diagnostically mixed disturbed group versus well controls) on factor scores from the Mothers' Project Rating Scales. Children ranged in age from 2 months to 5 years. Two child factors emerged and were tested. The first factor, Child Communicative Competence and Attentional and Social Abilities, included seven ratings: child social initiative, communicative competence, attentional abilities, social responsiveness, readability, cheerful disposition, and passivity. The second factor, Child Negative Affect and Behavior, included three ratings: amount of expressed negative affect, noncompliance and angry, hostile disposition.

Results indicated no maternal diagnostic group differences on either factor score; however, several effects of sociodemographic variables were noted. More educated mothers (high school education or higher), regardless of diagnostic status, had children who scored higher on Communicative, Attentional, and Social Abilities and lower on Negative Affect and

Behavior. Furthermore, children whose families were from the lowest SES scored higher on Negative Affect and Behavior than did children from low–middle or middle SES families.

Goodman (1987a) also tested the effects of maternal diagnostic status on ratings of children's interactions with their mothers using the Mothers' Project Rating Scales. Two-month to 5-year-old children of schizophrenic, depressed, and well mothers were observed interacting with their mothers during free play in the laboratory. The free-play situation was chosen because the previous study (Clark, 1983) found that unstructured situations give the broadest range of individual differences in contrast to more structured situations. Rather than factor scores, Goodman tested the effects of maternal diagnostic group on the set of 15 child competence items.

Contrary to Clark's findings, Goodman's results indicated that the maternal diagnostic group had an effect on the quality of children's interactions with their mothers. Children of schizophrenic mothers were less communicatively competent and had a higher activity level than children of both depressed and well mothers. Children of schizophrenic mothers were more angry, hostile, and anxious than children of well mothers (children of depressed mothers did not significantly differ from either other group). Furthermore, children of both schizophrenic and depressed mothers exhibited more negative affect than children of well mothers. These findings were most marked in the younger children in the sample. However, the unique effects of schizophrenia, as opposed to maternal psychopathology (both schizophrenia and depression), diminished as children got older; i.e., for infants and toddlers, children of schizophrenic mothers looked the worst. In contrast, for preschool-aged children, children of both schizophrenic and depressed mothers looked less competent relative to those of well mothers.

Goodman (1987a) and Clark (1983) also tested maternal diagnostic group differences using Burton White's (White, Kaban, and Attanucci, 1979) conceptualization and measurement of social competence from the Harvard Pre-School Project. Based on observations of hundreds of 1- to 6-year-old children from middle and lower SES families, White and his colleagues identified five aspects of social competence relevant to a child's interactions with adults: gaining adult attention, using adults as a resource, expressing affection and hostility to adults, engaging in role play, and expression of pride and pleasure in accomplishments. While competent children demonstrated all of these behaviors, the most competent children were those who early on developed the ability to appropriately rely on getting and maintaining adult attention. These competent children were able to use socially acceptable methods of engaging adults, particularly after attempting a difficult task. When the child succeeded in his or her effort, with or without adult assistance, the competent child was likely to express pride in the accomplishment.

Using a summary scaled score across the five social competence behaviors, Clark (1983) found an effect of maternal diagnostic group. Children of a diagnostically mixed group of psychotic mothers were less socially competent than children of well mothers. No differences were found as a function of sociodemographic factors.

Goodman (1987a) found differences on three out of five of White's social competence behaviors. Children of schizophrenic mothers less often expressed both affection and hostility to their mothers than children of depressed or well mothers. Children of schizophrenic and depressed mothers also engaged in less role play and less often used their mothers as resources. When results were analyzed by age of child, those results were replicated for the youngest children. However, among preschool and early school-aged children (2–7 years old) it was the depressives' offspring who scored significantly lower than the other groups on role play and showing pride in product.

Sameroff et al. (1984) included several measures of qualities of social interaction between children and their parents. At 4 and 12 months of age, infants were observed interacting with their mothers at home. At both ages, no effects were found for mother's diagnostic group on infant behavior in interaction with their mothers. Children of disturbed parents were found to be no less spontaneous, responsive, happy, active, or playful. There were also no differences in amount of crying, clinging, or whimpering. However, at 12 months of age, several social status and severity/chronicity effects were noted. Children of more severely or chronically ill mothers, regardless of diagnosis, were less spontaneous and playful. Black infants, all of whom were from low SES families, were less spontaneous, less happy, more clinging, more mobile, and fussier than white infants of both low and middle SES. Children were also observed at 48 months during a maternal teaching task; however, these results have not yet been reported.

McNeil and his colleagues (McNeil, 1986) in the Swedish longitudinal study also observed infants' interactions with their mothers at several points during the child's first year. Infant children of mothers with a history of hospitalization for nonorganic psychosis showed less social contact with their mothers as early as 3 days postpartum relative to children of well mothers. Other results have not yet been reported in detail.

In summary, evidence from observations of children's social and emotional competence in structured and unstructured interactions supports the conclusion that offspring of schizophrenic parents are at risk; however, the effects of parental psychopathology in general, severity and chronicity, and sociodemographic factors are also implicated. Effects specific to off-spring of schizophrenic parents were most often apparent in very young children (i.e., <2 years old). These young children were judged to be less communicatively competent and more active, anxious, angry, and hostile. In interactions with their mothers, they were affectively flat and with-drawn, engaged in little anticipatory role play, and less often used their mothers as resources than did children of parents with other disorders or well parents. Beyond infancy, interactive qualities seem to be more gen-erally related to parental psychopathology (not schizophrenia *per se*) and severity, chronicity, and sociodemographic variables. Sameroff and his colleagues' failure to find effects specific to schizophrenia, even in the youngest children, may have been due to their reliance on counting sampled behaviors rather than a qualitative rating scale. Discrete behav-iors may be inadequate to tap the unique qualities of interactive systems.

High-Risk Children's Interactions with Others

Studies of children's interactions with their disturbed or well mothers do not clarify whether the differences found in children's quality of inter-actions are due to stable individual differences in the children or are attributable to the child's behavior in reaction to the mother. An important question is whether or not the quality of the child's interaction is the same with other adults as with the mother. Based on Bowlby's work (1982), Sroufe (1988) questions whether or not the child takes the expectations regarding relationships acquired during interactions with the mother into his or her relationships with other adults and, eventually, peers. To what extent does the quality of the child's social competence vary as a function of the interactive partner? Are offspring of schizophrenic parents less attractive, interesting, or skilled in engaging others relative to comparison groups?

Unfortunately, researchers have not tested these specific hypotheses; however, several researchers have collected pertinent data on children's interactions with other adults, but it has not yet been analyzed or reported. For example, Fish (1987a,b) gathered clinical impressions of observations of the interactions of children of schizophrenic parents with their mothers and compared them with their interactions with the researcher; however, those data were never analyzed. Similarly, Cohler has not yet reported results comparing observations of children of psychotic parents interacting with their therapeutic nursery teacher with their interactions with their mothers. Furthermore, Goodman (1986) observed children of schizophren-ic, depressed, and well mothers interacting with their case worker using the same rating scale as for children interacting with their mothers; those data have also not yet been analyzed.

One study compared the quality of peer interactions of children of schizophrenic parents with children of well parents. Cohler *et al.* (1987), using White's social competence measure, observed children interacting with their peers in a therapeutic nursery school setting. They found that children of a diagnostically mixed group of psychotic mothers had significantly greater difficulty than children of well mothers in imitating positive peer examples and in getting other children to follow their example.

EVIDENCE FOR SOCIAL AND EMOTIONAL COMPETENCE: CLINICAL AND DIAGNOSTIC ASSESSMENTS

Research on children of schizophrenic mothers has produced evidence bearing on social and emotional competence not only from observations of children's interactions, but also from neonatal behavioral responsivity, behavioral style (temperament), social and emotional behaviors during developmental assessments, adaptive behavior, and clinical–diagnostic evaluations. For the most part, researchers studying high-risk children have been interested in these variables as evidence of the early effects of being genetically vulnerable to disorder and/or being reared by a schizophrenic parent. Children of schizophrenic parents are likely to face many emotional challenges. They may be genetically predisposed to physiological over-reactivity (Mednick, 1967; Mednick *et al.*, 1984), forced to cope with more separations from their mothers due to her psychiatric hospitalizations, and deprived of an interactive partner who would provide the guidelines, which are necessary for healthy social and emotional development.

Another reason for interest in variables such as behavioral responsivity, behavioral style, and adaptive behavior is the potential to elucidate ways in which children may cope with vulnerabilities. Abilities to regulate affect and arousal, to communicate about emotions, and to adapt to changing circumstances are important milestones in emotional and social development. Furthermore, individual differences exist in the personal qualities and characteristics by which one reacts to stressors (Rutter, 1983). However, none of the research on children at risk for schizophrenia has provided direct evidence on how or to what extent behavioral style or other social or emotional competence variables may modify the outcome, i.e., serving as protective factors.

A related point is that behavioral responsivity and behavioral style may be an important component in the development of parent–child relationships. From a transactional point of view, or goodness-of-fit notion, infants affect the quality of interaction by way of the parent's reaction to the infants behavior or style. In Rutter's work with families of mentally ill patients, children with adverse temperamental characteristics were twice as likely as other children to be the target of parental criticism (Rutter, 1979). Thus, temperament may be a risk factor in its role in affecting parent–child interaction (Rutter, 1983). Furthermore, Kagan (1983) proposes that temperament factors influence children's responses to potentially stressful situations.

Both neonatal behavioral responsivity and children's behavioral style are considered to be largely constitutional or genetic in origin. Thus, at least as assessed at birth, they cannot be considered to be the effects of differential rearing conditions. Later assessments of behavioral style may reflect influences of the environment to some extent and also may be influenced by perceptions of the mother—the typical informant.

Brazelton

Four of the prospective high-risk studies included the Brazelton (1973) Neonatal Behavioral Assessment Scale (NBAS). The NBAS, typically administered when the infant is between 48 and 72 hours old, measures several behavioral responses, including emotional regulation, alertness, cuddliness, and response to stimuli. (Other items assessed, including neurological reflexes, motor maturity, tremulousness, and the like, are not addressed here; they are the subject of Chapter 3, earlier in this volume.)

Offspring of schizophrenic parents showed no significantly greater signs of abnormal behavioral or affective response in three of the four studies using the NBAS. Sameroff et al. (1984) found maternal diagnostic group effects on only one of four relevant NBAS scales. Specifically, the infants of both depressed mothers and personality-disordered mothers had lower self-quieting ability. Schizophrenic offspring did not differ from normals. Similarly, Hans et al. (1987) found no maternal diagnostic group differences in the NBAS behavioral scale scores in the Jerusalem Infant Development Study, which compared 3-day-old infants of schizophrenic, affective-disordered, personality-disordered/neurotic, and well control mothers. However, at 14 days of age, infants of schizophrenic mothers were more easily consoled than infants of all of the other groups combined. Furthermore, a subgroup of infants of schizophrenic mothers scored lower, as shown on scatterplots, than the other groups. Further lack of support for indications of abnormal behavioral or affective response comes from S. H. Goodman (unpublished data), who, in a small sample for whom NBAS scores were available (n = 12), found no diagnostic group differences.

In contrast, D'Angelo et al. (1983) found that the 2-day-old infants of schizophrenic mothers were more irritable and showed significantly less alertness, consolability, cuddliness, and capacity to self-quiet than did infants of either recurrent major depressive-disordered or well mothers. However, those findings were mainly attributable to the subgroup of offspring of schizophrenic mothers who had been voluntarily placed in foster care by the mothers.

Thus shortly after birth, a discrete subgroup of infants of schizophrenic mothers were behaving differently: less cuddly and less consolable. In D'Angelo et al.'s (1983) sample, the behavioral differences may have contributed to the schizophrenic mother's decision to place her infant with an adoptive family. Indeed, these behaviorally difficult babies may carry greater genetic risk as was noted by Sameroff and Zax (1973). It should also be noted that data on medication during pregnancy was not available in any of these studies, and this should be included as a factor in future studies.

Temperament

Four of the studies included measures of infant or child temperament. Temperament is a measure of individual differences in behavioral style, or the *how* of behavioral responsivity to different situations (Thomas and Chess, 1977). Temperamental differences are considered to be at least partly genetically determined (Torgesen and Kringlen, 1978). In infancy, a common measure of temperament is the Carey and McDevit (1977) Infant Temperament Questionnaire, which is administered to the mother. The instrument produces nine scales of infant behavior: activity, rhythmicity, adaptability, approach (versus withdrawal), threshold to stimulation, intensity of response, mood, distractibility/soothability, and persistence.

Sameroff et al. (1984) found maternal diagnostic group differences on several of the Carey Temperament Scales when the children were 4 and 48 months old. However, at 4 months, none of the diagnostic group differences were attributable to schizophrenia. At 4 months, depressed mothers reported that their infants were more active and more distractible; personality-disordered mothers also reported that their infants were more active and more persistent. At 48 months, schizophrenic mothers rated their children as less approaching than did the well control mothers. Depressed mothers rated their children as more intense. Several effects were due to chronicity and severity, regardless of diagnostic status. At 4 months, more chronically ill mothers, compared to mothers with less chronic illness, described their infants as more active, irregular, withdrawn, intense, and negative in mood, with lower levels of adaptability and threshold to stimulation. Also at 4 months, severity of the mothers' illness was associated with their ratings of their infants as more active, less adaptable, having a lower threshold to stimulation, more intense, more negative in mood, and more persistent. Lower social status was also associated with poorer temperament in that lower SES mothers rated their infants as having a lower threshold and higher intensity of responses than did higher SES mothers. At 48 months, higher severity was associated with less rhythmicity, adaptability, and persistence and a lower threshold to stimulation. Higher chronicity was related to lower adaptability and threshold to stimulation.

Hans et al. (1987) also used the Carey Infant Temperament Interview when children in their sample were 4 and 8 months old. Only one parental diagnostic group effect was found on any of the nine scales. Mothers who had affective disorders or whose husbands had affective disorders described their children to be more negative in mood.

Goodman (Goodman and Van Buskirk, 1986) found maternal diagnostic group differences on three of the Carey Scales when the babies were between 3 and 8 months old. Schizophrenic mothers rated their babies as more negative in mood and less approachable than did depressed mothers, and less adaptable than did well mothers. Depressed mothers also rated their babies as less approachable than did well mothers. Severity of mothers' emotional disturbance did not influence their temperament ratings.

D'Angelo et al. (1983), with the Carey Scales, found that infants of schizophrenic mothers were significantly less adaptive, active, and rhythmic than those of mothers with recurrent, major depressive disorders or of well mothers. These differences were apparent at 2, 4, and 6 moths of age. At 8 months, the infants of schizophrenic mothers continued to be less adaptive than infants of well mothers. However, as with their NBAS data, nearly all of the variability in the Carey scores was found to be attributable to the subgroup of schizophrenic offspring who had been placed in foster care by 4 months of age. At the time of their placements, the infants were perceived by their biological mothers as temperamentally difficult. In contrast, the schizophrenic offspring who continued to be reared by their biological mothers only scored lower on one scale—activity—and only at the 2-month assessments.

The results of the four sets of data on infants' temperament ratings by their schizophrenic mothers are difficult to interpret. Three groups of researchers, Sameroff et al. (1984), Goodman and Van Buskirk (1986), and D'Angelo et al. (1983), found some schizophrenic-specific effects, at least on a subgroup, yet Hans et al. (1987) did not. Furthermore, depressed mothers often rated their babies as having more difficult temperaments. In addition, Sameroff et al. (1984) found more effects due to chronicity and severity than any specific diagnosis, although Goodman and Van Buskirk (1986) and D'Angelo et al. (1983) did not. The divergent findings are surprising given that all four studies used the same measurement instrument. While the studies differed in sociodemographic characteristics of their samples, this provides no obvious explanation for the contradictions.

Social and Emotional Behaviors

For three of the studies, the examiner who administered the individual IQ test to the child also scored the children on social and emotional behaviors observed during the testing session. Sameroff *et al.* (1984) and Goodman and her colleagues (Johnson, 1989; Johnson and Goodman, in preparation) scored these observations using the Infant Behavior Record (IBR) accompanying the Bayley Scales of Infant Development. Cohler *et al.* (1987) used equivalent measures.

IBR data from the Rochester study are available from when the children were 4, 12, and 30 months old. At 4 months, no effects were due to maternal schizophrenia. The only diagnostic group effect showed that children of depressed mothers were less responsive to people than those of well mothers. Furthermore, more severe and chronic maternal illness (regardless of diagnosis) was related to poorer response to people and more severe illness was related to less happy mood during the testing. At 12 months, the only diagnostic group effect was that children of depressed mothers had better reactions to the examiner than those of well mothers. More chronicity was also related to better response to the examiner. Higher severity was related to poorer response to objects and lower reactivity. At 30 months, the only diagnostic group effect was due to schizophrenia: Children of schizophrenic mothers showed lower reactivity than did those of well mothers. Both higher severity and chronicity were also related to lower reactivity, and higher chronicity was associated with poorer response to the examiner.

In Goodman's study (Johnson, 1989; Johnson and Goodman, in preparation), scores from the IBR were analyzed using the factor scores generated by Matheny (1980): test affect and task orientation. Tests for effects of maternal diagnostic group were conducted separately for the youngest children (2–30 months) and older children (31–66 months). No maternal diagnostic group effects were found for younger children on either test affect or task orientation. Among the older children, children of schizophrenic mothers scored significantly lower than children of well mothers on test affect and lower than children of both well and depressed mothers on task orientation.

Significant age of child effects suggest a developmental lag hypothesis. Specifically, higher scores for older children than younger children were found only for children of well mothers on test affect, and children of well or depressed mothers on task orientation; i.e., on both scales, older children of schizophrenic mothers looked and behaved more like younger children, whereas older children of well mothers and, to some extent, children of depressed mothers were looking more mature relative to their younger counterparts. Cohler *et al.* (1987) collected comparable data on children's response to IQ testing using the Infant and Child Behavior Checklist. They found that children of psychiatrically ill mothers, relative to those of well mothers, were significantly more reactive to failure, significantly more hesitant in situations where they were unfamiliar with the test stimuli, asked for more help, required greater reassurance to perform adequately on the tasks, were more inhibited in their response to the test situation, showed greater difficulty maintaining attention to tasks in the testing session, more often became distressed on not being able to solve a problem, and more often became aggressive in the testing situation. Unfortunately, Cohler's results do not allow for conclusions about effects that are specific to schizophrenia.

In summary, while results, again, are mixed, studies of children's social and emotional behaviors during testing indicate that at least by the age of 30 months, offspring of schizophrenic parents may behave in manners that are less suitable to optimal performance on cognitive-intellectual tasks than other children. An intriguing notion is that of a developmental lag, whereby with increasing age children of schizophrenic parents may be less adaptive to such structured situations.

Adaptive Behavior

Both the Rochester and the Jerusalem studies assessed adaptive behavior of the children using Seifer *et al.'s* (1981) Rochester Adaptive Behavior Inventory (RABI). The RABI is a semistructured interview used to obtain detailed, behavior-specific maternal reports of the child's adaptive social behavior. A global rating is obtained as well as scores on 11 scales, including cooperation with family members, cooperation with others, friendships, timidity, and fearfulness.

Sameroff *et al.* (1984) administered the RABI at 30 and 48 months of age. At 30 months, they found maternal diagnostic group effects on 5 of the 10 scales, but only one effect was due to maternal schizophrenia. Children of schizophrenic mothers and children of depressed mothers were more depressed than those of well mothers. All other effects were due to depression in mothers relative to well controls: less cooperative in the family and with others, more bizarre, and engaged in more imaginary play. Severity and chronicity of maternal illness, regardless of diagnosis, were related to even more of the scores: less cooperation in the family and with others, more timidity, more fearfulness, more bizarre behavior, more whiny behavior, and more depression. More chronicity and severity were also associated with poorer global ratings of adjustment. By 48 months, several changes occurred regarding diagnostic group effects. Children of both schizophrenic and depressed mothers were more bizarre, whiny, and depressed than those of well mothers. Children of schizophrenic mothers were also less demanding of their mothers than those of well mothers. Children of depressed mothers also had poorer global ratings and were less cooperative in the family and with others. Both severity and chronicity were again associated with poorer global ratings and several specific indices of maladjustment.

In the Jerusalem study, the RABI was not administered until the children were 7 years old. At that time, only one diagnostic group difference was found: children of schizophrenic parents were described by their parents as more fearful than were children in the well-parents control group and the personality-disorder/neurosis group (Hans *et al.*, 1987).

Overall, children of schizophrenic mothers apparently were no less well-adapted than children of other-disordered or well parents. Children of depressed parents showed lower adaptive behavior than controls. Severity and chronicity, regardless of diagnosis, were also important factors.

Clinical Diagnostic Evaluations

The ultimate index of failures in social and emotional functioning is the presence of psychopathology. Yet psychopathology in children as young as those in this review is rare and extremely difficult to reliably diagnose. Therefore, most of the studies delayed the inclusion of diagnostic procedures until the children were in middle childhood. This is true for the Rochester study, the Jerusalem study, and the Thresholds Mothers' Project.

In the author's project, a child psychiatrist, who was blind to the diagnostic status of the mother, observed and interacted with the children and interviewed the mother and the case worker assigned to the family. Based on a combination of information from all sources, he determined the diagnostic status of the children using DSM-III criteria. Such diagnoses are considered extremely tentative because of the children's young age and the potential biases introduced by the necessity of the child psychiatrist to interview the mother, and thereby forming an opinion of her diagnostic status, and because the same psychiatrist conducted the evaluation all three times.

As expected, rates of diagnoses were extremely low: 4% when the children were between 2 months and 5 years old, 2% 1 year later, and 10%

another year later. These percentages represent a total of 15 children who received a diagnosis at any of the three times. Only one child of a well mother received a diagnosis at any time—an attention-deficit disorder in a 7-year-old. Children of both schizophrenic and depressed mothers were equally more likely to be diagnosed relative to children of well mothers. The most common diagnoses were developmental disorder and attention-deficit disorder with hyperactivity (ADD-H). Marcus (1986) noted that ADD-H resembles the pattern of motor, perceptual, and attention deficits often found in offspring of schizophrenic parents who eventually have schizophrenic breakdowns; however, caution is required in interpreting this finding. For example, some children who received a diagnosis at one of the first two assessment phases were judged as not having a disorder at a later assessment phase, reflecting the difficulty in obtaining reliable diagnoses in the context of large expected developmental changes.

In the Swedish study, McNeil and Kaij (1987) used the Children's Global Assessment Scale (CGAS; Shaffer et al., 1983) to evaluate offsprings' "mental status" at 6 years of age. Scores on the CGAS range from 1 to 100, with scores ≤70 indicating "mental disturbance." The scores on the CGAS were found to be significantly lower in the combined high-risk group relative to well controls. Among the diagnostic groups, the children of schizophrenic or postpartum psychotic mothers had significantly lower mean CGAS scores than did those of their matched well controls. CGAS scores <71 were significantly more frequent in children of schizophrenic mothers than in comparison groups or well controls. Specifically, 82% of the children of schizophrenic mothers scored within the range of mental disturbance, compared with 15% of children of affective-disordered mothers, and 28% of the combined well control groups.

Rates of diagnosable conditions are extremely low in children <7 years old. The findings in the Goodman project are consistent with expected rates, especially when low reliability is considered. Yet McNeil and Kaij's (1987) finding, using a dimensional rather than categorical index of pathology, provides strong support for the conclusion that children of schizophrenic mothers, at least by the age of 6 years, are showing more psychological disturbance than comparison or control groups.

QUALITY OF PARENTING BY SCHIZOPHRENICS AND ITS ROLE IN CHILDREN'S SOCIAL AND AFFECTIVE DEVELOPMENT

Stress-diathesis is currently the most viable model for the etiology of schizophrenia (Rosenthal, 1970; Wynne, 1978). Thus, in studies of offspring of schizophrenic parents, with the inherent genetic vulnerability, it is important to delineate aspects of the environment that place children at risk. Relationship variables are increasingly accepted as necessary to account for the mechanisms through which a parent's pathology may interfere with the child's healthy development. Among the nonbiological factors potentially involved in the development of psychopathology, the study of parent–child relationships has strong clinical, theoretical, and empirical backing (cf. Jacob, 1987).

From an interpersonal systems perspective (Hoffman, 1981), the symptoms and other attributes of schizophrenia can be conceptualized as incompatible with quality parenting. Schizophrenia may affect parenting in that the schizophrenic is likely to be withdrawn and passively interacting with the environment, presumably resulting in emotional unavailability or unresponsiveness to the child. Also, delusions may involve the child, thereby exposing the child to the incongruent affect often associated with schizophrenia.

Parenting by Schizophrenic Mothers

Some researchers tested hypotheses on the effects of schizophrenia on a woman's parenting attitudes and behavior. Both interview and observational studies have yielded results indicating that parenting by women diagnosed as schizophrenic is of poorer quality relative to controls with no mental illness and sometimes relative to an affective-disordered comparison group. Cohler *et al.* (1980) found that hospitalized schizophrenic mothers of babies differed from well controls in attitudes regarding reciprocity. On the one hand, schizophrenic mothers were more likely than well mothers to believe that they can understand and meet the baby's demands for physical care; on the other hand, schizophrenic mothers were more likely to believe that it is difficult for parents to respond to babies' demands for reciprocity. Thus, although not observed as part of this study, schizophrenic mothers would be less likely to engage in back-and-forth smiling play.

Sameroff *et al.* (1984) also studied parenting attitudes and beliefs. They had mothers complete the Parental Attitude Research Instrument (Schaefer and Bell, 1958), a measure of parenting attitudes, when the children were 30 months old. None of the diagnostic groups differed significantly from each other; however, severely ill mothers, regardless of diagnosis, had more authoritarian, more hostile-rejecting, and less democratic attitudes. When the children were 48 months old, mothers were administered the Concepts of Development Questionnaire (Feil and Sameroff, 1979) and the Kohn (1969) parental values measure. Schizophrenic mothers and all severely ill mothers and low SES mothers, regardless of diagnosis, had less advanced concepts of child development. Severely and chronically ill mothers and low SES mothers, regardless of diagnostic status, expressed more conforming parental values.

Observational studies provide more direct support that attributes of schizophrenia affect parenting. Cohler and his colleagues (Clark, 1983; Cohler et al., 1987) compared quality of mothers' interactions with their children using the Mothers' Project Rating Scales of Mother–Child Interaction. They found that groups of mentally ill women were less affectively involved and responsive and less consistent in their caretaking behaviors and styles, but displayed no more negative affect or behavior, in interactions with their children relative to well mothers. Furthermore, regardless of diagnostic status, lower SES mothers were less affectively involved and responsive.

Goodman (Goodman and Brumley, 1990) found some of the same effects and some different effects in a similar study to the one just described. Schizophrenic, depressed, and well mothers were observed interacting with their 2- to 18-month-old or 18-month-old to 5-year-old children. Interactions were scored with the Mothers' Project Rating Scales. Schizophrenic mothers were found to exhibit less affectional involvement and responsiveness with their children than well mothers, with depressed mothers scoring in between. Schizophrenic mothers' interactions were also characterized as less angry and hostile than either other group. No maternal diagnostic group differences were found on maternal tenseness and rigidity. Neither severity of disturbance nor mother's education explained a significant amount of the relationship of mother's diagnosis with any of the three factor scores. Nor were there any interactions of maternal diagnosis group and child age in effects on parenting.

The quality of the child-rearing environment, measured by the Home Observation for Measurement of the Environment (HOME) Inventory (Bradley and Caldwell, 1979, 1981; Bradley, 1985), was also found to differ as a function of the mother's diagnostic status (Goodman and Brumley, 1990). Schizophrenic mothers provided poorer quality of child-rearing relative to well mothers, with depressed mothers scoring in between. Neither child's age, mother's education, nor severity of disturbance had significant effects. Subscale analyses indicated that schizophrenic mothers were less responsive and provided poorer quality physical environment, less play stimulation, and less overall variety of stimulation. On one scale, depressed mothers had the lowest scores. Depressed mothers avoided punishment and discipline more than well mothers, with schizophrenic mothers scoring in between. More severely disturbed mothers were also more likely to avoid punishment and discipline.

Effects of Schizophrenic Parenting on Children's Social and Affective Development

The research reviewed to this point provides indirect evidence for the role of parenting in the effects of schizophrenic parents on their young children; i.e., children of schizophrenic parents have a wide range of deficits and delays in social and emotional development, which would be better conceptualized as the broad band of effects of inadequate parenting than as early signs of inherited risk for schizophrenia. Furthermore, parenting attitudes, beliefs, and behaviors by schizophrenics have been found to be undesirable. Compared to knowledge of parenting qualities required for healthy social and emotional development (Maccoby, 1980), schizophrenic parents expose their children to qualities of parenting that are likely to create exactly the problems that researchers are finding.

However, further evidence is needed to impute parenting variables as mechanisms of risk, even for the specific area of child competence of social and affective functioning. Two studies provide data to that effect. The first included children who are older than those who are the focus of this study; however, it is included here because studies that directly link mechanisms of risk and child social–emotional functioning in offspring of schizophrenic parents are rare.

As part of the Lyman Wynne's University of Rochester Child and Family Study, Fisher and Jones (1980) found specific areas of family functioning that were related to child social competence. Subjects were 61 7- and 10-year-old sons of previously hospitalized schizophrenics ($n = 23$), affective psychotics ($n = 11$), and nonpsychotic ($n = 27$) patients (mothers and fathers). All of the children came from families with intact marriages and middle to upper–middle SES. Parents and all children in the home worked together on a consensus problem-solving task—the Family Rorschach. Family variables, scored from transcripts, included agreement/disagreement, negative/positive relationship, clarity, task focus, nonacknowledgment, and parental communication deviance (Doane *et al.*, 1982). Social–emotional behavior was measured with a variety of peer and teacher scales, including scores for friendliness, intrusiveness, social competence, and a summary score. Data were analyzed with parental diagnostic groups combined and, thus, cannot be taken as specific to families with a schizophrenic parent.

The hypothesized relationship between child social–emotional competence (grouped as high, medium, and low) and family interaction variables was found between only two of the four social–emotional behaviors and one of the seven family variables. Friendlier children, and those who were, overall, higher on social–emotional competence, had families who used less parental communication deviance. Fisher and Jones interpret the role of parental communication deviance as emphasizing the importance of the development of adequate attention skills in children's social–emotional development (Wynne *et al.*, 1977). When all of the family variables were considered together, the summary index of child social–emotional behavior was significantly predicted by an equation that included (in order of entrance) task focus, positive relationship, parental communication deviance, and clarity ($R = 0.47$, $p = 0.005$). An important contribution of the Fisher and Jones (1980) study is the finding that different sets of family variables predicted specific aspects of child behavior, i.e., cognitive/intellectual versus social–emotional. Thus, in the search for predictors of child competence or, conversely, the development of psychopathology, in the children of schizophrenic parents (or those with other severe pathologies), it is important to specify the level and focus of measurement.

The other study that linked mechanisms of risk with social–emotional development in offspring of schizophrenic parents was part of the author's Emory University Project PACT. It was hypothesized that poorer quality mother–child interaction (Mothers' Project Rating Scales factor scores) and less adequate child-rearing environments (HOME Inventory) would be related to poorer child social competence.

Of the three factor scores measuring the mother's interaction with her child, one was found to have a significant effect on one of the five social behavior scale scores. Mothers who were higher on affectional involvement and responsiveness had children who engaged in more role play. Neither of the other two factor scores—maternal tenseness or anger and hostility—had significant effects on any of the child social behavior scores.

Of the five HOME Inventory subscales and the total score, all but one of the significant effects on children's social behavior were due to the scale of maternal responsiveness. Maternal responsiveness had a significant positive effect on four of the five social behavior scores: showing pride in accomplishment, engaging in role play, showing affection and annoyance, and using the mother as a resource, which was predicted by both maternal responsiveness and a negative effect of punishment and discipline. The effect sizes ranged from $R^2 = 0.09$–0.25. None of the other HOME scales had significant effects on any of the children's social behavior scales.

The data were taken a step further to test the hypothesis that poorer quality mother–child interactions and less adequate child-rearing environments will have a greater effect on child outcome than will mother's diagnosis. Results were consistent with predictions for three of the five social behavior measures: showing pride in accomplishments, engaging in role play, and using the adult as a resource. For those three variables, mother's diagnosis did not influence outcomes while parenting practices did. The amount of variance due to parenting was a significant increment over the mother's diagnosis, yet the mother's diagnosis did not account for a significant increment in variance over parenting variables. The subset of parenting variables that accounted for the significant findings were maternal responsiveness either alone or in combination with maternal tenseness; i.e., the mother's lack of responsiveness significantly negatively influenced her child in showing pride in accomplishments or in using the mother as a resource more so than did the mother's diagnosis. Furthermore, the mother's lack of responsiveness, combined with tenseness and rigidity, significantly negatively influenced her child's tendency to engage in role play more so than did the mother's diagnosis.

As with Fisher and Jones (1980), specific aspects of parenting were found to affect components of child competence. Effect sizes also differed by aspect of child competence, indicating that the parenting variables measured vary in their amount of influence depending on the competence variable. While not the subject of this review, it was interesting to note that child IQ was found to be better predicted by the mother's diagnosis than by parenting.

CONCLUSIONS

A developmental psychopathology perspective emphasizes that the expression of children's vulnerabilities should differ as a function of their developmental stage. Thus, children will be differentially responsive to aspects of their environment because of developmental changes in their cognitive, affective, and social functioning. These developmental factors influence both how children perceive, interpret, and respond to their environments and the needs that children require to be satisfied by their environments.

Infants and preschool children cope with rearing by a schizophrenic parent both affectively and cognitively. During infancy, children's affect states are regulated by patterns of events (e.g., feeding, changing, holding) that facilitate transitions from states of alertness to restfulness (Gianino and Tronick, 1985). Bizarre and unpredictable behavior from a mother may act as an arousing event, a stressor, which would disrupt the infant's emotional equilibrium and development of schemata regarding caretaking. The initial response may be alertness, affective and motoric disorganization, and strong negative affect, which might be labeled as fear (Kagan, 1983; Maccoby, 1983). Repeated exposure to a predictable stressor may lead to withdrawal and dull affect (Berlyne, 1960). However, by its nature, bizarre and unpredictable behavior cannot become routine or predictable to an infant incapable of drawing categorical inferences across interactive instances.

Kagan's (1983) scheme of developmental changes in children's vulnerability to stressors can be applied to the circumstances of a child being raised by a schizophrenic mother. As noted in the review, children of schizophrenic mothers are exposed to less reciprocity, affection, responsiveness, consistency, and stimulation. For very young infants, the response to such parenting is likely to be a state of uncertainty. Being unable to assimilate the events into beginning schemata, the infant will be alert, inhibiting motor or vocal responses, and may become fussy. By 9–12 months of age, infants can establish schemata more quickly, thus leaving the child more aware of discrepancies between usual and unusual events and more likely to protest such discrepancies. Therefore, without even considering infant temperament, the stage is set for negative mother–child interactions. Mothers who are less affectionate and responsive interacting with babies who are more fussy or withdrawn should produce less securely attached children. In addition, by 2–3 years of age, children are aware of the amount of attentiveness with which they are treated and are beginning to empathize with the emotional states of others.

A transactional model (Sameroff, 1975) aids the interpretation of the effects of maternal schizophrenia on child social–emotional development. All of the available data support the conclusion that schizophrenia in the mother, alone, is not tied to differences at birth and shortly thereafter in infants' behavioral responsivity, emotional capacity, or behavioral style. However, infants of more severely or chronically ill women (perhaps because of drug effects *in utero*) and of lower SES women do look worse than others. On the other hand, schizophrenic women are parenting their babies less adequately than women with other disturbances or no disturbances. Schizophrenic mothers are less responsive, both emotionally and simply in terms of back-and-forth interchanges, display less affect (positive or negative), provide less stimulation, and have lower expectations for their babies.

By 1 year of age, schizophrenic offspring, or at least a subgroup of schizophrenic offspring, are looking different from others in many ways. They initiate interactions less often and are less socially competent, less cheerful, more passive, less responsive, and less readable in interactions with their mothers. They often give the impression of being rather dull, as if they are turned off from their interpersonal world. Among the older children studied, however, the conclusion is that by the time children are 2–2.5 years old, maternal psychopathology in general, severity, chronicity, and low SES negatively impact children's social and emotional development. The only exception was some evidence of a developmental lag, resulting in older offspring of schizophrenic parents being less well-adapted to structured cognitive-intellectual tasks.

Both theory and data help to explain why this developmental pattern occurs. Evidence was found for poor parenting as one mechanism to account for problems in children's social and emotional development. Furthermore, quality of parenting was significantly more important than mother's diagnostic classification. However, proportions of variance accounted for in child outcome were small. Thus, poorer parenting of schizophrenic mothers apparently has a negative effect on their early development. However, after the first year or two, all children appear to be equally vulnerable to poor parenting, regardless of their mother's psychiatric diagnostic status.

The little evidence on peer relations in schizophrenic offspring further supports the developmental hypothesis; i.e., schizophrenic offspring's early interactions are likely to be characterized by neglect from peers as well as self-initiated social isolation or withdrawal.

The genetic vulnerability of offspring of schizophrenic parents may be such that they are more reactive to their environments, especially in the first year or two of life. This conclusion, of course, is compatible with Mednick's (1967; Mednick et al., 1984) finding of greater physiological reactivity in schizophrenic offspring.

The findings support a stress-diathesis model for the development of psychopathology in offspring of schizophrenic parents. The truly at-risk children are likely to be those who are slow to mature emotionally and lagging in the development of social competence and whose mothers are unresponsive, uninvolved, and have lower expectations for their children. While genetic factors may predispose schizophrenic offspring to be more reactive to poor parenting, or less resilient, the evidence points more to quality of parenting as the mechanism that sets the course for the development of psychopathology or adjustment problems.

More research is needed to clarify the possible pathways for the development of psychopathology and other negative outcomes in children of schizophrenic parents. It is essential that all future research use highly specific measures of both predictor and outcome variables. Both Fisher and Jones (1980), studying older children, and Goodman and Brumley (1990), studying younger children, found that different aspects of parenting were differentially predictive of specific child outcomes. Global indices of both parenting and child outcome are confusing and best avoided.

Furthermore, measures of both sets of variables, parenting and child outcome, must be more developmentally sensitive than has often been true in past research. For example, maternal responsiveness may be most important for the younger children, whereas parental communication deviance is more critical for the older children. Compatible with a developmental psychopathology point of view is the idea of measuring intermediate outcomes in children. These may be intermediate outcomes in a developmental course leading to the onset of schizophrenia. Alternatively, assessment of intermediate outcomes may elucidate variable patterns of development whereby some children recover from early lags in development, perhaps in relation to identifiable protective factors.

More research is also needed to distinguish any aspects of parenting that are specific to schizophrenia, other forms of psychopathology, or, alternatively, a multiple-risk model (Rutter, 1979; Sameroff et al., 1987). It is likely that a dimensional, rather than a categorical approach to assessing psychopathology will clarify the phenomenon (Harder et al., 1980). Harder et al. (1980) found that, for school-aged children, continuous measures of impairment were more related to child functioning than DSM-III diagnoses. The next step needed is to include a sophisticated analysis of parenting in the measurement of impairment, in order to be even more relevant to the search for risk factors for problems in social and emotional development in the children.

Finally, it is apparent from the review that much work needs to be done before researchers can confidently inform program planners on how best to design preventive interventions for young at-risk children. Suggestions at this point can only be tentative. Specifically, families could be selected for participation based on characteristics of both the child and the parent. High-risk children should be screened for the occurrence of poor or delayed social competence. Among babies and young children, it is important to be alert for withdrawn, passive, unresponsive children who, by their very nature, will not call attention to themselves. Disturbed parents should be screened to identify those who are unresponsive, are emotionally flat in interactions with their children, provide little stimulation, and have low developmental expectations. The most effective interventions are likely to be those modeled after those of the National Center for Clinical Infant Programs of Greenspan and his colleagues (Greenspan and Greenspan, 1989; Lieberman, 1989; Lieberman and Pawl, 1988). The needs of severely emotionally disturbed parents and their young children are compelling. Researchers are gradually clarifying both the risks for abnormal or delayed social and affective development and the mechanisms for such vulnerabilities, whether they are specific to offspring of schizophrenics or equally true for children with severely chronically ill parents in general. The value of the findings to this point should satisfy those who have been skeptical of this line of research.

ACKNOWLEDGMENT

The author's work has been supported by grants from the NIMH: R01MH25042 and RO1MH40541.

REFERENCES

Ainsworth, M. D. S. (1973). The development of mother–infant attachment. In B. M. Caldwell and H. N. Riccuti (Eds.), *Review of child development research* (Vol. 3, pp. 1–94). Chicago: University of Chicago.

Ainsworth, M. D. S., Blehar, M. C., Waters, E., and Wall, S. (1978). *Patterns of attachment: A psychological study of the strange situation.* Hillsdale, NJ: Erlbaum.

Berlyne, D. E. (1960). *Conflict, arousal, and curiosity.* New York: McGraw-Hill.

Bowlby, J. (1982). *Attachment and loss, Vol. 1: Attachment* (2nd ed.). New York: Basic Books.

Bradley, R. H. (1985). The HOME Inventory: Rationale and research. In J. Stevenson (Ed.), *Recent research in developmental psychopathology.* Book supplement to the *Journal of Child Psychology and Psychiatry,* No. 4. Oxford: Pergamon.

Bradley, R. H., and Caldwell, B. (1979). Home observation for measurement of the environment: A revision of the preschool scale. *American Journal of Mental Deficiency, 84,* 235–244.

Bradley, R. H., and Caldwell, B. (1981). The HOME Inventory: A validation of the preschool scale for black children. *Child Development, 52,* 708–710.

Brazelton, T. B. (1973). *Neonatal Behavioral Assessment Scale.* London: Heinemann.

Brazelton, T. B., Koslowski, B., and Main, M. (1974). The origins of reciprocity. In M. Lewis and L. A. Rosenblum (Eds.), *The effects of the infant on its caregivers.* New York: Wiley.

Carey, W. B., and McDevitt, S. C. (1977). Revision of the Infant Temperament Questionnaire. *Pediatrics, 61,* 735–739.

Clark, R. (1983). Interactions of psychiatrically ill and well mothers and their young children: Quality of maternal care and child competence. Unpublished doctoral dissertation, Northwestern University, Evanston, IL.

Clark, R., Musick, J., Stott, F., and Klehr, K. (1980). The Thresholds Mothers' Project: Rating scales of mother–child interaction. Unpublished manuscript, The Thresholds Mothers' Project, 2700 N. Lakeview Ave., Chicago, IL.

Cohler, B., Gallant, D., Grunebaum, H., Weiss, J., and Gamer, E. (1980). Childcare attitudes and development of young children of mentally ill and well mothers. *Psychological Reports, 46,* 31–46.

Cohler, B. J., and Musick, J. (1984). Psychopathology of parenthood: Implications for mental health of children. *Infant Mental Health Journal, 4,* 140–164.

Cohler, B. J., Stott, F. M., and Musick, J. S. (1987). From infancy to middle childhood: The Thresholds Mothers' Project. Paper prepared for the Schizophrenic High-Risk Consortium Conference (May 1987), Newport, RI.

D'Angelo, E. J., Krock, L. A., O'Neill, L. D., and Boyle, M. P. (1983). Developmental and temperamental characteristics of infants at risk for serious psychopathology. In J. D. Call, E. Galenson, and R. L. Tyson (Eds.), *Frontiers of infant psychiatry* Vol. 11, pp. 190–200. New York: Basic Books.

Doane, J. A., Jones, J. E., Fisher, L., Ritzler, B., Singer, M. T., and Wynne, L. C. (1982). Parental communication deviance as a predictor of competence in children at risk for adult psychiatric disorder. *Family Process, 21,* 211–223.

Feil, L. A., and Sameroff, A. J. (1979). Mother's conception of child development: Socioeconomic status, cross-cultural, and parity comparisons. Paper presented at the meeting of the American Psychological Association (August 1979), New York.

Field, T. F., and Sostek, A. (Eds.). (1983). *Infants born at risk: Physiological, perceptual, and cognitive processes.* New York: Grune & Stratton.

Fish, B. (1987a). Infant predictors of the longitudinal course of schizophrenic development. *Schizophrenia Bulletin, 13,* 395–410.

Fish, B. (1987b). Pandysmaturation as an infant predictor of schizotypal development. Paper presented at the meeting of the Risk Research Consortium in Schizophrenia (May 1987), Newport, RI.

Fish, B., and Alpert, M. (1962). Abnormal states of consciousness and muscle tone in infants born to schizophrenic mothers. *American Journal of Psychiatry, 119,* 439–445.

Fisher, L., and Jones, J. E. (1980). Child competence and psychiatric risk: 2. Areas of relationship between child and family functioning. *Journal of Nervous and Mental Disease, 168,* 332–337.

Garmezy, N., Masten, A., Ferrarese, N., and Nordstrom, L. (1978). The nature of competence in normal and deviant children. In M. W. Kent and J. E. Rolf (Eds.), *The primary prevention of psychopathology* (Vol. 3). (pp. 23–43). Hanover, NH: University Press of New England.

Gianino, A. F., and Tronick, E. Z. (1985). The mutual regulation model: The infant's self and interactive regulation and coping and defensive capacities. In T. R. Field, P. McCabe, and N. Schneiderman (Eds.), *Stress and coping.* Hillsdale, NJ: Erlbaum.

Goldstein, M. (1980). The course of schizophrenic psychosis. In O. G. Brim and J. Kagan (Eds.), *Constancy and change in human development* (pp. 325–358). Cambridge, MA: Harvard University Press.

Goodman, S. H. (1984a). Children of disturbed parents: A research based model for intervention. In B. J. Cohler and J. Musick (Eds.), *Interventions with psychiatrically disabled parents and their young children.* San Francisco: Jossey-Bass.

Goodman, S. H. (1984b). Children of disturbed parents: The interface between research and intervention. *The American Journal of Community Psychology, 12,* 663–687.

Goodman, S. H. (1986). Primary prevention with children of severely disturbed mothers: Progress report. Unpublished manuscript, Emory University, Atlanta, GA.

Goodman, S. H. (1987a). The Emory University Children of Disturbed Parents Project. Paper presented at the Schizophrenia High-Risk Consortium Conference (May 1987), Newport, RI.

Goodman, S. H. (1987b). Emory University Project on children of disturbed parents. *Schizophrenic Bulletin, 13,* 411–424.

Goodman, S. H., and Brumley, H. E. (1990). Schizophrenic and depressed mothers: Relational deficits in parenting. *Development Psychology, 26,* 31–39.

Goodman, S. H., and Van Buskirk, A. (1986). Schizophrenic and depressed mothers' ratings of their children's temperament. Unpublished manuscript, Emory University, Atlanta, GA.

Greenspan, S., and Greenspan, N. T. (1989). *The essential partnership: How parents and children can meet the emotional challenges of infancy and childhood.* New York: Viking Penguin.

Grossman, K. E., Grossman, K., and Huber, F. (1981). German children's behavior toward their mothers at 12 months and their fathers at 18 months in Ainsworth's Strange Situation. *International Journal of Behavioral Development, 4,* 157–181.

Hans, S., Marcus, J., and Auerbach, J. (1987). Jerusalem Infant Development Study. Paper presented at the meeting of the Schizophrenia Consortium Conference on Risk in Infancy (May 1987), Newport, RI.

Harder, D. W., Kokes, R. F., Fisher, L., and Strauss, J. S. (1980). Child competence and psychiatric risk: 4. Relationships of parent diagnostic classifications and parent psychopathology severity to child functioning. *Journal of Nervous and Mental Disease, 168,* 343–347.

Hoffman, L. (1981). *Foundations of family therapy: A conceptual framework for systems change.* New York: Basic Books.

Jacob, T. (1987). *Family interaction and psychopathology: Theories, methods, and findings.* New York: Plenum.

Johnson, D. W. (1989). The intellectual strengths and weaknesses of young offspring of schizophrenic and depressed mothers. Unpublished doctoral dissertation, Emory University, Atlanta, GA.

Johnson, D. W., and Goodman, S. H. (in preparation). Effects of schizophrenic and depressed mothers on their young children's intellectual functioning. Unpublished manuscript.

Kagan, J. (1983). Stress and coping in early development. In N. Garmezy and M. Rutter (Eds.), *Stress, coping, and development in children* (pp. 191–216). New York: McGraw-Hill.

Kohn, M. L. (1969). *Class and conformity: A study in values.* Homewood, IL: Dorsey.

Lieberman, A. F. (1989). Preventive intervention with anxiously attached mothers and infants. Presented at Society for Research in Child Development (April 27–30, 1989), Kansas City, MO.

Lieberman, A. F., and Pawl, J. H. (1988). Clinical applications of attachment theory. In J. Belsky and T. Nezworksi (Eds.), *Clinical implications of attachment.* (pp. 327–351). Hillsdale, NJ: Erlbaum.

Maccoby, E. E. (1980). *Social development: Psychological growth and the parent–child relationship.* New York: Harcourt Brace Jovanovich.

Maccoby, E. E. (1983). Social–emotional development and response to stressors. In N. Garmezy and M. Rutter (Eds.), *Stress, coping, and development in children.* New York: McGraw-Hill.

Marcus, J. (1986). Schizophrenic and attention deficit disorder (ADD): An answer to Dr. Koffman. *Schizophrenia Bulletin, 12,* 337–339.

Marcus, J. Auerbach, J., Wilkinson, L., and Burack, C. M. (1981). Infants at risk for schizophrenia: The Jerusalem Infant Development Study. *Archives of General Psychiatry, 38,* 703–713.

Marcus, J., Hans, S. L., Nagler, S., Auerbach, J. G., Mirsky, A. F., and Aubrey, A. (1987). Review of the NIMH Israeli Kibbutz-City Study and the Jerusalem Infant Development Study. *Schizophrenia Bulletin, 13,* 425–438.

Matheny, J. A. (1980). Bayley's Infant Behavior Record: Behavioral components and twin analyses. *Child Development, 51,* 1151–1167.

NcNeil, N., and Blennow, G. (1983). Offspring of women with nonorganic psychoses: Development of a longitudinal study of children of high risk. *Acta Psychiatrica Scandinavica, 68,* 234–250.

McNeil, T. F. (1986). A prospective study of postpartum psychoses in a high-risk group: 1. Clinical characteristics of the current postpartum episodes. *Acta Psychiatrica Scandinavica, 74,* 205–216.

McNeil, T. F., and Kaij, L. (1984). Offspring of women with nonorganic psychoses. In N. F. Watt, E. J. Anthony, L. C. Wynne, and J. E. Rolf (Eds.), *Children at risk for schizophrenia: A longitudinal perspective* (pp. 465–481). New York: Cambridge University Press.

McNeil, T. F. and Kaij, L. (1987). Swedish High-Risk Study: Sample characteristics at age 6. *Schizophrenia Bulletin, 13,* 373–382.

McNeil, T. F., Kaij, L., Malmquist-Larsson, A., Naslund, B., Persson-Blennow, I., McNeil, N., and Blennow, G. (1983). Offspring of women with nonorganic psychoses: Development of a longitudinal study of children at his risk. *Acta Psychiatrica Scandinavica, 68,* 234–250.

McNeil, T. F., Naslund, B., Persson-Blennow, I., and Kaij, L. (1985). Offspring of women with nonorganic psychosis: Mother–infant interaction at three-and-a-half and six months of age. *Acta Psychiatrica Scandinavica, 71,* 551–558.

Mednick, S. A. (1967). The children of schizophrenics: Serious difficulties in current research methodologies which suggest the use of the "high-risk group" method. In J. Romano (Ed.), *The origins of schizophrenia* (pp. 179–200). New York: Exerpta Media Foundation.

Mednick, S. A., Cudeck, R., Griffith, J. J., Talovic, S. A., and Schulsinger, F. (1984). The Danish High-Risk Project: Recent methods and findings. In N. F. Watt, E. J. Anthony, L. C. Wynne, and J. E. Rolf (Eds.), *Children at risk for schizophrenia: A longitudinal perspective* (pp. 21–47). New York: Cambridge University Press.

Mednick, S. A., Mura, E., Schulsinger, F., and Mednick, B. (1971). Perinatal conditions and infant development in children with schizophrenic parents. *Social Biology (Suppl.), 18,* S103–S113.

Musick, J. S., Stott, F. M., Spencer, K. K., Goldman, J., and Cohler, B. J. (1985). Maternal factors related to vulnerability and resiliency in young children at risk. In E. J. Anthony and B. Cohler (Eds.), *The invulnerable child.* (pp. 229–252). New York: Guilford.

Naslund, B. Persson-Blennow, I., McNeil, T. F., Kaij, L., and Malmquist-Larsson, A. (1984a). Deviations on exploration, attachment, and fear of strangers in high-risk and control infants at one year of age. *American Journal of Orthopsychiatry, 54,* 569–577.

Naslund, B., Persson-Blennow, I., McNeil, T. F., Kaij, L., and Malmquist-Larsson, A. (1984b). Offspring of women with nonorganic psychosis: Fear of strangers during the first year of life. *Acta Psychiatrica Scandinavica, 69,* 435–444.

Naslund, B., Persson-Blennow, I., McNeil, T. F., Kaij, L., and Malmquist-Larsson, A. (1984c). Offspring of women with nonorganic psychosis: Infant attachment to the mother at one year of age. *Acta Psychiatrica Scandinavica, 69,* 231–241.

Persson-Blennow, I., Naslund, B., McNeil, T. F., and Kaij, L. (1986). Offspring of women with nonorganic psychosis: Mother–infant interaction at one year of age. *Acta Psychiatrica Scandinavica, 73,* 207–213.

Persson-Blennow, I., Naslund, B., McNeil, T. F., Kaij, L., and Malmquist-Larsson, A. (1984). Offspring of women with nonorganic psychosis: Mother–infant interaction at three days of age. *Acta Psychiatrica Scandinavica, 70,* 149–159.

Ricks, D. F., and Berry, J. C. (1970). Family and symptom patterns that precede schizophrenia. In M. Roff and D. F. Ricks (Eds.), *Life history research in psychopathology* (Vol. 1), Minneapolis: University of Minnesota Press.

Rosenthal, D. (1970). *Genetic theory and abnormal behavior.* New York: McGraw-Hill.

Rutter, M. (1979). Protective factors in children's responses to stress and disadvantage. In M. W. Kent and J. E. Rolf (Eds.), *Primary prevention of psychopathology, Vol. 3: Social competence in children,* (pp. 49–74). Hanover, NH: University Press of New England.

Rutter, M. (1983). Stress, coping, and development: Some issues and some questions. In N. Garmezy and M. Rutter (Eds.), *Stress, coping, and development in children.* (pp. 1–42). New York: McGraw-Hill.

Sameroff, A. J. (1975). Early influences on development: Fact or fancy? *Merrill-Palmer Quarterly, 21,* 221–236.

Sameroff, A. J., Barocas, R., and Seifer, R. (1984). The early development of children born to mentally-ill women. In N. F. Watt, E. J. Anthony, L. C. Wynne, and J. E. Rolf (Eds.), *Children at risk for schizophrenia: A longitudinal perspective* (pp. 482–514). New York: Cambridge University Press.

Sameroff, A. J., Seifer, R., and Zax, M. (1982). Early development of children at risk for emotional disorder. *Monographs of the Society of Research in Child Development, 47.*

Sameroff, A. J., Seifer, R., Zax, M., and Barocas, R. (1987). Early indicators of developmental risk: Rochester Longitudinal Study. *Schizophrenia Bulletin, 13,* 383–394.

Schaefer, E. S., and Bell, R. Q. (1958). Development of a parental attitude research instrument. *Child Development, 29*, 339–361.

Seifer, R., and Sameroff, A. J. (1982). A structural equation model analysis of competence in children at risk for mental disorder. In H. Moss, R. Hess, and C. Swift (Eds.), *Early intervention programs for infants. Prevention in Human Services, 1*, 85–97.

Seifer, R., Sameroff, A. J., and Jones, F. (1981). Adaptive behavior in young children of emotionally disturbed women. *Journal of Applied Developmental Psychology, 1*, 251–276.

Shaffer, D., Gould, M. S., Brasic, J., Ambrosini, P., Fisher, P., Bird, H., and Aluwahlia, S. A. (1983). A children's global assessment scale (CGAS). *Archives of General Psychiatry, 40*, 1228–1231.

Sroufe, L. A. (1988). The role of infant-caregiver attachment in development. In J. Belsky and T. Netzworski (Eds.), *Clinical implications of attachment.* (pp. 18–40). Hillsdale, NJ: Erlbaum.

Sroufe, R. A., and Waters, E. (1977). Attachment as an organizational construct. *Child Development, 48*, 1184–1199.

Stern, D. N. (1985). *The interpersonal world of the infant.* New York: Basic Books.

Stern, D. N., Hofer, L., Haft, W., and Dore, J. (1985). Affect attunement: The sharing of feeling states between mother and infant by means of inter-modal fluency. In T. Field and N. A. Fox (Eds.), *Social perception in infants.* (pp. 249–268). Norwood, NJ: Ablex.

Stott, F., Musick, J., Clark, R., and Cohler, B. (1984). Developmental patterns in the infants and young children of mentally ill mothers: Infant development. *Infant Mental Health Journal, 3*, 27–36.

Thomas, A., and Chess, S. (1977). *Temperament and development.* New York: Brunner/Mazel.

Torgesen, A. M., and Kringlen, E. (1978). Genetic aspects of temperamental differences in infants. *Journal of the American Academy of Child Psychiatry, 17*, 433–444.

Tracy, R., Lamb, M., and Ainsworth, M. D. S. (1976). Infant approach behavior as related to attachment. *Child Development, 47*, 571–578.

Tronick, E., and Adamson, L. (1980). *Babies as people: New findings on our social beginnings.* New York: Collier Books.

Vaughn, B. E., Egeland, B., Sroufe, L. A., and Waters, E. (1979). Individual differences in infant–mother attachment at 12 and 18 months: Stability and change in families under stress. *Child Development, 50*, 971–975.

Vaughn, B. E., Gove, F. L., and Egeland, B. (1980). The relationship between out of home care and the quality of infant–mother attachment in an economically disadvantaged population. *Child Development, 51*, 1203–1214.

Waters, E. (1981). Traits, relationships and behavioral systems: The attachment construct and the organization of behavior and development. In G. Barlow, K. Immelman, M. Main, and T. L. Petrinovich (Eds.), *Proceedings of the Bielefeld Interdisciplinary Conference: Development of Behavior.* Cambridge: Cambridge University Press.

White, B. L., Kaban, B. T., Attanucci, J. S. (1979). *The origins of human competence: The final report of the Harvard Preschool Project.* Lexington, MA: Lexington Books.

Wynne, L. C. (1978). From symptoms to vulnerability and beyond: An overview. In L. C. Wynne, R. L. Cromwell, and S. Mattysse (Eds.), *The Nature of Schizophrenia; new approaches to research and treatment.* New York: John Wiley & Sons.

Wynne, L. C., Singer, M. T., Bartko, J. J., and Toohey, M. L. (1977). Schizophrenics and their families: Recent research on parental communication. In J. M. Tanner (Eds.), *Developments in psychiatric research* (pp. 254–286). London: Hodder & Stoughton.

PART II

Childhood and Adolescence

OVERVIEW

The chapters in this section highlight two important points: first, vulnerability to schizophrenia can be manifested in multiple functional domains during childhood and, second, a broad range of levels of childhood adaptation occur in schizophrenia. The chapters by Winters, Cornblatt, and Erlenmeyer-Kimling and Harvey both demonstrate that a variety of cognitive impairments may predate the onset of clinical symptoms. In the domain of social behavior, Watt and Saiz present evidence indicating that many adult-onset patients are significantly impaired during childhood and adolescence. Thus, vulnerability appears to manifest itself diffusely, rather than being restricted to a specific functional domain.

With respect to the range of childhood functional adaptations occurring in schizophrenia, these chapters show that it is extremely broad. The spectrum extends from the full-blown clinical syndrome of schizophrenia, as described by Asarnow and her colleagues, to highly adaptive functioning, as revealed in the follow-back studies discussed by Watt and Saiz. The striking diversity in the childhood and adolescent functioning of patients lends further support to the assumption that schizophrenia is heterogeneous with respect to etiology.

Copyright © 1991 by Academic Press, Inc.
All rights of reproduction in any form reserved.

Childhood-Onset Schizophrenia: Developmental Perspectives on Schizophrenic Disorders

Joan Rosenbaum Asarnow
Robert F. Asarnow
Nancy Hornstein
Andrew Russell

This chapter reviews current literature on childhood-onset schizophrenia. Although we briefly summarize the general literature, our focus is on a series of studies conducted at UCLA with a cohort of children who were diagnosed with schizophrenia or schizotypal personality disorder prior to 14 years of age (for reviews of the general literature, see Fish and Ritvo, 1979; Russell, in press; Tanguay and Asarnow, 1985; Werry, 1979, 1989). We first review research focusing on clinical presentation, onset, early developmental patterns, course, and treatment. Next, we summarize a series of studies aimed at describing hypothesized psychobiological vulnerability factors and psychosocial stressors and elucidating the links between psychobiological dysfunctions and the development of schizophrenia in childhood.

Our studies of childhood-onset schizophrenia have been stimulated by the belief that studying this very early onset form of schizophrenia may be a particularly promising way to increase our understanding of the schizo-

95

Copyright © 1991 by Academic Press, Inc.
All rights of reproduction in any form reserved.

phrenic disorders. This belief is partly based on prior findings of a twofold increase in the aggregation of schizophrenic disorders among the first-degree relatives of schizophrenic children (onset before 14 years of age) when compared with adult-onset cases (Kallman and Roth, 1956; Kolvin, 1971). Thus, similar to findings for a number of genetically transmitted diseases, early onset of schizophrenia may be associated with a heavy genetic loading for the disorder. Although these data require confirmation, they suggest that childhood-onset schizophrenia may be a more severe form of the disorder, with an increased genetic liability and possibly greater genetic homogeneity. Schizophrenic children, therefore, may comprise a particularly informative group for isolating etiological pathways for certain schizophrenic disorders.

Schizotypal children have been included in these studies to permit examination of risk factors and precursor states to schizophrenia. Links between schizotypal and schizophrenic disorders are suggested by the accumulating literature on children at risk for schizophrenia. This research indicates that schizotypal symptoms such as social isolation, inadequate rapport, and subtle signs of thought disorder may be childhood precursors of adult-onset schizophrenia (for reviews, see Asarnow, 1988; Garmezy, 1974; Goldstein and Asarnow, 1986; Watt, 1984). Results from the Danish adoption studies indicating elevated rates of schizotypal personality disorders in the biological relatives of schizophrenics (Kety *et al.*, 1978) further support an association between these syndromes.

It is important to note at the start that research on childhood-onset schizophrenia has been scant and difficult to interpret due to two major factors. First, prior to the introduction of DSM-III and ICD-9, childhood-onset schizophrenia, autism, and a variety of other syndromes were lumped under the general category of "childhood schizophrenia." Because of this early failure to differentiate among the childhood psychotic disorders, most of the research conducted before the introduction of DSM-III and ICD-9 criteria contained heterogenous diagnostic groups composed of schizophrenic and autistic children. Consequently, this early research is difficult to evaluate.

A second factor that has impeded research on childhood-onset schizophrenia is the relative rarity of the disorder. Although precise epidemiological figures are needed, childhood-onset schizophrenia is very rare. Published prevalence rates for schizophrenia with preadolescent onset range from 0.19 (Burd and Kerbeshian, 1987) to 1–2/10,000 (Beitchman, 1985). As might be expected from these prevalence data, even in large metropolitan areas, persistent efforts over several years are needed to generate adequate sample sizes.

CLINICAL PRESENTATION

Sufficient data now support the conclusions that (1) "schizophrenia" as seen in adults can be reliably diagnosed in children and (2) schizophrenic and autistic disorders can and should be clearly differentiated. Table 5.1 (drawn from Russell *et al.*, 1989) summarizes the clinical presentations of 35 schizophrenic children seen in the UCLA Child Psychiatry Clinical Research Center. When inspecting this table, it is important to recall that

TABLE 5.1. Frequencies and Percentages of Schizophrenic Children Presenting with Key Symptoms

	Frequency	%
Auditory hallucinations	28	80
Command	24	69
Conversing voices	12	34
Religious	12	34
Persecutory	9	26
Commenting voices	8	23
Visual hallucinations	13	37
Olfactory hallucinations	2	6
Somatic hallucinations	2	6
Delusions	22	63
Persecutory	7	20
Somatic	7	20
Bizarre	6	17
Reference	5	14
Grandiose	4	11
Thought insertion	4	11
Control influence	3	9
Mind reading	3	9
Thought broadcasting	2	6
Thought control	1	3
Religious	1	3
Thought disorder	14	40
Hallucinations and delusions	19	54
Hallucinations and thought disorder	10	29
Delusions and thought disorder	—	—
Hallucinations, delusions, and thought disorder	8	23
Marked deterioration in functioning	35	100
Signs of illness over >6 months	35	100

Note: Data included in this table are drawn from Russell *et al.* (1989).

both DSM-III and DSM-III-R criteria require the presence of characteristic hallucinations, delusions, and/or thought disorder. Consequently, it is not surprising that these children showed very high rates of hallucinations and delusions.

As fully described in Russell *et al.* (1989), the symptom ratings were based on the results of semistructured interviews conducted with the child and his or her parents or caregiver in conjunction with a thorough review of collateral information including current and prior clinical records, school and teacher reports, and results of psychological testing. Interviews were conducted using the Interview for Childhood Disorders and Schizophrenia (ICDS), an interview compiled by Russell *et al.* (1989) to provide full coverage of schizophrenic and schizotypal symptoms as well as the other major childhood psychiatric disorders. Although this interview draws from a variety of sources, the ICDS is based primarily on the Childhood Version of the Schedule for Affective Disorders and Schizophrenia—Present State version (Puig-Antich and Chambers, 1978; Chambers *et al.*, 1982) and the Diagnostic Interview Schedule for Children and Adolescents (Herjanic and Campbell, 1977; Welner *et al.*, 1987). Inter-rater reliabilities for DSM-III diagnoses and symptom ratings were adequate, as revealed by the following k values based on analyses of independent ratings for 23 cases: diagnosis of schizophrenia, k = 0.88; delusions, k = 1.0; auditory hallucinations, k = 0.69; thought disorder, k = 0.86; blunted or inappropriate affect, k = 0.56; disorganized behavior, k = 0.47.

As shown in Table 5.1, this sample of schizophrenic children clearly met DSM-III criteria. Among the major positive symptoms, auditory hallucinations were the most common, followed by delusions and marked thought disorder, respectively. As seen in adults, these symptoms overlapped considerably, with the largest group showing evidence of both hallucinations and delusions.

Comorbidity, the presence of codiagnoses, is commonly reported in studies of childhood psychiatric disorders and has also been apparent in our schizophrenic samples. In the Russell *et al.* (1989) group, 68% (*n* = 24) of the sample presented with codiagnoses. Major codiagnoses included conduct disorder (*n* = 10), atypical depression (*n* = 9), dysthymic disorder (*n* = 4), enuresis/encopresis (*n* = 5), sexual/physical abuse (*n* = 2), elective mutism (*n* = 1), separation anxiety disorder (*n* = 1), and oppositional disorder (*n* = 1). Although how the presence of associated syndromes in the presence of such a severe psychotic disorder should be interpreted is unclear, it is important to recognize that even schizophrenia occurs in association with other syndromes and symptoms.

ONSET, PRECURSOR STATES, AND
EARLY SYMPTOM DEVELOPMENT

The diagnosis of schizophrenia prior to 8 years of age is rare. Although schizophrenic symptoms have been reported to occur as early as 3 years (Russell et al., 1989), to our knowledge the youngest age of onset reported in the literature for the full-blown disorder is 4.9 years (Russell et al., 1989). However, determining whether or not very young children are experiencing symptoms such as hallucinations and delusions, which depends primarily on verbal report for their evaluation, is difficult. This problem is compounded by the frequent discrepancies between reports obtained from children and their parents, and the fact that parents are often unaware of such private symptoms as hallucinations and delusions. Hopefully, as child-assessment procedures continue to be developed, questions concerning the age and mode of onset will be further elucidated.

Although some children who develop schizophrenia appear to experience acute onset of disorder, the majority of children appear to have been chronically impaired or to show insidious onset patterns (for an excellent review, see Werry, 1989). Our work has generally been consistent with that of others in indicating that schizophrenic children tend to show chronic patterns of dysfunction or insidious onset patterns and relatively poor levels of premorbid adjustment. In our sample (Asarnow and Ben-Meir, 1988), schizophrenic and schizotypal children differed from depressed children in their early tendencies toward social withdrawal, poor peer relationships, low levels of scholastic achievement, poor school adaptation, few interests, and histories of nonacute onset patterns.

Watkins et al. (1989) conducted detailed analyses of the history of symptom development in an early subset of the UCLA sample. Their results indicated that schizophrenic children frequently showed early language abnormalities and delays, motor delays and hypotonia, bizarre responses to the environment, and lack of social responsiveness during infancy. During early childhood, the histories of schizophrenic children were characterized by problems with extreme mood lability, inappropriate clinging, unexplained rage reactions, and hyperactivity. Later, symptoms of formal thought disorder and flat or inappropriate affect first emerged, followed by the development of characteristic hallucinations and delusions. Formal thought disorder was not reported before 6 years of age, and hallucinations and delusions usually occurred only after 9 years of age, supporting the view that developmental changes exert significant influences on the expression of schizophrenic symptoms.

These analyses, like the comorbidity data, raise questions concerning the overlap between different syndromes. Notably, the early symptoms of language abnormalities and delays, bizarre responses to the environment, and lack of social responsiveness identified in the Watkins *et al.* (1989) analyses resemble those required for DSM-III and DSM-III-R diagnoses of autism and pervasive developmental disorder. Consequently, it is not surprising that some cases of schizophrenia have been reported in UCLA samples among children who originally presented with diagnoses of autism or pervasive developmental disorder (PDD; Petty *et al.*, 1984). Given the controversy that has raged about associations between these syndromes, it is important to add that the majority of childhood-onset schizophrenics do not appear to have shown earlier autism or PDD syndromes. Nor do the majority of children with PDD develop schizophrenia, a point that is underscored by Burd and Kerbeshian's (1987) finding of no cases of schizophrenia in their statewide (North Dakota) survey of children with early histories of PDD. The observation of occasional overlap between autistic and schizophrenic syndromes and symptoms over time suggests that early autism or PDD does not protect against the later development of schizophrenia. However, no evidence demonstrates an increased risk of schizophrenia among autistic and PDD children, underscoring the need to clearly differentiate between these syndromes. Finally, qualitative differences may exist between the type of early language disturbance found in some of the UCLA cohort of schizophrenic children and that typically found in autistic children.

It is interesting to note that the childhood symptoms of extreme mood lability, unexplained rage reactions, and hyperactivity identified in the Watkins *et al.* (1989) cohort of childhood-onset schizophrenics are also similar to those described in the childhood histories of adolescents who develop bipolar disorders. More specifically, Strober *et al.* (1988) have identified a subgroup of bipolar adolescents who showed prepubertal onset of clinically diagnosable psychopathology. For the most part, these children showed patterns of extreme mood lability, intermittent explosive outbursts, hyperactivity, and disruptive behavior. These similarities are particularly noteworthy given recent reports that some children originally diagnosed with early-onset schizophrenia received diagnoses of schizoaffective or bipolar disorders at later follow-up evaluations (Eggers, 1989; Werry, 1989).

Future research is needed to resolve the issue of the apparent overlap in the behavioral precursors identified for these different DSM-III-defined syndromes. This early overlap may reflect diagnostic imprecision and/or problems with our current systems of psychiatric diagnosis. Alternatively, certain symptoms, such as problems with mood regulation and behavioral control, may lack diagnostic specificity, and, like fever, may signal the onset of a diverse set of illnesses.

CLINICAL HETEROGENEITY

Extensive research literature with adult schizophrenics demonstrates that premorbid adjustment is useful for predicting prognosis and for separating schizophrenics into groups that show different performance and symptom patterns. Consequently, another approach adopted in our work has been to examine premorbid adjustment and onset patterns within our cohort of schizophrenic and schizotypal children. These analyses (Asarnow and Ben-Meir, 1988) indicated that the functioning of children with schizophrenia spectrum disorders and children with depressive disorders overlapped. Interestingly, the subgroup of schizophrenic and schizotypal children showing both relatively low levels of impairment and relatively good premorbid adjustments tended to present with depressive symptoms.

Although sample size limitations require that this finding be viewed with caution, it is intriguing given (1) results indicating that depressive symptoms tend to be associated with better outcomes in schizophrenic samples (Kydd and Werry, 1982; for review of adult literature, see Stephens, 1978) and (2) DeLisi et al.'s (1987) data suggesting that Research Diagnostic Criteria schizoaffective disorder and schizophrenia with a depressive component may comprise an etiological subtype of schizophrenia.

Another potentially useful dimension for subgrouping schizophrenic children is suggested by Bettes and Walker's (1987) report that low IQ in psychotic children is associated with high levels of negative symptoms, such as social withdrawal and affective flattening, and lower levels of positive psychotic symptoms such as hallucinations, delusions, and formal thought disorder. To date, we have not examined the positive/negative symptom distinction in our work. However, those children with the lowest levels of premorbid and intellectual functioning may comprise a subgroup with prominent negative symptoms. This possibility is intriguing given research with adults indicating that high levels of negative symptoms are associated with poorer prognoses, poorer response to neuroleptic medications and structural brain impairment, which results in loss of function (see Bettes and Walker, 1987).

COURSE

Despite the crucial importance of data on the longitudinal course for establishing the validity of our psychiatric syndromes, data on course and prognosis in childhood-onset schizophrenia are limited. The data that do exist are summarized in Table 5.2. Again, it is important to note that we have excluded earlier data from this review where there was confusion between DSM-III adult-type schizophrenia and other childhood-onset psychotic syndromes (for detailed reviews of earlier data, see Fish and Ritvo, 1979; Werry, 1979).

The data presented in Table 5.2 are drawn from two studies. The studies by both Eggers (1978, 1989), carried out in Germany, and Kydd and Werry (1982), conducted in New Zealand, relied to some extent on retrospective diagnoses and/or earlier diagnoses made on the basis of more variable diagnostic procedures than those currently employed. Additionally, some children were found to have developed schizoaffective or bipolar disorders at subsequent follow-ups. However, these data do indicate poor outcomes in 50–60% of cases.

The data presented above are generally consistent with preliminary data from our follow-up study of children initially hospitalized with diagnoses of schizophrenia or schizotypal personality disorder (Asarnow et al., 1988). This study is still in progress and only preliminary results regarding rates of rehospitalization and out-of-home placement are available (Asarnow et al., 1988b). Our preliminary data were collected using telephone interviews conducted with families and caretakers of 18 schizophrenic and schizotypal children. Because the outcomes were similar for schizophrenic and schizotypal children, we combined the data for these

TABLE 5.2. Longitudinal Course in Studies of DSM-III Type Childhood-Onset Schizophrenia

Study	Sample size	Range of diagnosis	Age range	Length of follow-up	% in Remission	% Moderate to poor outcome
Eggers (1978)	57	Bleulerian first-rank (includes 16 cases later diagnosed as schizoaffective)	7–13 years	mean = 15 years range = 6–40 years	20%	50%
Kydd and Werry (1982)[a]	18	DSM-III— schizophrenia or schizophreniform (includes some cases later diagnosed as bipolar disorder)	6–15 years	mean = 4.6 years range = 1–9 years	40%	60%

[a]A larger more recent follow-up based on the Kydd and Werry (1982) sample is in progress, which deletes cases of misdiagnosed bipolar disorder (Werry, 1989).

two groups into one group, which we refer to as children with schizophrenia spectrum disorders.

The cumulative probability of out-of-home placement for children with schizophrenia spectrum disorders in comparison with children with depressive disorders (major depression or dysthymic disorder) is shown in Fig. 5.1. Inspection of Fig. 5.1 reveals that out-of-home placement was very common for schizophrenic and schizotypal children. Although all but two children were sent home at discharge, within 13 months of hospital discharge, 57% of the schizophrenic and schizotypal children were placed out of their homes. Placement was usually in residential treatment centers for an extended period of time (the range was 560–730 days, with some children still in placement) and was typically precipitated by out-of-control behavior. Rates of out-of-home placements were significantly higher for children with schizophrenia spectrum disorders than for children with depressive disorders. Moreover, when depressed children were placed, they tended to be placed in nontherapeutic settings such as boarding schools or foster homes. Rehospitalizations were more common among the depressed children than the schizophrenic children. Two schizophrenic children, however, were rehospitalized after discharge because, even after long hospitalizations, they were judged to be too disturbed to be safe at home. Five schizotypal children were rehospitalized within 2.5 years of

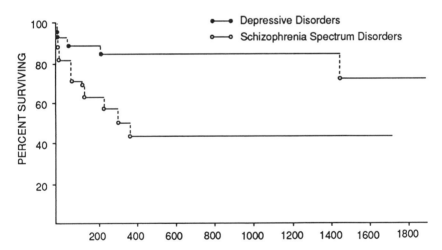

Figure 5.1. Results of a survival analysis of probability of out-of-home placement for children with schizophrenia spectrum disorders and children with depressive disorders. "Percent surviving" refers to the number of children remaining in their homes (not placed). Observations were censored at the point of any rehospitalization because rehospitalization would decrease the likelihood of placement at that time. [Copyright Lawrence Erlbaum, 1989.]

discharge. Reasons for rehospitalization included out-of-control behavior (four cases), suicide attempts (one case), and concerns about depression (one case).

Although these data are consistent with our working hypothesis that childhood-onset schizophrenia is a particularly severe form of the disorder, our data on symptomatology and social adjustment (still in progress) are crucial for clarifying the developmental patterns shown by our schizophrenic and schizotypal children (J. R. Asarnow, M. J. Goldstein, N. Hornstein, and M. Tompson, in preparation).

TREATMENT

Crucial questions for future research concern whether or not treatment influences prognosis in childhood-onset schizophrenia, and, if so, what form of treatment or treatment combinations are most beneficial. Unfortunately, our search of the literature revealed no adequately controlled studies of the efficacy of pharmacologic interventions with adequate samples of DSM-III-diagnosed schizophrenic children. Despite this lack of empirical data, our follow-up data are consistent with those from other centers in indicating that a large proportion of schizophrenic children are being treated with combinations of ongoing therapy and antipsychotic medications (Hornstein *et al.*, in progress).

Table 5.3 summarizes the treatment histories of 15 of the children for whom we have follow-up data based on interviews with parents and children, as well as treatment questionnaires sent to mental health providers. These children, ten boys and five girls, were admitted to the hospital between the ages of 7 and 13 years, and given initial diagnoses of schizophrenia. The length of the follow-up periods to date vary from 1 to 5.5 years. This study is naturalistic, and treatment is provided by mental health practitioners in the patients' communities, according to their own standards and practices.

Inspection of Table 5.3 reveals that all of these children had received psychosocial intervention in terms of conventional therapies prior to and during their hospitalization, and a majority continued in individual and/or family therapy after hospitalization. Eighty-seven percent received psychotropic medications prior to hospitalization, and approximately half received stimulant medications (amphetamines or methylphenidate). This is an interesting observation for two reasons: (1) We can conjecture that early symptoms in these children included problems with attention and/or hyperactivity, and (2) stimulants may precipitate or exacerbate psychotic symptoms in susceptible individuals (Rapoport and Kruesi, 1985). This observation underscores the need for further longitudinal re-

TABLE 5.3. Summary of Treatment Received by Schizophrenic Children

Therapy	Prehospitalization		Hospitalization		Posthospitalization	
	%	Frequency	%	Frequency	%	Frequency
Psychosocial treatment						
Total in therapy	100	15	100	15	93	14
Individual	73	11	100	15	93	14
Family	40	6	100	15	47	7
Both	40	6	100	15	47	7
Group	0	0	13	2		
Pharmacotherapy						
Total on medications	87	13	100	15	87	13
Neuroleptics	47	7	93	14	87	13
Lithium	0		7	1	27	4
Tegretol	0		0		7	1
Tricyclic antidepressants	7	1	7	1	13	2
Benzodiazepines	20	3	0		7	1
Catapress	0		0		7	1
Stimulants	47	7	7	1	0	
Combinations	27	4	33	5	53	8

[a]All children receiving combinations of medications had a neuroleptic as one of the medications. Column percentage does not equal 100% due to the fact that children frequently received multiple medications and psychosocial treatments.

search into childhood psychiatric illnesses to increase recognition of prodromal states and early manifestations of the illness. It also highlights the possibility that some schizophrenic children may be receiving pharmacological treatments that may be exacerbating their problems. Although these children were all hospitalized at UCLA or affiliated hospitals, it is interesting to note that during and following hospitalization most children were treated with neuroleptic medications alone or in combination with other medications. In this small sample, 6 of the 14 children on neuroleptics experienced possible side effects. Two children had dystonic reactions definitely related to the medications, and four had abnormal movements of uncertain etiology. Given the apparently widespread use of neuroleptics in the treatment of schizophrenic children, a clear priority for future research is establishing their efficacy, their effect on development, and their potential for serious and irreversible side effects. This will aid in a realistic assessment of the potential risks and benefits of a particular type of treatment.

One possible interpretation of the observation that over half of these children were on combinations of neuroleptics along with other medications posthospitalization is that the neuroleptics alone were not sufficient to manage the symptoms of these children. In this context, it is important to recall the high rates of out-of-home placements and rehospitalizations reported above. Among this group of 15 schizophrenic children, 12 have required out of home placements, rehospitalizations, or day-hospital programs. Clearly, these children have remained severely affected by their illness, despite the treatment they have received.

THE SEARCH FOR ETIOLOGICAL PATHWAYS

Our studies of childhood-onset schizophrenia have been motivated partly by the hope that studies of this early onset form of the disorder would prove particularly informative. Although there are some conflicting data (Pope *et al.*, 1982; Abrams and Taylor, 1983; Coryell and Zimmerman, 1988), it is generally agreed that the bulk of current evidence supports the view that (1) some forms of schizophrenia are familially transmitted and (2) what is transmitted is not restricted to schizophrenic psychosis but may also include personality characteristics like those defined by the diagnostic construct of schizotypal personality disorder. Moreover, as Cloninger (1987) and others have pointed out, current evidence allows rejection of the hypothesis that all schizophrenia is due to a single major locus defect. Consequently, schizophrenia will probably prove to be genetically heterogeneous. Multiple genes or sets of genes may contribute to the liability to schizophrenia.

Also, the developmental pathways from genotype to phenotype will probably be complex and characterized by multiple interactions between genetic and environmental factors, with no single cause sufficient to produce schizophrenia. The set of potential environmental factors is broad, encompassing both the biological effects of the intra-uterine environment and stress during delivery and the psychosocial influences of the family, peers, and life events. Thus, we will need to elucidate the processes by which genetically transmitted predispositions and vulnerabilities interact developmentally with environmental factors to determine (1) whether or not an individual develops a schizophrenic disorder and, if so, when, and (2) the level of psychosocial functioning once the disorder develops.

From a developmental perspective, individuals vulnerable to the disorder may be particularly sensitive to environmental or biological stressors during critical periods. Biosocial stressors that occur during one developmental period may be more pathogenic than at other ages. This concept is illustrated by Mednick *et al.'s* (1988) report suggesting that viral infections occurring during the second trimester of pregnancy may be associated with increased risk of schizophrenia. In contrast, viral infections during other stages of pregnancy apparently are not associated with the same levels of risk.

A major obstacle to understanding the pathophysiology and complex etiologies of the schizophrenic disorders is uncertainty over the precise phenotype (or phenotypes) for these disorders. This problem is highlighted by family and twin studies, which indicate that estimates of the familial aggregation and heritability of schizophrenia vary according to the narrowness or breadth of the definition of schizophrenia (cf. Gottesman and Shields, 1982; Kendler, 1980). The question of which sets of symptoms, dysfunctions, and diagnostic conventions best define syndromes with common etiologies and responses to treatment has yet to be resolved.

Next we summarize a set of studies that examine impairments in certain aspects of attention and information processing (AIP), which are hypothesized to tap core central nervous system defects associated with risk for schizophrenic disorder. Following that, we summarize what we have learned from studies of parent and family attributes and processes, which are hypothesized to represent both psychosocial stressors and reflections of underlying psychobiological vulnerability.

AIP Impairments as a Possible Genetic Marker of Schizophrenia

R. Asarnow and his colleagues have attempted to develop measures that tap the central nervous system defect hypothesized to underlie the symptoms of schizophrenia. This work has focused on studies of impairments in certain aspects of AIP because of converging evidence that a number of AIP tasks show promise as indices of genetic liability for schizophrenia. This evidence derives from three major sources. First, several studies have shown that AIP impairments are found not only in acutely disturbed schizophrenic patients but also in schizophrenic patients during the postpsychotic states of the disorder, suggesting that AIP impairments do not merely reflect the generalized dysfunction associated with an acute psychotic state. Second, results from several high-risk studies have indicated that a subset of children considered to be at risk for schizophrenia by virtue of having at least one schizophrenic parent show AIP impairments (Asarnow, 1983; Nuechterlein, 1983; Erlenmeyer-Kimling and Cornblatt, 1987) Finally, nonaffected adult relatives of adult-onset schizophrenia probands also show impairment on a number of AIP tasks (e.g., Wood and Cook, 1979), some of which have also detected impairment in children at risk for schizophrenia. Thus, some evidence indicates familial aggregation of AIP impairments among the first-degree relatives of schizophrenic patients.

Clearly, familial aggregation is not necessarily an indication of genetic transmission. For example, shared environmental factors as diverse as exposure to neurotoxic viruses or exposure to severe psychosocial adversity could also contribute to familial aggregation of behavioral disorders. Two recent studies provide additional evidence indicating that certain AIP tasks may tap a genetically transmitted predisposition to schizophrenic disorders. These studies employ two of the classic research strategies—twin and adoption methods—used to disentangle genetic and environmental effects on human behavior. The AIP tasks used in these studies were a Continuous Performance Test (CPT) and a forced-choice, partial-report Span of Apprehension Task. The CPT measures the ability to sustain attention (for a review, see Nuechterlein, in press) and requires subjects to monitor a display to detect an intermittently presented target stimulus. In the CPT used in the studies below, the stimuli were perceptually degraded and presented briefly (e.g., 50 msec) on a computer monitor. Performance on the partial-report Span of Apprehension Task provides an index of the rate of visual information processing (for a review, see Asarnow *et al.*, in press). The Span of Apprehension Task requires subjects to indicate which of two predesignated target letters are present in arrays of tachistoscopically (e.g., 50 msec) presented letters. The number of nontarget stimuli in the arrays are varied.

A recently completed Swedish study (Bartfai *et al.*, submitted) of normal female monozygotic and dyzotic co-twins reared either together or apart indicated that individual differences are highly heritable ($h^2 = 0.74$). Moreover, more than half the genetic variance in span performance is genetically independent of IQ. These data suggest that a number of genes can determine in the general population (in the absence of acquired central nervous system disease) individual differences in performance on the Span of Apprehension Task and similar tasks.

Preliminary findings from the Finnish Adoptive Study (for a description of this project, see Tienari *et al.*, 1987) provide more direct evidence that the AIP impairments detected in the unaffected relatives of schizophrenic probands may be genetically transmitted. In this study, genetic and environmental factors are disentangled by prospectively studying the offspring of schizophrenic mothers and the offspring of parents without a history of schizophrenic disorder. The offspring were adopted away early in life. A study (Moring *et al.*, 1991) of a small subset of this sample indicates that a significantly greater proportion of the adoptees with a schizophrenic biological mother performed deviantly on the Span of Apprehension Task *or* the CPT than did the adoptees whose biological parents were not schizophrenic. Collectively, the results of these two recent studies are consistent with the hypothesis that certain AIP tasks may index a genetically transmitted predisposition to schizophrenic disorder.

Do schizophrenic children show impairments on the AIP tasks that appear to tap a genetically indexed predisposition to schizophrenic disorder? To answer this question in the first of a series of three studies, schizophrenic, mental age (MA) matched normal children and a group of younger normal children were administered the same span task used in the studies described above (for a more detailed description, see Asarnow and Sherman, 1984). Inspection of Fig. 5.2, which presents Span of Apprehension Task data for the three groups, indicates that for all groups performance decreases as the number of letters in the array increases. At all array sizes, except the one-letter array, the schizophrenic children detected significantly fewer target stimuli than the MA-matched normals. The schizophrenic and younger normal groups did not differ from each other on any of the arrays.

That schizophrenic children show the same kind of impairment on the span task as other groups of individuals vulnerable to adult-onset schizophrenia suggests that childhood-onset schizophrenia falls on the continuum of the "schizophrenia spectrum." In general, impaired information

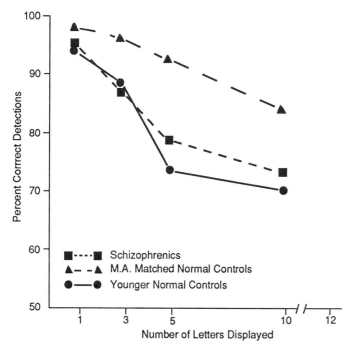

Figure 5.2 Partial-report span task: Mean number of correct detections of the target stimulus as a function of the number of letters displayed for schizophrenic and mental age-matched (M. A. Matched) and younger normal children. [Reprinted, with permission, from R. F. Asarnow and T. Sherman (1984) and the Society for Research in Child Development, Inc.]

processing tends to be a characteristic of those adult schizophrenics with a poor premorbid history (Cromwell, 1975). That schizophrenic children are also impaired suggests that attentional impairments are characteristic of the more severe forms of schizophrenia, i.e., those with the earliest onset and with the poorest prognosis.

Two additional studies tried to identify the cognitive processes underlying the impaired Span of Apprehension Task performance of schizophrenic children. First, a 12-letter array version of the span task was constructed in which task parameters were manipulated to isolate the contribution of four cognitive processes tapped by the Estes and Taylor (1964) Span of Apprehension Task: (1) information-acquisition strategies, (2) stimulus discrimination skills, (3) general response biases, and (4) fatigue/learning effects.

The results of this study suggested that the impaired performance of the schizophrenic children on the Estes and Taylor Span of Apprehension Task is *not* due to (1) a general fatigue habituation effect (they showed the same increase in accuracy level over four trial blocks as the other two groups of subjects), (2) the differential effects of some response bias (they showed the same response bias as the other two groups of children), or (3) poor stimulus discrimination skills (they responded in the same fashion as the two groups of normal children to the number of letters adjacent to the target stimulus). All three groups detected fewer target stimuli when the target was adjacent to five letters than when it was not immediately adjacent to any other letters.

Schizophrenic children and MA-matched normal children also apparently used the same information-acquisition strategies. As shown in Fig. 5.3, both the MA-matched controls and the schizophrenic children were more likely to detect the target stimuli when they were presented in the upper half of the screen than when they were presented in the lower half of the screen. In contrast, the younger normal children showed an equal probability of detecting the target stimuli across stimulus locations. Thus, in one important way the schizophrenic children differed from the younger children. These results suggest that the schizophrenic children were using the same information-acquisition strategy as that employed by the older MA-matched normal control group, but less efficiently since their overall performance levels were lower than those of the MA-matched controls. Additionally, the fact that schizophrenic children in both studies showed impaired performance relative to children who were matched to them on general intellectual abilities indicates that their information-processing impairments were not simply reflecting global impairments of intellectual abilities.

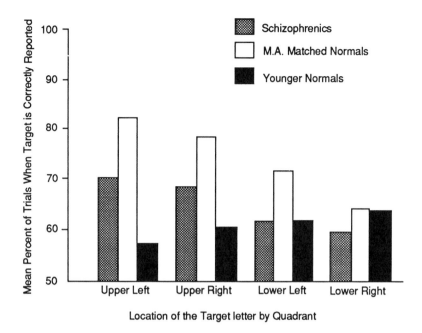

Figure 5.3 Partial-report span task: Mean percentage of trials when the target stimulus is correctly detected as a function of target letter location for schizophrenic and mental age-matched (M. A. Matched) and younger normal children. [Reprinted, with permission, from R. F. Asarnow and T. Sherman (1984) and the Society for Research in Child Development, Inc.]

What accounts for the reduced efficiency in the information-acquisition strategies of schizophrenic children? A third study examined the extent to which the impairments shown by schizophrenic children were due to deficient iconic and/or immediate memory. Iconic memory refers to a short-lasting (<300 msec), large-capacity memory store for visual stimuli, whereas immediate memory is typically thought to have a slightly longer persistence and less capacity. Stimuli are automatically entered into iconic/immediate memory without requiring active encoding. Information decays from iconic/immediate memory unless it is actively processed (e.g., rehearsed). This study used a full-report span task that makes greater demands on iconic and immediate memory and fewer demands on early attentive process by requiring subjects to report all of the tachistoscopically presented letters they can remember seeing. Schizophrenic children did not differ from the MA-matched controls in the number of letters reported in the full-report span task, suggesting that the impaired performance of schizophrenic children on partial-report span tasks was not due to deficient iconic and/or immediate memory.

Importantly, the results of this third study also indicate that subjects did not perform on the partial report span by simply naming all the letters they could retrieve from iconic and/or immediate memory. Detecting the target on a partial-report span task requires processing each stimulus to the point at which it can be determined whether it is a T or F. The mean number of letters reported (two to four) on the full-report span task is far less than the number of letters that had to be processed (six to nine) on the 12-letter partial-report span task to yield the detection rates obtained in experiment II.

In summary, schizophrenic children show impairments on the partial-report Span of Apprehension Task that apparently are associated with problems in the efficiency of their information-acquisition strategies. What strategies do children use to perform on partial-report span tasks? The data from experiment I suggest that all groups of subjects were engaged in serial search when performing this partial-report span task. Serial processing demands focal attention. It is characterized by the direction of attention serially to different locations, to integrate the features within the same spatio-temporal "spotlight" into a unitary percept C. One of the defining characteristics of a serial mode of processing is that there is an incremental cost (increased reaction time or errors) when subjects are required to detect targets in displays with increasing numbers of distractors (Treisman and Gelade, 1980). This is exactly what happens on the span task in experiment I. As the number of distractors increased from 0 to 2 to 4 to 9, the target detection rates for all groups decreased. Moreover, the fact that the schizophrenic children and the younger normals showed a greater "cost" with increased number of distractors than MA-matched normals suggests that their serial search is either initiated more slowly or employed less efficiently than that of the older control group.

A convergent result emerges from experiment II. When the target is in the upper quadrants, as opposed to the lower quadrants, both the schizophrenics and the MA-matched normals showed a significantly greater probability of correctly detecting the target. This suggests that both the schizophrenics and older normals consistently began their serial search in the upper quadrants and that their iconic image of the stimulus display faded before they could adequately process the lower quadrants.

From these data, we cannot determine whether the advantage of the older normals is due to their having found a better set of features to search for or all groups searched for the same set of critical features but the older normals were more efficient in either the initiation or application of their search. Cash *et al.* (1972) suggested that schizophrenic adults may have special difficulty in ignoring irrelevant features and, thus, may have problems with tasks involving speeded search. On the other hand, evidence suggests that schizophrenics may be delayed in the initiation of visual search (Russell *et al.*, 1980).

The results of these studies suggest that schizophrenic children, like other schizophrenic individuals, show information-processing impairments under conditions that entail controlled processing. Controlled processes (which are distinguished from automatic processes) are momentary sequences of mental operations that (1) are under the subject's control and (2) make demands on a central, limited pool of information-processing capacity.

Diagnostic Specificity of AIP Impairments

The AIP impairments found in schizophrenic children are robust and have some degree of diagnostic specificity. They can be detected by a number of cognitive tasks that make extensive demands on momentary processing capacity, including a number of subtests from the Wechsler Intelligence Scale for Children—Revised (WISC-R). The scores of schizophrenic children on the "distractibility factor" of the WISC-R were (1) significantly lower than those of a sample of nonretarded autistic children matched to the schizophrenic children in full-scale IQ, (2) below the range of normal children, and (3) significantly lower than the scores they obtained on the verbal comprehension and perceptual organization factors of the WISC-R (Asarnow *et al.*, 1987). Schizophrenic and schizotypal children also scored significantly lower on the WISC-R "distractibility factor" than did depressed children (Asarnow *et al.*, 1988a). The subtests included in the "distractibility" factor make extensive demands on controlled attentional processes because of their requirements for working memory, attention, and speed of responding.

Schizophrenic children made significantly more perseverative errors than MA-matched normals on the Wisconsin Card Sorting Test (Schneider and Asarnow, 1987). When schizophrenic children were taught the relevant sorting strategy on the Wisconsin Card Sorting Test, nonperseverative errors (random responding) increased relative to the trials administered before they were taught the strategy. The same manipulation had no effect on autistic and normal children. Thus, providing task-relevant information to the schizophrenic child, whose momentary processing capacity is already overburdened, may further encumber processing resources, resulting in the seemingly paradoxical effect of further impairing performance.

In summary, our studies to date indicate that schizophrenic children, like certain schizophrenic adults, may suffer from limitations in processing capacity. This may compromise the schizophrenic child's ability to process complex social/affective stimuli. In the next section, we review research examining the extent to which schizophrenic children are exposed to certain complex social/affective stimuli, which are hypothesized to act as psychosocial stressors.

Studies of Parent and Family Attributes

One of the more robust findings in studies of families of adult schizophrenics is that interpersonal communications in some of the families are often unclear and confusing. If, as suggested by our review of the AIP research, schizophrenic children are impaired in their ability to process complex stimuli, vague and confusing communication patterns may be particularly stressful. Conversely, parents attempting to communicate with schizophrenic children, who may themselves be struggling with their AIP impairments, may find it particularly difficult to maintain clear communication patterns.

Much of the research on communication patterns in families of adult schizophrenics has employed measures of communication deviance (CD). As defined by Singer and Wynne (1965), CD refers to a confusing, unclear communication style that leads to a disruption in the focus of attention. Singer and Wynne's theory of CD views it as the counterpart at the interpersonal level of cognitive and thought disorder at the individual level. Communication in families of schizophrenics is thought to be disturbed at the attentional level when a shared focus of attention is established. When communication fails at this level, the child is hypothesized to become confused about "what he is hearing and what he should think" (Singer *et al.*, 1978; 500), and the likelihood of thought disorder and disturbed attention in the child are thought to increase.

In the first study, to our knowledge, examining CD in rigorously diagnosed DSM-III-defined childhood-onset schizophrenics, Asarnow *et al.* (1988a) found that CD was significantly more frequent in parents of schizophrenic and schizotypal children than in parents of children with depressive disorders. Thus, like the data on AIP in childhood-onset schizophrenic, our results indicate patterns similar to those found in families of adult-onset schizophrenics (Doane, 1978; Jacob, 1975; Liem, 1980; Wynne *et al.*, 1977).

The CD measure used in the Asarnow *et al.* (1988a) study was scored from parents' responses to the Thematic Apperception Test (TAT), which is administered to each parent individually in the absence of the disturbed child. Consequently, responses on the TAT-CD measure are not likely to reflect the immediate influence of the child's behavior. It is interesting to note, therefore, that schizophrenic and schizotypal children from high-level CD families tended to be the most severely impaired (as indexed by Global Adjustment Scale scores) and to show the greatest AIP deficits (as indexed by scores on the "distractibility" factor of the WISC-R).

Similar patterns were identified in families of adult-onset schizophrenics. Wagener *et al.* (1986) found that mothers of schizophrenic patients with AIP impairments (as measured by a partial-report Span of Apprehension Task) tended to have higher levels of CD than did mothers of schizophrenic patients without AIP impairments. Additionally, mothers with elevated CD scores tended themselves to have AIP problems measured by a partial-report span task.

These data suggest that those schizophrenic and schizotypal children with the most severe attentional impairments are most likely to be reared in environments where they are exposed to confusing unfocused communications. This combination of impaired attention and environmental attributes that tax attentional processes might further potentiate developing attentional dysfunction and psychosocial impairment. Indeed, this association among parental CD, child impairment, and poorer attention is precisely the pattern observed in our sample of schizophrenic and schizotypal children.

Family patterns are clearly bidirectional, with parental behavior affecting children and child behavior affecting parents. Consequently, we have examined direct parent–child interactions in an effort to clarify processes that may contribute to the patterns described above. Tompson *et al.* (1990) compared communication patterns during a Family Rorschach Task among families of schizophrenic, schizotypal, and depressed children. In the Family Rorschach Task, families were asked to look at an inkblot (card VIII) and come to agreement regarding "what it looks like, reminds family members of, or resembles." This task has been used to assess communication patterns in the families of schizophrenic adults (Loveland *et al.*, 1963; Shapiro and Wild, 1976; Carter *et al.*, 1987).

Tompson *et al.* (1990) compiled a scoring system for this task drawn from the Doane and Singer (1977) CD scoring manual for the consensus Rorschach and the Thought Disorder Index (Arpoleda and Holzman, 1985; Johnston and Holzman, 1979; Solovay *et al.*, 1986). This scoring system was designed to tap three types of communication problems hypothesized to play an important role in schizophrenic disorders: (1) behavior reflecting difficulties maintaining attention to task, or "attentional drift" (e.g., interruptions, extraneous questions or remarks, nonverbal disruptive behavior, task set shift); (2) problems with communication clarity and commitment to ideas (e.g., hopping around among responses, confusion or abandoned remarks, mind-reading responses); and (3) speech indicative of thought disorder (e.g., contaminations, clang associations, peculiar logic).

Results from the Tompson *et al.* (1990) study underscored the salience of thought disorder and communication problems in schizophrenic and schizotypal children. When compared with depressed children, schizophrenic and schizotypal children exhibited significantly more thought disorder and disturbed attention during the Family Rorschach Task. Alternatively, despite the fact that parents of schizophrenic and schizotypal children showed higher rates of CD on the TAT-CD index than parents of depressed children, the two groups of parents were similar in the communication patterns and levels of thought disorder that they exhibited during the interaction task.

Evidence of thought disturbance is one of the criteria for diagnosing schizophrenic and schizotypal disorders. However, it is important to note that our measures of deviant thought and communication patterns were derived from a setting different from that employed to make diagnoses, and our ratings were made by raters who were blind to the child's diagnosis. Thus, our findings highlight the fact that families and others attempting to interact with schizophrenic and schizotypal children are frequently confronted with children who show disordered thinking and difficulties maintaining attention. These difficulties are likely to be manifested across a variety of social situations and to have an impact on the child's social relationships and adjustment. Our findings also underscore another similarity between adult- and child-onset schizophrenia. Consistent with Bleuler's (1950) view that thought disorder is a core feature of adult schizophrenic illness, our schizophrenic and schizotypal children showed elevated levels of thought disorder.

What accounts for the cross-study discrepancies with respect to parental behavior? This question remains to be resolved through future research. However, a few possible explanations merit note. First, the TAT-CD measure is a multifactorial measure that heavily weighs problems with perceptual distortions (factor 2) and major integration and closure problems (factor 6). Our interactional communication measure was very sensitive to the communication problems of our highly disturbed children but may not have been sensitive to the more subtle communication problems tapped by the TAT-CD measure. Also, the demand characteristics of our interactional task may have served to suppress communication features that were evident in the individual TAT sessions. In this regard, it is important to recall that our study involved psychiatrically hospitalized children who were generally severely distressed and, because of their hospitalizations had reduced contact with their families.

Another aspect of family transactions involving schizophrenic and schizotypal children is the impact of the child's disturbance on parental functioning. Asarnow and Horton (1990) found that parents of our psychiatric inpatients with schizophrenia spectrum and depressive disorders described disruption in their family lives, social relationships, leisure activities, and work functioning. Mothers experiencing high levels of disruption tended to lack close supportive intimate relationships and to have children with the most chronic disorders. These findings underscore the need to provide support and assistance for parents as well as their troubled children.

CONCLUSIONS

In this chapter, we reviewed research on childhood-onset schizophrenia and schizotypal personality disorder, with an emphasis on our research programs. The following conclusions can be offered.

1. Children do present with schizophrenic and schizotypal disorders like those seen in adults.

2. Schizophrenic and schizotypal children show severe and relatively enduring impairments.

3. Sound empirical data to inform our treatment decisions is urgently needed.

4. Schizophrenic children can be differentiated from normal controls and psychiatric contrast groups using measures found in previous research to characterize adult-onset schizophrenia.

These conclusions are consistent with our working hypothesis that childhood-onset schizophrenia represents a particularly severe form of schizophrenia. However, our review underscores the relatively early stage of our knowledge, as well as the crucial questions that await future research. How does the age of onset of the disorder affect subsequent cognitive, social, and emotional development? What determines age of onset? How stable are the patterns shown by schizophrenic and schizotypal children as they progress through adolescence and enter adulthood? What environmental and individual factors predict the course of childhood-onset schizophrenic and schizotypal disorders? How do early psychobiological vulnerability factors interact with stress and protective factors in the environment to determine the developmental course of these disorders? What are the most effective treatment strategies for these children and their families? Answers to these questions are crucial for advancing our understanding of the schizophrenic disorders.

ACKNOWLEDGMENTS

The research described in this chapter was supported by grants from the John D. and Catherine T. MacArthur Foundation to Robert Asarnow, Joan Asarnow, and the UCLA node of the Network on Risk and Protective Factors in Major Mental Disorders, and by NIMH grant MH30897 to the UCLA Child Psychiatry Clinical Research Center.

REFERENCES

Abrams, R. and Taylor, M. A. (1983). The genetics of schizophrenia: A reassessment using modern criteria. *Archives of General Psychiatry, 140,* 171–175.

Arboleda, C., and Holzman, P. S., (1985). Thought disorder in children at risk for psychosis. *Archives of General Psychiatry, 79*(36), 1315–1323.

Asarnow, J. R. (1988). Children at risk for schizophrenia: Converging lines of evidence. *Schizophrenia Bulletin, 14*(4), 613–631.

Asarnow, J. R., and Ben-Meir, S. (1988). Children with schizophrenia spectrum and depressive disorders: A comparative study of onset patterns, premorbid adjustment, and severity of dysfunction. *Journal of Child Psychology and Psychiatry, 29,*(A), 477–488.

Asarnow, J. R., Goldstein, M. J., and Ben-Meir, S. (1988a). Parental communication deviance in childhood onset schizophrenia spectrum and depressive disorders. *Journal of Child Psychology & Psychiatry, 29*(6), 825–838.

Asarnow, J. R., Goldstein, M. J., Carlson, G. A., Perdue, S., Bates, S., and Keller, J. (1988b). Child-onset depressive disorders: A follow-up study of rates of rehospitalization and out-of-home placement among child psychiatric inpatients. *Journal of Affective Disorders, 15,* 245–253.

Asarnow, J. R., and Horton, A. (1990). Coping and stress in families of child psychiatric inpatients: Parents of children with depressive and schizophrenia spectrum disorders. *Child Psychiatry and Human Development, 21,* 145–157.

Asarnow, R. F. (1983). The search for the psychobiological substrate of schizophrenia: A perspective from studies of children at risk for schizophrenia. In R. Tartar (Ed.), *The child at psychiatric risk.* (00–00). New York: Oxford University Press.

Asarnow, R. F., Granholm, E., and Sherman, T. (in press). Span of apprehension in schizophrenia. In S. Steinhauer, J. Gruzelier, and J. Zubin (Eds.), *Handbook of schizophrenia: Neuropsychology, psychophysiology and information processing.* Amsterdam: Elsevier.

Asarnow, R. F., and MacCrimmon, D. J. (1982). Attention/information processing, neuropsychological functioning and thought disorder using the acute and partial recovery phases of schizophrenia: A longitudinal study. *Psychiatry Research, 7,* 309–319.

Asarnow, R. F., and Sherman, T. (1984). Studies of visual information processing in schizophrenic children. *Child Development, 55,* 249–261.

Asarnow, R. F., Tanguay, P. E., Bott, L., and Freeman, B. J. (1987). Patterns of intellectual functioning in non-retarded autistic and schizophrenic children. *Journal of Child Psychology and Psychiatry, 28,* 273–280.

Bartfai, A., Pederson, N., Asarnow, R., and Schalling, D. (submitted). Genetic factors for a marker of schizophrenia: A twin study of span of apprehension.

Beitchman, J. H. (1985). Childhood schizophrenia: A review and comparison with adult-onset schizophrenia. *Psychiatric Journal of the University of Ottawa, 8,* 25–37.

Bettes, B. A., and Walker, E. (1987). Positive and negative symptoms in psychotic and other psychiatrically disturbed children. *Journal of Child Psychology & Psychiatry, 28,* 555–568.

Bleuler, E. (1950). *Dementia praecox, or the group of schizophrenias.* New York: International Universities Press.

Burd, L., and Kerbeshian, J. (1987). A North Dakota prevalence study of schizophrenia presenting in childhood. *Journal of the American Academy of Child and Adolescent Psychiatry, 26,* 347–350.

Callaway, E., and Naghdi, S. (1982). An information processing model for schizophrenia. *Archives of General Psychiatry, 3,* 339–347.

Carter, L., Robertson, S. R., Ladd, J., and Alpert, M. (1987). The family Rorschach with families of schizophrenics: Replication and extension. *Family Process, 26,* 461–474.

Cash, T. F., Neale, J. M., and Cromwell, R. L. (1972). Span of apprehension in acute schizophrenics: Full-report procedure. *Journal of Abnormal Psychology, 3,* 322–326.

Chambers, W. J., Puig-Antich, J., Tabrizi, M., and Davies, M. (1982). Psychotic symptoms in prepubertal major depressive disorder. *Archives of General Psychiatry, 39,* 921–927.

Cloninger, C. R. (1987). Genetic principles and methods in high-risk studies of schizophrenia. *Schizophrenia Bulletin, 13,* 515–523.

Coryell, W., and Zimmerman, M. (1988). The heritability of schizophrenia and schizoaffective disorder: A family study. *Archives of General Psychiatry, 45,* 323–327.

Cromwell, R. L. (1975). Assessment of schizophrenia. In M. Rosenzweig and L. Porter (Eds.), *Annual review of psychology.* (pp. 593–619). Palo Alto, CA: Annual Reviews.

DeLisi, L. E., Goldin, L. R., Maxwell, M. E., Kazuba, D. M., and Gershon, E. S. (1987). Clinical features of illness in siblings with schizophrenia or schizoaffective disorder. *Archives of General Psychiatry, 44,* 891–896.

Doane, J. A. (1978). Family interaction and communication deviance in disturbed and normal families: A review of research. *Family Process, 17,* 357–376.

Doane, J. A., and Singer, M. T. (1977). *Communication deviance scoring manual for use with consensus Rorschach.* Unpublished manuscript, University of Rochester, Rochester, New York.

Eggers, C. (1978). Course and prognosis of childhood schizophrenia. *Journal of Autism and Childhood Schizophrenia, 8,* 21–36.

Eggers, C. (1989). Schizo-affective psychoses in childhood: A follow-up study. *Journal of Autism and Developmental Disorders, 19,* 327–342.

Erlenmeyer-Kimling, L., and Cornblatt, B. (1987). The New York High-Risk Project: A follow-up report. *Schizophrenia Bulletin, 13,* 451–461.

Estes, W. K., and Taylor, H. A. (1964). A detection method and probabilistic models for assessing information processing from brief visual displays. *Proceedings of the National Academy of Sciences USA, 52,* 446–454.

Fish, B., and Ritvo, E. (1979). Psychosis in childhood. In J. D. Noshpitz (Ed.), *Basic handbook of child psychiatry* (Vol. 3, pp. 294–304). New York: Basic Books.

Garmezy, N. (1974). Children at risk: The search for the antecedents of schizophrenia: Part II. Ongoing research programs, issues, and intervention. *Schizophrenia Bulletin, 1,* 55–125.

Goldstein, M. J., and Asarnow, J. R. (1986). Prevention of schizophrenia: What do we know? In J. P. Barter and S. Talbot (Eds.), *Primary prevention: The state of the art* (pp. 85–116). Washington, DC: American Psychiatric Press.

Gottesman, I. E., and Shields, J. (1982). *Schizophrenia: The epigenetic puzzle.* Cambridge: Cambridge University Press.

Green, W. H., and Padron-Gayol, M. (1986). Schizophrenic disorder in childhood: Its relationship to DSM-III criteria. In C. Shagass (Ed.), *Biological psychiatry 1985* (pp. 1484–1486). Amsterdam: Elsevier.

Herjanic, B., and Campbell, W. (1977). Differentiating psychiatrically disturbed children on the basis of a structured interview. *Journal of Abnormal Child Psychology, 5,* 127–134.

Holzman, P. S. (1987). Recent studies of psychophysiology in schizophrenia. *Schizophrenia Bulletin, 13,* 49–76.

Hornstein, N., Asarnow, J., and Goldstein, M. J. (in progress). Survey of treatment practices for schizophrenic children.

Jacob, T. (1975). Family interaction in disturbed and normal families: A methodological and substantive review. *Psychological Bulletin, 82,* 33–65.

Johnston, M. H., and Holzman, P. S. (1979). *Assessing schizophrenic thinking: A clinical and research instrument for measuring thought disorder.* San Francisco: Jossey-Bass.

Kallman, F. J., and Roth, B. (1956). Genetic aspects of preadolescent schizophrenia. *American Journal of Psychiatry, 112,* 599–606.

Kendler, K. S. (1980). Familial aggregation of schizophrenia and schizophrenia spectrum disorders: Evaluation of conflicting results. *Archives of General Psychiatry, 45,* 377–383.

Kety, S. S., Rosenthal, D., Wender, P. H., Schulsinger, F., and Jacobsen, B. (1978). The biological and adoptive families of adoptive individuals who became schizophrenic: Prevalence of mental illness and other characteristics. In L. C. Wynne, R. L. Cromwell, and S. Matthysse (Eds.), *The nature of schizophrenia* (pp. 25–37). New York: John Wiley.

Kolvin, I. (1971). Psychoses in childhood—A comparative study. In M. Rutter (Ed.), *Infantile autism: Concepts, characteristics, and treatment.* Edinburgh: Churchill Livingstone.

Kydd, R. R., and Werry, J. S. (1982). Schizophrenia in children under 16 years. *Journal of Autism & Developmental Disabilities, 12,* 343–357.

Liem, J. H. (1980). Family studies of schizophrenia: An update and commentary. *Schizophrenia Bulletin, 6,* 429–455.

Loveland, N. T., Wynne, L. C., and Singer, M. T. (1963). The family Rorschach: A new method for studying family interaction. *Family Process, 2,* 187–215.

Mednick, S.A., Machon, R. A., Huttunen, M. O., and Bonnett, D. (1988). Adult schizophrenia following pre-natal exposure to an influenza epidemic. *Archives of General Psychiatry, 45,* 189–192.

Moring, J., Asarnow, R., Nuechterlein, K., Wynne, L. L., and Tienari, P. (1991). Information processing impairments in Finnish adopted-away offspring of schizophrenic mothers and control mothers. Paper presented at the 1991 meeting of the International Congress on Schizophrenia Research, Tuscon, Arizona.

Neale, J. M., and Oltmans, T. F. (1980). *Schizophrenia.* New York: John Wiley.

Nuechterlein, K. H. (1977). Reaction time and attention in schizophrenia: A critical evaluation of the data and theories. *Schizophrenia Bulletin, 13,* 373–428.

Nuechterlein, K. H. (1983). Signal detection in vigilance tasks and behavioral attributes among offspring of schizophrenic mothers and among hyperactive children. *Journal of Abnormal Psychiatry, 92,* 4–28.

Nuechterlein, K. H. (in press). Vigilance in schizophrenia and related disorders. In S. Steinhauer, J. Gruzelier, and J. Zubin (Eds.), *Handbook of schizophrenia: Neuropsychology, psychophysiology and information processing.* Amsterdam: Elsevier.

Nuechterlein, K. H., and Dawson, M. E. (1984). Information processing and attentional functioning in the developmental course of schizophrenic disorders. *Schizophrenia Bulletin, 10,* 160–203.

Petty, L. P., Ornitz, E. M., Michelman, J. D., and Zimmerman, E. G. (1984). Autistic children who become schizophrenic. *Archives of General Psychiatry, 41,* 129–135.

Pope, H. G., Jone, J. M., Cohen, B. M., and Lipinski, J. F. (1982). Failure to find evidence of schizophrenia in first degree relatives of schizophrenic probands. *American Journal of Psychiatry, 139,* 826–828.

Puig-Antich, J., and Chambers, W. (1978). *The schedule for affective disorders and schizophrenia for school-aged children (Kiddie-SADS)*. New York: New York State Psychiatric Association.

Rapoport, J. L., and Kruesi, M. J. P. (1985). Organic therapies. In H. I. Kaplan and B. J. Sadock (Eds.), *Comprehensive textbook of psychiatry* (4th ed., pp. 1793–1798). Baltimore, MD: Williams & Wilkins.

Russell, A. (in press). Schizophrenia. In S. R. Hooper, G. W. Hynd, and R. E. Mattison (Eds.), *Assessment and diagnosis of child and adolescent psychiatric disorders: Current issues*. Englewood Cliffs, NJ: Lawrence Erlbaum.

Russell, A. T., Bott, L., and Sammons, C. (1989). Phenomenology of schizophrenia occurring in childhood. *Journal of the American Academy of Child & Adolescent Psychiatry, 23*(31), 399–407.

Russell, P. N., Consedine, C. E., and Knight, R. G. (1980). Visual and memory search by process schizophrenics. *Journal of Abnormal Psychology, 2*, 109–114.

Rutter, M. (1972). Childhood schizophrenia reconsidered. *Journal of Autism and Childhood Schizophrenia, 2*(4), 315–337.

Schneider, S. G., and Asarnow, R. F. (1987). A comparison between the cognitive/neuropsychological impairments of non-retarded autistic and schizophrenic children. *Journal of Abnormal Child Psychology, 15*, 211–224.

Shapiro, L. N., and Wild, C. M. (1976). The product of the Consensus Rorschach in families of male schizophrenics. *Family Process, 15*, 211–224.

Singer, M. T., and Wynne, L. C. (1965). Thought disorder and family relations of schizophrenics. IV. Results and implications. *Archives of General Psychiatry, 12*, 201.

Singer, M. T., Wynne, L. C., and Toohey, M. L. (1978). Communication disorders and the families of schizophrenics. In L. Wynne, R. L. Cromwell, and S. Matthysse (Eds.), *The nature of schizophrenia* (pp. 499–511). New York: John Wiley.

Solovay, M. R., Shenton, M. E., Gasperetti, C., Coleman, M., Kestenbaum, E., Carpenter, J. T., and Holzman, P. S. (1986). Scoring manual of the thought disorder index. *Schizophrenia Bulletin, 12*, 483–496.

Stephens, J. H. (1978). Longterm prognosis and followup in schizophrenia. *Schizophrenia Bulletin, 4*, 25–47.

Strober, M., Morrell, W., Burroughs, J., Lampert, C., Danforth, H., and Freeman, R. (1988). A family study of bipolar I illness in adolescence: Early onset of symptoms linked to increased familial loading and lithium resistance. *Journal of Affective Disorders, 15*, 255–268.

Tanguay, P. E., and Asarnow, R. F. (1985). Schizophrenia in children. In A. J. Solnit, D. J. Cohen, and J. E. Schowalter (Eds.), *Psychiatry: 2 Child psychiatry* (pp. 1–10). Philadelphia: J. B. Lippincott.

Tienari, P., Sorri, A., Lahti, I., Naarala, M., Wahlberg, E., Moring, J., Pohjola, J., and Wynne, L. C. (1987). Interaction of genetic and psychosocial factors in schizophrenia: The Finnish Adoptive Study. *Schizophrenia Bulletin, 13*, 477–484.

Tompson, M., Asarnow, J., Goldstein, M., and Milkowitz, D. J. (1990). Thought disorder and communication problems in children with schizophrenia spectrum and depressive disorders and their parents. *Journal of Child Clinical Psychology, 19*, 159–168.

Treisman, A. M., and Gelade, G. (1980). A feature integration theory of attention. *Cognitive Psychology, 97*, 136–145.

Wagener, D. K., Hogarty, G. E., Goldstein, M. J., Asarnow, R. F., and Browne, A. (1986). Information processing and communication deviance in schizophrenic patients and their mothers. *Psychiatry Research, 18*, 365–377.

Watkins, J. M., Asarnow, R., and Tanguay, P. E. (1988). Symptom development in childhood onset schizophrenia. *Journal of Child Psychiatry, 29*, 865–878.

Watt, N. F. (1984). In a nut shell: The first two decades of high-risk research in schizophrenia. In N. F. Watt, E. J. Anthony, L. C. Wynne, and J. E. Rolf (Eds.), *Children at risk for schizophrenia: A longitudinal perspective* (pp. 572–596). New York: Cambridge University Press.

Welner, Z., Reich, W., Herjanic, B., Jung, K. G., and Amado, H. (1987). Reliability, validity, and parent–child agreement studies of the Diagnostic Interview for Children and Adolescents (DICA). *Journal of the American Academy of Child Psychology and Adolescent Psychiatry, 26,* 649–653.

Werry, J. S. (1979). The childhood psychoses. In H. Quay and J. S. Werry (Eds.), *Psychopathological disorders of childhood* (2nd ed.). New York: John Wiley & Sons.

Werry, J. S. (1989). *Child and adolescent schizophrenia.* Unpublished manuscript.

Wood, R. L., and Cook, M. (1979). Attentional deficit in the siblings of schizophrenics. *Psychological Medicine, 9,* 465–467.

Wynne, L. C., Singer, M. T., Bartko, J. J., and Toohey, M. L. (1977). Schizophrenics and their families: Research on parental communication. In J. M. Tanner (Ed.), *Developments in psychiatric research* (pp. 254–286). London: Hodder and Stoughton.

Zubin, J., Magaziner, J., and Steinhauer, S. R. (1983). The metamorphosis of schizophrenia: From chronicity to vulnerability. *Psychological Medicine, 13,* 551–571.

6

The Prediction of Psychiatric Disorders in Late Adolescence

Lynn Winters
Barbara A. Cornblatt
L. Erlenmeyer-Kimling

One major goal of prospective longitudinal studies of schizophrenia is the early identification of individuals at risk for the disorder. Identification of preschizophrenic individuals is of critical importance for both theoretical and therapeutic reasons. Several researchers have focused their efforts on identifying predictors, or markers, of later psychopathology (e.g., Erlenmeyer-Kimling and Cornblatt, 1978; Holzman, 1988; Mirsky, 1988; Winters *et al.*, 1981). While these studies have employed different research methods and strategies, they have in common the goal of identifying characteristics of the individual that reliably precede the onset of symptoms and, moreover, that are specific to schizophrenia and not related more generally to severe psychiatric disorders. Such work is expected to give us a better understanding of the developmental course of the disorder and, in addition, allow for the possibility of early therapeutic intervention.

One of the more promising potential markers of schizophrenia is attentional dysfunction. Studies of both schizophrenic patients and children at risk for schizophrenia have offered suggestive evidence that deficits in attention and information processing are of critical importance in at least

123

Copyright © 1991 by Academic Press, Inc.
All rights of reproduction in any form reserved.

one form of the illness (e.g., Asarnow and MacCrimmon, 1978, 1981; Chapman and McGhie, 1962; Cornblatt and Erlenmeyer-Kimling, 1984; Erlenmeyer-Kimling and Cornblatt, 1978; Freedman and Chapman, 1973; Grunebaum *et al.*, 1978; McGhie and Chapman, 1961; Nuechterlein, 1983; Orzack and Kornetsky, 1966). In addition, evidence from the New York High-Risk Project suggests that (1) these early deficits are stable over time among subjects at risk for schizophrenia (Cornblatt and Winters, 1987), (2) these deficits are related to adolescent adjustment (Cornblatt and Erlenmeyer-Kimling, 1986), and (3) this relationship may be specific to children at risk for schizophrenia (Cornblatt and Erlenmeyer-Kimling, 1986).

THE NEW YORK HIGH-RISK PROJECT

The New York High-Risk Project is a prospective longitudinal study of children at risk for schizophrenia or major affective disorder. Begun in 1971, this study has followed two samples of subjects at risk from childhood to young adulthood (Erlenmeyer-Kimling and Cornblatt, 1987). While it is still too early to draw firm conclusions regarding schizophrenia, we *can* evaluate our high-risk subjects in terms of their overall adjustment in adolescence.

The risk factor in this study is parental psychopathology, because the risk of schizophrenia among offspring of schizophrenic parents is higher than that among the general population (Erlenmeyer-Kimling, 1968; Rosenthal, 1971). Because most schizophrenic patients do *not* have a schizophrenic parent, children of schizophrenic parents who become schizophrenic themselves are an atypical group. However, they probably will not differ from the larger population of schizophrenics in basic attentional and cognitive, or biobehavioral functions (Erlenmeyer-Kimling *et al.*, 1984). Thus, following subjects who are considered to be at risk due to parental illness increases the probability of obtaining a *pre*schizophrenic subsample and offers the opportunity to chart the developmental course of the disorder.

The original sample in the New York Project, Sample A, began with 208 subjects; the replication sample, Sample B, began with 150 subjects. Each sample contains children of parents with schizophrenia or major affective disorder (the high-risk groups) and children of parents with no history of psychiatric disorder (the low-risk comparison group). Both samples have undergone several rounds of laboratory testing and interviewing and have been followed clinically through telephone interviews with a responsible adult family member at approximate 6-month intervals.

Previous reports of the results of this project have focused primarily on the attempt to identify early predictors, or biobehavioral markers, of psychopathology derived from Sample A (Cornblatt and Erlenmeyer-Kimling, 1984, 1985; Erlenmeyer-Kimling and Cornblatt, 1978; Erlenmeyer-Kimling et al., 1979, 1983; Rutschmann et al., 1977). This chapter examines developmental trends among subjects in Sample B on a measure of sustained attention and explores the relationship between attentional dysfunctions in childhood and behavioral adjustment in adolescence.

Subjects

The procedures for sample selection have been reported in detail elsewhere (cf. Erlenmeyer-Kimling and Cornblatt, 1987; Erlenmeyer-Kimling et al., 1984). High-risk subjects were selected by screening consecutive admissions at several state psychiatric facilities in New York. Patients who had one or more children from 7 through 12 years of age and who resided with their spouses were considered for the study. Patients with chronic alcoholism, drug addition, brain trauma, or psychoses of toxic origin were excluded. The children from Sample B, who are the subjects of this report, were white, English-speaking, had an IQ as measured by the Wechsler Intelligence Scale for Children—Revised (WISC-R; Wechsler, 1974) of at least 70, and had no history of psychiatric treatment or evident psychiatric disturbance. Control subjects with the same age range and socioeconomic status were recruited. The control subjects were also white, English-speaking, from intact homes, had an IQ ≥70, showed no history of psychiatric problems, and had parents with no history of psychiatric problems prior to recruitment for the study.

Patient-parents were diagnosed according to the Research Diagnostic Criteria (Spitzer et al., 1975). The initial sample consisted of 45 subjects at risk for schizophrenia (HR-Sz), 40 subjects at risk for major affective disorders (HR-Aff), and 65 low-risk control subjects (NC). HR-Sz subjects were those with one or both parents diagnosed as schizophrenic, and, similarly, HR-Aff subjects were those with one or both parents diagnosed as having major affective disorders.

Measures

The subjects in Sample B have been tested in the laboratory on four separate occasions at approximately 2- to 3-year intervals; a fifth round of laboratory testing is now in the planning stages. Figure 6.1 shows the mean age of the sample at each round of testing.

Although the specific tasks employed differed somewhat from round to round, each testing session contained measures of attention and information processing. In addition, some form of the Continuous Performance

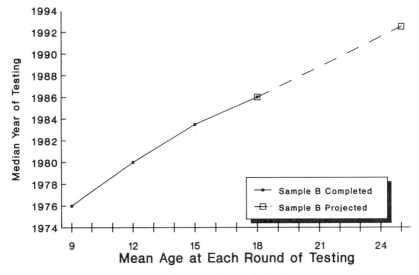

Figure 6.1   Mean age (years) of sample B at each round of Laboratory Testing. Mean age of the sample in 1992–93 is projected using the mean age of subjects tested in 1986–1987.

Test (CPT) was given in every round, with the CPT-Identical Pairs Version (CPT-IP; Cornblatt *et al.*, 1988) used in rounds 2, 3, and 4. The CPT-IP is a test of sustained attention. Subjects are required to watch a series of stimuli presented on a video monitor at a constant interstimulus interval of 1000 msec and to respond with a finger-lift from a response key whenever two consecutive stimuli are identical. The CPT-IP employs stimulus sets of either numbers or nonsense shapes presented with or without visual and auditory distractors in different subtests of 150 trials each.

Project social workers have conducted telephone interviews with the families of the subjects at frequent intervals since the beginning of the study. These interviews, plus interviews in person with the subjects during each round of testing, have provided the basis for ratings of behavioral adjustment. The Behavioral Global Adjustment Scale (BGAS; Cornblatt and Erlenmeyer-Kimling, 1984) assigns ratings in three areas of functioning: family relationships, peer interactions, and school (or work) functioning. Ratings are made by a clinician blind to parental diagnosis and are scored in the direction of health. They range from gross behavioral disturbance requiring hospitalization (a rating of 1) to above-average functioning in all three areas (a rating of 5) (for further details, see Cornblatt and Erlenmeyer-Kimling, 1984). For the purposes of these analyses, BGAS scores have been categorized as Healthy (ratings of 4 or 5), Moderately

Impaired (a rating of 3), and Severely Impaired (ratings of 1 or 2). While the Healthy and Severely Impaired categories are fairly straightforward, the intermediate category of Moderately Impaired functioning is less well-defined. This category reflects the presence of behavioral problems difficult to assess in terms of long-term adjustment. A rating of Moderately Impaired may reflect early signs of some later, more serious disturbance or, alternatively, reflect fairly transient problems of adjustment. Thus, when combining categories is necessary for the analysis, the more conservative approach of classifying Moderately Impaired subjects with the Healthy group has been taken. BGAS scores have been assigned to each subject through midadolescence. Assessment of adult functioning will be assessed through formal clinical interviews with the subjects during a later phase of the study.

LONGITUDINAL ANALYSES OF ATTENTION

Age-Appropriate Measures of Attention

Selection of an instrument that is age-appropriate for samples ranging from early childhood through adulthood poses a particular challenge. Both scale attenuation (i.e., ceiling and/or floor) effects and differences in the processes underlying performance at different ages make task selection and interpretation of results problematic for a number of domains of functioning (Nunnally, 1973; Schaie, 1973). While issues of item difficulty and test content are critical in many measures of higher cognitive and social functioning, the problems are minimized with tasks involving basic attentional or perceptual processes (Nunnally, 1973). The CPT-IP has been employed in three consecutive rounds of testing in Sample B, at 12, 15, and 18 years of age. When performance is measured using the signal detection index d', children at 12 years of age perform significantly above chance, yet the oldest subjects do not reach ceiling. Studies of normal adults and their adolescent children, and boys with attention-deficit–hyperactivity disorder from 6 through 12 years of age have also demonstrated the appropriateness of the CPT-IP across a wide age range, as well as its sensitivity to various types of psychopathology (Cornblatt et al., 1987, 1988).

Attentional Deviance Index

While age-appropriate measures are of concern to any longitudinal project, the need to define attentional *predictors* of illness is specific to high-risk research. The goal of high-risk studies is to identify the individuals who will ultimately develop schizophrenia. Although the subjects at risk, as a group, are expected to show a higher incidence of schizophrenia in adulthood, the majority of them will not become schizophrenic. We must, therefore, attempt to identify the subgroup of subjects that is genuinely liable to the disorder. As attentional measures hold some promise as predictors, we can hypothesize that the subjects who are most deviant on the attentional measures are those most likely to be at risk (Erlenmeyer-Kimling *et al.*, 1979). Thus, the absolute level of performance of a group of subjects on an attentional task at any given age is not at issue. What is at issue is the performance of a subgroup of particularly deviant subjects relative to the performance level of a normal control group. With that in mind, the Attentional Deviance Index (ADI) has been employed to identify the individuals who are outliers, i.e., those whose performance is much worse than normal subjects of the same age on a variety of attentional measures.

The ADI is a composite deviance score, combining measures of relative performance for an individual subject across all available tests of attention. Any score falling below the 5th percentile of the NC group is considered deviant. The ADI is the total number of response measures on which the individual is deviant. For round 1 of testing on Sample B, the ADI included 18 different measures of performance on two versions of the CPT (for details on selection of CPT measures, see Rutschmann *et al.*, 1986) and 4 from the Visual-Aural Digit-Span Task (Koppitz, 1977). The ADI calculated in later rounds includes performance indices limited to various subtests of the CPT-IP (Cornblatt and Winters, 1987).

Estimation for Missing Data

Whether due to equipment failure or a subject's reluctance to return for additional laboratory testing, missing data poses a particular problem for longitudinal analyses. Several approaches to dealing with partial data have been advocated, each with its own advantages and limitations (e.g., see Schaie, 1973). While sample attrition for the New York High-Risk Project has been relatively low, laboratory data are not complete for all subjects in the sample. Two approaches to this problem have been examined in our data analyses: analysis of complete cases only and estimation of missing data points using maximum likelihood procedures.

Use of complete cases only is the simplest approach, and, where sample attrition is relatively small, it is an acceptable approach to longitudinal data analysis. However, when there is reason to believe that missing subjects may be systematically different from those remaining in the study, as is likely when the target subjects are at risk for severe psychosis, generalization of results based on complete cases only is problematic. In addition, the use of complex tasks, with several subtests given at several points in time, increases the probability of accidental data loss for one or more of these data points. Loss of a single data point in a multifactorial design will result in the elimination of the subject from the analysis even though data are available for the subject for most of the cells of the design.

An alternate approach to using only complete cases is the use of one of several possible estimation procedures to substitute values for missing data. In the present report, the analyses of variance reported were done using maximum likelihood procedures (BMD Program PAM; BMDP, 1985) to estimate scores for missing data. Available scores on the CPT-IP were used to estimate missing values within each subject group separately. This resulted in a longitudinal sample of 115 subjects; 29 HR-Sz, 35 HR-Aff, and 51 NC. Examination of the pattern of missing data shows that the proportion of incomplete cases is comparable among all three subject groups. Analyses of variance using complete cases and those using estimates for missing data show the same pattern of results. Analyses of age changes in CPT-IP performance illustrate the usefulness of such estimation procedures.

Age Changes in the CPT-IP

Performance on the CPT-IP was measured using the signal detection index d' (Cornblatt et al., 1989). Collapsing across all three rounds of testing, HR-Sz subjects do more poorly than either NC or HR-Aff subjects ($p < 0.05$ using the Scheffes' procedure); the NC and HR-Aff groups do not differ. However, a significant group × round interaction [$F(4,244)$ 2.48, $p < 0.05$] shows that the developmental trajectories of the three groups differ. This interaction is shown in Fig. 6.2.

Performance among HR-Sz subjects is worse than NC subjects at each round of testing. HR-Aff subjects do as well as the NC subjects during rounds 2 and 3; however, their performance relative to the NCs declines between rounds 3 and 4. Post hoc comparisons reveal that by round 4 (at a mean age of 18 years), the scores of the HR-Aff group resemble those of the HR-Sz group more closely than those of the NC group. These comparisons are shown in Table 6.1.

These differences suggest that attentional deficits among HR-Sz subjects are an enduring trait, present in early childhood and stable over time, while among HR-Aff subjects they occur later, during adolescence. However, the relevance of this pattern of performance on the CPT-IP to development of schizophrenia rests on the assumption that the observed group differences result from the poorer performance of a subgroup of HR-Sz subjects possessing a genuine liability to schizophrenia or related dis-

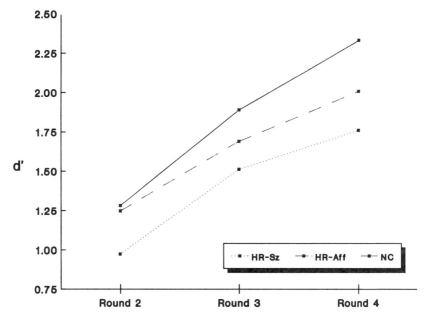

Figure 6.2   Sample B: Group × round interaction on CPT-IP d'.

orders that is reflected in their performance on tests of attention. The first step in verifying the soundness of this assumption is to identify the attentionally deviant subjects.

Results of Analyses Using The ADI

As noted above, attentional deviance has been defined in terms of the subjects' performance relative to NC subjects on the group of attentional measures. Analyses using the ADI have been completed for the first three rounds of testing in Sample B; preliminary analyses have been conducted on round 4 data. Results from Sample A strongly suggest that deviant attentional performance at 9 years of age is more common among HR-Sz subjects than among either HR-Aff or NC subjects. Moreover, HR-Sz subjects have a higher mean ADI (Cornblatt and Erlenmeyer-Kimling, 1986; Erlenmeyer-Kimling *et al.*, 1983). While the results in Sample B are weaker, the same pattern emerges: A higher percentage of subjects in the HR-Sz group fall into the attentionally deviant group (Cornblatt *et al.*, 1989). This is shown in Fig. 6.3.

Use of the criterion of extreme performance, however, has a built-in liability. Extremely poor performance, while relatively infrequent, is still

TABLE 6.1 *Post Hoc* Analyses of the Round × Group Interaction for d′

Comparison[a]	Round		
	2	3	4
HR-Sz vs. NC	$p < .05$	$p < 0.01$	$p < 0.01$
HR-Aff vs. NC	ns	ns	$p < 0.05$
HR-Sz vs. HR-Aff	ns	ns	ns

ns, not significant.
[a]Scheffe′ *post hoc* tests were used for these comparisons.

possible by chance. Regression toward the mean would predict that individual subjects who are outliers on the initial round of testing are unlikely to be outliers in later rounds. If it is a genuine trait, attentional deviance must be stable over time. A fair question to ask, then, is whether or not these attentionally deviant subjects at 9 years of age remain deviant performers throughout the course of the study.

Analyses of attentional deviance on the CPT-IP for subjects with complete data on rounds 1–3 of the study suggest that the overwhelming majority of NC subjects (94%) show attentional deviance on, at most, one round of testing; only 6% are deviant on two rounds, whereas none are deviant on all three. These results are consistent with expectations on purely statistical grounds. Similarly, the vast majority of HR-Aff subjects

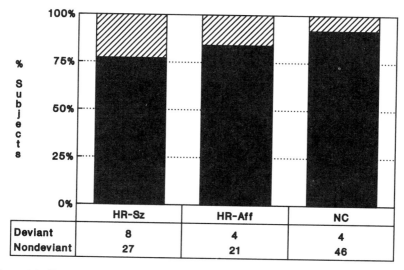

Figure 6.3 Percent of each group exhibiting attentional deviance. ■■■, Nondeviant; ▨▨▨, Deviant.

(95%) are deviant on zero or one round of testing and only a single subject deviant on two; none are deviant on all three rounds. In contrast, of the 18 HR-Sz subjects who completed all testing, 22% were deviant in attentional measures on all three rounds; only 78% were deviant for only zero or one round. The relationship between group membership and the number of rounds in which the subject was classified as attentionally deviant is statistically significant with $\chi^2(4) = 13.24$, $p = 0.01$ (Cornblatt *et al.*, 1989).

Preliminary analyses show that three of the four HR-Sz subjects who were deviant in the first three rounds of testing were again classified as deviant on CPT-IP measures at round 4; the fourth was hospitalized for schizophrenia and, thus, unavailable for testing. Moreover, all subjects classified as deviant in a later round of testing were also deviant in the initial round. Thus, these data offer further support for the argument that attentional dysfunction is an enduring characteristic of a subgroup of HR-Sz subjects and appears at an early age. In addition, the attentionally deviant subjects do seem to account for the observed group differences in CPT-IP performance noted earlier. Once the attentionally deviant subgroups are eliminated from the analyses, the remaining nondeviant subjects fail to show any group differences on d′ (Cornblatt and Winters, 1987).

EARLY ATTENTIONAL DEVIANCE AND ADOLESCENT ADJUSTMENT

Our results so far show that we can identify a subgroup of HR-Sz subjects that exhibits early and stable attentional deficits as measured by the CPT-IP. Next, it is necessary to ask whether or not attentional deficits are useful as predictors of later adjustment. As noted above, all subjects in the New York High-Risk Project were evaluated periodically on their behavioral adjustment using the BGAS. Thus, although formal psychological evaluations have not yet been completed on these subjects, we can evaluate behavioral adjustment in adolescence.

Sensitivity and Specificity of the ADI

One approach to determining the potential usefulness of the ADI as a predictor is to estimate the sensitivity and specificity of the measure. Sensitivity, in this instance, refers to the proportion of poorly adjusted adolescents who were classified as attentionally deviant in childhood. It is thus a measure of our accuracy in identifying individuals at risk for problems in adjustment (i.e., true positives). Specificity, on the other hand, refers to the proportion of subjects labeled as *non*deviant who are, in fact,

TABLE 6.2 Sensitivity and Specificity of the Attentional Deviance Index[a]

	Severely impaired behavior	Normal or moderately impaired behavior
Attentionally deviant	True positives 5	False positives 9
Attentionally nondeviant	False negatives 11	True negatives 77

[a]ADI sensitivity = 31%; ADI specificity = 90%.

classified as healthy adolescents (i.e., true negatives). It is a measure of our accuracy in identifying individuals who are not at risk for adjustment problems in adolescence. While sensitivity is potentially important in identifying candidates for early intervention, a high degree of specificity is critical for avoiding inappropriate identification of healthy children as liable to severe mental disorder (Cornblatt and Erlenmeyer-Kimling, 1985; Cornblatt et al., 1989).

The sensitivity and specificity of the ADI based on testing at round 1 are shown in Table 6.2. While sensitivity is somewhat low (31%), it is close to the ADI sensitivity of 36% found in Sample A (Cornblatt and Erlenmeyer-Kimling, 1985). On the other hand, specificity is 90%, almost identical to a specificity of 91% found for Sample A (Cornblatt and Erlenmeyer-Kimling, 1985), and gives us a false-positive rate of only 10%. Thus, roughly 30% of the subjects who were attentionally deviant at 9 years of age show serious behavioral problems in adolescence.

While ADI sensitivity of 31% seems modest, it may still prove to be an effective screening procedure for two reasons. First, it is possible that these subjects represent the estimated 35–45% of adult schizophrenics who experience attentional dysfunctions (Asarnow and MacCrimmon, 1981; Orzack and Kornetsky, 1966). Moreover, they are individuals who are not otherwise identifiable as vulnerable to behavioral problems in adolescence. Early detection offers the possibility of intervention early enough to make such intervention effective. However, further increases in both sensitivity and specificity of the ADI are both desirable and possible.

Improving ADI Sensitivity and Specificity: Stability of Attentional Deviance and the Two-Factor Criterion

To improve the accuracy of the ADI, researchers have explored the use of deviance scores on more than one round of testing. This strategy assumes that stable deviance across time is more likely to be indicative of liability to later behavioral problems. When the criterion of deviant performance on at least two rounds of testing is used, sensitivity is improved to 38% and specificity to 96% (Cornblatt *et al.*, 1989).

While using deviance on two test sessions as the criterion for attentional deficits yields some improvement in sensitivity and specificity, essentially the same gain in accuracy can be achieved by the simple expedient of using *two* criteria for identifying vulnerable individuals: attentional deviance in early childhood *and* history of schizophrenia in the parents. Recall that the overwhelming majority of NC and HR-Aff subjects exhibited deviant ADI scores on only one round of testing, whereas stable attentional deviance is much more likely among the HR-Sz subjects. Thus, early attentional testing among high-risk children may prove to be an effective screening device for behavioral problems in adolescence.

Problems of Early Intervention

While attentional measures show promise as predictors of adolescent adjustment, two related issues must be addressed. One is the nature of these adolescent problems; the other is the nature and scope of an early intervention.

The prospective design of the New York High-Risk Project leaves us with the problem of measuring clinical outcome. Until the full sample has passed the age of greatest risk for both schizophrenia and major affective disorder, the relevance of our predictions to schizophrenia remains somewhat speculative. We have identified a significant proportion of adolescents exhibiting poor adjustment, but, at this point, we cannot conclude positively that these problems foreshadow schizophrenia *per se*. Whether these problems are a prelude to serious illness or are fairly transient adolescent disturbances will not be determined for several years.

The possibility that attentional dysfunctions are specific markers of schizophrenia gains some support from the Israeli high-risk study. Mirsky and his colleagues report that attentional deficits in childhood were characteristic of the HR-Sz subjects who later became schizophrenic but were not characteristic of those who subsequently developed affective disorders, or who were free of any psychiatric disorder at 25 years of age (Mirsky, 1988; Mirsky *et al.*, 1986).

The second issue concerns the intervention itself. While early intervention is an attractive goal, what type of intervention could be employed and when it should take place is unclear (Erlenmeyer-Kimling and Cornblatt, 1987). The answer will depend, at least in part, on the role that attention plays in the development of schizophrenia. Attentional dysfunction may be an early, subtle sign of schizophrenia resulting from the underlying disease process. On the other hand, problems in processing information may well play a causal role in the etiology of at least one type of schizophrenia, perhaps one that is characterized by a predominance of interpersonal difficulties. Recent analyses of structured interview data from a subset of subjects in Sample A who have reached adulthood provide some hints that early attentional dysfunction is related specifically to a tendency toward social isolation in HR-Sz subjects (Cornblatt and Erlenmeyer-Kimling, 1989).

SUMMARY

The results can be summarized briefly. Attentional deficits are more common among HR-Sz subjects than among either HR-Aff or NC subjects. These attentional deficits appear early, are stable over time, and are reliably associated with adjustment problems in adolescence within the HR-Sz group. While it is too soon to know whether or not these adjustment problems foreshadow schizophrenia, data from other studies and preliminary analyses of young adults in the New York High-Risk Project offer suggestive evidence that early attentional deficits are markers for a liability to schizophrenia.

REFERENCES

Asarnow, R., and MacCrimmon, D. (1978). Residual performance deficit in clinically remitted schizophrenics: A marker of schizophrenia? *Journal of Abnormal Psychology, 87,* 597–608.

Asarnow, R., and MacCrimmon, D. (1981). Span of apprehension deficits during the postpsychotic stages of schizophrenia: A replication and extension. *Archives of General Psychiatry, 38,* 1006–1011.

Chapman, J., and McGhie, A. (1962). A comparative study of disordered attention in schizophrenia. *Journal of Mental Science, 108,* 487–500.

Cornblatt, B., and Erlenmeyer-Kimling, L. (1984). Early attentional predictors of adolescent behavioral disturbances in children at risk for schizophrenia. In N. Watt, E. J. Anthony, L. Wynne, and J. Rolf (Eds.), *Children at risk for schizophrenia: A longitudinal perspective* (pp. 198–212). New York: Cambridge University Press.

Cornblatt, B., and Erlenmeyer-Kimling, L. (1985). Global attentional deviance as a marker of risk for schizophrenia: Specificity and predictive validity. *Journal of Abnormal Psychology, 94,* 470–486.

Cornblatt, B., and Erlenmeyer-Kimling, L. (1986). Following children at risk for schizhoprenia or depression: The New York High-Risk Project. In C. Shagass, G. Simpson, W. Bridges, R. Josiassen, D. Staff, and K. Weiss (Eds.), *Biological psychiatry 1985* (pp. 1481–1483). New York: Elsevier.

Cornblatt, B., and Erlenmeyer-Kimling, L. (1989). Attention and schizophrenia. *Schizophrenia Research, 2,* 58.

Cornblatt, B., Risch, N., Faris, G., Friedman, D., and Erlenmeyer-Kimling, L. (1988). The Continuous Performance Test, Identical Pairs Version (CPT-IP): I. New findings about sustained attention in normal families. *Psychiatry Research, 26,* 223–238.

Cornblatt, B., and Winters, L. (1987). Developmental trends in attentional performance. *Proceedings of the IXth Biennial Meetings of the International Society for the Study of Behavioural Development.* Tokyo, Japan: ISSBD.

Cornblatt, B., Winters, L., and Erlenmeyer-Kimling, L. (1989). Attentional markers of schizophrenia: Evidence from the New York High-Risk Study. In S. Schultz and C. Tamminga (Eds.), *Schizophrenia: Scientific progress* (pp. 83–92). New York: Oxford University Press.

Cornblatt, B., Winters, L., Maminski, B., and Greenhill, L. (1987). Methylphenidate-SR: Effects on sustained attention in ADDH males. *Proceedings of the 34th Annual Meeting of the American Academy of Child and Adolescent Psychiatry.* Washington, DC: AACAP.

Dixon, W., Brown, M., Engleman, L., Frane, J., Hill, M., Jennrich, R., and Toporek, J. (1985). *BMDP Statistical Software: 1985 Printing.* Berkeley, California: University of California Press.

Erlenmeyer-Kimling, L. (1968). Studies on the offspring of two schizophrenic parents. In D. Rosenthal and S. Kety (Eds.), *The transmission of schizophrenia* (pp. 65–83). New York: Wiley.

Erlenmeyer-Kimling, L., and Cornblatt, B. (1978). Attentional measures in a study of children at high-risk for schizophrenia. *Journal of Psychiatry Research, 14,* 93–98.

Erlenmeyer-Kimling, L., and Cornblatt, B. (1987). Implications for preventative intervention from prospective research on children at risk for schizophrenia. In J. Steinberg and M. Silverman (Eds.), *Preventing mental disorders: A research perspective* (pp. 90–107). Rockville, MD: NIMH.

Erlenmeyer-Kimling, L., Cornblatt, B., and Fleiss, J. (1979). High-risk research in schizophrenia. *Psychiatric Annals, 9,* 79–111.

Erlenmeyer-Kimling, L., Cornblatt, B., and Golden, R. (1983). Early indicators of liability to schizophrenia in children at high risk. In S. Guze, F. Earls, and J. Barrett (Eds.), *Childhood psychopathology and development* (pp. 247–261). New York: Raven Press.

Erlenmeyer-Kimling, L., Marcuse, Y., Cornblatt, B., Friedman, D., Rainer, J. and Rutschmann, J. (1984). The New York High-Risk Project. In N. F. Watt, E. J. Anthony, L. C. Wynne, and J. Rolf (Eds.), *Children at Risk for Schizophrenia: A Longitudinal Perspective* (pp. 169–189). New York: Cambridge University Press.

Freedman, B., and Chapman, L. (1973). Early subjective experience in schizophrenic episodes. *Journal of Abnormal Psychology, 82,* 46–54.

Grunebaum, H., Cohler, G., Kauffman, C., and Gallant, D. (1978). Children of depressed and schizophrenic mothers. *Child Psychiatry and Human Development, 8,* 219–228.

Holzman, P. (1988). A single dominant gene can account for schizophrenia and eye movement dysfunctions in the family. In D. Dunner, E. Gershon, and J. Barrett (Eds.), *Relatives at risk for mental disorder* (pp. 299–314). New York: Raven Press.

Koppitz, E. (1977). *The Visual Aural Digit Span Test.* New York: Grune & Stratton.

McGhie, A., and Chapman, J. (1961). Disorders of attention and perception in early schizophrenia. *British Journal of Medical Psychology, 34,* 103–117.

Mirsky, A. (1988). The Israeli High-Risk Study. In D. Dunner, E. Gershon, and J. Barrett (Eds.), *Relatives at risk for mental disorder* (pp. 279–296). New York: Raven Press.

Mirsky, A., Duncan, C., Silberman, E., Nagler, S., Kugelmass, S., Sohlberg, S., and Shotten, J. (1986). Early neuropsychological and other behavioral predictors of later psychotic disorders. In C. Shagass, G. Simpson, W. Bridges, R. Josiassen, D. Staff, and K. Weiss (Eds.), *Biological psychiatry 1985* (pp. 1118–1120). New York: Elsevier.

Nuechterlein, K. (1983). Signal detection in vigilance tasks and behavioral attributes among offspring of schizophrenic mothers and among hyperactive children. *Journal of Abnormal Psychology, 92,* 4–28.

Nunnally, J. (1973). Research strategies and measurement methods for investigating human development. In J. Nesselroade and H. Reese (Eds.), *Life span developmental psychology: Methodological issues* (pp. 87–109). New York: Academic Press.

Orzack, M., and Kornetsky, C. (1966). Attention dysfunction in chronic schizophrenia. *Archives of General Psychiatry, 14,* 323–326.

Rosenthal, D. (1971). A program of research on heredity in schizophrenia. *Behavioral Science, 16,* 191–201.

Rutschmann, J., Cornblatt, B., and Erlenmeyer-Kimling, L. (1977). Sustained attention in children at risk for schizophrenia. *Archives of General Psychiatry, 34,* 571–575.

Rutschmann, J., Cornblatt, B. and Erlenmeyer-Kimling, L. (1986). Sustained attention in children at risk for schizophrenia: Findings with two visual continuous performance tasks in a new sample. *Journal of Abnormal Child Psychology, 14,* 365–385.

Schaie, K. W. (1973). Methodological problems in descriptive developmental research in adulthood and aging. In J. Nesselroade and H. Reese (Eds.), *Life span developmental psychology: Methodological issues* (pp. 253–280). New York: Academic Press.

Spitzer, R., Endicott, J., and Robins, E. (1975). *Research Diagnostic Criteria (RDC) for a selected group of functional disorders (2nd ed.).* New York: New York State Psychiatric Institute.

Wechsler, D. (1974). *The Wechsler Intelligence Scale for Children—Revised.* New York: The Psychological Corporation.

Winters, K., Stone, A., Weintraub, S., and Neale, J. M. (1981). Cognitive and attentional deficits in children vulnerable to psychopathology. *Journal of Abnormal Child Psychology, 9,* 435–453.

Cognitive and Linguistic Functions of Adolescent Children at Risk for Schizophrenia

Philip D. Harvey

Adolescence is a period of numerous developmental changes, and it marks the transition to adulthood. Similarly, adolescence is the time when the initial symptoms of schizophrenia manifest themselves in the same manner as those seen in adult schizophrenic patients. As a result, studies of adolescents at risk for schizophrenia can potentially identify aspects of cognitive, linguistic, and neuropsychological performance that most immediately precede the onset of symptoms. Thus, adolescence is potentially the critical period in the premorbid course—the time when those individuals who will eventually develop schizophrenia can best be differentiated from those who will not. Consequently, aspects of behavior in adolescence may offer the most promising and powerful indicators of risk for the disorder.

Based on evidence indicating that schizophrenia tends to be familial and possibly genetic in its transmission, significant attention has been paid to studies of the relatives of schizophrenic patients. Focusing on children of schizophrenics allows for studies of individuals whose functioning is not yet affected by epiphenomenal variables such as medication, institu-

139

Copyright © 1991 by Academic Press, Inc.
All rights of reproduction in any form reserved.

tionalization, and other consequences of the development of the schizo-phrenic illness. This high-risk methodology, initially proposed by Med-nick and McNeil (1968) and adopted by Mednick and Schulsinger (1968), has a number of advantages, including the avoidance of epiphenomenal influences and the assets of a prospective approach. The major limitation of the method is that, by definition, the sample is atypical, because most schizophrenics do not have a schizophrenic parent. Another limitation is the massive amount of data typically collected over an extended period of time; risks to the strategy include both financial and conceptual. The major conceptual risk is that the investigator must choose the variables in advance, hoping these variables will turn out to be informative decades later.

Many studies of offspring of schizophrenics have selected samples of very young children, and some have even enrolled subjects at birth (e.g., Fish, 1987). Most researchers have wanted to observe the developmental course of their subjects for an extended period—from early childhood, through adolescence, into adulthood—and through the full age of risk for the disorder. This chapter focuses on high-risk children during the adoles-cent period. Of specific interest is the continuity of language and cognitive performance by these children, the importance of these deficits for predic-tion of adult outcome, and the validation of these performance patterns through comparison with both psychotic and remitted schizophrenic pa-tients. Also of interest is the preliminary outcome data available from some of the studies.

STUDY OF LANGUAGE AND COGNITION IN THE HIGH-RISK PARADIGM

The study of language and cognition in adult schizophrenics has a long and somewhat complex history (Harvey and Neale, 1983). These investiga-tions were initially predicated upon Bleuler's (1911/1950) notions of the centrality of associative loosening and thinking disorders in schizophre-nia. Since that time, newer models with more sophisticated premises have appeared, and presently substantial information about the cognitive func-tioning of adult schizophrenics is available (Callaway and Naghdi, 1982; Neale and Oltmanns, 1980).

The study of language and cognition in the high-risk paradigm largely follows the theorizing of Meehl (1962), as adapted by Zubin and Spring (1977). Meehl described the language and cognitive functioning of non-psychotic schizophrenia spectrum members ("schizotypes") as reflecting "cognitive slippage." This process is one whereby the communication and, by inference, the underlying logical and cognitive operations of certain individuals are subtly deviant. Meehl assumed that this language dysfunction reflected the actual genetic vulnerability, and that the presence of cognitive slippage could identify an at-risk individual. In Zubin and Spring's formulation of schizophrenia from a "markers" perspective, stable aspects of functioning are identifiable as indicators of vulnerability to the disorder. Other aspects of the patient's presentation may vary as a function of psychotic episodes, life stress, etc., yielding a behavioral presentation that is a mixture of both stable and fluctuating behaviors.

Given Meehl's (1962) assumption that communication disorders and subtle deficits in thinking are stable aspects of the presentation of schizophrenia spectrum members who are not currently symptomatic, the use of language and cognitive deficits as markers of vulnerability to the disorder may be feasible. Meehl hypothesized that vulnerability is genetically transmitted and marked by certain identifiable language behaviors. Thus, linguistic and cognitive variation within families of schizophrenics could be hypothesized to covary with genetic vulnerability to schizophrenia or other disorders within the schizophrenia spectrum (e.g., schizotypal personality disorder).

To be an effective marker of vulnerability, a linguistic or cognitive performance characteristic must be present and relatively stable through the course of the disorder (for a comprehensive discussion of this issue, see Nuechterlein and Dawson, 1984). The premorbid period is a critical one, because it is the period wherein an effective primary prevention intervention could be applied. The adolescent period, therefore, is usually the final time period before the onset of the disorder (except in cases with a particularly early age of onset).

A problem with the majority of the data reviewed in this chapter is that they come from either cross-sectional studies or short-term longitudinal studies that were conducted before the onset of the clinical disorder in the subjects. There are no studies to date where the results of a premorbidly administered comprehensive cognitive and linguistic assessment have been related to onset of schizophrenia or other spectrum disorders. This type of analysis is required to establish the association between cognitive and linguistic functioning and risk for schizophrenia or spectrum disorders. The study closest to attaining this goal is the New York High-Risk Project (Erlenmeyer-Kimling and Cornblatt, 1987; Erlenmeyer-Kimling et al., 1989), which is discussed below.

The subjects in the studies reviewed in this chapter generally range from 13 to 18 years of age; thus, they span the entire range of ages that could be considered adolescence. In cases where more specific analyses of the data were performed on the basis of age, those specifications will be mentioned.

SPECIFIC CONTENT AREAS INVESTIGATED
IN ADOLESCENTS

The main area of psychological investigation in adolescents at risk for schizophrenia has been attentional functioning. These studies have examined the abilities of subjects to sustain attention, to focus selectively on information while ignoring irrelevant information, and to process perceptual stimuli rapidly. Many of these studies have compared children at risk for schizophrenia with children vulnerable to other disorders (e.g., affective disorder) to determine the specificity of deficits to risk for schizophrenia. In addition, some studies have compared the children on multiple attentional indices to identify a subgroup of the high-risk sample characterized by broad impairment. This method has the advantage of identifying a subsample of children whose attentional performance resembles that subgroup of adult schizophrenics who tend to show multiple attentional impairments. A shortcoming of this approach is that not all adult schizophrenics are globally impaired on attentional tasks, and, in fact, some adult schizophrenics appear to be relatively normal in all aspects of attentional functioning.

Some attentional studies of high-risk adolescents have examined the performance of the subjects in a longitudinal manner. This approach allows for both validation of classifications of children who are identified as deviant at a particular point in time and assessment of predictive validity. If deviance classifications in adolescence are to be useful in identifying risk for the development of spectrum disorders in adulthood, establishing stable deviance classifications is a necessary precondition. Some of the studies reviewed below have begun that process, with promising results.

Fewer studies of linguistic functioning in adolescents at risk have been conducted than studies of attention, and, as a result, they are less promising to this point. Many studies of children at risk have focused almost entirely on cognition and have ignored speech performance. This approach may have been based on notions that language and cognition are isomorphic, a perspective with many conceptual problems (e.g., see Hotchkiss and Harvey, 1986). It is also possible that researchers correctly noted that adolescents at risk for schizophrenia very rarely manifest communication disorders at the level that meets criteria for "formal thought disorder" (Harvey et al., 1982; Weintraub, 1987). Few objective measures of "subclinical" naturalistic linguistic dysfunction were available at the time of the development of most high-risk projects, which may explain the lack of such studies.

In the following sections, data that bear on cognitive, attentional, and linguistic functioning during the adolescent period in subjects at risk for schizophrenia are reviewed. Because no adult outcome studies of high-risk children are yet complete, validation information is presented from adult literature that bears on the similarity between deficits in individuals who are postpsychotic and those in adolescents who are at risk. In addition, the predictive validity of preadolescent cognitive functioning for adolescent behavior problems is reviewed, with an emphasis on determining the utility of cognitive signs for prediction of later maladjustment, including problems that are not specifically "schizophrenic" in character.

Attentional Functioning

Attention is, in general, a broadly and sometimes vaguely defined construct. In research on risk for schizophrenia, attentional tasks have included (1) serial recall tasks designed to measure selective attention and freedom from distractibility, (2) sustained attention tasks [typically the Continuous Performance Test (CPT) or visual search tasks], and (3) measures of rapid information processing, such as the Span of Apprehension Task. Many of the high-risk studies have not yet published the results from the assessments of their samples during adolescence, so studies in the area at present are relatively few.

Selective Attention/Distractibility

Numerous studies of distractibility in schizophrenia have suggested that symptomatic schizophrenics are quite susceptible to the effects of irrelevant auditory information during serial recall tasks (e.g., Oltmanns and Neale, 1975; Oltmanns, 1978). In addition, deficits on these tasks are temporally stable in psychotic patients during an episode (Harvey *et al.*, 1988) and are apparently responsive to medication (Oltmanns *et al.*, 1979).

In contrast to these patterns of results with adult patients, preadolescent children at risk for schizophrenia manifest relatively inconsistent patterns of distractibility in serial recall tasks. For example, Winters *et al.*, (1981) found that children (from late childhood through 18 years of age) of schizophrenics were more distractible than children of normals on a digit-span distraction task but were not more distractible than children of affect-disordered parents. However, Erlenmeyer-Kimling and Cornblatt (1979) reported that preadolescent children of schizophrenics were not more distractible than children of normals on a very similar task. Although sample and task variations could be considered responsible for these divergent results, the robustness of the adult findings contrasts with these findings. Similarly, the fact that Winters *et al.*'s (1981) and Erlenmeyer-Kimling and Cornblatt's (1979) tasks were *not* matched for discriminating power would probably tend to increase, rather than suppress, differences between children of schizophrenics and those of normals.

In one study to date that reported specifically on distractibility in adolescent high-risk subjects (13–18 years of age), Harvey *et al.* (1981) found that children of schizophrenics were not only more distractible than children of normals, but also their performance patterns were parametrically similar to those of adult schizophrenics, as reported by Frame and Oltmanns (1982) and Oltmanns (1978). This performance deficit was a notable flattening of the primacy portion of the serial position curve for recall of digit information presented in the presence of distraction. This flattening was interpreted by Harvey *et al.* (1981) to reflect a tendency for rehearsal, or other aspects of controlled, voluntarily accessed information processing, to be vulnerable to the effects of irrelevant information. This interpretation is similar to that advanced by Oltmanns (1978) with respect to the performance patterns of adult schizophrenics.

A possibility is that distractibility is an aspect of schizophrenic predisposition that emerges later than childhood in the developmental course of the disorder. Weinberger (1987) posits a neurodevelopmental model of schizophrenia, specifying that identical predispositions may be manifested differently over time, as a function of various developmental events and stressors. While Weinberger's model focuses specifically on the implications of prefrontal dysfunction and the attendant consequences for dopaminergic activity, the logic can apply to various aspects of behavior.

A recent follow-up study has suggested that distractibility is a robust phenomenon in adult schizophrenics, regardless of their clinical state. Harvey *et al.* (1990) reported that at an 8-month follow-up, nonpsychotic and psychotic schizophrenic patients did not differ in degree of distractibility. This is in contrast to manic patients who were distractible only if they were psychotic. This finding is similar to that of Frame and Oltmanns (1982), who reported that word-span performance was relatively stable in schizophrenics from the acute admission stage to the point where they were ready for discharge from the hospital (about 7 weeks later).

In summary, selective attention/serial recall deficits are reportedly present in adolescents at risk for schizophrenia, although the findings regarding younger children are inconsistent. Given the recent findings that clinical state in adult schizophrenics is not associated with the extent of distractibility, the latter variable may hold promise as a marker of vulnerability. As a result, a possible interpretation is that distractibility is a developmental feature of adolescent risk for schizophrenia and that deficient selective attention ability may be an emergent aspect of the adolescent risk period.

Sustained Attention/Vigilance

Deficits in the ability to sustain attention have been a noted feature of schizophrenia since the descriptions of Kraepelin (1919) and Bleuler (1911, 1950). In fact, several investigations have suggested that sustained attention deficits are present in both remitted and currently psychotic schizophrenic patients (e.g., Asarnow and MacCrimmon, 1978), lending credence to the idea that deficits in sustained attention are a marker of vulnerability to the disorder. The typical task used to measure sustained attention is the CPT, usually administered in the visual modality. In the CPT, the subject is instructed to maintain attention to a continuous series of stimuli, usually numbers or letters, while searching for either a single target item (e.g., a "7") or a series of items (e.g., a "3" followed by a "7"). The typical dependent measures are (1) failure to identify a target stimulus when presented (an error of omission) and (2) misidentification of a non-target as a target (an error of commission). In addition, some researchers (e.g., Nuechterlein, 1977) have suggested that signal detection analyses of response sensitivity are the best way to examine the data.

Interestingly, high-risk studies have uniformly found that preadolescent children of schizophrenics are more deviant in their performance on the CPT than children of normals (e.g., Nuechterlein, 1983; Rutschmann *et al.*, 1977; also see Chapter 6, earlier in this volume), in contrast to the results of the selective attention studies presented above. One published report on sustained attention in adolescents (13 years of age and older) at risk found no CPT differences between children of schizophrenics and children of normals (Asarnow *et al.*, 1977). The sample in that study was quite small (nine children of schizophrenics), however, suggesting caution in the interpretation of the findings. In contrast, Winters and her colleagues (Chapter 6, this volume) report that CPT performance deficits persisted in the New York Project high-risk subjects as they entered adolescence. In fact, the deficits became more pronounced in the three successive testing sessions, where the mean age of the high-risk and control groups increased from 12 to 18 years. It is possible that differences in task difficulty are responsible for these differences in findings on CPT performance. More so than in any other area of high-risk research, study-to-study variations in the methodology used in the CPT are tremendous. For example, in the Asarnow *et al.* (1977) study, where adolescents at risk were found to be unimpaired, the task demands simply required a response whenever a specified target digit was presented on the screen. In contrast, the New York High-Risk Project's CPT is a much more difficult task, requiring a response whenever the same playing card appears twice in succession on the screen. Keeping in mind that the average age at last assessment of the New York children was 18 years, whereas the Asarnow *et al.* (1977) children averaged 16, task characteristics may indeed have contributed to the differences in findings.

A different type of vigilance task was used by Winters *et al.* (1981) in the Stony Brook High-Risk Project. That task, labeled a visual search task, required the subjects to search a visual array for a predetermined target letter. Target information was presented continuously, under the control of the subject, and high- and low-similarity irrelevant information was presented simultaneously with the target stimuli. Adolescent (13 years of age and older) children of schizophrenics were considerably slower than children of normals in their rate of identification of the target stimuli. Younger children were slower than the adolescents in both diagnostic groups, but age did not interact with diagnosis, suggesting no group-specific developmental effects.

Rapid Visual Processing

The rapid processing of visual information has been an area of substantial research interest in schizophrenia. Two main research paradigms have been used: the Backward Masking Task and the Span of Apprehension Task. The two are similar in that they require identification of information that is presented very briefly and, in the case of the Backward Masking Task, almost immediately obscured by irrelevant information.

Both of these tasks have been found to discriminate schizophrenics from normals, and schizophrenics' performance deficits persist on both tasks after remission of psychosis (Asarnow and MacCrimmon, 1978; Braff, 1981). Only the Span of Apprehension Task has been used with adolescent children of schizophrenics, although the Backward Masking Task has been used with other schizophrenia spectrum members.

The two studies using the Span of Apprehension Task with high-risk adolescents produced notably divergent results. The first report suggested that deficient performance on the Span of Apprehension Task discriminated children of schizophrenics from those of normals (Asarnow *et al.*, 1977). A second report found that adolescent children (13 years of age and older) of schizophrenics did not differ at all from children of normals (Harvey *et al.*, 1985). Harvey and his colleagues suggested that sample differences may have accounted for the differences in the results. The Asarnow *et al.* (1977) sample consisted of children who were all adopted away from their schizophrenic parents and, thus, they may have been more maladjusted.

The area of rapid visual processing has notably been particularly promising for identification of vulnerability indicators (Holzman, 1987). However, the Span of Apprehension Task apparently does not consistently reveal deficient performance on the part of adolescents at risk for schizophrenia. Deficits in Span of Apprehension Task performance may develop as one of the early aspects of the actual schizophrenic illness, rather than as an aspect of vulnerability. Such a perspective explains the findings that remitted patients manifest deficits while older children at risk do not. It should be noted that Asarnow *et al.* (1983) reported that subjects with no history of psychiatric disturbance who were deviant on the Span of Apprehension Task scored higher on the Minnesota Multiphasic Personality Inventory (MMPI) schizophrenia (#8) scale than nondeviant subjects.

In summary, there are indications that rapid visual processing deficits are associated with clinical schizophrenia, both in and out of episodes, but no evidence consistently indicates that adolescents at risk manifest these deficits. Further investigation in this area, including the use of the Backward Masking Task with this population, would be informative.

Verbal Performance

As noted above, numerous theorists assume that verbal deficits are a significant correlate of schizophrenia spectrum membership (Meehl, 1962; Singer *et al.*, 1978). It is somewhat surprising, therefore, that the majority of prospective studies of children at risk have not studied communication abnormalities directly. Three reported studies are relevant to the phenomenon, but two of these studies presented data on the same sample of children. The New York High-Risk Project (Erlenmeyer-Kimling and Cornblatt, 1987) assessed communication disorder in very late adolescence, and the resulting data should be particularly informative when available, because the New York sample is especially well assessed throughout childhood.

In one of the studies of communication disorder in children at risk for schizophrenia, Worland *et al.* (1979) evaluated subjects who ranged in age from 6 to 20 years. They administered the Rorschach and the Thematic Apperception Test (TAT) and compared the performance of the children of schizophrenics with children of medically and psychiatrically ill controls, as well as children of normals. Children of schizophrenics manifested more primitive Rorschach content and less aggressive TAT content than controls. Preadolescent children had more aggressive TAT content than did older subjects, but this age effect did not interact with parental diagnosis. These results suggest that children of schizophrenics have a tendency to produce responses with developmentally inappropriate content. Yet the phenomenon does not appear to be developmental in that no age-related changes were specific to the schizophrenic children.

In the other two studies of language behavior in adolescents at risk, speech abnormalities were examined in terms of the frequencies of several reference performance variables. Reference performance is the process by which spoken text is organized into a coherent framework (Halladay and Hasan, 1976). As adapted by Rochester and Martin (1979) for the examination of the speech of psychiatric patients, reference process analysis has demonstrated the ability to discriminate the speech of schizophrenic patients who were classified as thought-disordered from the speech of those who were not thought-disordered (Rochester and Martin, 1979). The typical variables examined are (1) explicit verbal references, which are references in speech to previously presented verbal material, and (2) reference failures, which are references in which the item that is being referred to is either unclear or ambiguous.

In one of the studies of speech in adolescents at risk for schizophrenia, Harvey *et al.* (1982) found that offspring of schizophrenics (13 years of age and older) made significantly more reference failures than children of normals. In addition, the high-risk children made fewer competent references and produced less speech overall. Harvey *et al.* (1982) characterized the speech of high-risk subjects as being more vague than that of normals, as well as having lower overall information content. The combination of these two tendencies led to a situation where the speech was confusing, unclear, and poorly elaborated, although not meeting traditional criteria for formal thought disorder.

In the other study of speech disorder in adolescents (Neale *et al.*, 1985), the Harvey *et al.* (1982) speech data were correlated with performance on an analog test of language ability—the word communication test. This test, initially developed by Cohen and Cahmi (1967), was later adapted by Smith (1971). The overall format of the word communication test is like a "password" game, wherein the speaker is given a set of two words with one specified as the referent and is asked to produce a clue to allow an imaginary listener to discriminate the referent. Some versions of the test use an open-ended format, where the speaker is asked to generate the clue spontaneously, whereas other versions provide a choice of two possible target words. The version of the test used in the study by Neale *et al.* (1985) was a two-item, forced-choice format with two types of clue sets. The task was initially developed by Kagan and Oltmanns (1981) so that the items in the two clue sets were comparable in discriminating power. In type I clue items, the correct clue is a higher-frequency associate of the referent than is the incorrect clue [e.g., Light Heavy (referent underlined), Bulb Weight (the correct choice and highest associate of the referent is "Bulb")], whereas in type II items the incorrect clue is a more frequent associate of the referent than is the correct clue [e.g., Star Sun (referent underlined)], Sky Movie [the correct choice but less frequent associate of the referent is "Movie"]. Thus, type I items can be solved simply by choosing the higher-frequency associate of the target, whereas type II items require that the subject ignore the higher-frequency associate and solve the item by selecting on the basis of contextual relationships. Kagan and Oltmanns (1981) found that adult schizophrenics are nondeviant on type I items, while making numerous errors on type II items.

Neale *et al.* (1985) found that children of schizophrenics made substantially more type II errors than type I errors, with this difference in performance discriminating them from children of normals. Interestingly, they found that these errors in an analog communication task were uncorrelated with reference failures in speech. Thus, despite the fact that children of schizophrenics made more reference failures and more word communication errors than children of normals, these two tendencies failed to overlap in the same sample. The possible implications of this finding are either that the referent communication task is not a correlate of actual linguistic failures in these at-risk adolescents, and hence lacks validity as a potential vulnerability marker, or that the task measures an aspect of deficient cognitive performance that is simply not correlated with linguistic failures. The results of the Neale *et al.* (1985) study also indicate that no relationship exists between measures of speech failures and the referent communication task in adult schizophrenics. It is nonetheless interesting that deficits on the referent communication task are specific to adolescents at risk for schizophrenia, relative to children of normals and children of affectively ill parents. The task may be measuring some aspect of cognitive dyscontrol that is correlated with the predisposition to schizophrenia, but in a way other than through linguistic dysfunction. Given that both genetic and nongenetic models of vulnerability to schizophrenia allow for substantial variation among individuals who are predisposed, it is entirely feasible that cognitive deficits could be uncorrelated within predisposed individuals. The validation of the referent communication task, therefore, will be in its association with schizophrenia spectrum disorders, based on eventual psychiatric outcome data from the Stony Brook Project.

In summary, the language performance studies of children at risk for schizophrenia yield evidence of deficits in adolescence. The characteristics of these verbal deficits are similar to the subtle language failures that are assumed by Meehl (1962) to reflect cognitive slippage in schizotypes.

Consequently, the use of linguistic deviance to predict eventual schizophrenic outcome in children at risk may be a promising strategy that can be validated with outcome data from the various high-risk projects.

CONSISTENCY OF DEVIANCE ACROSS MEASURES

A notable feature of adult schizophrenics is their tendency to manifest deviance on a variety of measures of cognitive, linguistic, and intellectual functioning. Although there are many possible explanations for this, including motivational deficits, drug side effects, and consequences of psychotic clinical state, it is also plausible that certain schizophrenics are globally deficient in their cognitive functioning. Similarly, a variety of factors could produce deficits on a single measure of psychological functions. In contrast to adult schizophrenics, however, children at risk are not affected by many factors that could have a causal effect on measures of psychological functioning.

Some investigators in the field of high-risk research have employed examinations of the consistency of cognitive and linguistic functioning across multiple measures. In so doing, they have hoped to identify a subgroup of their sample who, by virtue of their consistently impaired functioning, may be at higher risk to develop schizophrenia than the less impaired subjects in the sample.

In the first such examination of an adolescent high-risk sample, Asarnow et al. (1977) compared their group of nine fostered-out children of schizophrenics with comparison samples across a variety of attentional tasks. They found that five (55%) of their children of schizophrenics, in contrast to 10% of the foster control group and no members of the community control group, manifested deviance across a variety of attentional measures. However, as noted by Cornblatt and Erlenmeyer-Kimling (1985), the number of excessively deviant children of schizophrenics was notably higher than the predicted risk for development of adult schizophrenia and other spectrum disorders in the sample. Thus, either the attentional measures are overpredicting risk or, as suggested by Harvey et al. (1985), the sample manifests excessive deviance by virtue of its special, late-fostered status.

A similar approach was adopted by Winters et al. (1981). They compared their samples of children of schizophrenics, affectives, and normals across six cognitive, attentional, and intellectual measures. They reported that 44% of children of schizophrenics manifested deviance on three to six tasks, in contrast to the children of normals and affectives, who tended to be much less consistently deviant. Harvey et al. (1982) used the same approach to compare their nearly identical sample of adolescents on nine linguistic measures, noting that 39% of children of schizophrenics were deviant on four or more linguistic measures, with only 2% of the children of normals manifesting this level of deviance. Similarly, Nuechterlein (1983) reported that 29% of the children of schizophrenic mothers, in contrast to 11% of the nonschizophrenic psychiatric and 6% of the normal samples, fell into a consistently low-response sensitivity subgroup on sustained attention measures.

EARLY ATTENTION DEFICITS AS A PREDICTOR OF LATER MALADJUSTMENT

A highly creative use of this type of "global deviance" approach has been demonstrated by the New York research group and is described by Winters and her colleagues in Chapter 6 of this volume. They used an aggregated measure of attentional deviance at 12 years of age to predict behavioral problems in adolescence. Thus, they used cognitive dysfunction to longitudinally predict behavioral dysfunction in high-risk children. Specifically, very deviant attentional performance in children of schizophrenics and control samples was highly specific and moderately sensitive for identification of extremely disturbed behavior in adolescence. At the same time, the children of schizophrenics were much more likely to manifest both global attentional deviance and extremely disturbed behavior.

Two issues must be kept in mind when evaluating these results. The first is that for the results to have their utmost validity, the adolescent behavioral dysfunctions predicted by preadolescent global attentional deviance must themselves be precursors of schizophrenia spectrum disorders. Otherwise, the utility of the global deviance marker, quite sensitive and specific for the prediction of later behavioral problems, will not also include the identification of schizophrenia spectrum disorders. The second issue is that the long-term, cross-temporal stability of global attentional deviance is not well established. Also, the status of adolescent global attentional deviance in terms of its concurrent associations with behavioral maladaptation is unclear. If they truly mark vulnerability to schizophrenia, then global attentional deviations should be temporally stable and show concurrent validity.

The issue of predicting actual adult psychopathology in the New York sample was addressed in a recent paper by Erlenmeyer-Kimling *et al.* (1989). In this study, they used the Bayesian statistical methods initially employed by Golden and Meehl (1979) to identify putative schizoid taxon members from MMPI responses. The Bayesian analysis was applied to the attentional data from round 1 testing, in addition to intellectual and neuropsychological data collected in the same assessment. Using the statistical models, assignment as a member or nonmember of the schizoid taxon was completed. Then the hypothetical assignments to taxon membership were compared with actual early-adulthood outcome data. Of the children of schizophrenics who had been hospitalized by early adulthood, 72% were predicted to be taxon members by the battery of attentional/neuropsychological tests. Children of schizophrenics who had "no major problems" were selected for taxon membership exactly half as often, i.e., 36%. The relationship between functional status and taxon selection was close to random in the affective control sample and in the children of normals, as would be expected if the indicators were specific to problems within the schizophrenia spectrum and not related to maladjustment in other types of samples.

Thus, global attentional and neuropsychological deviance in preadolescence appears to predict maladjustment in adolescence and eventual behavioral problems afterward. It would be interesting for this research group to relate the adolescent adjustment measures to the results of the early adult assessment of their sample. Both seem to validate the global attentional dysfunction construct as the most robust predictor of maladjustment; knowing if both attentional deviance and adolescent maladjustment precedes adult psychopathology would be interesting as well.

Some unpublished data from the Stony Brook Project address the issue of the stability of attentional deficits. These data (Winters *et al.*, 1985) involve a reevaluation of the children assessed in the Winters *et al.* (1981) paper at a 2.5-year follow-up interval. The stability of the estimates of global deviance for children of schizophrenics was quite impressive. For example, 86% of the children who were nondeviant at time 1 were also nondeviant at time 2, and 61% of the nondeviant cases at time 2 had also been considered nondeviant at time 1. Of the children of schizophrenics who manifested global dysfunctions at time 1, 61% were also deviant at time 2, and 67% of the children who were deviant at time 2 were also deviant at time 1. In total, 27% of the sample of children of schizophrenics were deviant at both time periods. These data suggest that there is reasonable stability of global attentional dysfunction and, in addition, argue against the criticisms of risk overprediction raised by Cornblatt and Erlenmeyer-Kimling (1985). Remarkably, the proportion of high-risk children who were deviant at both time periods in the Stony Brook Project is identical to the proportion of globally attentionally deviant children in the New York study, and both are only 2% lower than the estimate of children with extreme attentional deviance from the Nuechterlein (1983) high-risk sample.

These data suggest that global deficits in attentional functioning are relatively stable over a follow-up interval during adolescence. Thus, cognitive deficits are not secondary to transitory fluctuations in performance at a single testing session, adding to their potential to be genuine markers of vulnerability. However, it must be kept in mind that stable attentional deficits are not schizophrenia. Only outcome data relating these adolescent performance characteristics to adult schizophrenia spectrum outcomes can validate these aspects of performance as true markers of vulnerability. The data from Winters and her colleagues (Chapter 6, this volume), however, are very reassuring with respect to the predictive validity of early attention dysfunction and later maladjustment within the schizophrenia spectrum. It is also encouraging to see that the number of high-risk children in the New York sample who manifest consistent attentional deviance through adolescence is identical to the estimates of two earlier studies that identified deviant subgroups. Thus, the estimates of the number of children of schizophrenics who are attentionally deviant before and through the period of adolescence is about 25–30%, in many ways similar to the risk of schizophrenia spectrum disorders that would be predicted for this type of sample (Rosenthal, 1970).

PROFILE OF PERFORMANCE DURING THE ADOLESCENT RISK PERIOD

Adolescent children of schizophrenics manifest a variety of attentional and linguistic impairments. Compared with children of normals, they manifest difficulty in sustaining their attention to relevant information and are easily distracted by irrelevant stimuli. Some evidence suggests that they do not process information as rapidly as do children of normals. In addition, their speech may be vague, lower in information value, and at times disconnected. Only a subset of children of schizophrenics manifest this behavioral profile, but those that do tend to show significant behavioral problems in adolescence and in early adulthood. These deficits probably do not develop abruptly in adolescence but, rather, are part of a pattern of deviation that can be detected with appropriately sensitive tests early in development. Although some deficits may first appear in adolescence (e.g., distractibility in auditory processing), too few studies have presented data on this population to make this claim.

CONCLUSIONS

At the present time, it is impossible to make the definitive statement that attentional and linguistic deficits are a part of the premorbid developmental course of schizophrenia. It is likely that some attentionally and linguistically impaired children of schizophrenics will never manifest a psychotic episode but, rather, will present, over the course of their lives, as stable "schizotypes" or as manifesting schizotypal personality disorder.

However, it is obvious that these deficits are related to schizophrenia in some way: The individuals manifesting them are related to schizophrenics and some presumably carry genetic predispositions to schizophrenia. Right now, however, given the lack of outcome data, we are unsure if these various aspects of performance are truly markers of vulnerability. Even if they are markers of vulnerability, whether they are specific to schizophrenia or spectrum outcomes is not clear.

The most recent studies, as cited above, suggest that attentional failures are potentially valid means to identify individuals predisposed to schizophrenia who will manifest later maladjustment. In fact, the more deviant a child of a schizophrenic is, the more likely that he or she will in fact be hospitalized as a young adult. But no single aspect of attentional performance has been demonstrated to be a valid marker of vulnerability. In addition, the interrelations among various attentional and linguistic variables are not yet understood. The data from the New York High-Risk Project, as replicated in other investigations, suggests that global attentional failures mark vulnerability to schizophrenia in children of schizophrenics, and that there is a consistently identifiable group of these individuals at risk who will manifest adjustment problems as adolescents and who may eventually develop schizophrenia at a higher rate than their nonattentionally impaired counterparts. These findings suggest that high-risk research has begun to fill its immense potential as a means to identify, and possibly intervene with, the most vulnerable children of schizophrenics.

ACKNOWLEDGMENTS

The author thanks Ken C. Winters and Sheldon Weintraub for allowing him to cite their unpublished data.

REFERENCES

Asarnow, R. F., and MacCrimmon, D. (1978). Residual performance deficit in clinically remitted schizophrenics: A marker of schizophrenia? *Journal of Abnormal Psychology, 87,* 597–608.

Asarnow, R. F., Nuechterlein, K. H., and Marder, S. R. (1983). Span of apprehension performance, neuropsychological functioning, and indices of psychosis-proneness. *Journal of Nervous and Mental Disease, 171,* 662–669.

Asarnow, R. F., Steffy, R., Cleghorn, J. M., and MacCrimmon, D. J. (1977). An attentional assessment of foster children at risk for schizophrenia. *Journal of Abnormal Psychology, 86,* 267–275.

Bleuler, E. (1911/1950). *Dementia praecox or the group of schizophrenias.* New York: International Universities Press.

Braff, D. L. (1981). Impaired speed of information processing in unmedicated schizotypal patients. *Schizophrenia Bulletin, 7,* 499–508.

Callaway, E. S., and Naghdi, S. (1982). An information processing model for schizophrenia. *Archives of General Psychiatry, 39,* 339–347.

Cohen, B. D., and Cahmi, J. (1976). Schizophrenic performance in a word-communication task. *Journal of Abnormal Psychology, 76,* 240–246.

Cornblatt, B., and Erlenmeyer-Kimling, L. (1985). Global attentional deviance as a marker of risk for schizophrenia: Specificity and predictive validity. *Journal of Abnormal Psychology, 94,* 470–486.

Erlenmeyer-Kimling, L., and Cornblatt, B. (1979). Attentional measures in a study of children at high risk for schizophrenia. *Journal of Psychiatric Research, 14,* 93–98.

Erlenmeyer-Kimling, L., and Cornblatt, B. (1987). The New York High-Risk Project: A follow-up report. *Schizophrenia Bulletin, 13,* 451–461.

Erlenmeyer-Kimling, L., Golden, R., and Cornblatt, B. (1989). A taxometric analysis of cognitive and neuromotor variables in children at risk for schizophrenia. *Journal of Abnormal Psychology, 98,* 203–208.

Fish, B. (1987). Infant predictors of the longitudinal course of schizophrenic development. *Schizophrenia Bulletin, 13,* 395–410.

Frame, C. F., and Oltmanns, T. F. (1982). Serial recall by schizophrenic and affective patients during and after psychotic episodes. *Journal of Abnormal Psychology, 91,* 311–318.

Golden, R. R., and Meehl, P. E. (1979). Detection of the schizoid taxon with MMPI indicators. *Journal of Abnormal Psychology, 88,* 217–233.

Halladay, M. A. K., and Hasan, R. (1976). *Cohesion in English.* London: Longman.

Harvey, P. D., Docherty, N. M., Serper, M. R., and Rasmussen, M. (1990). Cognitive deficits and thought disorder: II. An eight-month followup study. *Schizophrenia Bulletin. 16,* 147–156.

Harvey, P. D., Earle-Boyer, E. A., and Levinson, J. C. (1988). Cognitive deficits and thought disorder: A retest study. *Schizophrenia Bulletin, 14,* 58–66.

Harvey, P. D., and Neale, J. M. (1983). The specificity of thought disorder to schizophrenia: Research methods in their historical perspective. In B. A. Maher (Ed.), *Progress in experimental personality research* (Vol. 12). pp. 153–180. New York: Academic Press.

Harvey, P. D., Weintraub, S., and Neale, J. M. (1982). Speech competence of children vulnerable to psychopathology. *Journal of Abnormal Child Psychology, 10,* 373–388.

Harvey, P. D., Weintraub, S., and Neale, J. M. (1985). Span of apprehension deficits in children vulnerable to psychopathology: A failure to replicate. *Journal of Abnormal Psychology, 94,* 410–413.

Harvey, P., Winters, K., Weintraub, S., and Neale, J. M. (1981). Distractibility in children vulnerable to psychopathology. *Journal of Abnormal Psychology, 90,* 298–304.

Holzman, P. S. (1987). Recent studies of psychophysiology in schizophrenia. *Schizophrenia Bulletin, 13,* 49–76.

Hotchkiss, A. P., and Harvey, P. D. (1986). Linguistic analyses of speech disorder in psychosis. *Clinical Psychology Review, 6,* 155–178.

Kagan, D. L., and Oltmanns, T. F. (1981). Matched tasks for measuring single-word referent communication: The performance of patients with schizophrenic and affective disorders. *Journal of Abnormal Psychology, 90,* 204–212.

Kraepelin, E. (1919). *Dementia praecox and paraphrenia.* Edinburgh: E & S. Livingstone.

Mednick, S. A., and McNeil, T. (1968). Current methodology in research on the etiology of schizophrenia: Serious difficulties that suggest the use of the high-risk group method.

Psychological Bulletin, 70, 681–693.

Mednick, S. A., and Schulsinger, F. (1968). Some premorbid characteristics related to breakdown in children with schizophrenic mothers. *Journal of Psychiatric Research, 6,* 267–291.

Meehl, P. E. (1962). Schizotaxia, schizotypy, schizophrenia. *American Psychologist, 17,* 827–838.

Neale, J. M., and Oltmanns, T. F. (1980). *Schizophrenia.* New York: Wiley.

Neale, J. M., Oltmanns, T. F., and Harvey, P. D. (1985). The need to relate cognitive deficits to behavioral referents of schizophrenia. *Schizophrenia Bulletin, 11,* 286–291.

Nuechterlein, K. H. (1977). Reaction time and attention in schizophrenia: A critical evaluation of the data and the theories. *Schizophrenia Bulletin, 3,* 373–428.

Nuechterlein, K. H. (1983). Signal detection in vigilance tasks and behavioral attributes among offspring of schizophrenic mothers and among hyperactive children. *Journal of Abnormal Psychology, 92,* 4–28.

Nuechterlein, K. H., and Dawson, M. (1984). Information processing and attentional functioning in the developmental course of schizophrenic disorders. *Schizophrenia Bulletin, 10,* 160–203.

Oltmanns, T. F. (1978). Selective attention in manic and schizophrenic psychoses: The effect of distraction on information processing. *Journal of Abnormal Psychology, 87,* 212–225.

Oltmanns, T. F., and Neale, J. M. (1975). Schizophrenic performance when distractors are present: Attentional deficit or differential task difficulty. *Journal of Abnormal Psychology, 84,* 204–209.

Oltmanns, T. F., Ohayon, J., and Neale, J. M. (1979). The effect of medication and diagnostic criteria on distractibility in schizophrenia. *Journal of Psychiatric Research, 14,* 81–91.

Rochester, S. R., and Martin, J. R. (1979). *Crazy talk: A study of the discourse of schizophrenic speakers.* New York: Plenum.

Rosenthal, D. (1970). *Genetic theory and abnormal behavior.* New York: McGraw-Hill.

Rutschmann, J., Cornblatt, B., and Erlenmeyer-Kimling, L. (1977). Sustained attention in children at risk for schizophrenia. *Archives of General Psychiatry, 34,* 571–575.

Singer, M. T., Wynne, L. C., and Toohey, M. L. (1978). Communication disorders and the families of schizophrenics. In L. C. Wynne, R. C. Cromwell, and S. Mathysse (Eds.), *The nature of schizophrenia: New approaches to research and treatment.* New York: Wiley Interscience.

Smith, E. E. (1971). Associative and editing processes in schizophrenia. *Journal of Abnormal Psychology, 75,* 182–186.

Weinberger, D. R. (1987). Implications of normal brain development for the pathogenesis of schizophrenia. *Archives of General Psychiatry, 44,* 660–669.

Weintraub, S. (1987). Risk factors in schizophrenia. *Schizophrenia Bulletin, 13,* 439–450.

Winters, K. C., Persons, W., and Weintraub, S. (1985). A longitudinal analysis of cognitive and attentional disorders in children at risk for psychopathology. Unpublished manuscript, State University of New York at Stony Brook. [Cited by permission.]

Winters, K. C., Stone, A. A., Weintraub, S., and Neale, J. M. (1981). Cognitive and attentional deficits in children vulnerable to psychopathology. *Journal of Abnormal Child Psychology, 9,* 435–453.

Worland, J., Lander, J., and Hesselbrock, V. (1979). Psychological evaluation of clinical disturbance in children at risk for psychopathology. *Journal of Abnormal Psychology, 88,* 13–26.

Zubin, J., and Spring, B. (1977). Vulnerability: A new view of schizophrenia. *Journal of Abnormal Psychology, 86,* 103–126.

Longitudinal Studies of Premorbid Development of Adult Schizophrenics

Norman F. Watt
Christopher Saiz

Explanation of schizophrenic disorder has plagued scientists and clinicians for centuries. In its acute form the disorder can be devastatingly incapacitating, and in its chronic form it can virtually nullify an entire adult life. From a human perspective, it is fortunately quite rare, with a lifetime morbid risk of about 1% in populations throughout the world (Gottesman and Shields, 1982). However, that epidemiological fact conspires with the fact that the onset of the disorder hardly ever occurs before 15 years of age (Slater and Cowie, 1971), creating a conceptual nightmare for psychopathologists, some of whom trace the origins of the disorder to early childhood (Laing and Esterson, 1971) and many of whom begin their search for causes at the point of conception or before (Gershon *et al.*, 1981).

The explanatory quest in almost any domain of clinical science begins retrospectively with a search for reliable covariation between antecedents and consequences. The quest then proceeds from there hopefully to prospective investigation of the presumably critical antecedents, to explain the pathological processes and ultimately control them either after the fact

Copyright © 1991 by Academic Press, Inc.
All rights of reproduction in any form reserved.

(through treatment) or before the fact (through preventive intervention). When the primary causes are separated by one (or even two) generations from the manifest disorder, scientists are confronted with a formidable intellectual challenge that requires persistence, ingenuity, and, in many cases, a lifetime commitment to the quest.

Our task here is to review longitudinal studies of premorbid development in adult schizophrenics, focusing primarily on retrospective accounts based on childhood records, sometimes referred to as follow-back, or follow-up, studies, but also including some prospective studies of children at high risk for schizophrenia, which are naturally much smaller in number. Our primary objective is to summarize the most promising premorbid markers of the disorder and, where possible, to discuss some of their theoretical implications.

DATED CONCEPTIONS OF THE LONGITUDINAL COURSE OF SCHIZOPHRENIC DISORDERS

Regression Theories

There is an appealing symmetry and parsimony in a theory with several variations that was especially popular among clinical psychiatrists in the middle decades of this century (Goldstein, 1948; Vigotsky, 1934; von Domarus, 1944; Werner, 1948). It was based on a principle of regression: In certain forms of psychopathology, notably schizophrenia and aphasia, the language of adults regresses to a more primitive, concrete level. Brown (1958) argued that this principle is a corollary of the popular developmental "law of linguistic progression," which holds that progression from the concrete to the abstract characterizes the evolution of the species from animals to humans, the historical development of contemporary languages, and the transformation of children into adults. Part of the attraction of this conception was that, if language declines with mental disorder according to the regression principle, it could be adduced as evidence to support the inference that language progresses in *normal* development according to the general law, showing increasing mastery of abstraction with age, civilization, and phylogenetic advancement. Parallel hypotheses of psychodynamic regression had, of course, won prominent attention for psychoanalytic theory in earlier decades of this century (Freud, 1917). There are several testable premises of such regression theories, the most important of which is the notion that linguistic decline in psychopathological conditions retraces the path of linguistic growth, rather than taking some other course. Some evidence has supported this premise (Klorman and Chapman, 1969; Willner, 1965) but other studies have not (Benjamin and Watt, 1969; Watt, 1971), and regression theories have been benignly neglected, for the most part, during the last two decades.

Regression formulations have died a slow death partly because they were consonant with Kraepelin's (1919) authoritatively promulgated etiological theory (incurable disease leading to inexorable deterioration) and partly because many of the behavioral symptoms in deteriorated schizophrenics *appear* regressive. Kraepelin's conceptual hegemony has slowly diminished, and recent evidence of favorable clinical outcomes (reviewed below) has gradually undermined the conviction that schizophrenia (properly diagnosed) inexorably leads to "defect states." Regression hypotheses also endure because, prior to the revolution in hospital practices that began in the mid-1950s, intrinsic features of the course of schizophrenic disorders were extremely difficult to distinguish from extrinsic behavioral manifestations more appropriately attributable to the stultifying effects of chronic incarceration.

Follow-Up Studies of Child Guidance Clinic Populations

Also in the middle decades of this century, a popular method used to approximate an account of premorbid development in schizophrenia was to examine childhood records of people seen in child guidance clinics who were subsequently hospitalized for schizophrenic disorders. The predominant pattern found in most of those studies was the shy, withdrawn, "shut-in" preschizophrenic personality type (Birren, 1944; Bowman, 1934; Frazee, 1953; Gardner, 1967; Ricks and Nameche, 1966; Wittman and Steinberg, 1944). Moreover, Birren (1944) and Nameche *et al.* (1964) found that among preschizophrenic children, those with apathetic or schizoid tendencies had poorer psychiatric prognosis after breakdown than those who were aggressive and committed social transgressions against the community. These findings were not very secure because child guidance clinic clients are not representative of our general population, include disproportionate numbers of boys, and, depending on the child's age when seen at the clinic, may display behaviors that are actually prodromal symptoms of psychosis rather than genuine antecedents of schizophrenia.

Two studies cast some doubt on how frequently shy, withdrawn children become schizophrenic as compared to other types of children. Morris *et al.* (1954) followed 54 subjects (drawn from Dallas Child Guidance Clinic records) for periods of 16–27 years. About two-thirds of them were satisfactorily adjusted adults and about one-third were marginally adjusted. Only two were considered to be mentally ill: one diagnosed schizophrenic in a mental hospital and the other still managing in the community. Most of the subjects were still quiet and retiring but were self-supporting and stable in their employment, which tended to be sheltered. Michael *et al.* (1957) followed 606 boys (drawn from the same clinic) whom they classified as introverts, extraverts, and ambiverts, following the classification scheme of Bellak and Purcell (1946), who had found, among 100 dementia praecox patients, 35 distinctly extravert, 28 distinctly introvert, and 37 ambivert prepsychotic personalities. Michael *et al.* (1957) found that the introverted boys were more intelligent and were seen at an earlier age in the clinic than the other groups, which might have some bearing on psychiatric outcome. When these boys were followed from 14 to 29 years after being seen at the clinic, only 1 of the 164 introverts was hospitalized for schizophrenia and none for any other form of mental illness, whereas 6 of the 174 ambiverts were schizophrenic and 6 were hospitalized for other mental illness, and 3 of the 268 extraverts were schizophrenic and 8 were hospitalized for other mental illness.

Several follow-up studies of antisocial or sociopathic children found substantial numbers of them eventually hospitalized for schizophrenia (McCord *et al.*, 1962; Morris *et al.*, 1956; O'Neal and Robins, 1958; Robins, 1966). Many of the studies cited previously also found evidence of antisocial patterns, but these findings tended to be discounted until school-based studies were published in the last two decades. Even dating back to the last century, interpersonal frictions have been prominently featured in the characterization of schizoid temperament, which has been widely accepted as a common foundation for schizophrenic disorder (Gottesman and Shields, 1982), but the introverted features of that pattern have been stubbornly given preference by clinical scholars as a more discriminating indicator of later breakdown or prognosis for recovery after breakdown. This may be attributable to residual effects of Kraepelin's (1919) views of the course of the disorder.

Early School-Based Follow-Back Studies

Kasanin and Veo (1932) examined grade school records of male and female preschizophrenics. Although they lacked a control group, they described about 20% as showing positive characteristics of popularity, confidence, and leadership, whereas about 25% were definitely peculiar, about 25% had milder maladjustments, and about 25% were seclusive but caused no difficulties in school. Bower *et al.* (1960) interviewed the high school teachers of 44 schizophrenic veterans and 44 normal controls. They found the two groups to differ significantly on 16 of 20 interview variables, including the classic question "Did he like girls?" Among the schizophrenics, 50% had been markedly withdrawn, 20% had primarily acting-out problems, 20% had miscellaneous problems, and 10% had no marked difficulties. These authors argued that clinic-based follow-back studies might implicate antisocial or nuisance behavior more than their study did and feature less of the shy, withdrawn cases who present fewer management difficulties. However, because *control* groups drawn from clinic populations would tend to show more antisocial behavior than *control* groups drawn from school populations, the net effect would be to *under*emphasize the antisocial elements in the premorbid behavior of the schizophrenics seen in clinics and to *over*emphasize evidence of them at school. Corroborative evidence reported by Barthell and Holmes (1968) showed that preschizophrenic high school graduates had fewer social activities listed in their high school yearbooks than did normal controls. It is worth noting that these last two studies focused exclusively on behavior in high school, where significant signs of the precipitant phase of the disorder (Garmezy, 1970) might intrude to place a different cast on preschizophrenic behavior than would the earlier signs from the premorbid phase. For example, it is plausible to expect that abrasive behavior in the middle childhood years might elicit strong retaliative responses from the social network, leading to ostracism and/or voluntary seclusion in adolescence, as the onset of explicit psychosis approaches.

Systematic content analysis of *ad lib* comments written by teachers in cumulative school records for grades kindergarten to twelfth depicted preschizophrenic boys as scholastically underachieving, cheerless, uncooperative, antisocial, and defiant of authority, when compared with normal controls (Watt *et al.*, 1970; Watt and Lubensky, 1976). By contrast, preschizophrenic girls were described as emotionally immature, introverted, and socially insecure. The boys were clearly more obtrusive than the girls because their behavior created more difficulties for the teachers and others in school. Longitudinal analyses revealed that the patterns of social deviation were progressive over time, especially among the boys (Watt, 1972, 1978). Behavioral signs of emotional instability and passivity were already apparent in the girls during the first half of their school careers and became slightly more pronounced during the second half. The boys were not behaviorally discriminable from other boys in the elementary grades, but they became substantially more irritable, aggressive, negativistic, and rebellious (though *not* more introverted) as they approached adolescence. Watt offered the following summary of some implications from these findings:

> Without prejudging what the primary causes of these behavioral deviations might be, it is worth considering their potential *psychological* contribution to the ultimate schizophrenic disorder. Childhood and adolescence are periods of

experimentation and apprenticeship for adult living. A child normally acquires specific competencies, a particular style of relating to others, and a repertory of emotional habits and self-attitudes through various socializing experiences in the home, at school, and on the playground. The passive, introverted girl who abstains from participating may be deprived thereby of essential psychological growth. She may come to think of herself as one who does not or cannot do (the psychological difference may be slight) many things well. Having few friends and limited social experience may deprive her of important opportunities for learning how to calibrate her emotional expression to that of others, and leave her with fundamental doubts of her worthiness as a friend and lover. Similarly, the abrasive adolescent boy may be headed for troubled psychological waters. If his willfulness is indulged or ignored, he may never learn realistic limits for his desires. More likely, his antagonism will eventually elicit rejection and retaliation from his victims, leaving him feeling alienated, isolated and bitter. Neither eventuality is likely to lead to a mature sense of social reciprocity and self-esteem.

In effect, what has been argued here is that many preschizophrenics are characterologically immature children. Behaviorally, they may be indistinguishable from other immature children with different destinies (Watt, 1978: 165).

The notion of emotional immaturity offers an important theoretical contrast to the earlier regression formulations, namely, that *even as children* some schizophrenics may experience developmental arrest or delay in characterological development, which may at the very least presage their psychiatric destiny and perhaps even contribute functionally to its unfolding in young adulthood. We shall return later to this important theoretical shift.

Early Follow-Back Studies of Intellectual Development

Because disordered thinking is a cardinal feature of schizophrenia, the follow-back literature contains a substantial volume of studies of premorbid intellectual development. The results reported have been reasonably consistent, although not unequivocal. Schizophrenics have been found generally to have lower childhood intelligence than their classmates in school (Albee *et al.*, 1964; Bower *et al.*, 1960), although this finding was not replicated in a suburban population (Schaffner *et al.*, 1967), and lower childhood intelligence than their own siblings (Lane and Albee, 1965; Schaffner *et al.*, 1967). Pollack *et al.* (1970) found the same trends comparing schizophrenics with their siblings, but they also found similar (and stronger) results for patients with personality disorders. Therefore, they questioned whether or not lower childhood intelligence is specific to schizophrenic disorders. Watt and Lubensky (1976) found that preschizo-phrenics achieved lower IQs than matched classmates, but differences from their own siblings were not significant. The evidence weighs strongly against intellectual decline during childhood (Lane and Albee, 1970; Pollack *et al.*, 1970; Watt and Lubensky, 1976) and against intellectual deterioration after onset (Albee *et al.*, 1963; Batman *et al.*, 1966; Hamlin and Ward, 1965). The evidence of declining overall grade patterns and progressive academic failure (Bower *et al.*, 1960; Wittman and Steinberg, 1944; Watt and Lubensky, 1976) would be consistent with either a biological or motivational explanation of dysfunction.

Heath *et al.* (1965) found that schizophrenics whose psychiatric symptoms featured withdrawal and "turning against others" had lower childhood intelligence than their siblings, but schizophrenics with "turning against self" symptoms did not differ from their siblings. These authors inferred a connection between lower childhood intelligence and a "process" form of schizophrenia from that configuration of results. On the other hand, Watt and Lubensky (1976) found that childhood intelligence was not significantly related to length of hospitalization up to 4 years after the initial hospital admission, which challenges the value of premorbid intelligence as a prognostic sign.

We must conclude from this body of evidence that childhood intelligence is, at best, a weak and unreliable index of prognosis for schizophrenic disorders. A clue for unraveling the confusing melange of findings may be found in a relatively crude study by Astrup and Noreik (1966), who followed up a large cohort of schizophrenics for several decades after their initial hospital admission. Intake psychiatrists had made subjective binary classifications of all the patients, judging whether their intelligence was average or below average. More than three decades later, independent assessments classified their long-term psychiatric outcome on a five-point scale ranging from completely normal to severe deterioration. Intelligence was completely unrelated to outcome at four of the five levels of assessment, but below-average intelligence significantly predicted extreme personality deterioration or defect states. We might infer from this result that only a very limited subset of malignant schizophrenics show evidence of defective intelligence early in life.

Premature Parental Death

The premature death of a parent is obviously a stressful experience for a child and may have serious long-range consequences for later psychological development. Barry and Bousfield (1937) found that 28% of the schizophrenics in a large sample had lost one or both parents before 12 years of age. Subsequently, Barry (1949) hypothesized that bereavement prior to 8 years of age predisposes a child to psychotic breakdown in adulthood. Wahl (1956) corroborated the high frequency of bereavement among male schizophrenic naval personnel, although the largest portion occurred between 10 and 15 years of age. Granville-Grossman (1966) reviewed 13 studies published between 1944 and 1963 and found the results equivocal, concluding that the relationship between schizophrenia and childhood bereavement had not been established.

More recent evidence has also not settled the matter. Hilgard and Newman (1963) found significant loss of mothers only among schizophrenics with onset between 20 and 39 years of age, but Oltman and Friedman (1965) emphatically denied the relationship for schizophrenia (with supporting data) and challenged Hilgard and Newman's interpretation. Gay and Tonge (1967) found parental death associated with psychogenic (especially reactive depressive) rather than endogenous disorders, and specifically *not* with schizophrenia. Dennehy (1966) reported that bereavement was related to schizophrenia, depression, alcoholism, and drug addiction. A spate of investigations (Gregory, 1965; Munro and Griffiths, 1969; Pitts *et al.*, 1965) produced negative results regarding schizophrenia, although Pitts *et al.* (1965) did report a high frequency of parental deaths among schizophrenics with onset before 40 years of age, which was consistent with Hilgard and Newman (1963).

Jacobsen and Ryder (1969) cited studies associating parental loss in childhood with a variety of pathological outcomes, including psychoneurosis, suicide, addictions, schizophrenia, depression, anxiety reactions, sociopathy, poor employment record, and failure in the Peace Corps. Rahe and Gunderson (1974) contributed to evidence indicating that parental death generally plays a significant role in the genesis of psychopathology. Watt and Nicholi (1979) presented evidence on premature parental death from three independent studies, including 185 schizophrenics, 162 depressives, 368 neurotics, and 424 other disorders. They found that 23.8% of the schizophrenics had been bereaved in childhood, as compared with 14.2% of the depressives, 13.3% of the neurotics, and 11.3% of the other disorders. Parental death was found to occur earlier among schizophrenics than other patients and, in two studies, to be most frequent among schizophrenics with predominantly paranoid symptoms. They concluded that premature death of a parent may be a contributing factor in the etiology of schizophrenia.

Robins (1966) offered data to show that broken homes lead to adult pathology only if parental discord is involved, largely reflecting the *father's* behavior problems. Among a small sample of children with schizophrenic outcome in Robins' study, 17% had lost a parent prematurely, but this did not exceed the rates for other groups. Brill and Liston (1966) concluded that, although parental divorce and separation are significant pathogenic factors, parental death has not been demonstrated to contribute to psycho-pathology, regardless of which parent is lost or the age of the child when the loss occurred. A recent review of the literature on parental bereave-ment by Osterweis *et al.* (1984) concludes that bereaved children are most at risk for subsequent *depressive* disorders, making little mention of the connection with schizophrenia, and then further qualifies that conclusion by stating that the data linking early loss and adult depression are only suggestive.

CONTEMPORARY STUDIES OF DEVELOPMENTAL PRECURSORS, PROGNOSTIC SIGNS, AND OUTCOME

Recent Investigations

Taking advantage of previous follow-back and high-risk studies for guidance in devising a repertoire of vulnerability indicators for schizo-phrenia, Hartmann *et al.* (1984) successfully distinguished schizophrenic from nonschizophrenic outcomes among the 1000 boys originally exam-ined in the classic delinquency study by Glueck and Glueck (1950). De-tailed interview data and test responses had been collected in 1940–1942 for 500 "delinquents" and 500 "nondelinquent controls" 10–17 years of age. In follow-up studies of this sample, Hartmann and his colleagues located 24 adult schizophrenics, half from the index group and half from the control group. The childhood records for those 24 were matched for IQ, ethnicity, age at interview, and original grouping (delinquent or control) with records for 48 boys with nonschizophrenic outcomes and no evidence of schizophrenic disorder among their first-degree relatives.

The literature search by the authors yielded 30 possible "markers" of vulnerability, but only the 12 psychosocial indicators (comprising 49 specific items) were employed because information about them was avail-able in the childhood records. The two outcome groups differed significantly on the "indicator total score" ($t = 3.70$, $p < 0.001$) and on the "item total score" ($t = 3.00$, $p < 0.005$) but not at all on the "global prediction score" from the Rorschach protocols. Multiple regression analysis identified the following six indicator clusters as the best predictors (in descending order of power):

1. *Lack of historicity:* poor identity, lack of ambition and goal direction
2. *Anxiety:* inconsolable baby, scared, frequent nightmares, school anxi-ety
3. *Interpersonal difficulties:* considered by parents to be undependable

and hard to reach, little or no peer group relations

4. *Inappropriate anger:* self-directed anger, inexplicable outbursts, denial of obvious anger (questionable predictor)
5. *Lack of competence:* developmental delays, poor schoolwork, poor sense of competence
6. *Permeable boundaries:* easily distracted, daydreaming, tangential thinking, poorly integrated body image

Parallel regression analysis of the 49 component items showed the best prediction for these five items (in descending order of power):

a. Poor vocational ambitions
b. Cruelty or bullying
c. No role in group
d. Anxiety on the Rorschach (questionable predictor)
e. Poor adjustment to schoolmates

The average IQ of preschizophrenics was low (89.6) compared with the sample as a whole (93.3), so prediction was enhanced by excluding the 25% of the sample with IQs <85 because that reduced the number of false positives in the control group. Presumably, low intelligence is confounded with vulnerability to schizophrenia, so raising the intelligence threshold actually "purified" the predictive power of the indicators. Family history of schizophrenia was found in 25% of the preschizophrenics, and those six boys had higher scores on the indicators. (Controls were selected to exclude such family histories.) Using 23 items, 52 of 54 subjects (96%) with IQs >85 could be correctly assigned to outcome groups. Factor analysis yielded the strongest prediction from the following cluster of indicators: historicity (identity), object constancy (family relations), social relations, incompetence, and anhedonia.

Roff and Knight (1981) conducted another excellent follow-back study that was focused on family dynamics and childhood behavioral precursors of schizophrenia. There were three points of contact with the subjects: with a Child Guidance Clinic at an average age of 10.9 years, during military service hospitalization at 21.7 years, and at VA follow-up at 43.7 years. Good outcome was associated with *externalizing* childhood symptoms, high IQ, good school achievement, and absence of asocial behavior (apathy, seclusiveness, bizarre or inappropriate behavior, flat affect, and thought disorder). Poor outcome was strongly predicted by asociality and moderately by low IQ and school achievement, but externalizing behavior was a "protective" factor and internalizing behavior (anxiety, fears, somatic complaints, dependency problems, and inferiority feelings) was a neutral predictor.

Anxious and anxiety-inducing mothers combined with passive, uninvolved fathers (Parental Pattern I) were associated with internalizing symptoms, which were neutral outcome predictors but were *not* related to asociality, which *did* predict poor outcome. Asocial preschizophrenics had passive/uninvolved or critical/hostile fathers. Low IQ and poor school achievement were associated with anxious mothering (often justifiably so). Unfavorable outcome was predicted by maternal anxiety and maternal neglect. Adult outcome was strongly predicted by severity of family disturbance, whereas intact marriages and positive maternal behavior (approval, affection, helping, acceptance, attention, and understanding) were protective factors.

Path analysis revealed that severity of family disturbance directly influenced young adult social competence adversely and indirectly influenced outcome via the mediating effects of incompetence. Loss of parent prior to 6 years of age (half through divorce and one-third through premature parental death) was marginally related to poor outcome. The combination of anxious and neglectful mothering (labeled "aversive maternal control") was correlated with internalizing childhood symptoms and yielded seven of eight unfavorable outcomes. A second pattern featuring family disorganization and maternal irresponsibility and indifference produced asocial young adults and poor outcomes. This pattern reflected breakdown in family functioning rather than subtle forms of communication deviance. The authors reasoned that the constricted, internalized family pattern is likely to be over-represented in family studies because the families are intact. On the other hand, the chaotic, disorganized pattern would be over-represented in adoption studies, because those families are *not* intact. However, families can also be support systems, hence protective factors, as shown by the favorable effects of "intact family" and "mother positive" variables.

Harder *et al.* (1981) tested the hypothesis that higher aggregate levels of objective life-events stress before a first-time psychiatric admission for schizophrenia relates to good outcome. Vaillant (1964) had found precipitating stress factors were present in 75% of fully remitted cases but only in 31% of the less-than-fully remitted group, although his findings were challenged on methodological grounds (Serban, 1975). Other studies yielded equivocal results (Wallis, 1972; Rabkin, 1980). Harder *et al.* (1981) confirmed Vaillant's findings regarding the prediction of 2-year outcome for two of three diagnostic systems employed. The implication of these results presumably is that schizophrenic disorders lacking clear precipitating causes for breakdown are intrinsically more malignant than those with intense precipitating stresses, alluding to a familiar distinction between endogenous and exogenous etiology.

Refinements in the Study of Premorbid Competence

Obviously one of the most important objectives of studying the premorbid development of schizophrenics is to isolate reliable markers for accurate prognostic evaluation so that we can predict clinical course and outcome in advance and hopefully leverage that information scientifically to gain insights about the causes and possible treatments for the disorder. The most widely replicated prognostic indicator is probably premorbid competence (Herron, 1987; Watt et al., 1979). Research in the 1980s has provided very valuable refinements in our understanding of that construct and its relationship to outcome.

Westermeyer and Harrow (1986) studied the utility of the Zigler-Phillips Social Competence Scale for predicting psychiatric outcome in schizophrenic, schizo-affective, other psychotic, and nonpsychotic disorders. Schizophrenics had less premorbid social competence and poorer psychiatric outcome than the other three diagnostic groups, and all men showed less competence and poorer outcome than all women. Among the schizophrenics, superior social competence was associated with good overall outcome, good work adjustment, and fewer psychotic symptoms at follow-up 2 years after hospital discharge, but premorbid competence did not predict rehospitalization or social adjustment. The authors emphasized that the scale predicted work adjustment better than social functioning following release from the hospital.

Stoffelmayr et al. (1983) reexamined the relationship between premorbid social functioning and outcome in schizophrenia, utilizing a sophisticated method for cumulative analysis of published data. They found that premorbid functioning, as measured by a variety of prognostic scales, accounted for more than one-third of the variance in global outcome, with a cumulative correlation of 0.62. The authors argued that their cumulative analysis powerfully states the relationship between the two variables because it encompasses (in a single analysis) studies with a wide variety of research contexts, populations, modes of measurement, and length of follow-up, hence affording optimum generalization of the study's findings.

It was logical to question whether or not premorbid competence would lose some of its prognostic utility as a result of the narrowing of the diagnostic spectrum for schizophrenia with the introduction of DSM-III. Furthermore, it has long been questioned whether or not premorbid competence (e.g., as measured by age of onset, level of education, marital status, work history, type of occupation, and intelligence) predicts subsequent outcome because it comprises a measure of *early morbid process* rather than premorbid adjustment and, hence, stands as a proxy for assessing chronicity of illness *before* the onset of the manifest psychosis that requires hospitalization (Strauss and Carpenter, 1974, 1977). Harrow and Westermeyer (1987) reported that, as might have been expected, schizophrenic patients who meet DSM-III diagnostic criteria for the disorder do indeed have poorer outcome than those who meet only the DSM-II criteria. However, substantial heterogeneity remained in their DSM-III cohort, which preserved the value of premorbid competence as a prognostic index. The authors concluded that at the present time the premorbid phase cannot be delineated with certainty from the morbid phase in schizophrenia.

One of the most dramatic developments in the recent spate of lifetime follow-up studies (reviewed below) is the discovery that a substantial proportion of chronic schizophrenics recover from the disorder, even without the benefit of medication (Fenton and McGlashan, 1987b). This has introduced a new dimension to the problem of prognostication, because almost all of the established prognostic measures have focused on acutely ill schizophrenics and relatively short-term perspectives on outcome, where premorbid functioning and established chronicity have proven to be the best predictors of outcome (Fenton and McGlashan, 1987a). Studying a group of largely chronic inpatients from an exclusive private facility who were re-evaluated an average of 15 years after discharge, McGlashan (1986a) found that among patients with well-established disorders, indices of chronicity, such as duration of psychosis and length of previous hospitalization, lost their superordinate importance as predictors. Some "postmorbid" dimensions of outcome could still be predicted by their respective premorbid counterparts (e.g., social functioning) but with diminished specificity and power. The influence of premorbid state on later functioning was attenuated because many years had elapsed between the onset of illness and outcome. Four variables were consistently predictive across many individual outcome domains and global outcome: acquisition of skills, family history of schizophrenia, depressed mood, and psychotic assaultiveness. Acquisition of skills was predictive across all follow-up periods and most predictive of social functioning, symptoms, and employment at follow-up. Psychotic assaultiveness was the single best predictor of continued institutionalization over the follow-up period. A poor composite prognostic score based on these variables virtually guaranteed poor long-term outcome, but a good prognostic score did not necessarily ensure good outcome. Despite favorable outcomes in each domain for the good prognosis patients as a group, even some of those with the best prognosis remained at risk for persistent disability. With few exceptions, patients accruing relatively little social competence and life skills by the onset of illness were virtually assured of poor long-term functioning. Fenton and McGlashan (1987a) offered the following theoretical rationale for their findings:

... long-term outcome in chronic schizophrenic patients may result from a dynamic interplay between the highest level of premorbid interests, adaptive capacities, and productivity ever achieved (acquisition of skills) and the relative "virulence" of the illness as potentially reflected by genetic loading (family history), the presence of preservation of affect in psychopathology (depressed mood), and the degree to which the illness has eroded reality testing (psychotic assaultiveness) (Fenton and McGlashan, 1987a: 278).

Let us bear in mind for further consideration in the discussion below the now-familiar distinction drawn in this rationale between putatively *psychosocial* causes (acquisition of skills) and putatively *biological* causes (genetic loading), which are presumed to account for depressed mood and the erosion of reality testing.

Saugstad (1989) offered an encyclopedic review of research literature on social class, marriage, and fertility in schizophrenia, which is especially instructive for its survey of contemporary investigations and theoretical perspectives on a wide range of topics in Western Europe. The conclusion she drew from this massive compilation unfortunately goes far beyond the evidence reviewed, but it does explain the potential relevance to premorbid functioning in schizophrenia:

> The hypothesis is presented that the etiology of schizophrenia is neither simply genetic nor environmental, but neurodevelopmental. This hypothesis is based on recent advances in neurodevelopmental biology, which have called attention to the neuronal pruning that occurs in the central nervous system at puberty (elimination of about 40 percent of the neuronal synapses). Schizophrenia is hypothesized to be a disorder particularly affecting extremely late-maturing individuals, in whom greater than optimal neuronal pruning has resulted in excessively reduced synaptic density. In contrast, manic-depressive psychosis is considered a disorder affecting very early maturers (early puberty), in which prematurely abridged neuronal pruning leads to a redundancy of neuronal synapses (Saugstad, 1989: 37).

A potentially redeeming feature of this wildly speculative rationale is that the author seems to believe that the age of puberty, especially among lower-social class people, may be influenced through social policy and that, in individual cases, therapeutic decisions may be made to reduce the psychological handicaps of late-maturing schizophrenics. This review may be read profitably for things other than the author's etiological theory.

Roff and Knight (1980) correlated childhood IQ and aggressive social behavior in their Child Guidance Clinic sample of schizophrenics with outcome ratings and marital status in middle age. Neither IQ nor lack of aggressiveness (by themselves) was significantly correlated with either outcome measure, but the combination of low IQ and lack of aggressiveness did predict both outcome variables significantly. The authors concluded that " . . . the combination of low IQ, lack of aggressiveness, poor school achievement, and social maladjustment was predictive even in the absence of high schizoid syndrome scores reflecting prepsychotic disturbance" (Roff and Knight, 1980: 132). The latter observation was obviously intended to discount the potential criticism that the observed configuration comprised attenuated prodromal signs of psychosis and was not genuinely premorbid behavior.

Keefe *et al.* (1989) reported that poor premorbid sociosexual functioning in 69 chronic schizophrenic men was associated with ventricular asymmetry, greater severity of "negative symptoms," fewer "positive symptoms," and worse current social functioning during the course of schizophrenic illness. Although the title of their study purports to associate premorbid sociosexual functioning with "long-term outcome in schizophrenia," no evidence of the latter is presented. The most interesting finding concerns the correlation between premorbid asocial behavior and severity of negative symptoms (although the correlation actually presented is only marginally significant), which the authors interpreted as follows:

> The correlation of current negative symptoms, social impairment, and overall level of current psychopathology with poor premorbid sociosexual adjustment is consistent with the notion that schizophrenic patients with the worst social outcome differ from other schizophrenic patients not as a result of social deterioration after the onset of their psychosis but because of dispositional factors.
> . . . patients who demonstrate an earlier onset of such negative symptoms as sociosexual withdrawal are more likely to demonstrate severe social withdrawal in the later stages of their illness. Hence, regardless of whether sociosexual impairment before the onset of psychosis is viewed as part of a schizophrenic individual's predisposition to the illness or as an early expression of the disorder, the data we present are consistent with the notion that severe social deterioration in the end stage of schizophrenia is a result of predisposing factors (Keefe *et al.*, 1989: 209).

The logic of that causal conclusion is utterly elusive to these reviewers. This study certainly does not definitively establish a correlation between premorbid asocialty and "severe social deterioration in the end stage of schizophrenia"; however, even if we do assume such a correlation and concede that a configuration of negative symptoms at least presages such a defect state, a large leap of faith is still required to claim that one causes the other. Nevertheless, the hypothetical connection between premorbid social incompetence and a negative symptom syndrome offers an intriguing theoretical notion to which we shall return in the discussion below.

Studies of Samples at High Risk for Schizophrenia

A valuable and relatively recent perspective on the precursors of schizophrenia has been afforded by prospective studies of children and adolescents with elevated risk for schizophrenic disorders. A comprehensive summary of this research has already been published (Watt *et al.*, 1984), so this review briefly updates the previous reports and fills in a few studies that were omitted. Most high-risk investigations have studied children of schizophrenic parents, who are known to have substantially higher-than-average risk for the disorder themselves, but Chapman and Chapman (1987) have taken the novel approach of screening large numbers of college undergraduates with a variety of scales designed to measure processes theoretically associated with schizophrenic psychosis. These include physical anhedonia, perceptual aberration, impulsive nonconformity, and magical ideation. The most promising predictor of proneness to psychosis appears to be a combined scale of perceptual aberration (distortion in the perception of one's body and other objects) and magical ideation (the tendency to accept forms of causality that are not viewed as valid in our culture). Only a few prepsychotics have thus been identified so far, and distinguishing between proneness to schizophrenia and affective psychosis has been difficult.

Nuechterlein (1986) presents a useful review of both follow-back and high-risk studies. He summarizes a number of "particularly productive" studies of information processing but correctly concludes that, at this point, the types of deficits that specifically characterize children at risk for schizophrenia are not clearly delineated. He also cites an isolated study that suggests attentional and motor abnormalities at 8–14 years of age in early cases of schizophrenic breakdown in the Israeli High-Risk Project (Mirsky, 1985) and summarizes a large number of autonomic studies, but he concludes that " . . . at this point it appears that a simple relationship between electrodermal activity and risk for schizophrenia is unlikely among children of schizophrenic patients" (Nuechterlein, 1986: 137). He draws more encouraging conclusions from studies of premorbid social development, expressed emotion, and environmental factors that may potentiate schizophrenic vulnerability, most of which are covered in this chapter.

Harvey *et al.* (1986) found some consistency in research findings about auditory distractibility as a potential marker for schizophrenia, which is generally consonant with Meehl's (1962) conceptualization of cognitive slippage as an attribute of schizotypy. Although unclear and ambiguous communication characterizes schizophrenia across various stages of the illness, word-association studies indicate that associative deficits are not related to the development of schizophrenia in predisposed individuals (however, for contradictory evidence, see Parnas *et al.*, 1982, described below). These authors conclude that no definite psychological markers of schizophrenia have yet been detected.

Similarly equivocal preliminary findings were reported from the New York High-Risk Project (Erlenmeyer-Kimling and Cornblatt, 1987) regarding measures of attention and information processing, neuromotor functioning, electrodermal processes, evoked potentials, and the association between children's psychological adjustment and the severity of their parents' disorder. However, they did find that the mean IQ of the first five high-risk children to be hospitalized was 11 points lower than the mean for the high-risk group as a whole, a result that is consistent with the follow-back literature and one worthy of further pursuit.

A plausible and more promising result focusing narrowly on thought disorder was found in the Copenhagen High-Risk Project (Parnas and Schulsinger, 1986). Children of schizophrenic mothers were evaluated at 15 years of age by a psychiatrist for various aspects of thinking, including coherence, intelligibility and speed in their train of associations, concentration, attentiveness, and so on. Independent psychiatric reassessments of the same children 10 years later, when 48% were diagnosed as having serious psychiatric disorders, yielded scores on two major factors in Wender's Thought Disorder Inventory. *Vagueness* reflected illogical, incoherent, and tangential thinking with poor transition between topics. *Richness of speech* indicated mainly excessive talkativeness bordering on neologisms. Cognitive disturbances in adolescence were significantly correlated with both factors in formal thought disorder observed in young adulthood, demonstrating continuity and gradual evolution in thought disorder from childhood to adult life.

In separate reports on the general psychological development of the children in the Copenhagen project, Parnas *et al.* (1982) and John *et al.* (1982) reported that school teachers described the preschizophrenics in the high-risk sample as having had difficulties in making friends (rejected by others), being uneasy about criticism, exhibiting difficulty in affective control by becoming easily upset, persisting in their excitement, disturbing the class by unusual behavior, and presenting disciplinary problems. Future schizophrenics were judged by their teachers to have had poor psychiatric prognoses. Borderline schizophrenics tended to be more deviant than normal subjects, but less deviant than schizophrenics. Items relating to shyness and withdrawal were not distinguishing factors in any comparison. Parents described the future schizophrenics as passive babies, showing poor concentration in play with toys and being impolite (hence disruptive). The authors concluded from these studies that defective emotional contact and formal thought disorder are important precursive signs of schizophrenia.

In a more recent general progress report, Mednick *et al.* (1987) added three more factors that they consider to be associated with increased risk for schizophrenic breakdown: family history of schizophrenia, unstable parenting and public institutional care, and perinatal trauma (referring mainly to pregnancy and birth complications).

Sameroff *et al.* (1987) found that cognitive, psychomotor, social, and emotional development of infants born to neurotic depressed mothers was worse than in the offspring of schizophrenic or personality-disordered mothers. Both social status and chronicity of maternal illness seemed to exert more powerful unfavorable influence on infant development than did maternal schizophrenia.

A series of reports from the NIMH–Israeli High-Risk Study, featured in the *Schizophrenia Bulletin* (e.g., Mirsky *et al.*, 1985), elicited observations and criticisms from three authors. Garmezy (1985) noted that the authors *claimed* evidence of "underlying deficits in attention, motor function and perceptual integration" in some of the offspring of schizophrenic parents, but the evidence was only suggestive and based on very small samples. Kety (1985) brought some of the findings to bear on the diathesis-stress model of schizophrenia, observing nine schizophrenia spectrum disorders among the 46 index subjects and none among the 44 controls, but no outcome differences between Kibbutz-reared and town-reared index subjects, both of which are compatible with a significant genetic contribution to causing schizophrenia. On the other hand, when all diagnosed mental illness was considered, the prevalence of disorder was greater in the index than in the control groups but also greater in Kibbutz-reared than in family-reared subjects, indicating both genetic and environmental influences. Breznitz (1985) pursued a similar observation, namely, that Kibbutz versus city differences in prevalence of disorder increased with age, suggesting "an interaction between the developmental sequence from premorbid to morbid states and some environmental factors associated with the Kibbutz environment" (Breznitz, 1985: 358). Hence, a significant proportion of the variance in the transition from being at risk to actually manifesting clinical symptoms seems to be controlled by environmental factors. Referring to the classical distinction between instrumental and expressive roles in the family (Parsons and Bales, 1955), Breznitz inferred that a schizophrenic parent may be able to handle the instrumental role in relation to a child or adolescent because relatively simple repetitive chores may shield the relationship from drifting into more disturbing expressive interchanges. In contrast, in the Kibbutz, many instrumental responsibilities are transferred to professional caretakers, leaving more "love time" for schizophrenic parents and, hence, more opportunity for deleterious impact on the child's development.

Weintraub's (1987) update on the Stony Brook High-Risk Project reported considerable deviance in family functioning, expressed in conflict, marital discord, and parenting skills (characteristic of the families with an ill parent), which was related to child adjustment. Children of schizophrenic parents showed many cognitive, attentional, and social impairments, although in most respects they were not easily distinguished from children of affectively disordered parents. At follow-up after 18 years of age, 23% of the offspring of schizophrenic parents exhibited DSM-III diagnoses, in contrast to 15% in the unipolar group, 20% in the bipolar group, and 10% of the normal controls.

In an interim progress report on the social, emotional, and intellectual development of the adolescent subjects in the New York High-Risk Project, Watt et al. (1982) reported that the offspring of schizophrenic parents showed greater interpersonal disharmony, less scholastic motivation, more emotional instability, and lower intelligence than the normal control subjects, but the group difference in introversion was not significant. Two of the four children with *two* schizophrenic parents had extremely low teacher ratings for scholastic motivation, harmony, emotional stability, and intelligence, and a third was rated extremely low on emotional stability, but none of them was extremely introverted. The absence of introverted behavior among the children of schizophrenic parents was interpreted to indicate that introversion—when it is observed—may best be construed not as a static typology of preschizophrenic character but as a dynamic phase in a process of coping and retreat that precedes schizophrenic breakdown, sometimes by many years.

Goldstein (1987a) offered the following concise summary of the interim reports from most of these high-risk projects:

> High-risk studies, most of which study offspring of a schizophrenic parent, suggest that signs of vulnerability to the disorder may emerge in early to middle childhood in neuromotor integration, attentional and information-processing abilities, and deviant social behavior. It is still not clear that these markers are specific to the subsequent development of schizophrenia. (Goldstein, 1987a: 157).

Role of Family Interaction in Precipitating Schizophrenic Breakdown

The potential of family relationships to contribute to schizophrenic disorder has been appreciated for most of this century (Meyer, 1910; Sullivan, 1931; Bateson et al., 1956). However, most of the empirical research designed to test theoretical formulations along these lines proved to be quite discouraging (Mishler and Waxler, 1968) until a series of investigations inspired by George Brown and his colleagues at the Maudsley Hospital in London (Brown *et al.*, 1962, 1972) began to draw attention convincingly to the concept of "expressed emotion." Both the theory and many of the intervening research findings about expressed emotion were explained comprehensively in a recent volume (Leff and Vaughn, 1985), so our discussion here will be limited to a succinct overview.

Expressed emotion refers to both the content and the expressive style of communications among family members. The family of a psychiatric patient is characterized as high in expressed emotion (high EE) if its members express criticisms, annoyance, dissatisfaction, hostility, or emotional overinvolvement toward the patient, especially if those attitudes are expressed emphatically. Lack of such rejecting or enmeshed attitudes earns a classification of low expressed emotion (low EE) for the family. An impressive array of studies in a variety of settings have demonstrated that high EE among family members predicts relapse within a year or two after discharge from the hospital (Brown *et al.*, 1972; Vaughn and Leff, 1976; Vaughn *et al.*, 1984). These findings have even been replicated among low-income, relatively unacculturated Mexican–American households, where many experts expect relatives to convey " . . . concerned but non-judgmental attitudes toward schizophrenic family members, with modest expectations for independent achievement, less stigma for incompetence, and consequently less anxiety, less decrement in self-esteem, and better outcome for those afflicted" (Karno *et al.*, 1987: 143). In the Karno *et al.* (1987) study, expressed emotion was more strongly related to relapse than was compliance with medications. By contrast, expressions of warmth and personal endorsement in the family's response to the illness are believed to protect against relapse in some families (Leff and Vaughn, 1985).

A survey of studies in this area found a 15% relapse rate associated with low EE in the family, compared with rates of 40–50% associated with high EE (Mintz *et al.*, 1987). Similar results have been obtained patients with depression, bipolar disorders, and obesity. Treatment programs directed at improving communication in the family do reduce relapse rates (Koenigsberg and Handley, 1986). Complex findings suggest that maintenance doses of neuroleptic drugs may lose their prophylactic effect for patients who return to high-EE family settings if exposed to powerfully stressful life events (Leff and Vaughn, 1981). Koenigsberg and Handley (1986) concluded that expressed emotion definitely predicts schizophrenic relapse, and successful interventions to reduce EE and reduce contact with high-EE relatives imply a causal role in precipitating relapse (e.g., via increased physiological arousal in the patients), but the relationship to negative symptoms (asociality, anhedonia, apathy, alogia, and inattentiveness)—which are often the targets of family criticism—has not yet been established.

Microanalytic studies of communication deviance (CD) and affective style have yielded convergent results. Lewis *et al.* (1981) examined videotaped interactions between parents and their disturbed, nonpsychotic adolescent children. Parents classified as high in CD failed to focus communication on the topic under discussion or share their feelings about those topics. They also were rigid and evasive in their nonverbal communications of affect toward the child. Other studies have suggested that a combination of such distortions in communication and relationship style are associated with increased risk for schizophrenia spectrum disorders later in life, although the particular form of the adolescent behavioral problem is not (Doane *et al.*, 1981; Goldstein, 1987b).

Not all investigations have confirmed the principal findings in this area. Parker *et al.* (1988) found that relapse was *not* predicted by high EE and challenged the causal proposition linking high EE with relapse. They suggested instead that a poor course of illness may elicit high EE in relatives, particularly in one-parent households, and account for the relapse as well, thus explaining the link between the two effects. Spiegel and Wissler (1986) actually found high expressiveness in families to be *negatively* related to relapse potential. They concluded with the following plausible analysis and recommendations:

> The mere expression of emotion may have either positive or negative consequences, depending on the type of emotion expressed. Therefore, merely advising patients to avoid their families or advising families to diminish their dialogue about emotional topics would not, on the basis of these data, be likely to diminish rehospitalization. It would seem more productive to counsel the family to find ways to express feeling openly while avoiding conflict, criticism, and overinvolvement. Furthermore, these findings may serve as an empirical base for selecting families with patients at high risk for decompensation; those who are low in shared expression of problems, cohesion, and recreational activities and high in conflict and independence. Such families and their patient members may especially benefit from appropriate intervention (Spiegel and Wissler, 1986: 60).

Goldstein (1987a) considers that the findings on expressed emotion have been replicated more often than not, although the origins of high-EE attitudes are not yet precisely understood. Family-based intervention programs, when combined with regular antipsychotic drug treatment, appear to reduce the risk for relapse in the short term, at least partly by reducing the negative affective climate in the family.

Lurking in the background of this fertile research domain is a critical, often unspoken question: If family relationships contribute to schizophrenic relapse, can they also be a primary cause of the disorder in the first place? Two recent studies suggest an affirmative reply. Burman *et al.* (1987) examined family relationships prior to the onset of psychopathology in the Copenhagen High-Risk Study. The family relationships of high-risk off-spring who later developed schizophrenia were perceived to be signifi-cantly less satisfactory than the family relationships of high-risk offspring later diagnosed as having schizotypal personality disorders or no mental illness. Their theoretical conclusion from these results was that both schiz-ophrenic and schizotypal disorders share a similar genetic predisposition for psychosis, and environmental factors (such as family relations) deter-mine whether or not the full schizophrenic syndrome develops.

Similar results were reported by Tienari *et al.* (1987). A nationwide Finnish sample of offspring of schizophrenic mothers given up for adop-tion was compared blindly with matched controls, i.e., adoptees born to nonschizophrenic biological parents. Among the 10 adoptees who sub-sequently became psychotic, 8 were offspring of schizophrenic mothers and 2 were control offspring (confirming the familiar genetic link). How-ever, no seriously disturbed offspring was found in a healthy or mildly disturbed adoptive family and nearly all the psychotic or seriously dis-turbed offspring were reared in disturbed adoptive families. The authors concluded that in genetically vulnerable children, distortions in family relations may potentiate their disposition to schizophrenia or, alterna-tively, a healthy family environment may be a protective factor that sup-presses their predisposition to schizophrenia. It must be conceded, how-ever, that correlational findings of this sort can not rule out the alternative inference that subtle precursive features of schizophrenic disorder are the primary cause of the abnormalities in family relations.

Changing Views on Clinical Outcome in an "Incurable, Deteriorating Disease"

Kraepelin (1919) tried to do us a favor by keeping the prognostic tale for schizophrenia as simple as possible, once it could be assured that the "correct" diagnosis had been made. Psychopathologists faithful to the Kraepelinian perspective would *assume* a chronic course of illness with residual symptoms and lasting deficits in work capacity, social relations, and self-care, so the prognostic challenge really boiled down to accurately diagnosing "true" schizophrenics, based on their social and family histo-ries and presenting clinical symptoms. Bleuler (1911) muddied the waters by suggesting that prediction of outcome might require at least a binary decision and that florid clinical symptoms were not an entirely dependable basis for making that decision. Now the most recent follow-up research suggests that heterogeneity of outcome in rigorously diagnosed schizophrenics is the rule, while progressive deterioration is the exception (McGlashan, 1986a, 1988; Harding *et al.*, 1987).

Harding *et al.* (1987) pointed out that the samples studied by Kraepelin and Bleuler were probably biased by selective attrition and, therefore, not representative of the complete range of possible outcomes for the disorder. They cited an instructive analysis by Cohen and Cohen (1984) on the "clinician's illusion." For example, the 2% of patients with the longest duration of illness can be found in a caseload 64 times more often than the 40% of the patients with the shortest duration of illness. (This is true for other disorders as well.) Clinicians also tend to think of prognosis in binary fashion (good or bad) with no intermediate ground. These authors pointed out the conceptual complexities that flow from recognizing the full range of heterogeneity in outcome during recent years:

> In understanding the more complex picture of chronicity, it has been difficult to separate the residual effects of the disorder, such as negative symptoms, the effects of institutionalization, socialization into the patient role, lack of rehabilitation, reduced economic opportunities, lowered social status, medication, lack of staff expectations of improvement, self-fulfilling prophecies, and loss of hope. The possibility also exists that negative symptoms and other so-called residual effects of schizophrenia may be a recrudescence of a person's premorbid personality after the episode of illness (Harding *et al.*, 1987: 482).

Finally, they concluded that only premorbid personality seems to have a consistently positive relationship with outcome across studies.

Ogawa *et al.* (1987) reported the most recent long-term follow-up results, ranging from 21 to 27 years after discharge. Among the index schizophrenics, 47% were fully self-supporting, compared with 22% intermediate outcomes and 31% still hospitalized. Clinically, they rated 31% recovered, 46% improved, and 23% unimproved. Among self-supporting patients, 96% were living in their own homes and 82% were married, although 41% were still under psychiatric care. They cited four studies between 1972 and 1987 that showed collectively 20–32% recovered versus 14–24% severely chronic, far short of Kraepelin's (1919) prescribed outcome rates. The authors attributed the increase in self-supporting cases to improved aftercare and neuroleptics, *not* to increase in complete recoveries.

Table 8.1 summarizes the results from six very long-term follow-up investigations reported by Harding *et al.* (1987) and Ogawa *et al.* (1987). The composite figures at the bottom of the table combine the results from the six separate studies, using weighted averages. They provide crude estimates of the aggregate proportions of schizophrenics found in each of three outcome categories, as measured several decades after the onset of the disorder. Contrary to both popular belief and professional dogma,

TABLE 8.1   Summary of Long-Term Outcome in Six International Studies of Schizophrenia

Researchers	Location	n	Mean years	Follow-up		
				% Recovered	% Improved	% Unimproved
Bleuler, M., 1972	Zurich, Switzerland	208	23	23	43	34
Huber et al., 1975	Bonn, West Germany	502	22	26	31	43
Ciompi and Müller, 1976	Lausanne, Switzerland	289	37	29	24	47
Tsuang et al., 1979	Iowa City, IA, United States	186	35	20	26	54
Harding et al., 1986	Waterbury, VT, United States	118	32	34	34	32
Ogawa et al., 1987	Gunma, Japan	130	24	31	46	23
Composite results		1433	28	27	32	41

almost three of every five schizophrenics either recover or improve significantly if they are followed at least two decades from the onset of their disorder.

Further refinements in long-term prognostication have been suggested by the Chestnut Lodge Follow-Up Study (McGlashan, 1986b). Outcome in the first decade after discharge was best predicted by premorbid competence, referring mainly to acquired skills, investment in and pursuit of vocational interests, and hobbies before illness. In predicting medium-range outcome up to two decades after discharge, the quality of family relations took on the greatest importance, reflecting both the family's role prior to the illness and its continuing contribution to the patient's support network. Genetic predisposition, as reflected in family history of schizophrenia, was the most salient predictor of longer-term outcome of three decades or longer. Signs and symptoms of manifest illness at or before index admission (including positive as well as negative symptoms) strongly predicted both medium- and longer-term outcomes, but indices of chronicity prior to or during the index admission were not predictive for any of the three outcome intervals, presumably because the range of chronicity was severely restricted by the sampling procedures employed. (All of the patients were chosen because of the extreme persistence in their course of illness.

The Prognostic Value of Negative Symptoms

A thorough discussion of the relation of negative schizophrenic symptoms to outcome would reach beyond the scope of this chapter because of its conceptual substance—they occur *during* and *after* the onset of psychosis—and because of the accelerated volume of research done in that area in the last decade. However, the reader interested in the precursors of malignant schizophrenia (and what mental health specialist is not?) will find profitable instruction in a historical and contemporary overview of the subject by Zubin (1985). He begins with elegantly heuristic definitions:

> Positive symptoms are behaviors that schizophrenic patients engage in, but normals do not. Negative symptoms, when inverted to their opposites (e.g., 'withdrawal' to 'sociability'), are behaviors which normals engage in but schizophrenic patients do not, or only in diminished fashion (Zubin, 1985: 462).

Zubin then proceeds to summarize many of the recent research findings relating these two clusters of symptoms to premorbid development, course of illness, response to treatment, and clinical outcome. The heart of his analysis focuses on the implications of the positive/negative distinction for clinical pathology, classification, etiological theory, and treatment. He concludes by questioning provocatively whether or not negative symptoms are indigenous to schizophrenic disorder. The ultimate answer to that profound question may very well presuppose advanced solutions to many of the enigmas that remain so elusive today.

In many respects, this important symptomatic distinction comprises in highly condensed form a transposition of the most fundamental theoretical issues that have been raised throughout this chapter about premorbid development in schizophrenia: issues relating to temperament, cognitive functioning, behavioral continuity, symptomatic permanence, biological causes, environmental influences, responsiveness to treatment, and—most importantly—the functional relation to outcome. We might speculate that at some future time the definitive review of premorbid development in schizophrenia may redefine the parameters of illness in order to expand the compass of antecedents that help us to "predict and control" this mysterious illness.

Let us caution against a seductive trend that is already visible in the recent plethora of research on negative symptoms, as well as in the vast literature on premorbid development we have just reviewed: the tendency to exclusively "biologize" the causes and the effects of factors that appear to have prognostic power. As a counterbalance to that temptation, we would endorse the sensitive analysis of Strauss *et al.* (1989), which proposes seven potential causes of negative symptoms that are primarily social and psychological: anxiety about relapse into positive symptoms, loss of hope and self-esteem, fear of impulsive or bizarre behavior, obstacles to new identity as a nonpatient, guilt for past dysfunction, threat of stressful social situations, and apprehension about being rendered helpless by the disorder. The authors also cite three potentially powerful environmental contributors to negative symptoms: institutionalization, the social benefit system, and the social stigmatization of mental illness.

Psychosocial causation can be a two-way street. Strauss *et al.* (1989) offer a plausible explanation of how negative symptoms can influence the course of schizophrenic illness:

> One possibility is that negative symptoms contribute to poor prognosis by cutting the person off from potentially helpful environmental resources. Although negative symptoms may help patients avoid or cope with certain aspects of their life situation, these symptoms may also generate positive feedback mechanisms that maintain or exacerbate the disorder with its dysfunction (Strauss et al., 1985). There is evidence, for example, that in several mental disorders work and social relationships may prevent decompensation or help people improve (Brown & Harris, 1978; Henderson, 1981; Breier & Strauss, 1984; Strauss, Loevsky, Glazer, & Leaf, 1981). Negative symptoms usually undermine functioning in these life contexts. Patients who are too withdrawn to work, who are too apathetic and without affect to form social ties, cut themselves off from the very sources that could provide motivation, structure, hope, material assistance, and advice. Furthermore, vocational rehabilitation programs often systematically exclude persons with low motivation. Even the treatment system may give up on the patient with negative symptoms, making fewer resources available (Strauss *et al.*, 1989: 131).

These authors conclude that negative symptoms are powerful factors, in part, because the stigma is great, treatment and prognostic recommendations are so discouraging, and the accumulation of demoralizing experiences (plus social and cognitive dysfunction) all conspire to frustrate continued engagement, involvement, and hope. Hence, potential biological correlates of negative symptoms only address *part* of the issue; social and psychological ramifications are also critical. Biologically oriented investigators need to recognize that interactional models need not *necessarily* diminish either the salience or the primacy of genetic and/or constitutional factors in explaining schizophrenic pathology, etiology, prognosis, or treatment. The same argument could be made with equal force regarding most of the social and cognitive and behavioral precursors that have been featured in this chapter.

CONCLUSIONS

A good place to begin and to end any discussion of schizophrenic disorders is to acknowledge candidly how little we know definitively about their causes, how they evolve, how to treat them, or how they will turn out. Such ignorance spawns more rather than less investigative efforts and the history of theory in this area is filled with promising myths, some truths, and much hypothetical conjecture awaiting disproof. Little more than a century ago, passionate dissertations were delivered on the conviction that schizophrenics are possessed by evil spirits and can only be cured through exorcism. Most lay people nowadays regard that explanation as preposterous. This chapter began with an indictment of regression theories, which commanded many adherents and much respect half a century ago. These were offered to explain the nature of intellectual disorder in schizophrenia, but they have given way to a more modern perspective, as explained by White and Watt (1981):

> In past years much attention was given to the concept of possible regression in schizophrenic thinking because of features that are reminiscent of children's thinking: simplicity, concreteness, overgeneralization, stimulus-boundness, distractibility, weak governance by principles of relevance. The general consensus now is that regression is neither an accurate description nor a good metaphor for schizophrenic thought (Brown, 1973). More significant is the clue provided by the weakness of sustained effort and attention (Oltmanns & Neale, 1978), as if schizophrenics could not regularly summon the mental energy necessary for the organization of thought of which they are still capable. Frankl (1955) has called attention to a very general characteristic of schizophrenic experience that he calls the 'passivizing of the psychic functions.' The patients feel helpless, observed, photographed, influenced, the passive object of things happening around them. They complain that the world has become shifting and kaleidoscopic; this perhaps signifies a kind of perceptual passivity in which all stimuli have a claim on attention and nothing an be excluded. They perform poorly on complex learning tasks with many alternatives because they cannot maintain the learner's active role of selecting the relevant and excluding the irrelevant. They fail in sustained abstract thinking because they do not muster the necessary degree of active control over intellectual processes. The passivizing of thought may be the most telling description of the change that characterizes schizophrenic mental operations. It is this that a biochemical or psychodynamic hypothesis must explain (White and Watt, 1981: 494–495).

If "passivizing" is a major key to the pathology in schizophrenic thinking, then a great deal of the follow-back literature is quite relevant for tracing its developmental precursors. The critical theoretical shift requires some distancing from our natural fixation on purely cognitive and neuroanatomical aberrations and new emphasis on the motivational aspects of schizophrenic thought disorder. Once past that conceptual hurdle, it is easy to see the relevance of the accumulation of studies of premorbid development.

We see in this example an illustration of the process of theoretical refinement that has evolved painstakingly over many decades of research. A similar illustration was cited in reviewing the early enthusiasm for the *schizoid* temperament as the cardinal pattern of premorbid personality development. That research was based predominantly on child guidance clinic samples of preschizophrenics, and effectively postponed for many years a full appreciation of the prevalence of the *stormy* premorbid pattern characterized by explosive, antisocial, or unpredictable behavior (Arieti, 1975). Perhaps some of the fixation on introversion can be explained by the popular belief in its characterological continuity or permanence, which complements the preconception of immutability in schizophrenia. More recent characterizations have emphasized complex discontinuities and delays or irregularities in character development, as contrasted with the full developmental arrest implied in most conceptions of schizoid character or the abrupt reversal in development that was clearly connoted by the regression theories.

The urgent yearning to find dependable continuities in development probably also accounts for the stubborn search to find extreme childhood defects in intelligence among preschizophrenics and for various correlates that have commanded much recent attention: abnormalities in perception, thinking, and attention deployment. Related to this is the panorama of fishing expeditions directed toward finding organic dysfunctions, variously referred to as neurointegrative defects, pandevelopmental retardation, neurological soft signs, motor abnormalities, electrodermal aberrations, and pregnancy and birth complications. Our quarrel here is not with the very justifiable search for genetic and constitutional bases of the disorder, which almost certainly will prove to be fruitful eventually, but with the inclination to oversimplify the accounts for whatever fish are ultimately captured in the nets. From our reading of the longitudinal research literature on schizophrenia, complex models for subtle effects, as illustrated by the dopamine hypothesis (Snyder, 1974), offer more promise to fit the data than do gross anatomical formulations, [e.g., about ventricular enlargement (Andreasen, 1987)].

A similar caveat is in order regarding oversimplification of psychosocial formulations as well, especially those that expect a high degree of specificity to schizophrenia, because the evidence weighs heavily in favor of a blurring across diagnostic lines in the signs, symptoms, causes, course, and outcome of disorder.

THE MOST PROMISING LEADS FOR
FURTHER RESEARCH ON PREMORBID DEVELOPMENT

Despite our healthy skepticism and impatience about the deficiencies in our knowledge, we must guard against jettisoning all the theoretical babies with the bath water. The box score that follows emphasizes heavily psychological and social factors in premorbid development because the published research literature is heavily tilted in that direction. It represents our distillation of the consensus of opinion about the most promising issues to pursue in future longitudinal research. They are purposely formulated in the most general language in order to be maximally inclusive.

1. Difficulties in developing social and work skills, acquiring mastery and competence to be self-reliant.

2. Emotional immaturity, especially in regard to interpersonal transactions with intimate friends and family, perhaps dating all the way back to early infancy.

3. Demoralization and lack of motivation or aspiration, especially in behavior and achievement at school.

4. Distortions in family relations, particularly in the rapport with parents and in disruptions of family structure.

5. Dyscontrol over anger and its expression.

6. Apathy, emotional blunting, or extreme seclusiveness at any period in the life cycle, especially if it is persistent.

7. Interference in the development of personal identity, confidence, and self-esteem.

8. Family history of schizophrenic disorder.

9. Subtle limitations in intelligence, judgment, perception, and reasoning.

10. Stressful life events.

11. Basic neurophysiological factors that influence thinking, emotion, and behavior.

Finally, let us lay to rest the most influential myth of all: All schizophrenic disorders are incurable diseases that follow an inexorable course of progressive deterioration. Most of them are not. If we cleanse our minds of long-standing prejudices and avoid boxing schizophrenic people in warehouses, most of them recover at least partially, even without our help.

REFERENCES

Albee, G. W., Lane, E. A., Corcoran, C., and Wernecke, A. (1963). Childhood and intercurrent intellectual performance of adult schizophrenics. *Journal of Consulting Psychology, 27,* 364–366.

Albee, G. W., Lane, E. A., and Reuter, J. (1964). Childhood intelligence of future schizophrenics and neighborhood peers. *Journal of Psychology, 58,* 141–144.

Andreasen, N. C. (1987). The diagnosis of schizophrenia. *Schizophrenia Bulletin, 13,* 9–22.

Arieti, S. (1975). *Interpretation of schizophrenia.* New York: Basic Books.

Astrup, C., and Noreik, K. (1966). *Functional psychoses.* Springfield, IL: Charles C Thomas.

Barry, H. (1949). Significance of maternal bereavement before age eight in psychiatric patients. *Archives of Neurology and Psychiatry, 62,* 630–637.

Barry, H., and Bousfield, W. (1937). Incidence of orphanhood among 1500 psychotic patients. *Journal of Genetic Psychology, 50,* 198–202.

Barthell, C., and Holmes, D. (1968). High school yearbooks: A nonreactive measure of social isolation in graduates who later became schizophrenic. *Journal of Abnormal Psychology, 73,* 313–316.

Bateson, G., Jackson, D. D., Haley, J., and Weakland, J. (1956). Toward a theory of schizophrenia. *Behavioral Science, 1,* 251–264.

Batman, R., Albee, G. W., and Lane, E. A. (1966). Intelligence test performance of chronic and recovered schizophrenics. *Proceedings of the 74th Annual Convention of the American Psychological Association.* Washington, DC: American Psychological Association. [Summary.]

Bellak, L., and Purcell, B. (1946). The pre-psychotic personality in dementia praecox. *Psychiatric Quarterly, 20,* 627–637.

Benjamin, T. B., and Watt, N. F. (1969). Psychopathology and semantic interpretation of ambiguous words. *Journal of Abnormal Psychology, 74,* 706–714.

Birren, J. (1944). Psychological examination of children who later became psychotic. *Journal of Abnormal and Social Psychology, 39,* 84–95.

Bleuler, E. (1911). *Dementia praecox or the group of schizophrenics* (J. Zinkin, trans.). New York: International Universities Press. [Reprinted in 1950.]

Bower, E. M., Schellhammer, T. A., Daily, J. A., and Bower, M. (1960). High school students who later became schizophrenic. *Bulletin of the California State Department of Education, 29,* 1–157.

Bowman, K. (1934). A study of the prepsychotic personality in certain psychoses. *American Journal of Orthopsychiatry, 4,* 473–498.

Breier, A., and Strauss, J. S. (1984). Social relationships in the recovery from psychotic disorder. *American Journal of Psychiatry, 141,* 949–955.

Breznitz, S. (1985). Chores as a buffer against risky interaction. *Schizophrenia Bulletin, 11,* 357–360.

Brill, N., and Liston, E. (1966). Parental loss in adults with emotional disorders. *Archives of General Psychiatry, 14,* 307–314.

Brown, R. (1958). *Words and things.* New York: Free Press.

Brown, R. (1973). Schizophrenia, language, and reality. *American Psychologist, 28,* 395–403.

Brown, G. W., Birley, J. L. T., and Wing, J. K. (1972). Influence of family life on the course of schizophrenic disorders: A replication. *British Journal of Psychiatry, 121,* 241–258.

Brown, G. W., and Harris, T. (1978). *Social origins of depression.* New York: Free Press.

Brown, G. W., Monck, E. M., Carstairs, G. M., and Wing, J. K. (1962). Influence of family life on the course of schizophrenic illness. *British Journal of Preventive and Social Medicine, 16,* 55–68.

Burman, B., Mednick, S. A., Machon, R. A., Parnas, J., and Schulsinger, F. (1987). Children at high risk for schizophrenia: Parent and offspring perceptions of family relationships. *Journal of Abnormal Psychology, 96,* 364–366.

Chapman, L. J., and Chapman, J. P. (1987). The search for symptoms predictive of schizophrenia. *Schizophrenia Bulletin, 13,* 497–503.

Cohen, P., and Cohen, J. (1984). The clinician's illusion. *Archives of General Psychiatry, 41,* 1178–1183.

Dennehy, C. (1966). Childhood bereavement in psychiatric illness. *British Journal of Psychiatry, 112,* 1049–1069.

Doane, J., West, K., Goldstein, M. J., and Rodnick, E. (1981). Parental communication deviance and affective style as predictors of subsequent schizophrenia spectrum disorders in vulnerable adolescents. *Archives of General Psychiatry, 38,* 679–685.

Erlenmeyer-Kimling, L., and Cornblatt, B. (1987). The New York High-Risk Project: A follow-up report. *Schizophrenia Bulletin, 13,* 452–461.

Fenton, W. S., and McGlashan, T. H. (1987a). Prognostic scale for chronic schizophrenia. *Schizophrenia Bulletin, 13,* 277–286.

Fenton, W. S., and McGlashan, T. H. (1987b). Sustained remission in drug-free schizophrenic patients. *American Journal of Psychiatry, 144,* 1306–1309.

Frankl, V. E. (1955). *The doctor and the soul.* New York: Alfred A. Knopf.

Frazee, H. (1953). Children who later became schizophrenic. *Smith College Studies in Social Work, 23,* 125–249.

Freud, S. (1917). Mourning and melancholia. In *Collected papers* (Vol. 4). London: Hogarth Press and the Institute of Psychoanalysis. [Reprinted in 1950.]

Gardner, G. (1967). The relationship between childhood neurotic symptomatology and later schizophrenia in males and females. *Journal of Nervous and Mental Disease, 144,* 97–100.

Garmezy, N. (1970). Process and reactive schizophrenia: Some conceptions and issues. *Schizophrenia Bulletin, 2,* 30–74.

Garmezy, N. (1985). The NIMH–Israeli High-Risk Study: Commendation, comments, and cautions. *Schizophrenia Bulletin, 11,* 349–353.

Gay, M., and Tonge, W. (1967). The late effects of loss of parents in childhood. *British Journal of Psychiatry, 113,* 753–759.

Gershon, E., Matthyse, S., Breakefield, X. O., and Ciaranello, R. D. (Eds.). (1981). *Genetic research strategies in psychobiology and psychiatry.* Pacific Grove, CA: Boxwood Press.

Glueck, S., and Glueck, E. (1950). *Unraveling juvenile delinquency.* New York: Commonwealth Fund.

Goldstein, K. (1948). *Language and language disturbances: Aphasic symptom complexes and their significance for medicine and theory of language.* New York: Grune & Stratton.

Goldstein, M. J. (1987a). Psychosocial issues. *Schizophrenia Bulletin, 13,* 157–171.

Goldstein, M. J. (1987b). The UCLA High-Risk Project. *Schizophrenia Bulletin, 13,* 505–514.

Gottesman, I. I., and Shields, J. (1982). *Schizophrenia: The epigenetic puzzle.* New York: Cambridge University Press.

Granville-Grossman, K. (1966). Early bereavement and schizophrenia. *British Journal of Psychiatry, 112,* 1027–1034.

Gregory, I. (1965). Anterospective data following childhood loss of a parent. *Archives of General Psychiatry, 13,* 99–120.

Hamlin, R. M., and Ward, W. D. (1965). Aging, hospitalization, and schizophrenic intelligence. *Proceedings of the 73rd Annual Convention of the American Psychological Association.* Washington, DC: American Psychological Association. [Summary.]

Harder, D. W., Gift, T. E., Strauss, J. S., Ritzler, B. A., and Kokes, R. F. (1981). Life events and two-year outcome in schizophrenia. *Journal of Consulting and Clinical Psychology, 49,* 619–626.

Harding, C. M., Zubin, J., and Strauss, J. S. (1987). Chronicity in schizophrenia: Fact, partial fact, or artifact? *Hospital and Community Psychiatry, 38,* 477–486.

Harrow, M., and Westermeyer, J. F. (1987). Process-reactive dimension and outcome for narrow concepts of schizophrenia. *Schizophrenia Bulletin, 13,* 361–367.

Hartmann, E., Milofsky, E., Vaillant, G., Oldfield, M., Falke, R., and Ducey, C. (1984). Vulnerability to schizophrenia: Prediction of adult schizophrenia using childhood information. *Archives of General Psychiatry, 41,* 1050–1056.

Harvey, P. D., Walker, E., and Wielgus, M. S. (1986). Psychological markers of vulnerability to schizophrenia: Research and future directions. In B. A. Maher and W. B. Maher (Eds.), *Progress in experimental personality research* (pp. 231–267). New York: Academic Press.

Heath, E. B., Albee, G. W., and Lane, E. A. (1965). Predisorder intelligence of process and reactive schizophrenics and their siblings. *Proceedings of the 73rd Annual Convention of the American Psychological Association.* Washington, DC: American Psychological Association. [Summary.]

Henderson, S. (1981). Social relationships, adversity, and neurosis: An anaysis of prospective observations. *British Journal of Psychiatry, 138,* 391–398.

Herron, W. G. (1987). At issue: Evaluating the process-reactive dimension. *Schizophrenia Bulletin, 13,* 357–359.

Hilgard, J., and Newman, M. (1963). Parental loss by death in childhood as an aetiological factor among schizophrenic and alcoholic patients compared with a non-patient community sample. *Journal of Nervous and Mental Disease, 137,* 14–28.

Jacobsen, G., and Ryder, R. (1969). Parental loss and some characteristics of the early marriage relationship. *American Journal of Orthopsychiatry, 39,* 779–787.

John, R. S. Mednick, S. A., and Schulsinger, F. (1982). Teacher reports as a predictor of schizophrenia and borderline schizophrenia: A Bayesian decision analysis. *Journal of Abnormal Psychology, 91,* 399–413.

Karno, M., Jenkins, J. H., de la Selva, A., Santana, F., Telles, C., Lopez, S., and Mintz, J. (1987). Expressed emotion and schizophrenic outcome among Mexican–American families. *Journal of Nervous and Mental Disease, 175,* 143–151.

Kasanin, J., and Veo, L. (1932). A study of the school adjustments of children who later in life became psychotic. *American Journal of Orthopsychiatry, 2,* 212–227.

Keefe, R. S. E., Mohs, R. C., Losonczy, M. F., Davidson, M., Silverman, J. M., Horvath, R. B., and Davis, K. L. (1989). Premorbid sociosexual functioning and long-term outcome in schizophrenia. *American Journal of Psychiatry, 146,* 206–211.

Kety, S. S. (1985). Comments on the NIMH–Israeli High-Risk Study. *Schizophrenia Bulletin, 11,* 354–356.

Klorman, R., and Chapman, L. J. (1969). Regression in schizophrenic thought disorder. *Journal of Abnormal Psychology, 74,* 199–204.

Koenigsberg, H. W., and Handley, R. (1986). Expressed emotion: From predictive index to clinical construct. *American Journal of Psychiatry, 143,* 1361–1373.

Kraepelin, E. (1919). *Dementia praecox and paraphrenia* (R. M. Barclay, trans.). New York: Robert E. Krieger. [Reprinted with an historical introduction in 1971.]

Laing, R. D., and Esterson, A. (1971). *Sanity, madness and the family* (2nd ed.). New York: Basic Books.

Lane, E. A., and Albee, G. W. (1965). Childhood intellectual differences between schizophrenic adults and their siblings. *American Journal of Orthopsychiatry, 35,* 747–753.

Lane, E. A., and Albee, G. W. (1970). Intellectual antecedents of schizophrenia. In M. Roff and D. F. Ricks (Eds.), *Life history research in psychopathology* (Vol. 1, pp. 189–207). Minneapolis: University of Minnesota Press.

Leff, J., and Vaughn, C. (1981). The role of maintenance therapy and relatives' expressed emotion in relapse of schizophrenia: A two-year follow-up. *British Journal of Psychiatry, 139,* 102–104.

Leff, J., and Vaughn, C. (1985). *Expressed emotion in families: Its significance for mental illness.* New York: Guilford Press.

Lewis, J. M., Rodnick, E. H., and Goldstein, M. J. (1981). Intrafamilial interactive behavior, parental communication deviance, and risk for schizophrenia. *Journal of Abnormal Psychology, 90,* 448–457.

McCord, W., Porta, J., and McCord, J. (1962). The familial genesis of psychoses. *Psychiatry, 25,* 60–71.

McGlashan, T. H. (1986a). The prediction of outcome in chronic schizophrenia: IV. The Chestnut Lodge Follow-up Study. *Archives of General Psychiatry, 43,* 167–176.

McGlashan, T. H. (1986b). Predictors of shorter-, medium-, and longer-term outcome in schizophenia. *American Journal of Psychiatry, 143,* 50–55.

McGlashan, T. H. (1988). A selective review of recent North American long-term follow-up studies of schizophrenia. *Schizophrenia Bulletin, 14,* 515–542.

Mednick, S. A., Parnas, J., and Schulsinger, F. (1987). The Copenhagen High-Risk Project, 1962–1986. *Schizophrenia Bulletin, 13,* 485–495.

Meehl, P. E. (1962). Schizotaxia, schizotypy, schizophrenia. *American Psychologist, 17,* 827–838.

Meyer, A. (1910). The dynamic interpretation of dementia praecox. *American Journal of Psychiatry, 21,* 385–403.

Michael, C., Morris, D., and Soroker, E. (1957). Follow-up studies of shy, withdrawn children. II. Relative incidence of schizophrenia. *American Journal of Orthopsychiatry, 27,* 331–337.

Mintz, L. I., Liberman, R. P., Miklowitz, D. J., and Mintz, J. (1987). Expressed emotion: A call for partnership among relatives, patients, and professionals. *Schizophrenia Bulletin, 13,* 227–235.

Mirsky, A. F., Silberman, E. K., Latz, A., and Nagler, S. (1985). Adult outcomes of high-risk children: Differential effects of town and kibbutz rearing. *Schizophrenia Bulletin, 11,* 150–154.

Mishler, E. G., and Waxler, N. E. (1968). *Interaction in families: An experimental study of family processes and schizophrenia.* New York: Wiley.

Morris, D., Soroker, E., and Burruss, G. (1954). Follow-up studies of shy, withdrawn children. I. Evaluation of later adjustment. *American Journal of Orthopsychiatry, 24,* 743–754.

Morris, H., Escoll, P., and Wexler, R. (1956). Aggressive behavior disorders of childhood: A follow-up study. *American Journal of Psychiatry, 112,* 991–997.

Munro, A., and Griffiths, A. (1969). Some psychiatric non-sequelae of childhood bereavement. *British Journal of Psychiatry, 115,* 305–311.

Nameche, G., Waring, M., and Ricks, D. F. (1964). Early indicators of outcome in schizophrenia. *Journal of Nervous and Mental Disease, 139,* 232–240.

Nuechterlein, K. H. (1986). Annotation: Childhood precursors of adult schizophrenia. *Journal of Child Psychology and Psychiatry, 27,* 133–144.

Ogawa, K., Miya, M., Watarai, A., Nakazawa, M., Yuasa, S., and Utena, H. (1987). A long-term follow-up study of schizophrenia in Japan, with special reference to the course of social adjustment. *British Journal of Psychiatry, 151,* 758–765.

Oltman, J., and Friedman, S. (1965). Report on parental deprivation in psychiatric disorders. *Archives of General Psychiatry, 12,* 46–56.

Oltmanns, T. F., and Neale, J. M. (1978). Abstraction and schizophrenia: Problems in psychological deficit research. In B. A. Maher (Ed.), *Progress in experimental personality research* (Vol. 8, pp. 197–243). New York: Academic Press.

O'Neal, P., and Robins, L. (1958). Childhood patterns predictive of adult schizophrenia: A 30-year follow-up study. *American Journal of Psychiatry, 115,* 385–391.

Osterweis, M., Solomon, F., and Green, M. (Eds.). (1984). *Bereavement: Reactions, consequences, and care.* Washington, DC: National Academy Press.

Parker, G., Johnston, P., and Hayward, L. (1988). Parental 'expressed emotion' as a predictor of schizophrenic relapse. *Archives of General Psychiatry, 45,* 806–813.

Parnas, J., Schulsinger, F., Schulsinger, H., Mednick, S. A., and Teasdale, T. W. (1982). Behavioral precursors of schizophrenia spectrum. *Archives of General Psychiatry, 39,* 658–664.

Parnas, J., and Schulsinger, H. (1986). Continuity of formal thought disorder from childhood to adulthood in a high-risk sample. *Acta Psychiatrica Scandinavica, 74,* 246–251.

Parsons, R., and Bales, R. F. (1955). *Family socialization and interaction process.* Glencoe, IL: Free Press.

Pitts, F. N., Jr., Meyer, J., Brooks, M., and Winokur, G. (1965). Adult psychiatric illness assessed for childhood parent loss and psychiatric illness in family members. *American Journal of Psychiatry, 121,* Suppl.

Pollack, M., Woerner, M. G., and Klein, D. F. (1970). A comparison of childhood characteristics of schizophrenics, personality disorders, and their siblings. In M. Roff and D. F. Ricks (Eds.), *Life history research in psychopathology* (Vol. 1, pp. 208–225). Minneapolis: University of Minnesota Press.

Rabkin, J. G. (1980). Stressful life events and schizophrenia: A review of the research literature. *Psychological Bulletin, 87,* 408–425.

Rahe, R., and Gunderson, E. (Eds.). (1974). *Life stress and illness.* Springfield, IL: Charles C Thomas.

Ricks, D. F., and Nameche, G. (1966). Symbiosis, sacrifice and schizophrenia. *Mental Hygiene, 50,* 541–551.

Robins, L. (1966). *Deviant children grown up.* Baltimore, MD: Williams and Wilkens.

Roff, J. D., and Knight, R. (1980). Preschizophrenics: Low IQ and aggressive symptoms as predictors of adult outcome and marital status. *Journal of Nervous and Mental Disease, 168,* 129–132.

Roff, J. D., and Knight, R. (1981). Family characteristics, childhood symptoms, and adult outcome in schizophrenia. *Journal of Abnormal Psychology, 90,* 510–520.

Sameroff, A., Seifer, R., Zax, M., and Barocas, R. (1987). Early indicators of developmental risk: Rochester Longitudinal Study. *Schizophrenia Bulletin, 13,* 383–394.

Saugstad, L. F. (1989). Social class, marriage, and fertility in schizophrenia. *Schizophrenia Bulletin, 15,* 9–43.

Schaffner, A., Albee, G. W., and Lane, E. A. (1967). Intellectual differences between suburban preschizophrenics and their siblings. *Journal of Consulting and Clinical Psychology, 31,* 326–327.

Serban, G. (1975). Relationship of mental status, functioning and stress to readmission of schizophrenics. *British Journal of Social and Clinical Psychology, 14,* 291–301.

Slater, E., and Cowie, V. (1971). *The genetics of mental disorders.* London: Oxford University Press.

Snyder, S. H. (1974). *Madness and the brain.* New York: McGraw-Hill.

Spiegel, D., and Wissler, T. (1986). Family environment as a predictor of psychiatric rehospitalization. *American Journal of Psychiatry, 143,* 56–60.

Stoffelmayr, B. E., Dillavou, D., and Hunter, J. E. (1983). Premorbid functioning and outcome in schizophrenia: A cumulative analysis. *Journal of Consulting and Clinical Psychology, 51,* 338–352.

Strauss, J. S., and Carpenter, W. T. (1974). The prediction of outcome in schizophrenia: II. Relationships between predictor and outcome variables. *Archives of General Psychiatry, 31,* 37–42.

Strauss, J. S., and Carpenter, W. T. (1977). Prediction of outcome in schizophrenia: III. Five-year outcome and its predictors. *Archives of General Psychiatry, 34,* 159–163.

Strauss, J. S., Hafez, H., Lieberman, P., and Harding, C. M. (1985). The course of psychiatric disorder: III. Longitudinal principles. *American Journal of Psychiatry, 142,* 289–296.

Strauss, J. S., Loevsky, L., Glazer, W., and Leaf, P. (1981). Organizing the complexities of schizophrenia: Concepts, measures, and implications. *Journal of Nervous and Mental Disease, 169,* 120–126.

Strauss, J. S., Rakfeldt, J., Harding, C. M., and Lieberman, P. (1989). Psychological and social aspects of negative symptoms. *British Journal of Psychiatry, 155,* 128–132.

Sullivan, H. S. (1931). The modified psychoanalytic treatment of schizophrenia. *American Journal of Psychiatry, 11,* 519–540.

Tienari, P., Sorri, A., Lahti, I., Naarala, M., Wahlberg, K. E., Moring, J., Pohjola, J., and Wynne, L. C. (1987). Genetic and psychosocial factors in schizoprhenia: The Finnish Adoptive Family Study. *Schizophrenia Bulletin, 13,* 477–484.

Vaillant, G. E. (1964). Prospective prediction of schizophrenic remission. *Archives of General Psychiatry, 11,* 509–518.

Vaughn, C., and Leff, J. P. (1976). The influence of family and social factors on the course of psychiatric illness: A comparison of schizophrenic and depressed neurotic patients. *British Journal of Psychiatry, 15,* 157–165.

Vaughn, C., Snyder, K. S., Jones, S., Freeman, W. B., and Falloon, I. R. H. (1984). Family factors in schizophrenic relapse: A California replication of the British research on expressed emotion. *Archives of General Psychiatry, 41,* 1169–1177.

Vigotsky, L. S. (1934). Thought in schizophrenia. *Archives of Neurological Psychiatry, 31,* 1063–1077.

von Domarus, E. (1944). The specific laws of logic in schizophrenia. In J. Kasanin (Ed.), *Language and thought in schizophrenia* (pp. 104–114). Berkeley: University of California Press.

Wahl, C. (1956). Some antecedent factors in the family histories of 568 male schizophrenics of the United States Navy. *American Journal of Psychiatry, 113,* 201–210.

Wallis, G. G. (1972). Stress as a predictor in schizophrenia. *British Journal of Psychiatry, 120,* 375–384.

Watt, N. F. (1971). Developmental changes in semantic interpretation of ambiguous words. *Journal of Abnormal Psychology, 77,* 332–339.

Watt, N. F. (1972). Longitudinal changes in the social behavior of children hospitalized for schizophrenia as adults. *Journal of Nervous and Mental Disease, 155,* 42–54.

Watt, N. F. (1978). Patterns of childhood social development in adult schizophrenics. *Archives of General Psychiatry, 35,* 160–165.

Watt, N. F., Anthony, E. J., Wynne, L. C., and Rolf, J. E. (Eds.). (1984). *Children at risk for schizophrenia: A longitudinal perspective.* New York: Cambridge University Press.

Watt, N. F., Fryer, J. H., Lewine, R. R. J., and Prentky, R. A. (1979). Toward longitudinal conceptions of psychiatric disorder. In B. A. Maher (Ed.), *Progress in experimental personality research* (pp. 199–283). New York: Academic Press.

Watt, N. F., Grubb, T. W., and Erlenmeyer-Kimling, L. (1982). Social, emotional, and intellectual behavior at school among children at high risk for schizophrenia. *Journal of Consulting and Clinical Psychology, 50,* 171–181.

Watt, N. F., and Lubensky, A. W. (1976). Childhood roots of schizophrenia. *Journal of Consulting and Clinical Psychology, 44,* 363–375.

Watt, N. F., and Nicholi, A., Jr. (1979). Early death of a parent as an etiological factor in schizophrenia. *American Journal of Orthopsychiatry, 49,* 465–473.

Watt, N. F., Stolorow, R. D., Lubensky, A. W., and McClelland, D. C. (1970). School adjustment and behavior of children hospitalized for schizophrenia as adults. *American Journal of Orthopsychiatry, 40,* 637–657.

Weintraub, S. (1987). Risk factors in schizophrenia: The Stony Brook High-Risk Project. *Schizophrenia Bulletin, 13,* 439–450.

Werner, H. (1948). *Comparative psychology of mental development.* Chicago: Follett.

Westermeyer, J. F., and Harrow, M. (1986). Predicting outcome in schizophrenics and non-schizophrenics of both sexes: The Zigler-Phillips Social Competence Scale. *Journal of Abnormal Psychology, 95,* 406–409.

White, R. W., and Watt, N. F. (1981). *The abnormal personality* (5th ed.). New York: Wiley.

Willner, A. (1965). Impairment of knowledge of unusual meanings of familiar words in brain damage and schizophrenia. *Journal of Anormal Psychology, 70,* 405–411.

Wittman, M., and Steinberg, D. (1944). A study of prodromal factors in mental illness with special reference to schizophrenia. *American Journal of Psychiatry, 100,* 811–816.

Zubin, J. (1985). Negative symptoms: Are they indigenous to schizophrenia? *Schizophrenia Bulletin, 11,* 461–469.

PART III

Adulthood: The Onset and Course of Clinical Symptoms

The chapters in this section explore the determinants of the phenomenology and course of schizophrenia. Richard Lewine, in Chapter 9, points out salient clinical differences between male and female patients and considers some theoretical approaches to the mechanisms subserving these differences. The impact of contextual factors on the course of schizophrenia is examined by Jeri Doane in Chapter 10. She presents persuasive evidence indicating that the patient's family environment is a significant predictor of the illness course. In Chapter 11, Ramzy Yassa examines the nature of late-onset schizophrenia and highlights the important implications of these late-onset syndromes for our conceptualization of the disorder. Finally, in Chapter 12, Courtenay Harding draws our attention to the significant intra-and intersubject variability in the long-term course and outcome of schizophrenia. She emphasizes that the illness is by no means uniformly characterized by a deteriorating course.

Together, these chapters provide compelling support for the notion that differences among schizophrenic patients may hold clues to etiologic determinants and processes. The sex and age differences discussed here suggest some biochemical mechanisms that may influence the nature and course of the illness. In addition, the apparent moderating influences of the family environment indicates that at least some schizophrenic patients are suffering from a stress-sensitive disorder.

193

Copyright © 1991 by Academic Press, Inc.
All rights of reproduction in any form reserved.

Ontogenetic Implications of Sex Differences in Schizophrenia

Richard R. J. Lewine

Sex biases in sample composition exist throughout the study of schizophrenia. Harry Stack Sullivan, for example, exclusively treated male schizophrenic patients. The generalizability of the results of every empirical study of VA schizophrenic patients is constrained by an almost complete reliance on male samples. These sample biases assume major significance in the face of accumulating evidence of systematic sex differences in premorbid development, onset age, clinical picture, medication response, and long-term outcome among schizophrenic patients. The first goal of this chapter is to review this evidence briefly, with a special emphasis on initial clinical onset, and to suggest that schizophrenia represents substantially different disorders in the sexes.

The second goal is to discuss the implications of sex differences for the study of the ontogenesis of schizophrenia. In particular, neurological involvement, in the form of nonspecific, diffuse cortical and/or subcortical abnormality, is implicated in male schizophrenic patients. Hormonal mechanisms, particularly those involving estrogen, seem particularly relevant in women with schizophrenia.

Finally, two themes that have general applicability to the study of psychopathology will be delineated. The first is that of searching for pro-

195

Copyright © 1991 by Academic Press, Inc.
All rights of reproduction in any form reserved.

tective mechanisms in disordered states. For good reason, the study of schizophrenia has led us to adopt the deficit model as an explanatory construct, from which the search for disordered structure and function follows logically. An alternative and potentially fruitful paradigm is to identify protective mechanisms suggested by sex differences in schizophrenia, especially because they may imply novel modes of treatment in addition to suggesting differences in etiological paths.

The examination of age-of-onset differences between female and male schizophrenics, for example, led Lewine (1981) and Seeman (1983) to conclude independently that schizophrenia in women may involve a "suppressor" (Lewine, 1981) or protective factor. That is, our understanding of psychopathology may require the elucidation of factors that prevent, slow, or mitigate a disease process (i.e., inhibitory factors). Similarly, adolescence has attracted considerable attention as an especially vulnerable period not only because it is the time of overt manifestation of the clinical syndrome for many schizophrenic patients, but also because adolescence is the time of biological and psychosocial graduation: Some processes are ending and others are beginning, with transition phases always presenting highly vulnerable developmental periods. We suggest below that typical adolescence may differentially bestow protective factors on women relative to men. Current research paradigms are not well suited to the study of such factors.

The second theme is that sex differences in schizophrenia may be a consequence of earlier biological maturation in women than in men (Lewine, 1990; Saugstad, 1989). The difference in age of onset of (and first hospitalization for) schizophrenia between men and women corresponds to the sex difference in age at biological maturity, approximately 2 years. Specifically, women have a later onset of schizophrenia by about 2 years than do men, yet women reach puberty approximately 2 years before men. This may be a coincidence or it may be a tantalizing clue to the relationship between maturational processes and the development of psychopathology. Perhaps early maturation serves to ameliorate (all other factors being equal) or delay schizophrenia. To examine this alternative construct, we must turn from the analysis of between-sex differences to within-sex comparisons of early and late maturers, a methodologically difficult task but one with considerable potential.

PREMORBID DEVELOPMENT

Researchers generally agree that men who develop schizophrenia have a significantly poorer premorbid development than do women (Klorman *et al.*, 1977; Lewine, 1981; Seeman, 1982; Zigler and Glick, 1986). The men, in contrast to the women, are less likely to have finished high school, dated or established enduring social relationships, married or remained married, and worked regularly. Zigler and Glick (1986) have suggested that some of these differences may be due to the previous scoring of employment history as an operational criterion of premorbid competence. Because a large proportion of women in earlier studies did not work outside the home ("housewives" in older coding schemes), they were not rated, and, hence, the quality of their work was not evaluated. In addition, clerical and sales positions, among which there is a large number of women, had been categorized as a higher level of work functioning in the original than in the revised version of the premorbid social competence scale. The current Phillips-Zigler scale of premorbid social competence lowers the status of these occupations; therefore, we can expect that studies of premorbid social competence using the revised scale may fail to yield as great a sex discrepancy in social competence as in the past.

Even if this is the case, researchers universally agree that marital status continues to discriminate between female and male schizophrenic patients; male schizophrenic patients are significantly less likely to have ever been married than female schizophrenics.

Premorbid differences, as typically assessed (retrospectively on a behavioral basis), may, of course, be a function of the disruptive effect of the presence of illness on usual functioning rather than a predisposing factor (i.e., a condition of development preceding the onset of schizophrenia). Because men are typically younger than women when the full clinical syndrome of schizophrenia manifests itself, the premorbid differences may reflect this earlier onset; in other words, schizophrenia begins to disrupt the normal developmental trajectory in men earlier than in women, and this disruption is what we are measuring, not level of competence before schizophrenia onset. Obviously, the earlier the intrusion of a disorder upon an individual's development, the less time that individual will have had to consolidate resources, build social skills, and generally establish a social position. If men and women were the same age at onset of schizophrenia, this argument predicts that the gender difference in marital status among schizophrenic patients would equalize.

We have found that even when age of onset is controlled, male schizophrenics are less likely to be married than female schizophrenics (R. Lewine and E. Walker, unpublished). Of 130 early-onset (operationalized as 25 years old or younger at first hospital admission) male schizophrenics, 88% had never been married; in contrast, only 59% of early-onset female schizophrenics had never been married.

A recent report from the Epidemiologic Catchment Area (ECA) collaborative study independently confirms this finding. The 1-year follow-up incidence of schizophrenia was 23 times higher in never-married men and 12 times higher in never-married women than in their married counterparts (Tien and Eaton, 1989). Age at schizophrenia onset is not, therefore, an adequate explanation for this consistently documented difference in marriage rates between female and male schizophrenic patients.

Another factor to consider under the rubric of premorbid, predisposing factors (acknowledging the uncertainty of the cause–effect relationship) is the biological integrity of the individual at schizophrenia onset. This term is meant to convey the extent to which the basic structural or functional mechanisms of the body have been compromised (e.g., poor nutrition, chronic stress, infections) in such a fashion as to lower the overall ability of the individual to resist or overcome illness.

Much of the evidence suggesting that men in general may be more compromised biologically than women emanates from the "high-risk" literature (see Watt *et al.*, 1984). Specifically, men who as adults are diagnosed with schizophrenia have been found to have been subject to a higher rate, than women, of birth and pregnancy complications and brain insults (Torrey and Torrey, 1980).

Green *et al.* (1987) assessed physical anomalies of the hair, ears, eyes, mouth, hands, and feet as indices of early cerebral insult. Although they found no sex differences in mean number of anomalies, they did find that early-onset (18 years of age or younger) schizophrenic patients had significantly more physical anomalies than later-onset patients. We can anticipate, given that men are younger than women at schizophrenia onset (see below), that Green's early-onset group was predominantly (if not exclusively) male; this is not reported in the study.

Furthermore, sex differences may exist in adult brain morphology that reflect sex-related differences in rate or pattern of neurodevelopment. Male schizophrenic patients have been reported in at least one study to have significantly smaller corpus callosum areas than female schizophrenics, a reversal of the typical sex difference in both psychiatric and normal control samples (Gulley *et al.*, 1989; Lewine *et al.*, 1990; Rossi *et al.*, 1989). [These data are still controversial because increased corpus callosum thickness in schizophrenia has also been reported by Nasrallah *et al.*, (1986) and Rosenthal and Bigelow (1972). However, the relationship between thickness and area has not been completely defined, nor have sex differences in the two corpus callosum parameters been delineated.] Such a difference, if confirmed, suggests a developmental disruption, which could range from a general and diffuse process reminiscent of Fish's (1984) "pandevelopmental delay" to a more circumscribed abnormality.

In summary, at the time of schizophrenia onset, men have, on average, less biological and psychosocial resources upon which to draw in coping with disorder than do women. Zigler and his colleagues have argued convincingly that this social competence differential holds across all diagnoses (Zigler and Glick, 1986). The theoretical interpretation of premorbid social competence differences are discussed in a later section.

ONSET AND FIRST HOSPITAL ADMISSION AGE

Documentation indicating that men are younger than women at onset of and at first hospital admission for schizophrenia is extensive (for detailed reviews see Eaton, 1985; Lewine, 1981, 1988a). Estimates of absolute age differences vary dramatically, with the general consensus converging on approximately a 2-year difference in mean age at first hospital admission. The decade of highest risk for schizophrenia is likewise later for women (about 24–35 years of age) than for men (about 14–25 years of age) (Lewine, 1988a). The ECA collaborative study cited earlier found that the 1-year follow-up incidence of schizophrenia peaked between 18 and 24 years of age for men and between 45 and 54 for women, an indication that earlier estimates (based on treated cases) may, if anything, have been too conservative (Tien and Eaton, 1989).

Several artifactual causes of this sex differential in timing have been examined and rejected (Lewine *et al.*, 1981, 1984, 1985; Burbach *et al.*, 1984; Lewine, 1980; Zigler and Glick, 1986). One interpretation is that deviant behavior is less tolerated in men than in women, thereby leading to the former's earlier hospitalization. Put another way, schizophrenic women may be more accepted by their environment than are men (Farina, 1981). The analysis of onset age, clearly more problematic to operationalize than first hospital admission age (Carpenter, 1987), yields a picture comparable with the hospital admission data; men are younger than women at reported age at first appearance of schizophrenic (psychotic) symptoms, disconfirming, in part, the psychosocial hypothesis (although the tolerance hypothesis could be extended to onset differences, namely, less environmental tolerance of male behavior leads to earliest onset of disorder in men than women).

Further disconfirming evidence is that the interval between reported symptom onset and first hospitalization is almost identical (about 4 years in one sample) for the sexes (Lewine, 1981; Burbach *et al.*, 1984). In other words, women and men are identifiably ill for the same length of time before they are first hospitalized. The differential tolerance hypothesis would predict that men would be hospitalized more quickly than women once the clinical syndrome had developed.

Variation in diagnostic criteria, while affecting the male : female ratio of diagnosed schizophrenia (Lewine *et al.*, 1984; Silverstein *et al.*, 1982;

Westermeyer and Harrow, 1984), does not seem to have an impact on onset or hospitalization age. The epidemiological data have been remarkably consistent across a wide spectrum of diagnostic criteria and, furthermore, across numerous historical periods (Eaton, 1985; Lewine, 1981, 1988a).

Empirical studies of the effect of diagnostic criteria on the male : female ratio of schizophrenia rates are consistent in showing an increased ratio with the use of increasingly stringent criteria. Lewine *et al.* (1984), for example, calculated the male : female ratio in a sample of 387 inpatients, each of whom received a diagnosis of schizophrenia by at least one of six diagnostic systems [ranging from the least stringent New Haven Schizophrenia Index (Astrachan *et al.*, 1971) to the highly stringent Feighner criteria (Feighner *et al.*, 1972)]. The New Haven Schizophrenia Index in this study yielded a ratio of 1:1, consistent with the larger sample's sex distribution. In contrast, the Feighner criteria yielded only seven schizophrenic patients, all male.

Burbach *et al.* (1984) used the same sample to analyze the pairwise concordance rates among the diagnostic systems by sex. They found that the average pairwise interdiagnostic system κ for men was twice (0.24) that for women (0.12). If diagnostic concordance reflects an underlying core trait of schizophrenia (Young *et al.*, 1982), then these data would suggest that men are "more schizophrenic" than women.

CLINICAL PICTURE AT ONSET–FIRST ADMISSION

Few of the empirical reports detailing sex differences in the clinical picture of schizophrenia have sampled acutely ill first-break patients; rather, the samples have tended to be chronically hospitalized patients. The clinical characterization of sex differences in this population has been mixed. On the one hand, schizophrenic men have been described as isolated, withdrawn, passive, and more likely than women to manifest negative or deficit symptoms (Pogue-Giele and Zubin, 1988). On the other hand, schizophrenic men have also been reported to be more antisocial and likely to commit suicide than schizophrenic women (Walker *et al.*, 1985; Zigler and Glick, 1986).

The issue of negative symptoms is especially interesting because it forces us to explore the utility of searching for differences in group means, in contrast to contextual or correlational analyses. Some investigators have reported no difference in the magnitude or severity of negative symptoms in female and male schizophrenics (see Pogue-Giele and Zubin, 1988). Examination of the correlational structure of negative symptoms and other clinical and demographic variables does seem to differ by sex even when absolute differences do not. Lewine and his colleagues (Lewine and Sommers, 1985) and Pogue-Giele (Pogue-Giele and Zubin, 1988) independently found that negative symptoms in female schizophrenics tended to be associated with depression and indices of good premorbid development and outcome, whereas in male schizophrenics the negative symptoms were associated with poor premorbid development and poor outcome.

Some of the inconsistency in the negative-symptom picture may be due to the inappropriate assumption that these symptoms represent a homogeneous syndrome (Bilder et al., 1985; Gibbons et al., 1985; Walker and Lewine, 1988). Dworkin (1990), for example, has reported no sex differences in the negative symptoms of affective flattening, alogia, avolition-apathy, and attentional impairment between male and female monozygotic proband twins and the concordant twins but did find that male schizophrenics were significantly more asocial and withdrawn than the female schizophrenics. As interesting as these findings are, it is impossible to disentangle the effects of differential responses to treatment, of institutionalization, and of secondary responses to the illness itself, from putative gender differences in development and course of disorder.

The longitudinal study of individuals at high risk for schizophrenia yields valuable information in this respect. Fish (1987), in reporting on the long-term follow-up of her risk infants, describes three of the sick high-risk infants as adult schizophrenics. The two men were both abnormally quiet at birth and apathetic and schizoid ever since; in contrast, the schizophrenic woman was quiet during the first month of life but went on to develop schizophrenia with a prominent affective component, including noncompliant and explosive behavior.

We have attempted to examine the initial presentation of schizophrenia in two independent, first-admission, large-sample, unpublished studies. In one case, the factor structure of negative symptoms in unmedicated schizophrenics is analyzed; in the other, symptom profile is examined as a function of onset age, which serves as a mediator of sex differences.

R. Lewine, R. Gibbons, D. Hedeker, and J. Davis (unpublished) conducted a secondary analysis of the NIMH collaborative study of phenothiazines in schizophrenia (Gibbons et al., 1985; NIMH Collaborative Study Group, 1964; Schooler, 1978) in which a subset of 93 women and 113 men, all on placebo, had had no previous hospitalizations. Confirmatory factor analysis was used to test the fit of a three-factor model (apathy, retardation, and loss of goal orientation) of negative symptoms (Gibbons et al., 1985) for women and men separately. The null hypothesis of equality of factor structures between men and women was rejected (χ^2 = 141.1, df = 104, p < 0.000): While the three-factor model adequately fit the data of the women (χ^2 = 52.0, df = 52, p < 0.474), the model could not account adequately for the male data (χ^2 = 96.3, df = 52, p < 0.0001) whereas a four-factor model did (χ^2 = 24.1, df = 17, p < 0.116) (apathy: apathy toward environment, apathy toward treatment and fixed facial expression; retardation: slow speech, slow movement, thought blocking, and poverty of speech; loosening of associations: wandering speech; and disorganization: incoherence, irrelevant speech, and inappropriate affect). The differences in mean symptom level between the sexes were not significant, suggesting that the pattern of symptom presentation was more discriminating than severity.

As a counterpoint, we found in an independent sample that absolute differences in negative symptoms between female and male schizophrenics were significant when age of onset (operationalized as age at first hospital admission) was used with sex as a defining feature of subtypes. R. Lewine and E. Walker (unpublished) examined symptom patterns in a sample of 561 first-admission schizophrenic patients divided into four subgroups by sex and by age at admission ("early" ≤25 years old and "late" >25). A significant sex by age interaction on a "withdrawal" factor (isolation, blunted affect, and dependency) reflected early-onset male schizophrenics having the highest factor score of the four groups ($F_{1,557}$ = 7.717, p = 0.006); early-onset female schizophrenics had the lowest "withdrawal" score. Additionally, of the four subgroups, late-onset male schizophrenics had the highest depression factor score. Sufficient data suggest that the developmental path to schizophrenia in men, especially among those with early onset, may be characterized by prominent apathy, amotivation, and withdrawal. Among women, affect plays a significant role, even if "negative" symptoms can be demonstrated.

RESPONSE TO TREATMENT

Very few treatment studies have specifically reported the analysis of sex effects; this, of course, fails to indicate whether sex was not analyzed or sex differences were not found. Prospective studies with this aim are therefore necessary.

The evidence among those investigations reporting sex-effect analyses is mixed. As summarized elsewhere in more detail (Lewine, 1988b), schizophrenic women tend to use more psychotropic medications and are more often on polypharmacy regimens, usually for the treatment of depression. Additionally, women may be more responsive or sensitive to antipsychotics as reflected in their requiring lower doses, controlling for body weight (Seeman, 1983, 1988), and not responding to placebo as strongly as men (Schooler, 1986).

One factor in treatment hyporesponse in men may be the presence of brain abnormality as indexed by enlarged lateral ventricles, the major portion of the structural system conducting cerebral spinal fluid through the brain. Several investigators have found that schizophrenic patients with significantly enlarged lateral ventricles tend to manifest more negative symptoms and to respond less well to antipsychotic medications than those whose ventricles are within the normal range (Crow, 1985; Luchins *et al.*, 1984; Pogue-Giele and Zubin, 1988; Walker and Lewine, 1988). If it is true that men are more likely to have brain abnormalities than women, and if the association between poor medication response and enlarged ventricles were systematically replicated (which it has not been), then we could speculate that the sex differences in treatment response could be accounted for in part by the limiting effect of brain abnormality in male schizophrenics.

The fact that female patients may have a form of schizophrenia that is very responsive to medication may be taken as *prima facie* evidence of the salience of a biochemical dysfunction, in contrast to the prominence of morphological–neurological factors in male schizophrenia. It is also important to remember that treatment response (or nonresponse) does not necessarily imply etiology. We can successfully treat broken bones with plaster and exercise, but this does not suggest that broken bones represent plaster and exercise deficits or abnormalities, an obvious point but one easily forgotten in the study of schizophrenia.

ONTOGENETIC PROCESSES

We know from a vast literature on normal development that men and women are similar in some areas and dissimilar in others (see Lewine, 1981, 1988b); in some respects, the choice of highlighting the dissimilar over the similar in the examination of sex differences in schizophrenia is a matter of preference, although one that we believe will lead to some insights about schizophrenia ontogenesis.

Zigler and his colleagues (Zigler and Glick, 1986) have presented an extensive array of data, all of which points to a higher level of psychosocial maturation among female than male schizophrenic patients. Set primarily in the developmental theory of Werner (1948) and initially articulated empirically by Phillips (1968), Zigler has been engaged in a decades-long effort to operationalize developmental organization. Three basic constructs have been delineated: premorbid social competence, role orientation, and action–thought continuum. Briefly stated, higher levels of development are reflected in higher levels of premorbid social competence (as measured by work history, social relationships, educational history, and age at first psychiatric hospitalization), a role orientation of turning against self (versus turning against others or withdrawal), and thought- (e.g., suicidal ideation, hallucinations) rather than action-based (e.g., suicidal attempt, physical assault) psychiatric symptoms. Female schizophrenics have emerged as more developmentally advanced than male schizophrenics on virtually every parameter examined.

Perhaps the most persistent sex difference to date is the earlier onset of, and hospitalization for, schizophrenia in men than women. We consider below some of the reasons for this timing difference and its implications for ontogeny.

Onset: A Nongenetic Process

Of particular fascination with respect to ontogeny is that onset does *not* seem to be under genetic control (Gottesman and Shields, 1983; Kendler and Robinette, 1983). That is, while zygosity affects the rate of concordance for schizophrenia (monozygotic twins being significantly more often concordant than dizygotic twins), age of onset is comparable between mono- and dizygotic affected twins and is no more highly correlated within monozygotic than within dizygotic twin pairs. In short, in searching for the cause of this age-related phenomenon and its implications for the development of schizophrenia, we must look toward the environment, as very broadly defined, to include possible early constitutional impairment.

Is genetic predisposition necessary? The diathesis-stress model has been the most frequently cited explanatory construct for schizophrenia during the last two decades. The simplest version of the model posits a necessary, but not sufficient, genetic predisposition (unknown nature other than statistical) that interacts with a broad range of potential stresses to produce the clinical picture of schizophrenia (Gottesman *et al.*, 1987). It has been argued that prevalence rates of (or risk for) schizophrenia are the same for women and men (Gottesman and Shields, 1983), despite Rosenthal's (1959) early presentation of data suggestive of a higher risk among women than men. Rosenthal found that female dizygotic twins were more likely to be concordant for schizophrenia than male dizygotic twins.

Two decades later, a similar sex difference is being supported in an independent sample and by a different investigator (Goldstein, 1989). In a restricted maximum likelihood latent class analysis of the Iowa-500 data (Tsuang and Winokur, 1975), Goldstein identified a group of male schizophrenics with deficit symptoms, low family morbidity risk, and birth during the winter months. This finding is consistent with a small, but growing body of evidence of a sporadic, or nonfamilial, form of schizophrenia (Kendler and Hays, 1982; Revely, 1985), which may be more common among men than women (Lewine, 1988a). Such a form of schizophrenia could be attributed to constitutional brain dysfunctions associated with putative birth and pregnancy complications and/or other evidence of brain abnormality in schizophrenic men (Torrey and Torrey, 1980).

Constitutional brain abnormality, by itself, could not account for schizophrenia because not every instance of early brain deviation results in schizophrenia. It may be, however, that nongenetic factors are particularly important in the shaping of schizophrenia in men.

Conversely, assuming Goldstein's provocative sex differences in schizophrenia risk are replicated, schizophrenia in women may more often be linked to a genetic predisposition. As in the case of male schizophrenia, a single factor (in this instance genetic liability) will not be sufficient to explain the development of schizophrenia in every individual, because up to 50% of monozygotic twins of (and hence genetically identical to) schizophrenic probands do *not* become affected. Something other than inherited predisposition must be necessary for the development of schizophrenia.

Biological Maturation

Several models incorporating maturational processes have been proposed to account for the timing of schizophrenia onset and these may be characterized as "trigger" models (Lewine, 1981, 1988a). That is, some factor in adolescence is assumed to account, in part, for the characteristic emergence of the clinical syndrome in adolescence, although it is widely recognized that the fundamental schizophrenic process may precede this formally identified syndrome by some years (Hanson et al., 1976; Carpenter, 1987).

Weinberger (1987) posits a latent lesion in the dorsolateral prefrontal cortex that is "brought on-line" with sexual maturation. Feinberg (1982/1983) suggests that schizophrenia involves an abnormality in synaptic pruning, the direction of which (too much or too little) is unspecified, during adolescence. Neither of these models, however, addresses the sex difference in schizophrenia onset. Saugstad (1989) is more specific on this point when she suggests that pubertal maturation coincides with the pruning of redundant synaptic connections. Because they mature later than women, men will be characterized by excessive elimination of synapses, a decrease in neural density (especially in the frontal lobes), and a consequent onset of schizophrenia that is earlier than in women. Obviously, a genetic predisposition must be assumed, lest all men become schizophrenic.

Simple maturational models, namely, those such as Saugstad's and Weinberger's that emphasize earlier puberty in women than men, must predict *later* onset in men than in women if maturation is assumed to trigger or speed schizophrenia ontogenesis. This is, of course, counter to the empirical findings. Therefore, we must conclude that the more logical hypothesis, if maturation is in fact related to schizophrenia onset, is that of a suppressor process. It seems clear that biological maturation must be examined from multiple points of view (such as puberty age, evidence of neurodevelopmental delays or accelerations, and adult changes as reflected in pregnancy and menopause) and specifically compared within sex to address the differences in onset age of schizophrenia.

Psychosocial Influences on Schizophrenia Ontogenesis

Efforts to identify psychosocial factors that serve as specific etiologies of schizophrenia have been notoriously unsuccessful; it is more reasonable to think of these influences as molders of the schizophrenia syndromes (Lewine, 1981, 1988a,b). Zigler, after briefly reviewing biological theories of sex differences in schizophrenia, concludes the following.

The period of puberty is as significant in the psychosocial realm as in the biological. It is a time of psychological readjustment to body changes and peers, especially heterosexual relationships, and increasing independence from parents. Social and work (usually in the form of school) demands are increasing at the very time when adolescents are experiencing surges in sexual and affective arousal that may threaten to overwhelm them. It is reasonable to expect, as many have (e.g., Arieti, 1974; Bellak, 1958; Watt *et al.*, 1984), that such a time is particularly difficult for the preschizophrenic who may already be experiencing identity and interpersonal difficulties.

The causative status of these psychosocial pressures is, however, problematic if we take their timing into account. If the psychosocial impact of puberty (recalling that it occurs, on average, 2 years earlier in girls than boys) hastens schizophrenia onset or intensifies its clinical manifestation, then we would expect that female schizophrenics would have an earlier onset than male schizophrenics, not the other way around as is the case (this assumes that "preschizophrenic" girls, on average, reach puberty at the same age as nonpreschizophrenic girls). We can, therefore, use the known sex difference in onset age to reframe the question: What psychosocial factors emerging during adolescence would provide women with protection against schizophrenia?

Sullivan (1962) wrote about the importance of adolescent "chums"; their absence, he suggested, played a key role in the ontogenesis of schizophrenia. The sociocultural changes in women's roles notwithstanding, we can still expect, as do Zigler and Glick (1986), that girls will be more oriented toward social interaction and personal relationships than boys. The relationships of boys are more likely to be focused on instrumental goals (e.g., sports, computer games), with less need for the establishment of interpersonal ties, and a consequent reduction in the opportunity for the self-conscious sharing of psychological experiences; boys are less likely to talk about their inner lives and experiences than are girls, for whom such exchange is an important part of the social fabric. To the extent that this is true, girls may experience greater support and connectedness (i.e., affiliation) for a longer period of time than do boys, thereby postponing schizophrenia onset. Obviously, such social interactions will not prevent schizophrenia. (Some might even argue that the intense pressure for peer conformity and the emphasis on interpersonal relationships would precipitate the breakdown of the preschizophrenic individual's self-system, which is particularly vulnerable in these areas.)

We offer these speculations about a psychosocial protective factor more as a model for the generation of new hypotheses, rather than as a substantive explanation of onset-age differences in schizophrenic men and women (although we consider the protective factor to be reasonable). The principle being articulated is that the "deficit" nature of schizophrenia should not blind us to the role of positive processes in the ontogenesis of schizophrenia. This group of disorders involves far more than a genetic predisposition or a constitutional vulnerability. As pointed out elegantly three decades ago (Meehl, 1962), schizophrenia is a complex product of multiple forces, so that exclusive focus on one path in ontogenetic development must necessarily omit critical information. Sex differences in schizophrenia provide us with a new way of examining schizophrenia that promises to yield interesting insights into both normal and abnormal development.

FUTURE DIRECTIONS

Although an extensive clinical descriptive literature already exists, a more detailed accounting of the initial presentation of schizophrenia and its early course in the two sexes is needed. The picture that has been drawn in this and previous reviews relies, for the most part, on *ad hoc* analyses or interpretation of data collected for other purposes. A prospective study including specific assessment of sex differences in first-break schizophrenic patients would be invaluable.

The problem of schizophrenia heterogeneity may be partially reduced by the formal incorporation of patient sex and age at onset (operationalized by age at first hospital admission) as diagnostic variables. Specifically, we have proposed a fourfold classification of early-onset male (the Kraepelinian prototype), early-onset female, late-onset male, and late-onset female (prototypical form) schizophrenics, with early being defined as 25 years of age or younger at first admission and late as over 25 at first admission (for justification, see Eaton, 1985; Lewine, 1981, 1988a). Such a classification has proved more useful than multiple regression (which considers age as a dimensional rather than as a dichotomous variable) in at least one study (R. Lewine and E. Walker, unpublished) in accounting for symptom variation.

To elucidate further the nature of differences between female and male schizophrenics in premorbid competence, it will be necessary to extend our studies to the schizophrenia spectrum. Specifically, we will want to examine schizotypal symptoms by sex because, by extension of the negative symptom literature, we anticipate that men would exhibit more schizotypal symptoms than women. If, as many assume, schizotypal characteristics are clinically and/or genetically linked to schizophrenia (Gunderson and Siever, 1985), then the study of schizotypal syndromes should help differentiate those sex differences in premorbid and clinical pictures that are a consequence of the disorder from those that are pre-existing and, perhaps, predisposing conditions.

Finally, we must begin to decompose the currently confounded effects of sex and biological maturation by within-sex comparisons of early versus late maturers (Lewine, 1990). This will require the development of a methodology that accurately and retrospectively dates the age of biological maturation, most often taken as puberty. Age of menarche is useful in this regard but is obviously limited to one sex. The attempt to devise such a methodology should add to our understanding of the onset and course of schizophrenia in men and women, as well as to normal development.

ACKNOWLEDGMENTS

Preparation of this chapter was supported, in part, by grants from the NIMH (MH44151, Lewine, PI), and the NARSAD (Walker, PI). I also thank Susan Maxwell for the preparation of the manuscript.

REFERENCES

Arieti, S. (1974). *Interpretation of schizophrenia.* New York: Basic Books.
Astrachan, B., Harrow, M., Adler, D., Brauer, T., Schwartz, A., Schwartz, C., and Tucker, G. (1971). A checklist for the diagnosis of schizophrenia. *British Journal of Psychiatry, 121,* 529–539.
Bellak, L. (Ed.). (1958). *Schizophrenia: A review of the syndrome.* New York: Logos Press.

Bilder, R., Mukherjee, S., Rieder, R., and Pandurangi, A. (1985). Symptomatic and neuropsychological components of defect state. *Schizophrenia Bulletin, 11*, 409–419.

Burbach, D., Lewine, R., and Meltzer, H. (1984). Diagnostic concordance for schizophrenia as a function of sex. *Journal of Consulting and Clinical Psychology, 52*, 478–479.

Carpenter, W. T. (1987). Review of the Tarrytown conference. *Schizophrenia Bulletin, 13*, 205–206.

Crow, T. (1985). The two-syndrome concept: Origins and current status. *Schizophrenia Bulletin, 11*, 471–486.

Dworkin, R. (1990) Patterns of sex differences in negative symptoms and social functioning consistent with separate dimensions of schizophrenic psychopathology. *American Journal of Psychiatry, 147*, 347–349.

Eaton, W. (1985). Epidemiology of schizophrenia. *Epidemiology Review, 7*, 105–125.

Farina, A. (1981). Are women nicer people than men? Sex and the stigma of mental disorders. *Clinical Psychology Review, 1*, 223–243.

Feighner, J., Robins, E., Guze, S., Woodruff, R., Winokur, G., and Munoz, R. (1972). Diagnostic criteria for use in psychiatric research. *Archives of General Psychiatry, 26*, 57–63.

Feinberg, I. (1982/1983). Schizophrenia: Caused by a fault in programmed synaptic elimination during adolescence. *Journal of Psychiatric Research, 17*, 319–334.

Fish, B. (1984). Characteristics and sequelae of the neurointegrative disorder in infants at risk for schizophrenia: 1952–1982. In N. Watt, E. Anthony, L. Wynne, and J. Rolf (Eds.), *Children at risk for schizophrenia: A longitudinal perspective.* Cambridge: Cambridge University Press.

Fish, B. (1987). Infant predictors of the longitudinal course of schizophrenic development. *Schizophrenic Bulletin, 13*, 395–410.

Gibbons, R., Lewine, R., Davis, J., Schooler, N., and Cole, J. (1985). An empirical test of a Kraepelinian vs. a Bleulerian view of negative symptoms. *Schizophrenia Bulletin, 11*, 390–396.

Goldstein, J. (1989). Gender and schizophrenia: Identification of the subtypes of the illness. *Schizophrenia Research, 2*, 9. [Abstract.]

Gottesman, I., McGuffin, P., and Farmer, A. (1987). Clinical genetics as clues to the "real" genetics of schizophrenia. *Schizophrenia Bulletin, 13*, 23–48.

Gottesman, I., and Shields, J. (1983). *Schizophrenia: The epigenetic puzzle.* Cambridge University Press: Cambridge.

Green, M., Satz, P., Soper, H., and Kharabi, F. (1987). Relationships between physical anomalies and age at onset of schizophrenia. *American Journal of Psychiatry, 144*, 666–667.

Gulley, L., Schwartzberg, D., Risch, C., and Lewine, R. (1989). Psychopathology and corpus callosal shape. *Schizophrenia Research, 2*, 161. [Abstract.]

Gunderson, J., and Siever, L. (1985). Relatedness of schizotypal to schizophrenic disorders. *Schizophrenia Bulletin, 11*, 532–537.

Hanson, D., Gottesman, I., and Heston, L. (1976). Some possible childhood indicators of adult schizophrenia inferred from children of schizophrenics. *British Journal of Psychiatry, 129*, 142–154.

Kendler, K., and Hays, P. (1982). Familial and sporadic schizophrenia: A symptomatic, prognostic and EEG comparison. *American Journal of Psychiatry, 139*, 1557–1662.

Kendler, K., and Robinette, C. (1983). Schizophrenia in the National Academy of Sciences National Research Council Twin Registry: A 16-year update. *American Journal of Psychiatry, 140*, 1551–1563.

Klorman, R., Strauss, J., and Kokes, R. (1977). The relationship of demographic and diagnostic factors to measures of premorbid adjustment in schizophrenia. *Schizophrenia Bulletin, 3*, 214–225.

Lewine, R. (1980). Sex differences in the age of symptom onset and first hospitalization in typical schizophrenia, schizophreniform psychosis, and paranoid psychosis. *American Journal of Orthopsychiatry, 50,* 316.

Lewine, R. (1981). Sex differences in schizophrenia: Timing or subtypes? *Psychological Bulletin, 90,* 432–444.

Lewine, R. (1988a) Gender and schizophrenia. In M. Tsuang and J. Simpson (Eds.), *Handbook of schizophrenia, 3.* Amsterdam: Elsevier.

Lewine, R. (1988b). The group of schizophrenias. In E. Blechman and K. Brownell (Eds.), *Behavioral medicine for women.* New York: Pergamon Press.

Lewine, R. (1990). Reflections on Saugstad's "Social Class, Marriage and Fertility in Schizophrenia." *Schizophrenia Bulletin, 16,* 171–174.

Lewine, R., Burbach, D., and Harrow, M. (1985). *Symptom onset–First hospital admission delay and outcome in schizophrenia.* Paper presented at the meeting of the American Psychological Association, Los Angeles.

Lewine, R., Burbach, D., and Meltzer, H. (1984). The effect of diagnostic criteria on the proportion of male to female schizophrenia. *American Journal of Psychiatry, 141,* 84–87.

Lewine, R., Gibbons, R., Hedeker, D., and Davis, J. (1987). Effect of anti-psychotic medication and sex on negative symptom factor structure in schizophrenia. Unpublished material, Illinois State Psychiatric Institute, Chicago.

Lewine, R., Gulley, L., Risch, C., Jewart, R., and Houpt, J. (1990). Sexual dimorphism, brain morphology and schizophrenia. *Schizophrenia Bulletin, 16,* 195–204.

Lewine, R., and Sommers, A. (1985). Negative versus positive symptoms in male and female schizophrenics. Paper presented at the meeting of the American Psychological Association, Los Angeles.

Lewine, R., Strauss, J., and Gift, T. (1981). Sex differences in age at first hospital admission for schizophrenia: Fact or artifact? *American Journal of Psychiatry, 138,* 440–444.

Lewine, R., and Walker, E. (1988). Sex and onset age as defining features of schizophrenia. Unpublished manuscript, Emory University, Atlanta, GA.

Luchins, D., Lewine, R., and Meltzer, H. (1984). Lateral ventricular size, psychopathology and medication response to the psychoses. *Biological Psychiatry, 19,* 29–44.

Meehl, P. (1962). Schizotaxia, schizotypy, schizophrenia. *American Psychologist, 17,* 827.

Nasrallah, H., Andreasen, N., Coffman, J., Olson, S., Dunn, V., Ehrhardt, J., and Chapman, S. (1986). A controlled magnetic resonance imaging study of corpus callosum thickness in schizophrenia. *Biological Psychiatry, 21,* 274–282.

NIMH Collaborative Study Group. (1964). Phenothiazine treatment in acute schizophrenia. *Archives of General Psychiatry, 10,* 246–261.

Phillips, L. (1968). *Human adaptation and its Failures.* New York: Academic Press.

Pogue-Giele, M., and Zubin, J. (1988). Negative symptomatology schizophrenia: A conceptual and empirical review. *International Journal of Mental Health, 16,* 3–45.

Revely, M. (1985). CT scans in schizophrenia. *British Journal of Psychiatry, 146,* 367–371.

Rosenthal, D. (1959). Some factors associated with concordance and discordance with respect to schizophrenia in monozygotic twins. *Journal of Nervous and Mental Disease, 129,* 1–10.

Rosenthal, R., and Bigelow, L. (1972). Quantitative brain measurements in chronic schizophrenia. *British Journal of Psychiatry, 35,* 259–264.

Rossi, A., Stratta, P., Gallucci, M., Passariello, R., and Casacchia, M. (1989). Quantification of corpus callosum and ventricles in schizophrenia with nuclear magnetic resonance imaging; a short pilot study. *American Journal of Psychiatry, 146,* 99–101.

Saugstad, L. (1989). Social class, marriage, and fertility in schizophrenia. *Schizophrenia Bulletin, 15,* 9–44.

Schooler, N. (1978). Antipsychotic drugs and psychological treatment in schizophrenia. In M. Lipton, A. DiMascio, and K. Killiam (Eds.), *Psychopharmacology: A generation of progress.* New York: Raven Press.

Schooler, N. (1986). Sex differences in placebo response in double-blind trial of antipsychotics. Presented at the Society for Research in Psychopathology, Cambridge, MA.

Seeman, M. (1982) Gender differences in schizophrenia. *Canadian Journal of Psychiatry, 27,* 107–112.

Seeman, M. (1983). Interaction of sex, age and neuroleptic dose. *Comprehensive Psychiatry, 24,* 125–128.

Seeman, M. (1988). Estrogens and schizophrenia. Presented as part of the symposium, "Gender Differences in Severe Psychopathology," at the American Psychiatric Association Annual Meeting, Montreal.

Silverstein, M., Warren, R., Harrow, M., Grinker, R. & Palewski, T. (1982). Changes in diagnosis from DSM-II to DSM-III. *American Journal of Psychiatry, 139,* 366–372.

Sullivan, H. S. (1962). *Schizophrenia as a human process.* New York: Norton.

Tien, A., and Eaton, W. (1989). Sociodemographic risk factors and psychopathologic precursors of the schizophrenia syndrome. *Schizophrenia Research, 2,* 21. [Abstract.]

Torrey, E., and Torrey, B. (1980). Sex differences in the seasonality of schizophrenic births. *British Journal of Psychiatry, 137,* 101–102.

Tsuang, M., and Winokur, G. (1975). The Iowa 500: Field work in a 35-year follow-up of depression, mania and schizophrenia. *Canadian Psychiatric Association, 20,* 359–365.

Walker, E., Bettes, B., Kain, E., and Harvey, P. (1985). Relationship of gender and marital status with symptomatology in psychotic patients. *Journal of Abnormal Psychology, 94,* 42–50.

Walker, E., and Lewine, R. (1988). The positive/negative symptom distinction in schizophrenia: Validity and etiological relevance. *Schizophrenia Research, 1,* 315–328.

Walker, E., and Lewine, R. (1990). The prediction of adult-onset schizophrenia from childhood home-movies. *American Journal of Psychiatry, 147,* 1052–1056.

Watt, N., Anthony, E., Wynne, L., and Roff, J. (Eds.). (1984). *Children at risk for schizophrenia: A longitudinal perspective.* Cambridge: Cambridge University Press.

Weinberger, D. (1987). Implications of normal brain development for the pathogenesis of schizophrenia. *Archives of General Psychiatry, 44,* 660–669.

Werner, H. (1948). *Comparative psychology of mental development.* New York: Follett.

Westermeyer, J., and Harrow, M. (1984). Prognosis and outcome using broad (DSM-II) and narrow (DSM-III) concepts of schizophrenia. *Schizophrenia Bulletin, 10,* 624–637.

Young, M., Tanner, M., and Meltzer, H. (1982). An empirical study of the diagnosis of schizophrenia. *Journal of Nervous and Mental Disease, 170,* 443–447.

Zigler, E., and Glick, M. (1986). *A developmental approach to adult psychopathology.* New York: Wiley & Sons.

Emotion and Attachment in Families of Schizophrenics: The Struggle for Recovery

Jeri A. Doane

Despite impressive advances in the neurosciences, schizophrenia continues to be a debilitating, life-long illness that touches nearly every aspect of the afflicted individual's life. Impairments in virtually all aspects of interpersonal functioning, work, sense of physical well-being, and day-to-day self-care make recovery from schizophrenia one of the most difficult tasks a human can face. Evidence accumulated in recent years points to the important role that the patient's family plays in this recovery effort. For many people with schizophrenia, the family remains one of the most reliable and consistent sources of meaningful human contact and support.

The role of the family in the course of a schizophrenic illness is a complex one, and the nature of the family's influence varies among patients. While some adult patients live with their family of origin, others have geographically separated and are struggling with varying degrees of independent living in the community. Despite this heterogeneity in the type and degree of family contact, most people with major psychiatric impairment have a common desire or yearning to seek sanctuary and sustenance from the family of origin, regardless of whether the family is

213
Copyright © 1991 by Academic Press, Inc.
All rights of reproduction in any form reserved.

actually capable or able to provide these things for the patient. It is this aspect of providing a sense of connectedness or belonging that is particularly significant for the patient with schizophrenia. Most patients with schizophrenia sooner or later turn to their families for support, care, and an ongoing experience of human contact. Despite the fact that schizophrenic patients are now released from hospitals after very brief periods of inpatient stay, they frequently either find their way back to homes of family members or remain in close contact with them.

This chapter focuses on the idea that the need for human contact and attachment is basic for the schizophrenic patient, and that disruptions of the schizophrenic's interpersonal world in this aspect will continue to influence his or her struggle for recovery of functioning as the patient progresses through various stages of the illness. Research on family emotional environment that views the need for attachment and bonds as primary is discussed in the context of this framework. Treatment studies aimed at correcting the negative emotional atmosphere are also reviewed in an effort to further understand treatment of patients and families suffering from a schizophrenic illness.

EXPRESSED EMOTION

In Great Britain, George Brown *et al.* (1962) reported a study of schizophrenic patients and their relatives in which the relatives' emotional responses toward the patient's behavior were rated. The relatives' responses were made while discussing with an interviewer familial problems involving the patient (e.g., his or her return home, relationships with other people in the family). The patients were followed for 1 year after that and family ratings of emotion toward the patient were used to predict relapse. Global measures of emotional overinvolvement were made as was a global measure of hostility, and both of these were associated with relapse in the patient. The methodological problems in this study were primarily that the interview used was quite unwieldy and naturalistic in nature; it took several hours to administer.

In 1972 Brown, Birley, and Wing carried out a more refined replication of this work in which they studied a sample of 101 consecutive cases of schizophrenia immediately after patients were discharged for hospitalized treatment of the acute state. Interviews were carried out with family members, and an index of family attitudes called expressed emotion (EE) was developed. Each family member was then rated on EE on the basis of an interview. The designation of high EE was based on the number of critical remarks the parent made about the patient, the degree to which he or she expressed hostility toward the patient, and the amount of excessive emotional overinvolvement with the patient or his or her illness. These investigators found that patients returning to live in high EE environments were three to four times more likely to relapse than patients returning to low EE homes. Brown *et al.* (1972) reported that, although degree of behavioral disturbance in the patient was also predictive of relapse, when a variant of multiple regression analysis was done, it was not as potent a predictor as the EE level of the patient's key relatives.

A prospective study of the predictive value of EE was carried out in 1976 by Brown's colleagues in London, Vaughn and Leff, who shortened Brown's lengthy interview technique for eliciting EE attitudes and substituted a more standardized interview for eliciting EE called the Camberwell Family Interview (CFI) (Vaughn and Leff, 1976a,b). This instrument has since become the standard instrument for evaluating the EE status of key relatives in studies of patients with a psychiatric illness. In the 1976 study by Vaughn and Leff, patients from families classified as high or low EE again varied dramatically in rate of relapse. Patients returning to high EE homes were three to four times more likely to relapse during the next 9 months than those returning to low EE households. This study also suggested that regular ingestion of neuroleptics, or a reduction in the amount of face-to-face contact between patient and relatives, narrowed the differences in relapse rate for patients from high and low EE homes.

This work on EE was quite exciting and provocative for family researchers who, until this time, had found it quite difficult to identify meaningful parameters of family life that were consistently related to course of illness. The British work on EE stimulated a number of replication studies that were designed to test whether or not the predictive validity measure would hold up cross-nationally and cross-culturally (Vaughn and Leff, 1976b; Brown *et al.*, 1972). A number of studies have since been published in western Europe and the United States suggesting that EE, as measured by the CFI, is indeed a good predictor of relapse in patients with schizophrenia. For example, Vaughn *et al.* (1984) carried out a carefully designed replication study of the British EE prediction studies in Los Angeles. This study found remarkably similar relapse rates for a sample of carefully diagnosed patients with schizophrenia.

Two EE prediction studies have reported negative results, but some investigators have criticized these replications on methodological grounds. A study by McCreadie and Phillips (1988) in Scotland reported no difference in relapse rates in patients living on their own with low EE or high EE relatives. There are methodological differences in this study that make comparison of these findings with other EE studies difficult, however. One of the problems includes definition of relapse. In the McCreadie study, relapse was defined by hospital readmission or an increase in medication. In the British and American studies, relapse has been defined by recurrence of schizophrenic symptoms as detected by the Present State Examination, a research diagnostic instrument designed for careful elicitation of core schizophrenic symptoms (Wing et al., 1974). In the Scottish study, the patients living in the community were also recruited when they were in a state of remission, in contrast to the British and American studies of EE where patients were studied shortly after hospital admission for clinical relapse. Thus, the Scottish study suggests that the meaning of EE may have different prognostic value depending on the point in the patient's illness at which the measures are obtained. One interpretation of the results is that perhaps it is high EE in the presence of an acute exacerbation of the illness that has a predictive relationship to subsequent relapse and not high EE attitudes per se. Perhaps the impact and meaning of high EE attitudes is different when it occurs only when the patient is in a remitted state and stronger emotionally.

The second study that has reported negative findings on EE was carried out in Australia by Gordon Parker et al. (1988). In this study of 57 schizophrenic patients who were assessed after admission to a hospital, it was found that relapse over the next 9 months was not predicted by household EE status. One of the problems in comparing these findings to other studies concerns which definition of relapse was used. As the authors themselves pointed out, clinical relapse was arbitrarily defined as an increase in two or more levels on the Present State Exam. Conclusions about whether or not a relapse occurred were based on two assessments that were 8 months apart with no assessment in between. Thus, it would be possible, for example, for a person to undergo a clinical relapse in month 4, recover over the next few months, and then be retested at month 8 when he or she was fully recovered and be judged as having had no clinical relapse at all. Because relapse was not continuously tracked as it was in the other EE studies, one might argue that these investigators have increased the risk for underestimating diagnosis.

Another study that is sometimes reported as failing to find the predicted relationship between high and low EE is MacMillan et al.'s (1986) study on first episodes of schizophrenia. Although the authors report that the components of EE fail to predict the outcome response to neuroleptic medication, in fact the data reveal that comparison of relapse rate in high versus low EE groups was statistically significant in the predicted direction. The fact that they found that prognostic factors of duration of illness preceding admission was also associated with course of illness does not negate the findings of the relationship between EE and relapse.

Perhaps the most useful conclusions to be drawn from this series of EE prediction studies is the hypothesis that the EE index reflects a complex web of family relationships and patterns of interaction that underlie some pathogenic process in the course of the patient's illness. This approach to interpreting EE would argue against the reification of the term EE, which has become relatively popularized in recent years in clinical circles in the United States. This notion of EE as indexing a much more complicated system of patterns and relationships in the family is supported by work on directly observed interaction among family members.

Interactional Studies of Family Emotional Climate

The findings of Vaughn and Leff (1976b) lead to the suggestion that EE attitudes in family members in fact reflected similar patterns of actual relating to the patient in terms of face-to-face verbal and nonverbal behavior. The further assumption was that the habitual patterns of criticizing the patient or displaying emotionally overinvolved attitudes with him or her was in some way etiologically linked to a deteriorating course in a person already diagnosed with schizophrenia. Studies that have demonstrated mixed findings with regard to this question of whether or not EE attitudes are a marker of actual behavior have now been carried out.

Affective Style

The CFI (Vaughn and Leff, 1967a), used to elicit data for EE ratings, yields measures of attitudes rather than direct affective communication. The CFI measures attitudes toward a patient, expressed within the context of an interview with a mental health professional. To look at emotional behavior more directly, this author developed a measure called affective style (AS) while working on a longitudinal research project headed by Goldstein at UCLA (Doane et al., 1981). This measure was designed to capture clinically meaningful affective attitudes and behaviors that were verbally expressed toward a patient during a face-to-face family interaction task. Some of the codes in this system overlap with the EE dimensions of criticism and emotional overinvolvement. A series of codes measuring different forms of support of the patient are also coded. Table 10.1 lists the positive and negative codes. As seen in the table, two different kinds of criticism codes exist. In addition, a measure of intrusion is obtained that, like guilt induction, has no direct parallel in the EE system of coding. Many guilt-inducing remarks are considered critical remarks in the EE coding scheme. The interpersonal analogue of emotional overinvolvement may be at least in part reflected by excessive intrusiveness on the part of the parent. With intrusion, one person speaks as an expert concerning the listener's thoughts, feelings, and motives.

TABLE 10.1.   Affective Style Codes

Positive affective style codes	Negative affective style codes
I. *Genuine Support* Conveys a committed, unconditional concern, love, or respect for the patient—unaccompanied by a request for behavior change. II. *Praise, Compliments, Acknowledgment of Accomplishments or Improvements* III. *Empathy* Accurate, supportive rephrasing of patients feelings, problems, etc. Parent adds something of him- or herself into the statement. IV. *Equalizing* Qualification of a child's negative self-statement in such a way that its negative impact is reduced, or the problem is put into perspective. V. *Generalizing* Conveys that others, perhaps even the parents, have the same or similar problems and difficulties VI. *Ego-Propping* Remarks intended to build the child's ego and self-esteem VII. *Siding* One parent aligns with the child during a three-way family conflict. VIII. *Owning Responsibility for Negative Impact* One parent overtly accepts responsibility for negative impact of his or her behavior on the child without being defensive. IX. *Defends Child to the Spouse* Third-person statements about the patient that contain a supportive element in the content.	I. *Criticism* A. Benign—Circumscribed, matter-of-fact, and usually directed toward specific incidents or sets of behavior. B. Personal—Unnecessary or overly harsh modifiers; reference to broad classes of behavior or reference to person's nature of character. II. *Guilt Induction* Conveys that the patient is to blame for some negative event *and* that the parent has been upset by it. III. *Intrusiveness* Implies knowledge of the person's thoughts, feeling states, or motives when in fact there is no apparent basis for such knowledge. A. Neutral—Non-critical tone; refers to patient's emotional states, ideas, or preferences. B. Critical—Contains a harsh critical component.

Family Assessment Procedures

To generate family interaction data for measuring AS, a specific assessment procedure is utilized. The family interaction task used is a modification of Strodtbeck's (1954) revealed differences technique, which elicits samples of clinically meaningful affective behavior during an emotionally charged discussion about a current problem or unresolved issue in the family. This involves first separating family members into different rooms where each family member is interviewed individually to generate problem issues that focus on family conflicts that are idiosyncratically relevant to that particular family. After an issue is identified, the interviewer asks the family member to pretend that the person involved in the problem is sitting in the room with him or her and to verbalize the issue while the tape recorder is running. This audiotaped recording of the family member's issue is then taken to the respective family member to whom it was directed, and he or she listens to the statement and is asked to respond to it. This response is recorded immediately after the initial statement. Two issue and response sequences are generated for each family member.

The family members are subsequently brought together into a lab where they sit and listen to one of these audiotaped sequences of statements. The family is then directed to discuss this problem for 10 minutes, to express their thoughts and feelings about it, and to try to solve the problem while the experimenter is out of the room. After 10 minutes the family is asked to discuss the second problem. One of the issues is generated by the patient and the other is generated by one of the parents. The order of presentation is counterbalanced across families. (For a more complete description of the procedure, see Miklowitz et al., 1984.)

Verbatim, typed transcripts are made from audiotapes of these interactions and are coded for AS (Doane et al., 1985). The data can be reduced in two ways. First, a categorical designation for each parent can be assigned based on whether or not the parent uses one of the negative marker codes of AS previously shown to be associated with increased risk for a poor course of illness (i.e., personal criticism, guilt induction, or excessive intrusiveness). Parental AS profiles are either benign or negative, and these parental classifications are then used to generate family classifications. Patients from negative AS profile families have been found in several studies to be at risk for poor course of illness (Albers et al., 1986; Doane et al., 1981, 1985; Miklowitz et al., 1988).

A second method of data reduction involves deriving cumulative counts of all supportive codes and all negative codes made by family members during the two interactions. Summary negative scores include all of the critical remarks, guilt-inducing statements, and intrusions. One can use these raw summary scores to assess changes in family functioning as a function of time or as a function of some kind of intervention (Doane et al., 1986). The negative score has been used in a validation study of EE in which it was found that parents classified as high EE on the CFI were in fact more inclined to use more negative AS codes during a face-to-face interaction than did low EE parents (Miklowitz et al., 1984; Valone et al., 1983).

Interestingly enough, two studies have found that the categorical designations of benign versus negative AS and low versus high EE are statistically independent (Miklowitz *et al.*, 1988; Valone *et al.*, 1983). This means that although the two measures overlap somewhat, they also, in fact, are quite independent. What this finding also suggests is that some high EE relatives may be able to inhibit their behavior when in the presence of the ill patient. One report has suggested that patients who return to homes where the parents have both high EE attitudes and negative AS profiles are at particularly high risk for clinical relapse than are patients who return to homes where both risk factors are not present (Miklowitz *et al.*, 1988). If one looks at the raw summary score of total negative AS statements, then parents rated as high EE are more negative in their AS than low EE parents are. Thus, this global index of emotional reactivity is associated with EE status. However, positive AS codes appear unrelated to either EE status or course of illness in the patient.

A recent study by Hahlweg *et al.* (1989) in West Germany reported additional validation for both EE and AS. A system called Kategoriensystem fuer Partnerschaftliche Interaktion (KPI) was used to measure verbal and nonverbal behavior in direct interaction in a study comparing low and high EE parents of schizophrenics with a recent onset of illness. The parents were compared on several dimensions of KPI that involved verbal and nonverbal codes that were conceptually similar to EE. When CFI data obtained 2 months prior to the interaction were used to compare subjects, no differences between groups were found. However, when a brief measure of EE (Magana *et al.*, 1986) obtained at or around the same time of the interaction was used to divide the parents, the overlap between the attitudes of behavior was statistically significant. This suggests that the EE measure may not always be a variable trait and that degrees and types of EE may change throughout the course of the patient's illness. This particular issue could not be addressed in this study.

In summary, one can say that some evidence exists for the validity of the EE measure. However, the issue of attitudes and behavior is a complex one and studies suggest that statistical correlation is lacking between the two categorical designations of risk. This in turn has implications for the treatment of families of schizophrenics in that intervention targeted at people who hold high EE attitudes *and* negative AS behaviors may be different than treatment goals for people who have only the negative attitude toward the patient and who can inhibit these attitudes when interacting with the child. It may be possible, for example, that parents in the latter category require less intensive forms of family therapy.

Patient Attributes Associated with EE Subtype

If high EE attitudes are associated with relapse, then this correlation may be due to a third variable such as severity of illness or the quality of the patient's symptoms at the time of discharge. Several studies have reported no relationship between severity of symptoms at discharge and likelihood of relapse with regard to low or high EE (Doane et al., 1985; Hogarty et al., 1986; Miklowitz et al., 1988; Tarrier et al., 1988). Miklowitz et al. (1983), however, did find that one high EE subgroup, emotionally overinvolved, was associated with ratings of poor premorbid adjustments in the patients and high levels of symptoms, as rated on the Brief Psychiatric Rating Scale (Overall and Gorham, 1962) at discharge. Parents designated in the overinvolved subgroup were placed there because they also did not have a high rating on criticism. Patients from families that had relatives who were categorized as high EE because of excessive criticism had better premorbid adjustment and symptom severity. Patients from this group were indiscriminable from patients in the low EE group in terms of symptoms and premorbid status. This study suggests a possible link between a poor premorbid child and the development of an overinvolved parenting style, perhaps initially aimed at compensating for the child's deficits or difficulties. This issue could not be addressed in this study, however, because it only included adults who already had an established history of illness.

It is reasonable to expect that family members can become emotionally overinvolved and upset by things other than symptoms. They may, for example, find the patient's verbal behavior irritating in some way. One can hypothesize that patients who have themselves more verbally high EE toward their parents are more likely to elicit and reinforce cycles of high EE from the parents. The issue of whether emotionally overinvolved attitudes contribute to poor prognosis or these attitudes are a result of having to care for a child with longstanding impairments in functioning remains unsettled. Studies that examine the role of patient variables in negative AS and EE are currently being carried out at Yale Psychiatric Institute.

A recent study by Strachan et al. (1989) analyzed the coping styles of patients from low and high EE families during a direct interaction task. The scheme measured autonomous, critical, supportive, self-affirming, and self-denigrating statements made by the patient during a direct interaction task with his or her parents. Their analysis revealed a significant relationship between measures of parental EE and AS and quality of patient coping. Patients from low EE or benign AS family environments tended to express either autonomous or neutral interactional behavior. In contrast, patients from high EE or negative AS families tended to express either externalizing (counter-criticism, a defensive search for blame in others) or self-denigration, and self-blame. The authors suggest that these data support the notion that the EE measure reflects transactional patterns between relatives and patients that are reciprocal and systemic, rather than unidirectional, as implied in the original EE studies.

Cross-Cultural EE

A recent cross-cultural replication of the original EE prediction results were reported by Karno *et al.* (1987) who measured criticism, hostility, and emotional overinvolvement in a sample of low-income, relatively unacculturated Mexican–American families of schizophrenics. The authors reported a lower level (41%) of high EE households among families of Mexican–Americans compared with rates reported for American families (67%; Vaughn *et al.*, 1984) and British samples (48%; Brown *et al.*, 1972; Vaughn and Leff, 1976b). After 9 months, 26% of the Mexican–American low EE patients had relapsed compared with 59% of the high EE patients, a statistically significant difference between groups. As with other EE studies, EE ratings were not correlated with symptom scores for the schizophrenic patients. This study provides additional evidence that EE is not merely a parental reaction to severe schizophrenic symptoms.

Causal Linkages

A number of questions remain unanswered regarding the relative contributions of patient and parental input to the resultant high or low EE atmosphere in the family. Further studies are needed to tease out the underlying complexities implied by labels such as high or low EE. The causal linkages between patient or illness variables and burdens on the families are relatively unexplored. Relatives often feel unfairly blamed and criticized by EE research, which implies that the parents are somehow to blame for the patient's inability to recover from the illness.

FAMILY-BASED INTERVENTION STUDIES

At approximately the same time as these EE studies of relapse began to emerge in the literature (1970s), several research investigations were underway that aimed to modify aspects of the family environment that were thought to be contributing to the increased risk for relapse in the patient (e.g., Falloon *et al.*, 1982; Hogarty *et al.*, 1986). All of these studies accepted the critical role of neuroleptic medication in the prevention of relapse in schizophrenia. At the same time each investigator acknowledged the fact that medication alone is not sufficient to prevent relapse in approximately 40% of patients during the first year following hospital discharge (Hogarty and Ulrich, 1977). The central question for each of these controlled treatment studies was whether or not the addition of a family therapy component to a maintenance neuroleptic regimen could improve the schizophrenic patient's chances for survival outside of the hospital. All four of these studies have provided dramatic evidence for the effectiveness of this combined approach to treatment. In all of these approaches, treatment has the relatively modest goal of preventing florid relapse. In none of these approaches are the investigators attempting to "cure" the illness as was often the aim in family therapy with schizophrenics in the 1950s and 1960s.

The first study reported was carried out by Goldstein *et al.* (1978), who studied young schizophrenic patients who were experiencing their first acute episode of the illness. Patients in this study were randomly assigned to one of two dose levels of injectable phenothiazine [moderate (25 mg) or low (6.25 mg) doses of fluphenazine enanthate] and either to receive or not receive a 6-week trial of crisis-oriented family therapy. Six months later patients were followed up and relapse rates for the four cells were compared. Patients in this study were not assessed for family risk variables such as EE; rather the intent of the study was to test the efficacy of combining low-dose and maintenance-dose neuroleptic medication with family therapy. Relapse rates during the 6-week trial of treatment were significantly different for the two groups: 0% for those in the high-dose/family therapy group and 24% for patients in the low-dose/no-therapy group. Relapse rate for the high-dose/no-therapy group was 17% and for the low-dose/therapy group 22%. After the 6-week intervention period, patients were treated in various, uncontrolled ways by their therapists since they were no longer actively participating in the study. This makes interpretation of their 6-month follow-up data somewhat difficult. Nevertheless, the authors report 6-month relapse rates that parallel those reported for the end of 6-week intervention: 0% relapse for patients in the high-dose/therapy group, and nearly 50% for those in the low-dose/no therapy group.

This study was important because it provided the first evidence that adding a family therapy component to neuroleptic medication could significantly reduce the probability of relapse beyond that expected when medication alone was used (approximately 40%). This study also provided suggestive evidence that even very minimal amounts of family intervention offered at critical periods in the early stages of the illness might help prevent the development of patterns of chronicity.

The report by Goldstein *et al.* (1978) brought a measure of enthusiasm to those studying ways to effectively treat schizophrenia. However, the study had limitations that left several questions unanswered. An important one was whether these protective effects of family therapy plus medication were short-lived or whether relapse could be prevented for a longer period of time due to the efforts to assist the family during that initial critical 6-month period. A related question concerned whether or not such brief treatment would be as effective with schizophrenics who had been ill for many years and who may have, as a consequence of the duration of illness, developed additional problems that were not quite so responsive to brief intervention.

In Great Britain, Leff *et al.* (1982) carried out a controlled treatment study of schizophrenic patients from predominantly high EE families. These investigators chose a somewhat different format for their family intervention—a relatives' group composed of both low and high EE family members. All but 2 of the 24 patients were maintained on long-acting injectable neuroleptic medication. Families in the control group received medication but no family therapy.

The high EE parents in the experimental treatment group were encouraged to discuss strategies for coping with their particular problems. Most families also received some in-house individual family therapy sessions, which were designed to help families reduce EE in the home environment. Patients were not involved in the family intervention component of this study, rather the program was targeted specifically for the relatives, most of whom were rated as high EE.

At the 9-month follow-up point only one (9%) relapse had occurred in the group receiving multifamily therapy, in contrast to 6 (50%) of the 12 patients receiving standard outpatient and no regular family therapy. Although these differences in relapse rates are quite striking, only half of the 12 high EE families in therapy converted to low EE. The authors also report that criticism was much more modifiable than emotional overinvolvement with the patient.

Leff and Vaughn (1981) reported a 2-year follow-up of this sample that provided evidence that the beneficial effects of their social interventions with families were evident 2 years later. The cumulative relapse rates for the 2-year period were 62% for high EE patients and 20% for low EE patients ($p < 0.02$). This means that the relationship between high EE and relapse persists for at least 2 years. They further reported a therapy effect at 2 years with patients from the family-treated group having a lower (20%) relapse rate than patients in the control group (no parent group, medication only, 78%).

The problem with this study was that the patients were not systematically included in the family treatment. This could be why only 50% of the families converted from high to low EE. Furthermore, the published reports imply that some but not all the experimental families also received extensive amounts of fairly unstructured, eclectic family therapy sessions in the context of home visits. Apparently there is no clear way to partition and assess the relative contributions of the group versus individual family therapy components in reducing risk for relapse. Leff *et al.* (1982) also reported that actual techniques varied from psychodynamic to behavior interventions. The Leff study did differ from the Goldstein study intervention in that a systematic psychoeducational component was included in the family treatment package. The approach used was also geared specifically toward lowering EE. In this sense the Leff study was somewhat more sharply defined conceptually than the Goldstein intervention.

In Pittsburgh, Hogarty et al. (1986) developed an intensive education and stress management program that aimed to lower the emotional climate of the home as well as develop manageable expectations for patient performance. Their treatment sought to "increase the stability and predictability of family life by decreasing the family's guilt and anxiety, increasing their self-confidence, and providing a sense of cognitive mastery through the provision of information concerning the nature and course of schizophrenia as well as specific management strategies thought to be helpful in coping with schizophrenic symptoms on a day-to-day basis" (Hogarty et al., 1986:634). These investigators tested this model of treatment in controlled trials of patients who were designated high risk for relapse on the basis of being rated as having high EE families. A unique and creative aspect of this program involved the inclusion of a social skills training component for the patient, which aimed to teach them how to avoid conflict and decrease behaviors thought to elicit high EE in family members. All 103 patients in the study received maintenance neuroleptic medication; most received injectable fluphenazine decanoate. Relapse rates for the first year following discharge from the hospital revealed a strong main effect for family treatment (19%), a main effect for social skills training (20%), and an additive effect for the combined conditions (0%). Control subjects received maintenance neuroleptics and supportive therapy from a psychiatric nurse clinical specialist. Their relapse rate was 41%, a rate quite similar to other reports of relapse rate in patients treated only with neuroleptics.

The family approach of Anderson et al. (1980) rests heavily on teaching the family to avoid placing stress on the patient. Patients are actively encouraged to rest and remain dependent for up to 6 months after the florid episode and then to begin very gradual steps toward re-entry into the community. The family members are educated about the nature of a schizophrenic illness and are encouraged to adopt tolerant, low-key, supportive behaviors and attitudes toward their disabled son or daughter. In the Anderson approach, the family component employed is less structured and task-specific than more comprehensive behaviorally oriented studies such as that by Falloon (Falloon et al., 1982).

In a carefully controlled study by Falloon et al. (1982, 1984, 1985) in California, 36 patients, predominantly from high EE families, were randomly assigned to either behaviorally oriented family therapy or a control condition of individual therapy. All patients were on maintenance doses of neuroleptic medication throughout the duration of the study.

The family management condition was carried out primarily in the homes, whereas the individual treatment was done in the clinic. Both treatments followed a common behaviorally oriented model in which communication and problem-solving training were core modules. Neither treatment condition concentrated on modifying EE or reducing affective communication, although a reduction in the level of emotional tension in the home would be expected in the family management condition as a side effect of learning more effective communication and problem-solving skills. For both groups, therapy was weekly during the first 3 months and ended with monthly maintenance sessions for the final 3 months of the 9-month treatment period.

Before each family entered into its respective psychosocial treatment protocol, a pretherapy family assessment task was carried out for each family. This was the direct interaction task described earlier in this chapter, in which two problems were discussed with an experimenter present. After the first 3 months of treatment, this procedure was repeated. These data were then scored for AS.

Families receiving family therapy had significantly lower levels of negative AS codes after 3 months of therapy than did parents of individually treated patients ($p < 0.005$) (Doane et al., 1986). The results also revealed evidence that the total number of negative AS codes actually increased over the early months after hospital discharge in parents who did not receive family therapy. One hypothesis about this finding was that as the months wore on, the patient and his or her illness became increasingly frustrating for the parents to deal with and the negative aspects of the family emotional climate may have intensified. Although this question could not be definitively tested in this study, if it were in fact true, then it would have important implications for treating schizophrenics from high EE families. Treatment programs that focused exclusively on family psychoeducation or "dynamic" forms of family therapy that encouraged the expression of intense affect might actually increase the patient's risk of relapse because they do not succeed in lowering the "resting level" of emotional tension in the home.

Average scores derived from group means do not permit assessment of an association between the reduction of negative verbal remarks by the parent and the likelihood of relapse in the patient offspring. To address these kinds of questions, a categorical method of assigning patients to risk groups was used to test whether or not patients from negative AS family profiles were more likely to relapse than patients from families classified as benign AS—no negative marker codes assigned to the parent(s). In a previous study of high-risk adolescents by Doane *et al.* (1981), the presence of one key marker variable from either parent during an interaction was found to be predictive of a poor outcome. Three of these negative AS codes are used as marker codes to define a parent's AS profile: personal criticism (one or more statements), guilt induction (one or more statements), and excessive neutral intrusiveness (six or more statements). A parent was categorized as negative if he or she exhibited one or more of these marker criteria and as benign if he or she had no marker codes. Benign AS *families* are those where both parents have benign AS profiles; negative AS families have one or more patients with a negative parent profile.

The AS data were obtained from family interactions carried out at both baseline and again 3 months after treatment had begun. Family AS pattern at the 3-month assessment point was the better predictor of relapse 9 months later. Nine of the 10 patients who had relapses came from homes with negative AS patterns at 3 months. Nine of these 10 were patients in the individual therapy condition. Family therapy failed to reverse negative AS profiles to benign for six families. These patients did not, however, suffer a relapse. The authors speculated that perhaps the reason for this was that these families required a longer period of time to absorb and integrate the family treatment and, thus, positive changes in the family could not be observed because family AS was not measured later than the 3-month point. This hypothesis could not be tested directly, however.

This study by Doane *et al.* (1981) demonstrated further support for the hypothesis that family emotional climate deleteriously influences the schizophrenic patient's recovery efforts because it measured parental behavior toward the patient and did not rely on inferences made from parental attitudes. The study also suggested that a subgroup of markedly relapse-prone patients could be identified prior to initiation of psychosocial treatment. The results did not suggest that negative AS causes relapse; however, they did, suggest that psychosocial factors may play an important contributory role in the course of the illness. In this sense, one can think of a negative emotional family climate as a nonspecific stressor that, theoretically, could affect the course of illness through an interaction with other variables known to affect the clinical course of schizophrenia. Viewing schizophrenia within the context of a stress vulnerability model means that if stressful environmental stimuli could be identified, the course of the illness might be improved. A stress vulnerability model posits a core biologic vulnerability to the illness that makes the individual vulnerable to stress overload (Liberman *et al.*, 1989).

In Great Britain, a recent study by Tarrier *et al.* (1988) tested the effectiveness of a behavioral family management approach in contrast to psychoeducation only and routine (minimal contact) treatment for patients from both high and low EE families. Low EE families received either education or routine treatment, as they were low-risk for relapse. There were no differences between these two groups in terms of education program or in relapse rates. However, the authors did report a considerable, although not significant, change from low EE to high EE in the group that did not receive psychoeducation. No relatives who received the two-session psychoeducation became high EE, which suggests that a brief psychoeducational program may be an effective intervention program for preventing relapse in low EE families. This hypothesis needs to be definitively tested, however.

The fact that some low EE relatives convert to high EE is consistent with the report by Doane *et al.* (1986), which showed that parents who did not receive family therapy significantly increased their negative remarks made to the patient during the 3 months after discharge from the hospital. Thus, in treating schizophrenia, it is important not to assume that families remain status quo with regard to levels of emotional reactivity when left as they were prior to hospitalization. Failure to provide family intervention is likely to result in an *increase* in emotional negativity in the home environment as time goes on for a substantial number of families. Given the enormous burdens and stresses inherent in caring for a chronically psychotic family member, these data are not surprising. Education alone was not effective in reducing risk of relapse for patients from high EE homes (43% relapsed). Patients from high EE families who received only minimal routine treatment from a local clinic had a relapse rate of 53%. All patients in the study received maintenance neuroleptic medication; 86% of them were on depot injection. None of the differences in relapse rate could be accounted for by differences in degree of medication compliance, rate of administration, or amount of dosage.

The two intensive family management groups were compared for high EE relatives. Both groups consisted of an initial phase comprised of two psychoeducation sessions followed by three sessions on stress management. This aspect of the treatment aimed to teach relatives to monitor sources of stress and their reactions to it, and to then attempt better ways of dealing with it. The two groups then received eight sessions of a goal-setting program, which involved teaching patients and families to identify problems and set goals to make necessary changes. The two treatment groups differed in the level of intervention—namely, one group discussed and received instruction about these new skills (symbolic) whereas the other group was required to actively role-play, practice, and document participation in treatment tasks (enactive). The overall aim of these behavioral interventions was to eliminate high EE behaviors on the part of the relatives and to modify aspects of the patient's behavior that seemed to elicit the high EE response. The relapse rates for patients in both of these groups were significantly lower (17% enactive and 8% symbolic) than for patients from high EE families receiving just education (42%) or only routine treatment (53%).

As with several of the other controlled treatment studies, this particular study used many patients who were already fairly chronically ill (mean number of admissions = 2.8; mean duration of illness = 6.3 years). Thus, the possibility remains that different results might have been found had they studied recent-onset schizophrenic patients. It is possible that high EE patterns of relating develop and become entrenched over a period of time as the patient's illness begins to establish itself as an enduring condition with serious impairments that have potential for creating chronic stress and burden on the family. Of 25 families who participated in the intensive family therapy treatment, 3 of them relapsed during the 9-month follow-up (12%). But if one includes drop-outs as treatment failures, this rate increases to 24% (6/25) for whom this family intervention was not entirely successful. One wonders about the characteristics of these families and whether or not they have unique attributes that make them particularly difficult to engage in treatment.

Tarrier et al. (1988) report that approximately half of the high EE relatives convert to low EE with just routine treatment of the patient or only minimal family psychoeducation. With the 9-month intensive family intervention, however, the percentage of high EE relatives who change to low EE was fairly consistent—from 93% at admission, to 8% at 4.5 months, and to 17% at 9 months for the symbolic group; and 93% to 50% to 29%, respectively, for the enactive group. These data point to the need for a high-quality, active, and fairly focused intensive family therapy program for patients living in high EE families. In interpreting the above figures, it is important to keep in mind that relatives of patients who relapsed during the 9-month follow-up period were excluded from these rates. Thus, although this presents a comparison of treatment effects on EE changes that are free of any reactive effect due to relapse, the figures necessarily underrepresent relatives whose EE stayed high throughout treatment for whatever reason. The question of whether the relative's EE is improving because the patient is getting better or becoming more socially skilled and functional remains to be answered by further research.

YALE PSYCHIATRIC INSTITUTE FAMILY STUDY

This author is involved in carrying out an ongoing prospective longitudinal study of the role of family factors in major psychiatric illness at the

Yale Psychiatric Institute (YPI) in New Haven, Connecticut. This study is quasi-naturalistic in design and employs repeated measures of a number of family attributes known to be implicated in probability of relapse for patients suffering from psychiatric illness. Most notably these include family emotional climate and communication deviance (CD) (Wynne *et al.*, 1977). The study is designed to address several basic research questions that have been left unanswered by the previous research on family factors and illness that is reviewed in this chapter. In particular, the focus is to try to understand some of the underlying complexity that is indexed by marker variables such as negative AS or high EE. To this end we have attempted to extend our knowledge about the role of family factors in course of illness by adding a new dimension of family functioning to the study of risk factors in schizophrenia—that of attachment and bonding.

The design of the study involves repeated assessments of these family attributes over time and assessment of three generations of the families. The long-term aim of this work is to learn more about the transmission of patterns of family interaction across generations, with particular attention focused on the ways in which intrafamilial patterns of attachment and EE are re-enacted in the course of long-term inpatient treatment. The notion of including measures of attachment and bonding in studies of familiar comes from clinical observations of the importance of both the internal and external object world for the severely ill patient. In particular, losses, or perceived or feared losses, play a crucial role in the patient's ability to recover from severe active episodes of psychosis.

In this study, the conceptual model for understanding schizophrenia assumes a biological base to the illness where the course and form of the disorder over the individual's lifetime depend in large part on the environmental experiences the individual incurs as he or she develops. The logic underlying the design is based on the gene–environment interaction model such as that suggested by Tienari *et al.*'s (1985, 1989) work in Finland, where adopted children at genetic risk for schizophrenia who become ill were those who were raised in chaotic or disturbed family environments. In the YPI study, the central hypothesis being tested is that intrafamilial attributes determine the extent to which the patient is able to sustain gains made in his or her social functioning while receiving hospital-based treatment. Patients returning to high contact with emotionally overreactive or negative families are predicted to be less able to sustain gains made in social functioning than are patients whose negative family attributes have been modified. The YPI study expands the gene–environment interaction model by integrating it with the hypothesis that crucial patterns of pathogenic, nonbiological as well as biological–genetic processes are passed from one generation to the next, contributing to the recurrence of schizophrenic illness.

Attachment in the Family

Attachment has been studied by Stern (1985), Ainsworth *et al.* (1978), and other empirical researchers who have operationalized Bowlby's (1982, 1988) concept of attachment by observing dyadic interactions between mothers and infants that seem to set the template for the emergence and consolidation of various patterns of attachment throughout adolescence and young adulthood (Main and Cassidy, 1988; Main *et al.*, 1985). The conceptual linkages of attachment to family risk factors have not been explored a great deal by researchers studying family factors in schizophrenia. The exception to this is work by Gordon Parker, a psychiatrist from Australia who has developed a measure for bonding and attachment that has been shown to be predictive of relapse in schizophrenics (Parker, 1983; Parker *et al.*, 1982) and other disorders (Parker *et al.*, 1979). In this study, patients were administered a simple 10-minute self-report measure. The patient scores his or her mother and father separately on 25 items designed to measure attachment and bonding. The score on the Parental Bonding Instrument (PBI) permits comparison of four parenting styles: (1) "affectionless control" (low care, high control); (2) "neglectful" (low care, low control), (3) "affectionate constraint" (high care, high control), and (4) "optimal" (high care, low control). Schizophrenic patients who relapsed were significantly more likely to have one or more parents with a high-risk PBI profile of affectionless control. For patients who stayed in contact with their families after discharge, the readmission rate was 75% for patients with one or more high-risk parents, compared with 25% for those who did not assign a parent to the affectionless control quadrant.

It could be inferred from the work on EE that the absence of hostile and/or critical attitudes toward a patient thereby implies a presence of an affectional bond. In fact, however, neither the EE coding system (Vaughn and Leff, 1976b) nor the AS interactional measure of emotional climate (Doane *et al.*, 1981) actually measure attachment. These emotional climate measures involve unidirectional assessment of parental criticism and rejection of the patient, intrusion, guilt induction, and emotional overinvolvement. Attachment, on the other hand, implies a bidirectional process in which both parties are drawn into reciprocal bonding and interaction (Stern, 1985; Bowlby, 1988). In general, researchers have neglected the bidirectional nature of affectional bonds that may exist or that have failed to develop between the schizophrenic and his or her family of origin.

Concepts such as emotional involvement, for example, are frequently assumed to reflect an overly strong attachment between the schizophrenic patient and the parent, usually on the part of the mother. Attempts to help the patient separate from the mother are often early targets of intervention. In the same vein, the clinician often assumes that overly dependent, symbiotic modes of patient–parent interaction reflect an emotional closeness or bond.

Wynne's Epigenetic Model of Relational Systems

Wynne (1984) has presented an epigenetic model for understanding the development of enduring relational systems. In his model, four major processes are outlined: attachment and caregiving, communicating, joint problem-solving, and mutuality. The initial epigenetic layer—attachment and caregiving—is primary, and when attachment has not taken place, a shared cognitive and affective perspective, necessary for more advanced and complex relational modes, cannot be established. With a nonexistent or negative attachment, the family may be arrested at the first stage of the epigenetic journey. A patient and his or her parent have no shared base of positive affective history, which each can take for granted when attempting to send and comprehend complex verbal and nonverbal communications. When the individuals in a family experience emotional security, communication styles become prominent in the day-to-day concerns of the family. As Wynne (1984) points out, however, family members must first be sufficiently emotionally attached to one another before they are willing to come together to learn communication skills or anything else.

Joint problem-solving, an even higher form of relating, presupposes not only an attachment, but also the acquisition of relatively successful communication skills in its family members. Joint goal-setting and problem-solving are key components of many contemporary forms of family-based treatments for schizophrenia reviewed earlier in this chapter. Wynne has suggested that the two major components of EE—emotional overinvolvement and criticism—can be understood as "special forms of attachment/caregiving that are likely to lead to dysfunctional communicating, problem-solving, and intimacy" (Wynne, 1984; 304). The implications of this theoretical linkage have not really been developed by Wynne. In the current ongoing study at the YPI, Diana Diamond and this author are pursuing the empirical study of this theoretical linkage (Doane and Diamond, 1990).

Yale Psychiatric Institute Study Design

Newly admitted patients and their families form three diagnostic groups: (1) a core group of young adults (aged 17–29 years) with a schizophrenia spectrum diagnosis, (2) a comparison group of young adults with affective disorders, and (3) a second comparison group of adolescents with primary diagnosis of conduct disorder, borderline personality disorder, or dysthymia. Only patients admitted for relatively long (approximately 1–2 years) periods of hospitalization are included in this study.

Patients and families participate in four 2-hour laboratory assessments in which a variety of measures are obtained, including parental AS, a measure that reflects interpersonal analogues of high EE attitudes and is derived from directly observed interaction with the patient. A negative family AS is characterized by relatively high levels of intensely critical, hostile, or intrusive verbal remarks. As mentioned earlier in this chapter, this measure has been used in several studies and has been found to be associated with increased risk for poor outcome. Family members' attitudes toward the patient and his or her illness are also obtained. In addition, interviews with family therapists are conducted at regular intervals, which permits the tracking of change in the ways that family members express emotion as family therapy progresses. Detailed methods for scoring the family therapist's ratings of family variables are presented in detail elsewhere (Doane *et al.*, 1988). Independent ratings of the patient's social functioning are made by the nursing staff at regular intervals throughout the course of hospitalization. Thus, the design permits the study of the sequence of changes that occur during hospitalization when both parents and the patient are receiving treatment simultaneously and all three are beginning to change their modes of interpersonal relating. When data collection is completed, it will be possible to look at the patient's progress over time and compare it in counterpoint fashion with changes in the family measures over time. Analysis of cause–effect sequences will be carried out to determine whether EE becomes higher or lower in response to improvements or deteriorations in the patient's state.

Intergenerational Assessment

The contribution of a genetically transmitted component to schizophrenia is not disputed by most contemporary researchers. At the same time, this body of work makes it clear that genetic transmission is not sufficient to account for all of the observed cases of schizophrenia. Environmental stressors may play a role in releasing the expression of this biologic vulnerability. Very little work has been done linking the worlds of genetics and family environmental stress in the study of schizophrenia. One notable exception is the work of Tienari *et al.* (1985, 1989) in Finland.

It is possible that the mere presence of a mentally ill relative in the parent's family of origin is a significant stressor that could lead to the parent becoming a more emotionally overreactive (negative AS) person in general. Alternatively, having a mentally ill relative may be totally unrelated to a person's tendency to relate in negative AS ways. These kinds of issues have not been addressed in the existing literature. One of the aims of the YPI study is to explore some of the possible mechanisms involved in the gene–environment interaction models of psychiatric illness. Understanding more about how genetic and environmental stressors interact to reduce risk for recovery will permit us to identify high-risk families of the mentally ill more easily and to provide them with appropriate interventions.

Genetic pedigree data are obtained through systematic family history interviews with the patient's parents. These data will be independently diagnosed for the presence of mental illness in the patient's relatives to ascertain whether or not the presence of mental illness in the parental nuclear family is associated with variables such as high CD, a tendency to use negative AS, or the presence of high EE attitudes.

Intergenerational biological transmission is not the only means of influencing the offspring in the family. Also in this study, the parents participated in a 1.5-hour semistructured interview (Diamond, 1986b) about their relationships with their own mothers and fathers. This author's colleague, Diana Diamond (1986a, 1987), has developed measures for use in this study that assess the quality of attachment and bonding between parent and child; the patient's parents are being administered these instruments. These measures are being studied in conjunction with family variables found in previous empirical studies to be associated with increased risk for poor outcome (EE, AS, CD) and other more traditional variables such as number of previous hospitalizations, severity of illness, and presence or absence of psychiatric illness in the first-degree relatives.

This transgenerational strategy permits an intergenerational analysis of patterns of attachment and bonding. These data will be studied in relation to other variables such as pedigree data on mental illness in the first- and second-degree relatives, patterns of interaction such as EE or AS, and outcome data on the patients 1 year after discharge. Patients are tracked for 1 year after they leave the hospital and are then administered a semistructured follow-up interview and a retest of certain key family measures.

The possibility that mental illness in one's family of origin increases the risk for developing "high-risk" parenting styles is one of the ideas that will be explored in this study. An equally plausible alternative hypothesis is that it is not so much the biologic risk that determines how one reacts to the ill child as it is the quality of emotional relating that one has experienced in the context of one's own family of origin. A healthy and warm attachment to one's parent may override any deleterious effects from that parent's psychiatric illness. These kinds of questions will be a major focus of this ongoing research investigation at the YPI.

Diagnostic Specificity versus Generalized Stressors

One of the unresolved issues in the area of family risk factors and major psychiatric disorder is the question of whether family variables known to increase risk for clinical relapse in schizophrenia are associated with specific psychiatric disorders or they are representative of a broader class of disorders such as depression, personality disorder, and substance abuse. Some evidence indicates that variables such as parental CD, as conceptualized by Wynne *et al.* (1977) are somewhat specific to schizophrenia or psychotic illness. In the YPI study, we are obtaining measures of these family risk factors from a comparison sample of young adults with borderline or depressed psychiatric disorders. A second comparison group of borderline and conduct-disordered adolescents is also being studied. Analyses on these clusters of variables will be carried out to determine whether or not they permit discrimination of one diagnostic group from the other.

State–Trait Questions

Another issue that will be addressed in this study is the notion of how stable these family variables are. Measures of CD are repeated at regular intervals, as are measures of attachment and bonding and family AS. Negative AS attitudes, as measured by a subset of items from the Kreisman Rejection Scale (Kreisman *et al.*, 1979), are also obtained. When the study is complete, it will be possible to study how these variables change over the course of the patient's illness as he or she enters into a period of recovery, around time of hospital discharge. Hopefully, these analyses will be useful in designing interventions that are better suited to the needs of the family.

Preliminary Studies

Preliminary studies have identified three subtypes of families, each of which suggests different treatment strategies. A more detailed discussion of these groups and their treatment implications is presented elsewhere (Doane and Diamond, 1989).

High-intensity families are characterized by very consistent patterns of negative AS: intrusion, criticism, emotional overinvolvement, and guilt-inducing behavior. Parents in these families are very emotionally over-involved with the patient throughout the course of treatment. They are clearly not detached or disengaged from the patient; they are positively attached to one another for the most part, across generations. The level of verbal activity is often quite chaotic and dramatic in these families.

A second group of families is labeled *disconnected*. These are families characterized by parents who demonstrate high EE characteristics such as rejection, criticism, and intrusion. They also appear to be very involved with the patient. However, this intensity appears not to derive so much from a positively attached, emotional overinvolvement as it does from frustrations and ruptures in bonds, or failures of attachment between parent and child. Family therapists consistently rate these families as disengaged and emotionally distant. Preliminary data suggest that problems in attachment and bonding are present across all three generational levels in many of these families; i.e., the patients themselves report disturbances in attachment with their parents; whereas the parents in turn report disturbed attachments in their family of origin.

In the last group, *low-intensity* families, parents show little evidence of entrenched high EE attitudes or behavior. They do display some criticism and occasional emotional overinvolvement but it does not tend to be excessive. In general, these are parents who seem to tolerate the stress of the patient's illness more readily. They seem to have derived some sense of mastery out of dealing with hardship in their own families of origin. The parents in these families have a more differentiated view of their own parents than do other parents in the study.

Treatment Issues

Wynne's (1984) epigenetic model, discussed earlier, suggests that the development of healthy and stable attachments are a necessary precursor to effective communication in the family. If this is true, then families in our disengaged subgroup should receive a family therapy approach targeted specifically toward attachment problems and not one that focuses exclusively on communication skills or problem-solving. Disengaged, unattached families pose a high risk for treatment failure. Patients from these families are not positively attached to their parents, although they may be in fairly frequent contact with them. The parents often seem to have less investment in maintaining a close relationship with the patient because they have not experienced things such as emotional overinvolvement and positive attachment in their previous family experience. Parents of patients in this group are often most comfortable with a disengaged relational style involving a high degree of distance from the patient. Although they may know intellectually that this is damaging to the patient, often they are unable to move beyond such a detached stance. The tragedy here, of course, is that often the patient is not at all comfortable with the parents' detachment and makes repeated and futile gestures to engage them. In a preliminary analysis, we have found that many of these patients show little improvement during intensive long-term treatment and they have a tendency to relapse fairly quickly after hospital discharge.

Clinicians can make a number of errors in attempting to treat families with attachment problems. The first one involves misdiagnosing a family problem as one of a parent–child dyad being fused and overly attached, when in fact a healthy attachment has not ever developed between the parent and child. Another example of treatment error involves focusing exclusively on structural and relational problems in the nuclear family and failing to address family-of-origin linkages to the current dysfunction in the family. Our subgrouping of families would also suggest that "high-level" psychoeducation and communication skills interventions are likely to be ill-suited to disengaged families. Psychoeducational or "high-level" problem-solving types of interventions presuppose a sufficient, positive attachment between parent and child. This particular aspect is consistent with a recently reported finding by Tarrier et al. (1988), who reported that psychoeducation alone had little impact on high EE families.

Treatment of the high-intensity family involves redirecting some of the emotional overinvolvement and criticism into forms of caring and positive bonding and teaching the family how to cope with emotional reactivity in its members. We have found that high-intensity families are often extremely slow to change and the clinician may want to think about making a long-term commitment to these types of families in planning treatment for the patient.

The low-intensity family seems to be a likely candidate for brief, psychoeducationally oriented forms of family treatment. In many cases, structured, collaborative educational work with these kinds of parents and patients can begin right away. One is not dealing with a long history of egosyntonic emotionally overinvolved patterns in these kinds of families nor does one have to struggle with angry feelings of resentment and bitterness about ruptured attachments or bonds that never developed. Instead, the parents of these patients are often more differentiated, and the patients in turn seem to be less emotionally tangled up with the parents, although they are usually quite dependent on them.

CONCLUDING REMARKS

Individuals with schizophrenia experience a course of development throughout their life span, just as do individuals without mental illness. The search for marker variables to identify children destined to develop schizophrenia will continue. With advances in the neurosciences, we will be increasingly able to learn about the biologic and genetic causes of the illness. Once the illness has manifested itself in young adulthood, however, we are faced with the problem of how to treat these patients most effectively. At the present time, we have no cure to offer. Most of the psychosocial interventions that seem effective in patients with schizophrenia involve a combination of maintenance neuroleptics and family therapy of some sort. Many of these approaches have been studied in patients who are at a point in their development where their illness has become fairly solidified and at least the beginnings of chronicity are occurring. However, we do have meaningful tools to offer schizophrenic patients who have already begun the chronic period of the illness in terms of medication and psychosocial treatment programs.

One area that deserves further study, however, is family treatment of the recent-onset case. We know very little about what goes on during the first year or two of the illness, and we know even less about the efficacy of various treatment options at this point. Ciompi (1988) has written about the notion that the initial florid, psychotic episode is really at the core of schizophrenia, and the way that this initial episode is handled afterward by the environment dictates the subsequent course and nature of the illness for the rest of the person's life. This notion seems to imply that we should treat the initial episode of schizophrenia as a traumatic event and apply intensive, focused treatment interventions to the patient and his or her family to minimize the trauma. It also suggests that we should provide continuing protection for the patient against postpsychotic deterioration and recurrence of the florid state. The factors likely to be important in this kind of effort may be quite different from those that are efficacious in the treatment and management of patients with long-standing chronic illness. It will be a challenge for investigators in the future to address these kinds of problems and to develop treatment approaches for schizophrenics that combine pharmacologic and family therapies in ways that aim the treatment at specific deficits in the patient as he or she exists in the developmental context of his or her family.

REFERENCES

Ainsworth, M. D., Blehar, M. C., Waters, E., and Wall, S. (1978). *Patterns of attachment: Assessed in the strange situation and at home.* Hillsdale, NJ: Lawrence Erlbaum.

Albers, L. J., Doane, J. A., and Mintz, J. (1986). Social competence and family environment: 15-year follow-up of disturbed adolescents. *Family Process, 25,* 379–389.

Anderson, C. M., Hogarty, G. E., and Reiss, D. J. (1980). Family treatment of adult schizophrenic patients: A psychoeducational approach. *Schizophrenia Bulletin, 6(3),* 490–505.

Barrowclough, C., and Tarrier, N. (1984). Psychosocial interventions with families and their effects on the course of schizophrenia: A review. *Psychological Medicine, 14,* 629–642.

Bowlby, J. (1982). *Attachment, Volume I of attachment and loss* (2nd ed). London: Hogarth Press.

Bowlby, J. (1988). *A secure base parent–child attachment and healthy human development.* New York: Basic Books.

Brown, G. W., Birley, J. L. T., and Wing, J. K. (1972). Influence of family life on the course of schizophrenic disorders: A replication. *British Journal of Psychiatry, 121,* 241–258.

Brown, G. W., Monck, E. M., Carstairs, G. M., and Wing, J. K. (1962). Influence of family life on the course of schizophrenic illness. *British Journal of Preventive and Social Medicine, 16,* 55–68.

Giompi, Luc. (1988). *The psyche and schizophrenia—The bond between affect and logic.* Cambridge: Harvard University Press.

Diamond, D. (1986a). *Attachment, bonding and separation—Individuation.* Unpublished Coding Manual, Yale University, New Haven, CT.

Diamond, D. (1986b). *Intergenerational family attachment interview schedule.* Yale University, New Haven, CT.

Diamond, D. (1987). *Attachment, bonding, and separation—Individuation scales.* Unpublished Rating Scales for Interview Data, Yale University, New Haven, CT.

Doane, J. A., and Diamond, D. (1989). *Intergenerational patterns of attachment/caregiving and expressed emotion—Implications for the treatment of schizophrenia.* Unpublished manuscript.

Doane, J. A., and Diamond, D. (1990). Family environment and severe psychiatric disorder— An intergenerational approach. *Yale Psychiatric Quarterly, 2–3,* 17–21.

Doane, J. A., Goldstein, M. J., Falloon, I. R. H., and Mintz, J. (1985). Parental affective style and the treatment of schizophrenia: Predicting course of illness and social functioning. *Archives of General Psychiatry, 42,* 34–42.

Doane, J. A., Goldstein, M. J., Miklowitz, D., and Falloon, I. R. H. (1986). The impact of individual and family treatment on the affective climate of families of schizophrenics. *British Journal of Psychiatry, 148,* 279–287.

Doane, J. A., Hill, W. L., Kaslow, N., and Quinlan, D. (1988). Family system functioning (FSF): Behavior in the laboratory and the family treatment setting. *Family Process, 27,* 213–227.

Doane, J. A., West, K. L., Goldstein, M. J., Rodnick, E., and Jones, J. E. (1981). Parental communication deviance and affective style—Predictors of subsequent schizophrenia-spectrum disorders in vulnerable adolescents. *Archives of General Psychiatry, 38,* 679–685.

Falloon, I. R. H., Boyd, J. E., and McGill, C. W. (1984). *Behavior family management of mental illness: Enhancing family coping in community care.* New York: Guilford.

Falloon, I. R. H., Boyd, J. L., McGill, C. W., Williamson, M., Razani, J., Moss, H. B., Gilderman, A. M., and Simpson, G. M. (1985). Family management in the prevention of morbidity of schizophrenia. *Archives of General Psychiatry, 42,* 887–896.

Falloon, I. R. H., Boyd, J. L., McGill, C. W., Razani, J., Moss, H. B., and Gilderman, A. M. (1982). Family management in the prevention of exacerbations of schizophrenia: A controlled study. *New England Journal of Medicine, 306,* 161–164.

Goldstein, M. J., Rodnick, E. H., Evans, J. R., May, P. R. A., and Steinberg, M. R. (1978). Drug and family therapy in the aftercare of acute schizophrenics. *Archives of General Psychiatry, 35,* 1169–1177.

Hahlweg, K., Goldstein, M. J., Nuechterlein, K. H., Magana, A. B., Mintz, J., Doane, J. A., Miklowitz, D. J., and Snyder, K. S. (1989). Expressed emotion and patient-relative interaction in families of recent onset schizophrenics. *Journal of Consulting and Clinical Psychology, 57(1),* 11–18.

Hogarty, G. E., Anderson, C. M., Reiss, D. J., Kornblith, S. J., Greenwald, D. P., Javna, C. D., and Madonia, M. J. (1986). Family psychoeducation, social skills training, and maintenance chemotherapy in the aftercare treatment of schizophrenia. I. One-year effects of a controlled study on relapse and expressed emotion. *Archives of General Psychiatry, 43,* 633–642.

Hogarty, G. E., and Ulrich, R. F. (1977). Temporal effects of drug and placebo in delaying relapse in schizophrenic outpatients. *Archives of General Psychiatry, 34,* 297–301.

Karno, M., Jenkins, J. H., De LaSelva, A., Santana, F., Telles, C., Lopez, S., and Mintz, J. (1987). Expressed emotion and schizophrenic outcome among Mexican–Americans, *Journal of Nervous and Mental Disease, 175(3),* 143–151.

Kreisman, D. E., Simmens, S. J., and Joy, V. D. (1979). Rejecting the patient: Preliminary validation of a self-report scale. *Schizophrenic Bulletin, 5,* 220–222.

Leff, J., and Vaughn, C. (1981). The role of maintenance therapy and relative's expressed emotion in relapse of schizophrenia. A two-year follow-up. *British Journal of Psychiatry, 139,* 102–104.

Leff, J. P., Kuipers, L., Berkowitz, R., Eberlein-Vries, R., and Sturgeon, D. (1982). A controlled trial of social intervention in the families of schizophrenic patients. *British Journal of Psychiatry, 141,* 121–134.

Liberman, R. P., Marshall, B. D., Marder, S., Dawson, M. E., Nuechterlein, K. H., and Doane, J. A. (1989). The nature and problem of schizophrenia. In A. S. Bellack (Ed.), *Schizophrenia: Treatment, management, and rehabilitation* (pp. 1–34). New York: Grune & Stratton.

MacMillan, J. F., Gold, A., Crow, T. J., Johnson, A. L., and Johnstone, E. C., IV. (1986). Expressed emotion and relapse. *British Journal of Psychiatry, 148,* 133–143.

Magana, A. B., Goldstein, M. J., Karno, M., Miklowitz, D. J., Jenkins, J., and Falloon, I. R. H. (1986). A brief method for assessing expressed emotion in relatives of psychiatric patients. *Psychiatry Research, 17,* 203–212.

Main, M., and Cassidy, J. (1988). Categories of response with the parent at age 6: Predicted from infant attachment classifications and stable over a one-month period. *Developmental Psychology, 24,* 415–426.

Main, M., Kaplan, N., and Cassidy, J. (1985). Security in infancy, childhood, and adulthood: A move to the level of representation. In I. Bretnerton and E. Waters (Eds.), *Growing points in attachments: Theory and research.* Monographs for the Society for Research in Child Development, Serial 209, 66–104. Chicago: University of Chicago Press.

McCreadie, R. G., and Phillips, K. (1988). The Nithsdale schizophrenia survey. *British Journal of Psychiatry, 152,* 477–481.

Miklowitz, D. J., and Goldstein, M. J. (1983). Premorbid and symptomatic characteristics of schizophrenics from families with high and low levels of expressed emotion. *Journal of Abnormal Psychology, 92,* 359–367.

Miklowitz, D. J., Goldstein, M. J., Falloon, I. R. H., and Doane, J. A. (1984). Interactional correlates of expressed emotion in the families of schizophrenics. *British Journal of Psychiatry, 144,* 482–487.

Miklowitz, D. J., Goldstein, M. J., Nuechterlein, K. H., Snyder, M. A., and Mintz, J. (1988). Family factors and the course of bipolar affective disorder. *Archives of General Psychiatry, 45,* 225–231.

Overall, J. E., and Gorham, D. R. (1962). The Brief Psychiatric Rating Scale (BPRS). *Psychological Reports, 10*, 799–812.

Parker, G. (1979). Parental characteristics in relation to depressive disorders. *British Journal of Psychiatry, 134*, 138–147.

Parker, G. (1983). *Parental overprotection: A risk factor in psychosocial development.* New York: Grune & Stratton.

Parker, G., Fairley, M., Greenwood, J., Jurd, A., and Silove, D. (1982). Parental representations of schizophrenics and their association with onset and course of schizophrenia. *British Journal of Psychiatry, 141*, 573–581.

Parker, G., Johnston, P., and Hayward, L. (1988). Parental "expressed emotion" as a predictor of schizophrenic relapse. *Archives of General Psychiatry, 45*, 806–813.

Stern, D. (1985). *The interpersonal world of the infant.* New York: Basic Books.

Strachan, A. M., Feingold, D., Goldstein, M. J., Miklowitz, D. J., and Nuechterlein, K. (1989). Is expressed emotion an index of a transactional process? *Family Process, 28*, 169–181.

Strodtbeck, F. L. (1954). The family as a three-person group. *American Sociological Review, 19*, 23–29.

Tarrier, N., Barrowclough, C., Vaughn, C., Bamrah, J. S., Porceddu, K., Watts, S., and Freeman, H. (1988). The community management of schizophrenia. *British Journal of Psychiatry, 153*, 532–542.

Tienari, P., Lahti, I., Sorri, A., Naarala, M., Moring, J., and Wahlberg, K. (1989). The Finnish adoptive family study of schizophrenia: Possible joint effects of genetic vulnerability and family environment. *British Journal of Psychiatry, 155, suppl 5*, 29–32.

Tienari, P., Sori, A., Lahti, I., Naarala, M., Wahlberg, K. E., Ronkko, T., Pohjola, J., and Moring, J. (1985). The Finnish adoptive family study of schizophrenia. *Yale Journal of Biology and Medicine, 58*, 227–237.

Valone, K., Goldstein, M. J., Norton, J., and Doane, J. A. (1983). Parental expressed emotion and affective style in an adolescent sample at risk for schizophrenia-spectrum disorders. *Journal of Abnormal Psychology, 92*, 399–407.

Vaughn, C. E., and Leff, J. P. (1976a). The influence of family and social factors on the course of psychiatric illness. *British Journal of Psychiatry, 129*, 125–137.

Vaughn, C. E., and Leff, J. P. (1976b). The measurement of expressed emotion in the families of psychiatric patients. *British Journal of Social and Clinical Psychology, 15, Part 2*, 157–165.

Vaughn, C. E., Snyder, K. S., Freeman, W., Jones, S., Falloon, I. H. R., and Liberman, R. P. (1984). Family factors in schizophrenic relapse: Replication in California of British research on expressed emotion. *Archives of General Psychiatry, 41*, 1169–1177.

Wing, J. K., Cooper, J. E., and Sartorius, N. (1974). *Measurement and classification of psychiatric symptoms.* London: Cambridge University Press.

Wynne, L. C. (1984). The epigenesis of relational systems: a model for understanding family development. *Family Process, 23(3)*, 297–318.

Wynne, L., Singer, M., Bartko, J., and Toohey, M. (1977). Schizophrenics and their families: Research on parental communication. In J. M. Tanner (Ed.). *Developments in psychiatric research: The widening perspectives* (pp. 254–286). London: Hodder and Stoughton.

11

Late-Onset Schizophrenia

R. Yassa

This chapter concerns late-onset schizophrenia; its conceptual, historical, and phenomenological aspects. Interest in late-onset schizophrenia has recently burgeoned in the United States, although this disorder has been of long-standing interest to European researchers. In addition to providing an overview of the evolution of theoretical perspectives on late-onset schizophrenia, empirical research on differential diagnosis, etiology, and prognosis is discussed. Several case studies are used to illustrate characteristics of the clinical onset and course.

HISTORICAL PERSPECTIVES

The concept of late-onset schizophrenia has evolved through many years of uncertainty and confusion. The term "paraphrenia" was first coined by Guislain to indicate a clinical entity that is roughly equivalent to our concept of schizophrenia (Hinsie and Campbell, 1974). Kraepelin (1971) defined paraphrenia as a condition characterized by marked delusions and many of the features of dementia praecox. However, paraphrenic patients exhibited fewer emotional and volitional disorders than did dementia praecox patients. Because 50% of the patients originally diagnosed as paraphrenic subsequently developed dementia praecox (Mayer, 1921; Mayer-Gross, 1932), the term fell in disuse for several years.

SCHIZOPHRENIA
A Life-Course Developmental Perspective
243
Copyright © 1991 by Academic Press, Inc.
All rights of reproduction in any form reserved.

Roth (1955) revived the terminology and defined the condition as a well-organized system of paranoid delusions with or without hallucinations existing in the setting of a well-preserved personality and affective response. The symptoms began after age 60 years in the majority of cases. He coined the term "late paraphrenia" for this group of patients. Kay and Roth (1961) divided their late paraphrenic patients into three groups: (1) delusions but no hallucinations; (2) delusions that were understandable in light of the patients' circumstances or following their prolonged social isolation; and (3) "endogenous paraphrenia where symptoms could not be attributed to social stressors or to long-term personality disorders."

Post (1966, 1978) also classified late paraphrenic patients into three categories: (1) paranoid hallucinosis, where auditory hallucinations and delusions of persecution were present; (2) the "schizophreniform syndrome," where paranoid experiences were more understandable, and (3) the "schizophrenic syndrome," which had Schneiderian first-rank symptoms. Thus, the concept of late paraphrenia developed in Europe over several years.

In the United States, however, this clinical entity was not well defined in the American classifications. The Diagnostic and Statistical Manual of Mental Disease (DSM-II) (American Psychiatric Association, 1968) did not have an age cutoff for the diagnosis of schizophrenia but did describe involutional paraphrenia as a paranoid psychosis characterized by delusion formation with onset in the involutional period. The DSM-III (American Psychiatric Association, 1980) did not recognize paraphrenia or involutional melancholia and restricted the definition of schizophrenia to onset before age 44 years. However, DSM-III-R (American Psychiatric Association, 1987) recognized the fact that schizophrenia may develop after age 45 years. The ICD-9 (World Health Organization, 1978) did not have an age cutoff for schizophrenia. It defined paraphrenia in a way similar to Roth's (1955) description and recognized that affective symptoms, if present, were not dominant. Thus, late-onset schizophrenia (paraphrenia) is now recognized as an entity in the classification of both European and American researchers, with well-defined criteria.

EPIDEMIOLOGY

Community Studies

The prevalence of suspiciousness and delusions in elderly populations in the community has been estimated to be as low as 4% (Christensen and Blazer, 1984; Blazer, 1989; Christison *et al.*, 1989) and as high as 17% (Lowenthal, 1964). On the other hand, the prevalence of late-onset schizophrenia in the community is estimated as varying between 0.1 and 0.5% (Kay et al., 1964; Blazer, 1989).

Prevalence in Psychiatric Settings

It is estimated that around 10% of first admissions to a psychiatric hospital after age 60 years exhibit schizophrenic symptoms of late onset (Post, 1967; Bridge and Wyatt, 1980a,b: Leuchter and Spar, 1985; Gurland and Meyers, 1988). In the psychogeriatric unit of Douglas Hospital Center (DHC; Montreal, Quebec, Canada), this author observed seven patients who developed schizophrenia after age 50 years among 288 first-admission patients over a 5-year period. This amounts to 2.4% of the units population. When age at first onset of schizophrenic symptoms is studied, it is noted that 13% of all schizophrenic patients present symptoms in their fifth decade, 7% in their sixth decade, and 3% thereafter (Harris and Jeste, 1988).

Thus, although rare in the community, late-onset schizophrenia comprises approximately 10% of admissions to a psychogeriatric unit.

CLINICAL PICTURE

The clinical picture of late-onset schizophrenia usually resembles that of early-onset paranoid schizophrenia (Post, 1978; Volavka, 1985). A mixture of paranoid delusions and auditory hallucinations in a well-preserved intellect and personality are the hallmarks of late-onset schizophrenia (Langley, 1975). First-rank Schneiderian symptoms have been reported but are not common (Post, 1966; Grahame, 1984; Jorgensen and Munk-Jorgensen, 1985; Gurland and Meyers, 1988). Thought disorder and flat and incongruous affect are rare (Langley, 1975; Gurland and Meyers, 1988; Jeste et al., 1988). Bizarre delusions similar to those reported in early-onset schizophrenia may be present, as seen in the following three cases.

Case 1. Mrs. A, a 72-year-old divorced mother of four, referred the onset of her problems to about 2 months prior to her first admission to the DHC, in April 1988. She felt that people wanted to harm her and heard voices speaking to her and commenting on her actions, ordering her not to leave the room. As a result, she locked herself in her room and prevented even her children from visiting her. While locked up, she believed that people were spying on her and monitored all her activities through microphones they put in her apartment. She also claimed to have contracted AIDS but did not have the symptoms because of her supernatural healing powers.

Mrs. A had no family or personal history of psychiatric conditions prior to this admission. She acknowledged that she had always been a loner and never trusted people. Clinically, no symptoms of depression or mania were noted, and her Mini Mental Status Exam (a simple test to detect dementia) scored 29 (out of 30 possible points). Laboratory investigations were unremarkable: HIV testing was negative, EEG normal, and brain CT scan normal.

Case 2. Mrs. B, an 82-year-old widow was brought to the DHC by her children. Two years prior to this admission, they noted the onset of a strange behavior in their mother: She would stare at them and inform them she was getting pregnant from their husbands. They also noted that she would stand in the corridors of her apartment immobile, refusing to eat because she heard Jesus ordering her not to eat. When examined in the hospital, she was found lying on her bed with her legs open and informed me that she was delivering babies. When I asked her to show them to me, she said that they were taken immediately for adoption. When asked how would she explain the fact that she was over 80 years old and still having babies, she answered: "Miracles happen."

The patient and her five daughters denied any previous psychiatric history. She was described as a sociable, caring mother. She developed deafness 8 years prior to admission. Again, all tests including brain CT scan and EEG were normal and her Mini Mental Status Exam scored 27.

Case 3. Mrs. C, a 68-year-old woman when first admitted to the DHC, stated that all her problems started 3–4 months prior to admission, when she noticed that wherever she moved, people were looking at her. This frightened her. Then, 2 weeks prior to admission she had dinner with a friend in a restaurant. Following this meeting, she began to think that people were poisoning her food and that certain people were putting spells on her to harm her. She even thought that people somehow (she does not know how) put a computer into her stomach to control her thoughts. The patient is described as a shy person who does not trust people and who joined an esoteric church group a few years prior to this admission. Again, all her tests were normal and her Mini Mental Status Exam score was 28.

"Phantom boarders" as a symptom of late paraphrenia has been reported (Rowan, 1984). The patient has a delusion of strange people boarding in his or her neighborhood. The following is a case example of this condition.

Case 4. Mrs. D was 72 years old when brought to the emergency room by her children. For 10 months, she had been feeling that the people who live above her have been controlling her mind, especially one woman. (The children said no tenants lived in the apartment and that it had been empty for several years.) She said that the woman and her husband had been quarreling all the time. The day of her admission she heard a bang and thought a gun went off. For the fourth time, she called the police. When they tried to convince her no one was there, she insisted they must have left for a trip. As a result, the patient was brought to the DHC. On examination, she was fully oriented and showed no other delusional behavior. All her tests were normal.

Depressive symptoms, accompanying paranoid delusions that are usually mood-incongruent, are common (Post, 1966, 1984; Gurland and Meyers, 1988). These symptoms will subside with treatment.

The premorbid personality of these patients is characterized by being lonely, unable to maintain relations with the opposite sex, suspicious, quarrelsome, and belonging to eccentric and esoteric cults (Post, 1966, 1967, 1978; Langley, 1975; Roth, 1989). Of 87 patients with late-onset schizophrenia, 26 were noted to have a "normal" premorbid personality (Langley, 1975).

ETIOLOGY OF LATE-ONSET SCHIZOPHRENIA

Female Gender

The majority of studies indicates that women are more prone to develop late-onset schizophrenia than men (Mayer, 1921; Bleuler, 1943; Roth and Morrissey, 1952; Roth, 1955; Fish, 1960; Kay and Roth, 1961; Grahame, 1984; Marneros and Deister, 1984; Rabins et al., 1984; Jeste et al., 1988; Pearlson and Rabins, 1988; Craig and Bregman, 1988). The male : female ratio is estimated at 1:11 (Rabins et al., 1984) and 1:12 (Kay and Roth, 1961). In contrast, men develop schizophrenia earlier in life and have a male : female ratio of 2:1 in early-onset schizophrenia (Yassa et al., 1990).

Several theories have attempted to explain this phenomenon. It is possible that women lose dopamine D2 receptors at a slower rate in older age than do men, thus leading to a relative excess of D2 receptors in older female patients (Wong et al., 1984). This may explain the higher prevalence of late-onset schizophrenia in women if we consider schizophrenia as a hyperdopaminergic condition (Pearlson and Coyle, 1983). On the other hand, Seeman and Lang (1990) have suggested that estrogens protect women in the premenopausal period. Estrogens have a dopaminergic effect. This protection is lost in the postmenopausal period, thus causing a higher prevalence of late-onset schizophrenia in women.

Genetic Factors

Several studies have indicated that patients with late-onset schizophrenia have a higher percentage of family history of psychoses than affective disorder. Funding (1961) found schizophrenia in 2.5% of relatives of 148 patients with paranoia. Kay (1963) studied 57 patients with late-onset schizophrenia and found 19% of the probands had one relative with schizophrenia. He estimated the risk among sibs to be about 5% and among children around 7%. However, this genetic loading seems to be less prevalent than in early-onset schizophrenia (Funding, 1961; Herbert and Jacobson, 1967; Kay et al., 1976; Roth, 1987). Naguib (1987), who studied human leukocyte antigens (HLAs) in late-onset schizophrenia, concluded that this condition may have a significant association with certain HLAs but "has a smaller genetic loading than early life onset patients and requires more environmental events" to express it.

Sensory Deficit

The association between deafness and paranoia was first noted by Kraepelin (Pearlson and Rabins, 1988). Since then, several authors have confirmed this finding (Post, 1965, 1973, 1978; Watt, 1985). Christensen and Blazer (1984) argued that sensory impairment may be a general risk factor to hallucinations and delusions in late life. Patients with late-onset schizophrenia have more auditory problems than patients with affective disorders (Post, 1966; Cooper et al., 1974; Cooper, 1976; Christensen and Blazer, 1984; Leuchter and Spar, 1985) or patients with early-onset schizophrenia (Leuchter and Spar, 1985).

When present, deafness often precedes the clinical onset of late-onset schizophrenia by many years (Cooper et al., 1974) and its etiology is usually conductive, due to chronic middle ear disease (Cooper et al., 1974; Pearlson and Rabins, 1988). Kay et al. (1976) described these patients as being socially deaf. This was confirmed by Post (1978) and Naguib and Levy (1987). These latter authors found social deafness more common in late-onset schizophrenia patients than in patients with affective disorders or normal controls. It should be noted that visual impairment has also been implicated by several authors in late-onset schizophrenia (Roth, 1955; Herbert and Jacobson, 1967; Christensen and Blazer, 1984; Leuchter and Spar, 1985).

The mechanisms by which sensory deficit leads to late-onset schizophrenia are poorly understood. The social isolation caused by sensory impairment may be the "straw that broke the camel's back" in an already predisposed individual.

DIFFERENTIAL DIAGNOSIS

It is generally agreed that late-onset schizophrenia is a condition characterized by a mixture of auditory hallucinations and paranoid delusions in a well-preserved personality and intellect, arising in the senium. However, the criterion for late-onset has differed from one investigator to another. According to DSM-III-R (American Psychiatric Association, 1987), the criterion for late-onset schizophrenia is 45 years and over. Some authors prefer to use a cutoff age of 60 years and older (Post, 1967; Grahame, 1984; Gurland and Meyers, 1988).

The differential diagnosis of delusions (particularly persecutory types) and hallucinations (auditory and visual) in the senium is an endless problem. Almost every condition arising in this age period may present with these symptoms. Notable among these conditions are late-onset bipolar disorder, transitional paranoid reactions, and the dementias. Late-onset bipolar disorder (Yassa et al., 1988a) is estimated to occur in 5–10% of all admissions to a psychiatric setting. It is characterized (as in younger age) by hyperactivity, grandiose delusions, and euphoria (Yassa et al., 1988b). It may or may not be preceded by depressive symptoms. However, the delusions may be mood-incongruent (Yassa et al., 1988b), and this condition responds well to lithium.

Delusions in the context of depressive illness may sometimes occur where they may be mood-incongruent and, thus, a condition akin to schizoaffective psychosis is described.

Transitional paranoid reaction was described by Post (1973). The condition is characterized by paranoid ideas with hallucinations and the belief that a plot exists against the patient. Most of the patients affected are socially isolated women. Thus, this condition may sometimes be misdiagnosed as late-onset schizophrenia.

A multitude of organic conditions may lead to the development of persecutory ideas and hallucinations (particularly of visual type). Among the causes of organic psychoses are alcoholic dementia, drug-induced (particularly anticholinergic drugs and steroids), metabolic (diabetes mellitus), endocrine (hypothyroidism, hypopituitarism, diabetes mellitus), nutritional (malnutrition, B_{12} deficiency), and postsurgical acute confusional states.

Dementia of old age needs special attention. Delusions of the persecutory type are common in Alzheimer's disease (Wragg and Jeste, 1989; Burns et al., 1990a). Cummings (1985) suggested that delusions in patients with organic conditions could be divided into four types: simple persecutory delusions, complex persecutory delusions, grandiose delusions, and delusions associated with specific neurological deficits. According to Cummings (1985), delusions resulting from damage to the limbic and subcortical structures are common. Hallucinations of the auditory and visual types are common among patients with senile dementia, Burns et al. (1990b) estimate them to occur in 10–13% of patients with Alzheimer's disease. Thus, the clinician should always differentiate late-onset schizophrenia from senile dementia, particularly in the early stages of the dementing process. The situation is rather complex, and several authors have argued both for and against a co-occurrence of various cerebral degenerative changes and late-onset schizophrenia (Pearlson and Rabins, 1988). Bleuler (1950) stated that cerebral lesions appeared many years after the clinical presentation of psychiatric symptoms. However, other authors could not confirm these findings (Ray and Roth, 1961; Blessed et al., 1968). In some patients initially diagnosed with late-onset schizophrenia, dementia develops, as discussed later. In addition, some cases fitting DSM-III-R criteria for late-onset schizophrenia may show mild cognitive disturbance (Miller et al., 1986). Thus, cognitive disturbances may be present in some patients who are otherwise diagnosed as late-onset schizophrenia.

COURSE AND PROGNOSIS

It is now generally accepted that the likelihood of a spontaneous, lasting recovery from late-onset schizophrenia is remote (Gurland and Meyers, 1988), but that psychotic symptoms can be brought under control using neuroleptic drugs in numerous cases (Roth, 1989). Thus, the course and prognosis are better now with the advent of neuroleptics.

Several studies have been conducted on the prognosis of late-onset schizophrenia. Post (1966) studied 73 cases of late-onset schizophrenia and found that complete remission occurred in 43 patients (59%), 22 (30%) recovered with residual symptoms, and 6 (8%) had a chronic course. Herbert and Jacobson (1967) studied 45 cases of late paraphrenia and found that 21 patients (46.6%) recovered fully and 16 (35.5%) had a chronic course. Blessed and Wilson (1982) found that 64.3% of 28 patients with a diagnosis of late-onset schizophrenia had full recovery and 35.7% (10 patients) remained chronically hospitalized after 2 years of follow-up. Rabins et al. (1984), following 35 patients with late-onset schizophrenia for a 2-year period, found that 20 (57%) recovered, 5 (14.3%) remained in the hospital, and 10 had recurrences (28.6%). Craig and Bregman (1988) found that 10 patients (31%) of 32 diagnosed with late-onset schizophrenia were discharged, while 5 (16%) remained chronically hospitalized.

Thus, across all studies, after a follow-up of 2–10 years, a total of 112 of 213 patients (48.5%) were discharged from the hospital, with figures as low as 31% (Craig and Bregman, 1988) and as high as 64% (Blessed and Wilson, 1982). On the other hand, about 20% (42 of 213 patients) remained in the hospital during the follow-up period, with figures as low as 8% (Post, 1966) and as high as 35% (Herbert and Jacobson, 1967; Blessed and Wilson, 1982).

Intellectual deterioration and dementia were noted in 10 patients (22%) in Herbert and Jacobson's (1967) study, 3 patients (10.7%) in Blessed and

Wilson's (1982) study, 17 patients (53%) in Craig and Bregman's (1988) study and 2 (4.8%) in Hymas *et al.*'s (1989) study.

Several studies have indicated prognostic features in their patient populations. The following were positively correlated with a good outcome: depression (Post, 1978; Craig and Bregman, 1988; Gurland and Meyers, 1988), assaultive behavior (Craig and Bregman, 1988), auditory hallucinations (Holden, 1987). On the other hand, organicity, sensory deficit, and visual hallucinations were found to be negatively correlated with a good outcome (Holden, 1987).

TREATMENT

Treating late-onset schizophrenia with neuroleptics is now considered imperative. As previously mentioned, spontaneous recovery is rare (Gurland and Meyers, 1988), although a sizable proportion of patients improve with neuroleptics (Harris and Jeste, 1988). Aggressive symptoms are reduced with these medications (Craig and Bregman, 1988), and psychotic symptoms (auditory hallucinations, delusions) are well controlled with antipsychotic drugs (Holden, 1987). Depressive symptoms appear to subside as the schizophrenic illness recedes with medication (Craig and Bregman, 1988; Roth, 1989).

There is no particular neuroleptic that has been found to be more efficacious than any other. The choice in these situations falls mainly on which medication causes fewer side effects than other medications. Hypotension may be common in these patients, thus caution should be used when prescribing sedative antipsychotic drugs (e.g., chlorpromazine). In addition, older patients are particularly susceptible to the development of extrapyramidal side effects, notably tardive dyskinesia (Waddington and Youssef, 1986; Yassa *et al.*, 1986). As with younger patients, there may be some benefit in prescribing intramuscular long-acting neuroleptics due to compliance issues (Raskind *et al.*, 1979); however, it is always advisable to start with smaller doses and increase the dose according to the patient's response and to maintain the patients on the minimum effective dose.

Due to the fact that many patients have had difficulties with interpersonal relationships, it may be important to explore psychodynamic issues and family dynamics to help the patient and his or her family to deal with the illness.

CONCLUSIONS

Late-onset schizophrenia is a clinical entity that differs from early-onset schizophrenia, not only in the age at onset but in other features as well, including the variables of gender, genetic factors, and clinical picture. Although the response to neuroleptics and prognosis are fair to good, no systematic studies conducted to date have compared neuroleptic treatment versus placebo in these patients. Also, few in-depth studies have aimed at exploring neuroradiological and biochemical parameters in these patients. We also need more refinement in the diagnostic tools to differentiate between affective and schizophrenia diagnoses, particularly in those cases with mixed symptoms. A point to explore further is the relationship between late-onset schizophrenia and dementia. Perhaps with the advent of the new magnetic resonance imaging we can explore the depths of the pathology of those patients presenting late-onset schizophrenic symptoms.

REFERENCES

American Psychiatric Association (1968). *Diagnostic and statistical manual of mental disorders* (2nd ed.). Washington, DC: American Psychiatric Press.

American Psychiatric Association (1980). *Diagnostic and statistical manual of mental disorders* (3rd ed.). Washington, DC: American Psychiatric Press.

American Psychiatric Association (1987). *Diagnostic and statistical manual of mental disorders* (3rd ed., revised). Washington, DC: American Psychiatric Press.

Blazer, D. (1989). Late-life schizophrenia and paranoid disorders. (quoted by C, Christison, G. Christison, and D. Blazer). In E. W. Busse, and D. Blazer (Eds.), *Geriatric psychiatry.*(pp. 403–414). Washington, DC: American Psychiatric Press.

Blessed, G., Tomlinson, B. E., and Roth, M. (1968). The association between qualitative measure of dementia and senile change with cerebral matter of elderly subjects. *British Journal of Psychiatry, 114*, 792–811.

Blessed, G., and Wilson, I. D. (1982). The contemporary natural history of mental disorder in old age. *British Journal of Psychiatry, 141*, 59–67.

Bleuler, E. (1950). Dementia praecox, on the group of schizophrenics. New York. International Universities Press (translated by J. Zinkin).

Bleuler, M. (1943). Late schizophrenic clinical pictures. *Fortschritte der Neurologie—Psychiatrie, 15*, 259–290.

Bridge, T. P., and Wyatt, R. J. (1980a). Paraphrenia: Paranoid states of late life. I—European research. *Journal of the American Geriatrics Society, 28*, 193–200.

Bridge, T. P., and Wyatt, R. J. (1980b). Paraphrenia: Paranoid states of late life. II—American research. *Journal of the American Geriatrics Society, 28*, 201–205.

Burns, A., Jacoby, R., and Levy, R. (1990a). Psychiatric phenomena in Alzheimer's disease. I: Disorders of thought content. *British Journal of Psychiatry, 157*, 72–76.

Burns, A., Jacoby, R., and Levy, R. (1990b). Psychiatric phenomena in Alzheimer's disease. II: Disorders of perception. *British Journal of Psychiatry, 157*, 76–81.

Christensen, R., and Blazer, D. (1984). Epidemiology of persecutory ideation in an elderly population in the community. *American Journal of Psychiatry, 141*, 1088–1091.

Christison, C., Christison, G., and Blazer, D. (1989). Late-life schizophrenia and paranoid disorders. In E. W. Busse, and D. Blazer (Eds.), *Geriatric psychiatry.* (pp. 403–414. Washington, DC: American Psychiatric Press.

Cooper, A. F. (1976). Deafness and psychiatric illness. *British Journal of Psychiatry, 129*, 216–226.

Cooper, A. F., Kay, D. W. K., and Curry, A. R. (1974). Hearing loss in paranoid and affective psychoses of the elderly. *Lancet, ii*, 851–854.

Craig, T. J., and Bregman, Z. (1988). Late-onset schizophrenia-like illness. *Journal of the American Geriatrics Society, 36*, 104–107.

Cummings, J. (1985). Organic delusions: phenomenology, anatomical correlations and review. *British Journal of Psychiatry, 146*, 184–197.

Fish, F. (1960). Senile schizophrenia. *Journal of Mental Science, 106*, 938–946.

Funding, T. (1961). Genetics of paranoid psychoses in later life. *Acta Psychiatrica Scandinavica, 37*, 267–282.

Grahame, P. (1984). Schizophrenia in old age (paraphrenia). *British Journal of Psychiatry, 145*, 493–495.

Gurland, B., and Meyers, B. (1988). Geriatric psychiatry. In J. A. Talbott, R. E. Hales, and S. C. Yudofsky (Eds)., *Textbook of psychiatry* (pp. 1117–1139). Washington, DC: American Psychiatric Press.

Harris, M. J., and Jeste, D. V. (1988). Late-onset schizophrenia: An overview. *Schizophrenia Bulletin, 14*, 39–55.

Herbert, M. E., and Jacobson, S. (1967). Late paraphrenia. *British Journal of Psychiatry, 113*, 461–469.

Hinsie, L. E., and Campbell, R. J. (1974). *Psychiatric dictionary*, 4th ed. New York: Oxford Univesity Press.

Holden, N. L. (1987). Late paraphrenia or the paraphrenias? A descriptive study with a 10-year follow-up. *British Journal of Psychiatry, 150*, 635–639.

Hymas, N., Naguib, M., and Levy, R. (1989). Late paraphrenia: A follow-up study. *International Journal of Geriatric Psychiatry, 4*, 23–29.

Jeste, D. V., Harris, M. I., Pearlson, G. D., Rabins, P., Lesser, I. M., Miller, B., Coles, C., and Yassa, R. (1988). Late-onset schizophrenia: Studying clinical validity. In D. V. Jeste, and S. Zisook (Eds.), *Psychosis and depression in the elderly. Psychiatric Clinics of North America, 11*, 1–14.

Jorgensen, P., and Munk-Jorgensen, P. (1985). Paranoid psychoses in the elderly: A follow-up study. *Acta Psychiatrica Scandinavica, 72*, 358–363.

Kay, D. W. K. (1963). Late paraphrenia and its bearing on the aetiology of schizophrenia. *Acta Psychiatrica Scandinavica, 39*, 159–169.

Kay, D. W. K., Beamish, P., and Roth, M. (1964). Old age mental disorders in Newcastle upon Tyne. *British Journal of Psychiatry, 110*, 146–158.

Kay, D. W. K., Cooper, A. F., and Garside, R. F. (1976). The differentiation of paranoid from affective psychoses by patient's premorbid characteristics. *British Journal of Psychiatry, 129*, 207–215.

Kay, D. W. K., and Roth, M. (1961). Environmental and hereditary factors in the schizophrenias of old age ("late paraphrenia") and their bearing on the general problem of causation in schizophrenia. *Journal of Mental Science, 107*, 649–686.

Kraepelin, E. (1971). *Dementia praecox and paraphrenia* (pp. 282–329). Translated by R. M. Barclay; edited by G. M. Robertson. Huntington, NY: Robert E. Krieger. [Original 1919.])

Langley, G. E. (1975). Functional psychoses. In J. G. Howells (Ed.), *Modern perspectives in the psychiatry of old age.* (pp. 348–353). New York: Brunner/Mazel.

Leuchter, A. F., and Spar, J. E. (1985). The late-onset psychoses: Clinical and diagnostic features. *Journal of Nervous Mental Disorders, 173*, 488–494.

Lowenthal, M. F. (1964). Lives in distress. New York: Basic Books.

Maineros, A., and Deister, A. (1984). The psychopathology of late schizophrenia. *Psychopathology, 17*, 264–274.

Mayer, W. (1921). On paraphrenic psychoses. *Zeitschrift fur die Gesamke Neurologie und psychiatrie, 71*, 187–206.

Mayer-Gross, W. (1932). *Die Schizophrenic.* In O. Bumke (Ed.), *Bumkes Handbuch der Geiskrankheiten* (Spez. 5). Berlin: Springer.

Miller, B. L., Benson, F., Cummings, J. L., and Neshkes, R. (1986). Late-life paraphrenia. An organic delusional syndrome. *Journal of Clinical Psychiatry, 47*, 204–207.

Naguib, M. (1987). Genetic markers in late paraphrenia: A study of HLA antigens. *British Journal of Psychiatry, 150*, 124–127.

Naguib, M., and Levy, R. (1987). Late paraphrenia: Neuropsychological impairment and structural brain abnormalities on completed tomography. *International Journal of Geriatric Psychiatry, 2*, 83–90.

Pearlson, G. D., and Coyle, J. T. (1983). The dopamine hypothesis and schizophrenia. In J. T. Coyle, and S. Enna (Eds.), *Neuroleptics, neurochemical, behavioral and clinical perspectives* (Vol. 3), *CNS pharmacology*, (pp. 297–324). New York: Raven Press.

Pearlson, G. D., and Rabins, P. (1988). The late-onset psychoses: Possible risk factors. In D. V. Jeste, and S. Zisook (Eds.), *Psychosis and depression in the elderly. Psychiatric Clinics of North America, 11*, 15–32.

Post, F. (1965). *The clinical psychiatry of late life.* Oxford: Pergamon Press.

Post, F. (1966). *Persistent persecutory states of the elderly.* Oxford: Pergamon Press.

Post, F. (1967). Aspects of psychiatry in the elderly. *Proceedings of the Royal Society of Medicine, 60*, 249–254.

Post, F. (1973). Paranoid disorders in the elderly. *Postgraduate Medicine, 3*, 52–56.

Post, F. (1978). The functional psychoses. In A. D. Isaacs, and F. Post (Eds.), *Studies in geriatric psychiatry.* (pp. 76–94). New York: John Wiley and Sons.

Post, F. (1984). Schizophrenic and paranoid psychoses. In D. W. K. Kay, G. D. Burrows (Eds.), *Handbook of studies on psychiatry and old age.* New York: Elsevier.

Rabins, P., Pauker, S., and Thomas, J. (1984). Can schizophrenia begin after age 44? *Comparative Psychiatry, 25*, 290–293.

Raskind, M. A., Alvary, C., and Herlin, S. (1979). Fluphenazine enanthate in the outpatient treatment of late paraphrenia. *Joural of the American Geriatrics Society, 27*, 459–463.

Roth, M. (1955). The natural history of mental disorder in old age. *Journal of mental Science, 101*, 281–301.

Roth, M. (1987). Late paraphrenia: Phenomenology and etiological factors and their bearing upon problems of the schizophrenic family of disorders. In N. E. Miller, and G. D. Cohen (Eds.), *Schizophrenia, paranoia and schizophreniform disorders in later life* (pp. 217–234). New York: The Guilford Press.

Roth, M. (1989). Delusional (paranoid) disorders. In T. D. Karaser (Ed.) *Treatments of psychiatric disorders: A task force report of the American Psychiatric Association* (Vol. 2, pp. 1609–1652). Washington, DC: American Psychiatric Press.

Roth, M., and Morrissey, J. D. (1952). Problems in the diagnosis and classification of mental disorders in old age. *Journal of Mental Science, 98*, 66–80.

Rowan, E. L. (1984). Phantom boarders as a symptom of late paraphrenia. *American Journal of Psychiatry, 141*, 580–581.

Seeman, M. V., and Lang, M. (1990). The role of estrogens in schizophrenia gender differences. *Schizophrenia Bulletin, 16*, 185–195.

Volavka, J. (1985). Late-onset schizophrenia: A review. *Comparative Psychiatry, 26*, 148–156.

Waddington, J., and Youssef, H. (1986). Involuntary movements and cognitive dysfunction in late onset schizophrenic outpatients. *Irish Medical Journal, 79*, 347–350.

Watt, J. A. G. (1985). Hearing and premorbid personality in paranoid states. *American Journal of Psychiatry, 142,* 1453–1458.

Wong, D. E., Wagner, H. N., and Dannals, R. E. (1984). Effects of age on dopamine and serotonin receptors measured by position tomography in the living human brain. *Science, 226,* 1393–1396.

World Health Organization (1978). *Mental disorders.* Glossary and guide to their classification in accordance with the Ninth Revision of the International Classification of Diseases. Geneva.

Wragg, R. E., and Jeste, D. V. (1989). Overview of depression and psychosis in Alzheimer's disease. *American Journal of Psychiatry, 146,* 577–587.

Yassa, R., Nair, N. P. V., and Iskandar, H. (1988a). Late-onset bipolar disorder. In D. V. Jeste, and S. Sizook (Eds.), *Psychosis and depression in the elderly. Psychiatric Clinics of North America, 11,* 117–131.

Yassa, R., Nair, V., Nastase, C., and Belzile, L. (1988b). Prevalence of biopolar disorder in a psychogeriatric population. *Journal of Affective Disorders, 14,* 197–201.

Yassa, R., Nair, V., and Schwartz, G. (1986). Early versus late-onset psychosis and tardive dyskinesia. *Biological Psychiatry, 21,* 1291–1297.

Yassa, R., Uhr, S., Jeste, D. (1990). Gender differences in chronic schizophrenia: Need for further research. In E. Light, and B. Leibowitz (Eds.), *Chronically mentally ill elderly* (in press).

Aging and Schizophrenia: Plasticity, Reversibility, and/or Compensation

Courtenay M. Harding

INTRODUCTION

This chapter briefly reviews five different but overlapping literatures: (1) normal aging of brain and body, (2) studies of pathological brain processes in schizophrenia, (3) catamnestic studies of the course of schizophrenia into the senium, (4) recent findings about adult development, and (5) research into late-onset schizophrenia. Together, they challenge many strongly held assumptions about the immutability, permanency, and irreversibility of schizophrenia and suggest a probable beneficial interaction with aging processes. Discussion of the implications for research and treatment is interwoven.

Old Mythologies Revisited

Several assumptions currently exist in the training and practice of American psychiatry about the processes involved in aging and schizophrenia. These assumptions include five interrelated concepts. (1) The brain and body are expected to succumb in normal aging to increasing

257
Copyright © 1991 by Academic Press, Inc.
All rights of reproduction in any form reserved.

performance deficits that are generated by subtle deterioration across multiple physiological systems and anatomical structures and are unpreventable and irreversible (Giaquinto, 1988). (2) Persons with repeated episodes of schizophrenia appear to decline generally toward marginal levels of functioning, which worsens as aging advances. (3) Thus, as the person with schizophrenia ages, the neurochemical and structural brain anomalies are expected to remain the same or deteriorate (Weinberger *et al.*, 1983). (4) Therefore, the young adult whose development is significantly delayed by such a severe psychiatric illness is generally unable to achieve full reconstitution of function and is denied further developmental gains as an older adult (Lamb, 1976). (5) Patients who defy such expectations by significantly improving or recovering after a chronic course or who become ill late in life after a long period of healthy functioning do not have schizophrenia (American Psychiatric Association, 1980).

Plasticity, Reversibility, and Compensation

These assumptions of decremental immutability persist despite counter-evidence from long-term studies of normal aging processes, the long-distance outcome of schizophrenia, and recent biochemical studies of the brain. Together, these studies contribute a new picture of plasticity, reversibility, and compensation achieved through longitudinal, biopsychosocial interactions. Such interactions can positively influence individual levels of psychological and physiological function across time. For example, many components of aging that were once considered the natural biological expression of advancing years, have been found to be due primarily to the "disuse and abuse" of the body and can be delayed or prevented altogether (Goldman, 1986). Brain research is also reporting significant alterations in cell structure and neurochemistry when the brain is subjected to impoverished or enriched environments (Kra, 1986). In addition, contrary to our expectations, very long-term follow-up studies of schizophrenic patients into advanced old age have shown about 50% of these subjects display not only cessation of symptomatology but also significant improvement or recovery in functioning regardless of the narrowness of diagnostic classification (Harding *et al.*, 1987b).

This chapter attempts to bring together such current research from a wide variety of separate disciplines to suggest a possible convergence in findings. The new empirical evidence may radically change our perceptions of aging and schizophrenic processes and has considerable implications for treatment and further research. It should be noted that the challenge to interweave the findings from these investigations in the space of one chapter necessitates the presentation of the large picture, leaving the discussion of subtleties, paradoxes, and complexities for a later time.

BIOLOGICAL AGING

New Evidence about Normal Aging Processes

Until recently, expectations about aging forecasted increasing losses of muscle strength, skeletal durability, agility, dexterity, memory and other cognitive functions, eyesight, and hearing acuity. These are added to a whole host of diseases that hasten one toward death either in an unfolding, genetically programmed sequence (Strehler *et al.*, 1971), by gene exhaustion (Medvedev, 1972), or by nucleic acid damage (Hayflick, 1975). Such were the convictions of the inevitability of this decremental model that until recently little research or treatment has been targeted toward geriatric subjects in the normal population (Birren, 1959; Botwinick, 1973; Butler, 1969). Only treated populations were investigated for specific disorders.

However, contemporary investigations such as the Baltimore Longitudinal Study (Department of Health, Education, and Welfare, 1978) have led to a new appreciation of the body's ability to prevent or postpone physical deterioration, to reclaim an earlier status, or to encourage the emergence of compensatory mechanisms. Interventions include improved diet and exercise regimens as well as occupational, social, and medical interventions (Comfort, 1976; Riley and Foner, 1968). Such person–environment interaction appears to reshape the ongoing individual life-course trajectory to a much larger extent than heretofore expected. Longitudinal research such as the Baltimore Study, which followed members of the general population over time, has injected significant balance and clarity into the broader picture of aging.

The Brain and Aging

Much of this longitudinal approach is missing in the study of normal brains as they age *in vivo*. *In vitro* studies are also difficult because fresh, nondiseased human brain tissue to study is lacking (Côté and Kremzner, 1983) and animal brains differ in their biochemical makeup. Few studies have been performed at autopsy of once healthy subjects suffering from sudden accidental deaths (Côté and Kremzner, 1983). Significant methodological hurdles exist such as the absence of broad-based samples, homogeneously defined subsamples, and samples followed longitudinally with repeated measures.

Positron emission tomography (PET) scans offer a new window on some brain processes, but findings can be misleading due to individual differences in the ability of the aging brain to increase enzymatic activity in response to stimuli (Côté and Kremzner, 1983), partially resulting in the decrease of glucose oxidation (Beck, 1978; Patch, 1977). This situation complicates the measurement of an ^{18}F-2-deoxy-2-fluoro-D-glucose compound, which is the key mechanism used to study brain function in PET scans (Ferris *et al.*, 1980; Côté and Kremzner, 1983: 29).

As research progresses, the brain's complexity is becoming more apparent. Over 36 neurotransmitters, in addition to neuroactive peptides and substances yet to be classified (such as adenosine), have been identified. Furthermore, each neuroactive compound (e.g., dopamine, acetylcholine, serotonin) can be a transmitter, a modulator, or a hormone, depending on its location and activity. We know how to measure only simple molecules and must often guess what it is we are looking at and where to find it in order to study it (Samorajski, 1977).

With these caveats in mind, current research on aging mechanisms suggest the possibility that enzymes regulating synthesis and degradation of neurotransmitters in the brain differentially change the available concentrations of transmitters. Postulated behavioral correlates of these changes include familiar aspects of aging such as impaired motor activity, mood changes, memory losses, altered sleep patterns, and loss of appetite (Côté and Kremzner, 1983). The assumption is that these changes are predictable and relentless, but considerable evidence indicates that the brain is in dynamic interaction with environmental influences in complex feedback loops (Kra, 1986; Samorajski, 1977). Furthermore, critical regulatory organs, such as the hypothalamus, have been found to age at different rates within different locations of the same organ (Frolkis *et al.*, 1972; Hasan *et al.*, 1974), adding considerable complexity to the picture.

In schizophrenia research, increases in dopaminergic and noradrenergic activity, as well as decreases in the γ-amino butyric acidic (GABAergic) system, have been implicated in the search for etiologic explanations (e.g., Freedman *et al.*, 1987; Jaskiw and Kleinman, 1988; Seeman *et al.*, 1984; Wyatt *et al.*, 1988). However, it is not clear whether these changes are (1) reflect interactions among transmitters in delicate feedback loops, (2) precursor enzyme dysfunction, (3) reuptake problems, (4) proliferation of receptor sites, and/or (5) primary or secondary to schizophrenia or psychoses in general.

Weinberger *et al.* (1979a,b) were among the first to show cerebral atrophy, ventricular enlargement, and wide cortical sulci in some patients with schizophrenia by computerized tomography studies. These findings have been replicated many times but may only represent a subgroup (Crow *et al.*, 1982). Position emission studies have reported reduced glucose metabolism in frontal lobes (e.g., Buchsbaum *et al.*, 1982). Wyatt and his colleagues point out: "It is not known, if there is actual loss of brain tissue or simply a failure for the brain to develop fully, or whether abnormality happens in neurons, glial, or both kinds of cells" (Wyatt *et al.*, 1988: 12). Heterogeneity of small samples, lack of longitudinal follow-along of the same patients, relatively primitive equipment (despite its high-tech appearance), and numerous methodological flaws persist in creating an exciting but frontier science.

Several investigators (e.g., Côté and Kremzner, 1983; Samorajski, 1977) suggest that the catecholamine system is the most susceptible to the aging process. They propose a decline in synthesis, as well as changes in the reuptake system and receptor sensitivity, all of which lead to a decrease in available dopamine (Bowen and Davison, 1983; Carlsson and Winblad, 1976). Other studies investigating normal aging brains have found increases in monoamine oxidase (MAO) levels (Nies *et al.*, 1973; Robinson *et al.*, 1972) and reductions in the activity of the noradrenergic (Lieberman *et al.*, 1972), serotonergic (Siow, 1985) GABA and cholinergic systems. These changes apparently occur differentially in a wide variety of brain locations (McGeer and McGeer, 1975).

Because neurotransmitters are less stable and more likely to diffuse than enzymes, research effort has focused on the enzyme systems to study aging effects. Radical changes in enzymes such as tyrosine hydroxylase, DOPA decarboxylase, glutamic acid decarbolase, and choline acetyl transferase in neurotransmitter systems (McGeer and McGeer, 1975) have been implicated in Parkinson's disease (McGeer and McGeer, 1976) and Huntington's disease (Bird and Iverson, 1974). Central cholinergic deficits may cause the senile dementias of Alzheimer's disease as well as substantial morphological changes and cell loss (Beck, 1978). However, the changes in the dopaminergic system and alterations in other neurotransmitter systems and enzymes [such as MAO (see Jeste *et al.*, 1982)] due to aging processes, while not helpful in their exaggerated form for victims of Parkinson's, Huntington's, or Alzheimer's disease, may contribute to the amelioration of schizophrenic symptomatology that has been observed by many long-term clinicians and documented by longitudinal studies (Bridge *et al.*, 1978). This possibility needs further investigation. Conversely, the maintenance of higher dopamine levels and lower MAO levels (the reverse of putative aging effects for each) may contribute to continued chronicity in a subgroup of schizophrenic patients.

Nobel laureate Gerald Edelman, Director of the Neurosciences Institute at Rockefeller University, has declared that "In the last 10 years . . . we have learned more about the brain than in all of history" (Hellerstein, 1988: 17), but it is abundantly clear that brain research is still a primitive science with a long road to travel. However, the decremental model appears to have been replaced by one of plasticity, reversibility, and compensation.

LONG-TERM OUTCOME OF SCHIZOPHRENIA

In the past 18 years, six major studies were conducted to ascertain the very long-term course of schizophrenia in the lives of 1500-plus subjects

(Bleuler, 1978; Ciompi and Müller, 1976; DeSisto *et al.*, in preparation; Harding *et al.*, 1987a,b; Huber *et al.*, 1979; Tsuang *et al.*, 1979). Each of these studies found wide heterogeneity in functioning within each cohort. Outcome ranged from deteriorated levels or improved status to full recovery. These variations even appeared in cohorts diagnosed with the narrow criteria of Feighner (Feighner *et al.*, 1972) and the DSM-III (American Psychiatric Association, 1980), as well as samples that had been considered chronic cases for many years prior to final assessment.

The Longest Study of Schizophrenia

The Lausanne Investigations have become the longest follow-up with subjects ranging up to 64 years after first admission. The subjects (*n* = 289) were diagnosed as having schizophrenia by a combination of Kraepelinian criteria (Kraepelin, 1902) and Bleulerian concepts (Bleuler, 1911), later modified by his son, Manfred Bleuler. Ciompi (1980) considered this modification to be narrower than either the DSM-I (American Psychiatric Association, 1952) or DSM-II (American Psychiatric Association, 1968) in the United States. The follow-up assessment included a clinical semistructured interview, a review of hospital records, and reports from other clinicians and proband families. Average age for the sample at follow-up was 75 years.

Of these subjects, 47% had only one hospitalization of less than 1 year, 23% spent more than 20 years in the hospital, and 49% were considered by the project's criteria to have had a favorable outcome. Of those with a favorable outcome, 27% were deemed recovered, achieving normal social, occupational, and behavioral levels; 22% were rated as mildly impaired in these spheres.

The Iowa 500 Study

The second longest study was conducted in the United States. Known as "the Iowa 500" (Tsuang and Winokur, 1975), 186 patients who were admitted between 1934 and 1944 were followed up an average of 35 years after their admissions. These cases were sifted from 515 consecutive schizophrenic admissions. Most of the patients (315) did not meet the narrowly constructed Feighner criteria for schizophrenia and were rejected. Of the 200 subjects who met the criteria, information on 14 was unobtainable. The final 186 subjects were followed up, along with 100 manic, 225 depressive, and 160 surgical control subjects, who served as comparison groups. Structured follow-up interviews were conducted, blind to original diagnostic status, with each subject and their first-degree relatives. The average age of the schizophrenia group at follow-up was 58 years. Outcome data showed that 67% of the schizophrenia group were still single and 58% were unemployed; 18% resided in a mental hospital with an additional 48% living in nursing or county homes. Fifty-five percent displayed incapacitating psychiatric symptoms (Tsuang et al., 1979). In the only report on overall functioning, Tsuang and Winokur (1975) indicated that, among 133 cases assessed up to that point, 53% had improved or recovered. However, that figure has since been reduced to 46% with the completion of the study. Those with the diagnosis of schizophrenia fared less well in comparison to the other diagnostic groups (e.g., affective and schizoaffective disorders) and to surgical controls from the general Iowan population.

The Vermont Study

The Vermont Longitudinal Research Project was a study of 269 very chronic individuals who were followed an average of 32 years after first admission, within a range encompassing 22–62 years (Harding et al., 1987a,b). In the early 1980s, 97% of the cohort members were studied. One hundred eighteen subjects retrospectively met the new DSM-III (American Psychiatric Association, 1980) criteria for schizophrenia. Assessments included both cross-sectional and longitudinal measures, obtained through structured interviews and record abstractions. All raters and interviewers were blind to either previous or follow-up data. Even with earlier indices of severe chronicity, 27% of these probands were rated by the Community Adjustment Scale to be fully recovered across behavioral, social, and occupational spheres (Harding, 1986; Harding et al., 1987b). An additional 35% were considered to be significantly improved in those spheres. Thus, an analysis utilizing the DSM-III to test its power in predicting uniformly poor outcome failed to do so. In fact, diagnosis per se, either DSM-I or DSM-III, washed out as a predictor over time (Harding et al., 1987b).

Manfred Bleuler's Study

The Burghölzli Hospital Study was conducted by Manfred Bleuler (1978) in Zurich, Switzerland. Two hundred eight patients were followed an average of 23 years. These subjects were representative of all patients admitted to the hospital in the years 1942–1943. Bleuler's criteria were considered to be much more restrictive than both his father's (Bleuler, 1978: 15–18; Ciompi, 1980: 607) and those of the DSM-I and DSM-II in America, but less exclusive than the Scandinavian systems proposed by Achté (1967), Holmböe and Astrup (1957), and Langfeldt (1960).

Outcome was assessed by M. Bleuler, himself, through clinical interviews. He established the criteria of "end-state," i.e., a stable level of functioning for at least 5 years prior to assessment. Fifty-three percent of all patients and 66% of his first-admission group recovered or significantly improved. Of the first admission group, 41% were socially impaired, with 54% of all patients displaying moderate to severe impairment in social functioning.

The Bonn Hospital Study

The fifth study was completed by the German team of Huber *et al.* (1979) at the University Psychiatric Hospital in Bonn. Five hundred and two subjects were followed out of the 758 patients admitted to the University Clinic between 1945 and 1959. The average for catamnestic years was 22.4 years. Assessment was made by semistructured interview and a review of hospital records. These investigations found 26% of their subjects were considered recovered at end-state, with an additional 31% significantly improved, for a total of 57% achieving a favorable status. Social outcome data revealed that 56% of the subjects were fully employed.

The World's Only Replication Study

The last major study to be described is the new Maine Longitudinal Research Project (De Sisto *et al.*, in preparation). This companion study to the Vermont Project contains 269 subjects from Augusta Mental Health Institute, matched to the Vermont probands for diagnosis, age, gender, and length of chronicity. After conducting interproject and intraproject rater reliabilities studies (using the same protocols and procedures), the Maine investigators accounted for 94% of their cohort, with an average of 37 years between hospitalization and follow-up. These patients achieved 48% significant improvement, without the comprehensive and pioneering rehabilitation program received by their counterparts in Vermont.

Implications of Long-Term Follow-Up Studies

The preceding six studies represent considerable methodological and design improvements over studies from earlier decades (Bachrach, 1976; Harding *et al.* 1987d; Shapiro and Shader, 1979; Stephens, 1970, Strömgren, 1961). The findings cut across studies and countries and indicate that one-half or more of each cohort significantly improves and/or recovers. Harding *et al.* (1987d) have identified myriad factors that contribute to persistent biased sampling and psychosocial artifacts. These perpetuate the picture of ongoing chronicity and cloud our view of the actual illness trajectory.

As an important addition to the cross-sectional picture of schizophrenia at a designated outcome point, M. Bleuler (1978), Ciompi (1980), and Huber et al. (1980) have identified 8–12 patterns of course and have estimated the percentages of patients falling in each category. Clustering of patients reveals the episodic nature of the illness in one-half of the subjects (Harding, 1988).

These data suggest, then, that the disorder is more a "prolonged illness then a chronic one" (Harding et al., 1987d) and joins many other illnesses in general medicine that are called chronic illnesses and that may remit or ameliorate over time. The possibility of underlying biopsychosocial corrective mechanisms which help restore the person to a more healthy state, add important considerations for the current research protocols, which, up to now, have assumed decremental immutability.

Further reports have described subsets of patients who display neither homogeneously poor nor good levels of function but who show complex combinations of dysfunction and adaptation, thus being heterogeneous within themselves. Strauss and Carpenter (1974) described this phenomenon as "open-linked" systems, in which domains best predicted themselves. For example, previous work function predicted current work function, but degree of severity of symptoms did not predict ability for current work as expected. This internal heterogeneity across domains of function within an individual suggests further complexities in brain mechanisms. For example, how is it that a person can be competent in a job while experiencing positive signs and symptoms of schizophrenia? Do these disparities reflect biochemical corrections and changes in some locations and not others? Do the differences in behaviors reflect positive or negative environmental influences, learning opportunities or lack of them, personality variables, the degree of acquisition of coping strategies, or an interaction of all four with brain chemistry (Harding et al., 1987d)? This new awareness will reshape future inquiries.

NEW CONCEPTS IN ADULT DEVELOPMENT

Normal Adult Development and Aging

As many developmentalists have shifted from the study of adolescents to various subgroups in adulthood, including the elderly, a new appreciation has emerged: the fact that "plasticity, resilience, discontinuity, regression, advancement, and compensation appear repeatedly across all ages" (Strauss and Harding, 1990). This is in contrast to the assumption of orderly hierarchical stages attached to specific ages (Hirschhorn, 1977; Neugarten, 1979). Stability and change occur across all stages of the life cycle in integral areas of function such as occupation (Belbin and Belbin, 1966; Riley and Foner, 1968; Comfort, 1976), social roles (Elder, 1974; Neugarten, 1979), intellectual strategies (Botwinick, 1973; Horn and Donaldson, 1980), physical status (Comfort, 1976; Maddox and Eisdorfer, 1962), sexual behavior (Masters and Johnson, 1966a,b), uses of the social milieu (Lowenthal and Boler, 1965; Lowenthal and Haven, 1968), personality development (Erikson, 1978; Loevinger, 1966; McCrae and Costa, 1988), and use of leisure time (Neugarten, 1974). All of these areas of functions ebb and flow across time within individuals.

Delayed Development

Dealing with repeated episodes of schizophrenia and surviving the impact of the illness is understood to be a long, difficult struggle. Much energy is expended in coping with the illness, severely reducing opportunities in work and relationships. This places the person significantly behind peers in many of the ongoing tasks of adult development; however, recorded cases show a variety of pathways on which these adults proceed, albeit slowly, in the direction of further development (Beiser *et al.*, 1972; Bleuler, 1978; Chittick *et al.*, 1961; Harding *et al.*, 1987c; Strauss and Harding, 1990). Some patients have reported that suddenly one day they "felt back to their old selves" (Brooks and Deane, 1960). They described these experiences in much the same manner as the subjective reports from patients experiencing nitrogen balance shifts a week after surgical anesthesia (Gann and Amaral, 1989). These occurrences may reflect biochemical events and give further clues about other aspects of brain functioning.

This more flexible approach to the course of schizophrenia allows someone who has a slow start because of coping with a prolonged severe illness seem not so out of step. In fact, other groups of people have delayed development in occupational or social domains. One example is the Olympic athlete, who generally has to learn a new occupation after age 30 years. Another would be physicians who emerge after years of concentrated study to learn new social behaviors (Havens, 1983). The point is that, over the years, various disenfranchised groups (such as children, adolescents, the middle-aged, the elderly, and women) have been stereotyped and underestimated, only later to be rediscovered, studied, and found to lead far richer, less predictable, and more complex lives than imagined.

Patients with prolonged and episodic illnesses have recently joined the groups to be reappraised. Also, it should be noted that current treatment systems are not geared, as they might be, to promote long-term turnaround of illness and expanded development. Operating with an acute versus chronic treatment dichotomy, the mental health system generally gives up. It decides on a custodial or maintenance approach to the person with an episodic and prolonged illness, ironically just as the illness may be beginning to lift. The person with newly released energy may begin a long-sought trajectory toward recovery and health in the absence of active treatment, yet often go unnoticed by the system or stymied by uncomprehending clinicians who seek to maintain stabilization at a large cost (McCrory *et al.*, 1980).

LATE-ONSET SCHIZOPHRENIA

Just as the patients who recover or significantly improve have been thought to have been misdiagnosed in the American classification systems, by the Feighner criteria (Feighner *et al.*, 1972) and the DSM-III (American Psychiatric Association, 1980), until recently, the diagnosis of schizophrenia could not be given if the illness began after the age of 45 years (American Psychiatric Association, 1987). Such patients were generally assigned other diagnoses, such as affective disorder, atypical paranoid disorder, or senile dementia. Although the onset of schizophrenia most generally occurs prior to 40 years of age, numerous American and European investigators have pointed to the clinical realities of patients who fit all criteria for schizophrenia but are older than 45 years (Bridge and Wyatt, 1980a,b; Fish, 1960; Gold, 1984; Grahame, 1984; Kay, 1963; Rabins *et al.*, 1984; Roth, 1955; Post, 1966; Volavka, 1985). Concerns have been raised that the misdiagnosis of such cases led to use of the wrong drugs and the mistaken expectation of irreversibility. Many of these cases might have shown a rapid response to phenothiazine treatment, hearing aids, or other modalities and could have returned many patients to their homes (Gold, 1984; Post, 1966; Roth, 1987; Rowan, 1984; Volavka, 1985).

The biochemistry of the mechanisms underlying late-onset schizophrenia might be postulated as the reversal of normal aging processes, i.e., increased dopamine and reduced MAO levels. This may produce an increased vulnerability to environmental stressors and sensory deficits that sometimes accompany aging, such as hearing loss, and may lead to suspiciousness and paranoia (Roth, 1987). An analogy to Type I diabetes with its onset in adolescence and Type II diabetes with its onset in later years might be considered an example of related illnesses with significantly different ages of onset and degrees of severity.

DISCUSSION

It is hoped that by interweaving several different literature bases, new directions will emerge in our understanding of the processes involved in aging and schizophrenia. These will reframe our assumptions and alter future research designs.

Empirical data have begun to challenge all five basic assumptions set forth at the beginning of this chapter. The normal aging brain and body are more resilient, plastic, and modifiable than previously assumed. The expected deterioration in aging may be prevented or altered significantly in interaction with the environment. Persons with repeated episodes of schizophrenia show a wide variety of outcome trajectories, not just the expected chronic course. Associated neurochemical and structural brain anomalies may not remain as permanent deficits but, rather, may be alterable over time. The person with delayed adult development has the potential to reconstitute lost skills, improve his or her level of function, and develop further.

The documentation of patients who defy the expected course and outcome provides the field with important information to be incorporated into diagnostic manuals, research protocols, and treatment strategies. For example, to draw more valid conclusions, biological researchers may need to study brain mechanisms longitudinally in both normal and affected subjects, instead of collecting cross-sectional slices and assays. The delicate feedback loops, which operate in the interface between the brain and the environment need further study. Presumably, the psychological status and coping abilities of the person are important modifiers of these ongoing processes (Strauss *et al.*, 1989). A greater appreciation of the body's ability to help correct or compensate for problems is also needed. The body's plasticity, mutability, and resiliency apparently are significant mechanisms but are currently neglected in the rush to study cross-sectional pathology.

Psychosocial researchers must form a critical partnership with the biologically oriented investigators in the field of psychopathology. With joint efforts, we will more likely come to understand the complex phenomena of aging and schizophrenia that have eluded us for so long. In addition, perhaps our treatment systems will be able to titrate care more effectively.

ACKNOWLEDGMENTS

This work was supported by NIMH grant #40607. The author thanks Drs. John Strauss and Malcolm B. Bowers for their thoughtful comments on earlier drafts of this manuscript, as well as Nancy Ryan and Carol Wersinger for typing.

REFERENCES

Achté, K. A. (1967). On prognosis and rehabilitation in schizophrenia and paranoid psychoses. *Acta Psychiatrica et Neurologica Scandinavica, Suppl.*, 196, Copenhagen: Munksgaard.

American Psychiatric Association (1952). *Diagnostic and statistical manual of mental disorders* (1st ed.). Washington, DC: American Psychiatric Press.

American Psychiatric Association (1968). *Diagnostic and statistical manual of mental disorders* (2nd ed.). Washington, DC: American Psychiatric Press.

American Psychiatric Association (1980). *Diagnostic and statistical manual of mental disorders* (3rd ed.). Washington, DC: American Psychiatric Press.

American Psychiatric Association (1987). *Diagnostic and statistical manual of mental disorders* (3rd ed., revised). Washington, DC: American Psychiatric Press.

Bachrach, L. L. (1976). A note on some recent studies of released mental hospital patients in the community. *American Journal of Psychiatry, 133(1),* 73–75.

Beck, C. H. (1978). Functional implications of changes in the senescent brain: A review. *Canadian Journal of Neurological Sciences, 5(4),* 417–424.

Beiser, M., Feldman, J. J., and Egelhoff, C. J. (1972). Assets and affects: A study of positive mental health. *Archives of General Psychiatry, 27,* 545–549.

Belbin, E., and Belbin, R. M. (1966). New careers in middle age. In *Proceedings of the 7th International Congress of Gerontology* (pp. 71–82). Vienna: Verlager Wiener Midizinischen Akademie.

Bird, E. D., and Iverson, L. L. (1974). Huntington's chorea: Post-mortem measurement of glutamic acid decarboxylase, choline acetyltransferase and dopamine in basal ganglia. *Brain, 97,* 459.

Birren, J. E. (1959). Principles of research in aging. In J. E. Birren (Ed.), *Handbook of aging and the individual.* Chicago: University of Chicago Press.

Bleuler, E. (1911). Dementia praecox oder Die Gruppe der Schizophrenien. In *Handbuch der Psychiatrie,* hrsg. von G. Aschaffenburg; Deuticket, Leipzig. Translated by Joseph Zinkin, 8th printing, 1968, New York: International Universities Press.

Bleuler, M. (1978). *Die schizophrenen Geistesstörungen im Lichte langjährigern Kranken-und Familiengeschichten.* Stuttgart, Georg Thieme 1972 Trans. Clemens SM, *The schizophrenic disorders, long term patient and family studies.* New Haven: Yale University Press.

Botwinick, J. (1973). *Aging and behavior: A comprehensive integration of research findings.* New York: Springer.

Bowen, D. M., and Davison, A. N. (1983). The failing brain. *Journal of Chronic Disease, 36,* 3–13.

Bridge, T. P., and Wyatt, R. J. (1980a). Paraphrenia: Paranoid states of late life, I. European Research. *Journal of the American Geriatrics Society, 28(5),* 193–200.

Bridge, T. P., and Wyatt, R. J. (1980b). Paraphrenia: Paranoid states of late life, II. American Research. *Journal of the American Geriatrics Society, 28(5),* 201–205.

Bridge, T. P., Cannon, E., and Wyatt, R. J. (1978). Burned-out schizophrenia: Evidence for age effects on schizophrenic symptomatology. *Journal of Gerontology, 33,* 835–839.

Brooks, G.W., and Deane, W. N. (1960). Attitudes of released chronic schizophrenic patients concerning illness and recovery as revealed by a structured post-hospital interview. *Journal of Clinical Psychology, 16(3),* 259–264.

Buchsbaum, M. S., Ingvar, D. H., Kessler, R., Waters, R. N., Cappelletti, J., van Kammen, D. P., King, A. C., Johnson, J. L., Manning, R. G., Flynn, R. W., Mann, L. S., Bunney, W. E., Jr., and Sokoloff, L. (1982). Cerebral glucography with positron tomography. *Archives of General Psychiatry, 39,* 251–259.

Butler, R. N. (1969). Age-ism: Another form of bigotry. *Gerontologist, 9,* 243–246.

Carlsson, A., and Winblad, B. (1976). Influence of age and time interval between death and autopsy on dopamine and 3 methoxy tyramine levels in human basal ganglia. *Journal of Neural Transmission, 38,* 271.

Chittick, R. A., Brooks, G. W., Irons, F. S., and Deane, W. N. (1961). *The Vermont story.* Burlington, VT: Queen City Printers.

Ciompi, L. (1980). Catamnestic long-term study on the course of life and aging of schizophrenics. *Schizophrenia Bulletin, 6(4)*, 606–618.

Ciompi, L., and Müller, C. (1976). Lebensweg und Alter Schizophrenen Eine Katamnestic Longzeitstudie bis ins Senium. Berlin: Springer-Verlag.

Comfort, A. (1976). *A good age*. New York: Crown Publishing.

Côté, L. J., and Kremzner, L. T. (1983). Biochemical changes in normal aging in human brain. *Advanced Neurology, 38*, 19–30.

Crow, T. J., Cross, A. J., Johnstone, E. C., and Owen, F. (1982). Two syndromes in schizophrenia and their prognosis. In F. A. Henn and H. A. Nasrallah (Eds.), *Schizophrenia as a brain disease*. New York: Oxford University Press.

De Sisto, M., Harding, C. M., McCormick, R. V., and Ashikaga, T. (in preparation). *The Maine longitudinal study of persons with severe mental illness, I. Methodology, matched selection and overall status 37 years later.*

Department of Health, Education, and Welfare (1978). *The Baltimore Longitudinal Study of the National Institute on Aging*, pp. 1–20. NIH 78-134. Washington, DC: Superintendent of Documents, U.S. Government Printing Office.

Elder, G. H., Jr. (1974). *Children of the great depression*. Chicago: University of Chicago Press.

Erikson, E. (Ed.) (1978). *Adulthood*. New York: W. W. Norton and Co.

Feighner, J. P., Robins, E., Guze, S. B., Woodruff, R. A., Winokur, G., and Munos, R. (1972). Diagnostic criteria for use in psychiatric research. *Archives of General Psychiatry, 26*, 57–63.

Ferris, S. H., de Leon, M. J., Wolf, A. P., Farkas, T., Christman, D. R., Reisberg, B., Fowler, J. S., MacGregor, R., Goldman, A., George, A. E., and Rampal, S. (1980). Positron emission tomography in the study of aging and senile dementia. *Neurobiology of Aging, 1*, 127–131.

Fish, F. (1960). Senile schizophrenia. *Journal of Mental Science, 106*, 938–946.

Freedman, R., Adler, L. E., Gerhardt, G. A., Waldo, M., Baher, N., Rose, G. M., Drebing, C., Nagamoto, H., Bickford-Wimer, P., and Franks R. (1987). Neurobiological studies of sensory gating in schizophrenia. *Schizophrenia Bulletin, 13(4)*, 669–678.

Frolkis, V. V., Bezrukov, V. V., Duplenko, Y. K., and Genis, E. D. (1972). The hypothalmus in aging. *Experimental Gerontology, 7*, 169.

Gann, D. S., and Amaral, J. F. (1989). Endocrine and metabolic responses to injury. In S. I. Schwartz, G. T. Shires, and F. C. Spencer (Eds.), *Principles of surgery* (Chap. 1, pp. 1–68). New York: McGraw-Hill.

Giaquinto, S. (1988). *Aging and the nervous system*. Chichester England: Wiley and Sons.

Gold, D. D. (1984). Late age of onset schizophrenia: Present but unaccounted for. *Comprehensive Psychiatry, 25(2)*, 225–237.

Goldman, A. P. (1986). Fitness and the aging process. *Newsweek, Sept. 1*, S22.

Grahame, P. S. (1984). Schizophrenia in old age (late paraphrenia). *British Journal of Psychiatry, 145*, 493–495.

Harding, C. M. (1986). Speculations on the measurement of recovery from severe psychotic disorder and the human condition. *The Psychiatric Journal of the University of Ottawa, 11(4)*, 199–204.

Harding, C. M. (1988). Course types in schizophrenia: An analysis of European and American studies. *Schizophrenia Bulletin, 14(4)*, 633–645.

Harding, C. M., Brooks, G. W., Ashikaga, T., Strauss, J. S., and Breier, A. (1987a). The Vermont longitudinal study of persons with severe mental illness: I. Methodology, study sample and overall status 32 years later. *American Journal of Psychiatry, 144(6)*, 718–726.

Harding, C. M., Brooks, G. W., Ashikaga, T., Strauss, J. S., and Breier, A. (1987b). The Vermont longitudinal research project: II. Long-term outcome functioning of subjects who retrospectively met DSM-III criteria for schizophrenia. *American Journal of Psychiatry, 144(6)*, 727–735.

Harding, C. M., Brooks, G. W., Ashikaga, T., Strauss, J. S., and Landerl, P. D. (1987c). Aging and social functioning in once chronic schizophrenic patients 22–62 years after first admission: The Vermont story. In N. E. Miller and G. D. Cohen (Eds.), *Schizophrenia and Aging* (pp. 74–83). New York: Guilford Press.

Harding, C. M., Zubin, J., and Strauss, J. S. (1987d). Chronicity in schizophrenia: Fact, partial fact or artifact? *Hospital and Community Psychiatry, 38(5)*, 477–486.

Hasan, M., Glees, P., and El-Ghazzawi, E. (1974). Age-associated changes in the hypothalamus of the guinea pig: Effect of dimethylaminoethyl p-chlorophenoxyacetate. An election microscope and histochemical study. *Experimental Gerintology, 9*, 153.

Havens, L. (November 1983). Grand Rounds, Department of Psychiatry, Yale School of Medicine. Connecticut Mental Health Center.

Hayflick, L. (1975). Current theories in biological aging. *Federation Proceedings, 34*, 9–13.

Hellerstein, D. (1988). Plotting a theory of the brain. *Time Magazine, May 22.* p. 17.

Hirschhorn, L. (1977). Social policy and the life cycle: A developmental perspective. *Social Service Review, 51*, 434–450.

Holmböe, R., and Astrup, C. (1957). A follow-up study of 255 patients with acute schizophrenia and schizophreniform psychoses. *Acta Psychiatrica et Neurologica Scandinavica, Suppl.* **115**, 32. Copenhagen: Munksgaard.

Horn, J. L., and Donaldson, G. (1980). Cognitive development in adulthood. In O. G. Brim and J. Kagan (Eds.), *Constancy and change in human development* (pp. 445–529). Cambridge: Harvard University Press.

Huber, G., Gross, G., and Schüttler, R. (1979). Schizophrenie. Verlaufs-und sozialpsychiatrische Langzeitunter-suchungen an den 1945 his 1959 in Bonn hospitalisierten schizophrenen Kranken. Monographien aus dem Gesamtgebiete der Psychiatrie. Bd. 21. Berlin: Springer-Verlag.

Huber, G., Gross, G., Schüttler, R., and Linz, M. (1980). Longitudinal studies of schizophrenic patients. *Schizophrenic Bulletin, 6(4)*, 592–605.

Jaskiw, G., and Kleinman, J. (1988). Postmortem neurochemistry studies in schizophrenia. In S. C. Schulz and C. A. Tamminga (Eds.), *Schizophrenia: A scientific focus*. New York: Oxford University Press.

Jeste, D. V., Kleinman, J. E., Potkin, S. G., Luchins, D. J., and Weinberger, D. R. (1982). Ex uno multi: Subtyping the schizophrenic syndrome. *Biological Psychiatry, 17*, 199–222.

Kay, D. W. (1963). Late paraphrenia and its bearing on the aetiology of schizophrenia. *Acta Psychiatrica Scandinavica, 39*, 159–169.

Kra, S. (1986). Aging myths: Reversible causes of mind and memory loss. New York: McGraw-Hill.

Kraepelin, E. (1902). Dementia praecox. In E. Kraepelin (Ed.), *Clinical psychiatry: A textbook for students and physicians* (6th ed.). Trans. by A. R. Diefendorf. (pp. 152–202). New York: Macmillan.

Lamb, H. R. (1976). Guiding principles for community survival. In H. R. Lamb (Ed.), *Community survival for long-term patients* (pp. 1–13). San Francisco: Jossey-Bass.

Langfeldt, G. (1960). Diagnosis and prognosis of schizophrenia. *Proceedings of the Royal Society of Medicine, 53*, 1047.

Lieberman, A. N., Freedman, L. S., and Goldstein, M. (1972). Serum-dopamine-β-hydroxylase activity in patients with Huntington's chorea and Parkinson's disease. *Lancet, 1*, 153–154.

Loevinger, J. (1966). The meaning and measurement of ego development. *American Psychologist, 21(3)*, 195–206.

Lowenthal, M. F., and Boler, D. (1965). Voluntary vs involuntary social withdrawal. *Journal of Gerontology, 20,* 363–371.

Lowenthal, M. F., and Haven, C. (1968). Interaction and adaptation intimacy as a critical variable. *American Sociological Review, 33,* 20–30.

Maddox, G., and Eisdorfer, C. (1962). Some correlates of activity and morale among the elderly. *Social Forces, 40,* S54–260.

Masters, W. H., and Johnson, V. E. (1966a). The aging female. In *Human sexual response.*. Boston: Little Brown & Co.

Masters, W. H., and Johnson, V. E. (1966b). The aging male. In *Human sexual response.* Boston: Little Brown and Co.

McCrae, R. R., and Costa, P. T. (1988). Age, personality and the spontaneous self-concept. *Journal of Gerontology (Social Sciences) 43(6),* S177–185.

McCrory, D. J., Connolly, P. S., Hanson-Meyer, T. P., Landolfi, J. M. S., Barone, F. C., Blood, A. H., and Gilsin, A. B. (1980). The rehabilitation crisis: The impact of growth. *Journal of Applied Rehabilitation Counseling, 11(3),* 136–139.

McGeer, E. G., and McGeer, P. L. (1975). Age changes in the humans for some enzymes associated with metabolism of catecholamines, GABA and acetylcholine. In J. M. Ordy and K. R. Brizzee (Eds.), *Neurobiology of aging* (pp. 287–305). New York: Plenum Press.

McGeer, P.L., and McGeer, E. G. (1976). Enzymes associated with the metabolism of catecholamines, acetylcholine and GABA in human controls and patients with Parkinson's disease and Huntington's chorea. *Journal of Neurochemistry, 26,* 65.

Medvedev, Zh. A. (1972). The repetition of molecular–genetic information as a possible factor in evolutionary changes of life span. *Experimental Gerontology, 7,* 227–238.

Neugarten, B. L. (1974). Age groups in American society and the rise of the young–old. *Annals of the American Academy of Political and Social Sciences, 415,* 187–198.

Neugarten, B. L. (1979). Time, age and the life cycle. *The American Journal of Psychiatry, 136(7),* 887–893.

Nies, A., Robinson, D. S., Davis, J. M., and Ravaris, C. L. (1973). Changes in monoamine oxidase in aging. In C. Eisdorfer and W. E. Fann (Eds.), *Psychopharmacology and aging* (pp. 41–54). New York: Plenum Press.

Patch, M. S. (1977). Age-dependent change in the oxidative metabolism in rat brains. *Journal of Gerontology, 32,* 643–646.

Post, F. (1966). *Persistant persecutory states of the elderly.* Oxford: Pergamon Press.

Rabins, P., Parker, S., and Thomas, J. (1984). Can schizophrenia begin after age 44? *Comprehensive Psychiatry, 25(3),* 290–294.

Riley, M. W., and Foner, A. (1968). *Aging and society* (Vol. 1). New York: Russell Sage Foundation.

Robinson, D. S., Nies, A., Davis, J. N., Bunney, W. E., Davis, J. M., Colburn, R. W., Bourne, H. R., Shaw, D. M., and Coppen, A. J. (1972). Aging monoamines, and monoamine–oxidase levels. *Lancet, 1,* 290–291.

Roth, M. (1955). The natural history of mental disorder in old age. *Journal of Mental Science, 101,* 281–301.

Roth, M. (1987). Late paraphrenia: Phenomenology and etiological factors and their bearing upon problems of the schizophrenic family of disorders. In N. E. Miller and G. D. Cohen (Eds.), *Schizophrenia and aging* (pp. 217–234). New York: Guilford Press.

Rowan, E. L. (1984). Phantom boarders as a symptom of late paraphrenia. *American Journal of Psychiatry, 141(4),* 580–581.

Samorajksi, T. (1977). Central neurotransmitter substances and aging: A review. *Journal of the American Geriatrics Society, 25(8),* 337–348.

Seeman, P., Ulpian, C., Bergeron, C., Riederer, P., Jellinger, K., Gabriel, E., Reynolds, G. P., and Tourtelotte, W. W. (1984). Biomodal distribution of dopamine receptor densities in brains of schizophrenics. *Science, 225,* 728.

Shapiro, R., and Shader, R. (1979). Selective review of results of previous follow-up studies of schizophrenia and other psychoses. In *Schizophrenia: An international follow-up study.* Geneva: World Health Organization.

Siow, B. L. (1985). Cerebral ageing, neurotransmitters, and therapeutic implications. *Singapore Medical Journal, 26(2),* 151–153.

Stephens, J. H. (1970). Long-term course and prognosis in schizophrenia. *Seminars in Psychiatry, 2,* 464–485.

Strauss, J. S., and Carpenter, W. T. (1974). The prediction of outcome in schizophrenia. *Archives of General Psychiatry, 31,* 37–42.

Strauss, J. S., and Harding, C. M. (1990). Relationships between adult development and the course of mental disorder. In J. Rolf, A. Master, D. Cicchetti, K. Nuechterlein, and S. Weintraub (Eds.), *Risk and protective factors in the development of psychopathology,* (pp. 514–535). New York: Cambridge University Press.

Straus, J. S., Rakfeldt, J. H., Harding, C. M., and Lieberman, P. D. (1989). Psychological and social aspects of negative symptoms. *British Journal of Psychiatry 155, (S5),* 100–106.

Strehler, B., Hirsch, G., Gusseck, D., Johnson, R., and Bick, M. (1971). Codon-restriction theory of aging and development. *Journal of Theoretical Biology, 33,* 429–474.

Strömgren, E. (1961). Recent studies of prognosis and outcome in the mental disorders. In P. Hoch and J. Zubin (Eds.), *Comparative epidemiology of the mental disorders.* New York: Grune & Stratton.

Tsuang, M. T., and Winokur, G. (1975). The Iowa 500: Field work in a 35 year follow-up of depression, mania and schizophrenia. *Canadian Psychiatric Journal, 20,* 389.

Tsuang, M., Woolson, R., and Fleming, J. (1979). Long-term outcome of major psychoses: I. Schizophrenia and affective disorders compared with psychiatrically symptom-free surgical conditions. *Archives of General Psychiatry, 36,* 1295–1301.

Volavka, J. (1985). Late-onset schizophrenia: A review. *Comprehensive Psychiatry, 26(2),* 148–156.

Weinberger, D. R., Torrey, E. F., Neophytides, A. N., and Wyatt, R. J. (1979a). Lateral cerebral ventricular enlargement in chronic schizophrenia. *Archives of General Psychiatry, 36(7),* 735–739.

Weinberger, D. R., Torrey, E. F., Neophytides, A. N., and Wyatt, R. J. (1979b). Structural abnormalities in cerebral cortex of chronic schizophrenic patients. *Archives of General Psychiatry, 36(9),* 935–939.

Weinberger, D. R., Wagner, R. L., and Wyatt, R. J. (1983). Neuropathological studies of schizophrenia: A selective review. *Schizophrenia Bulletin, 9(2),* 193–212.

Wyatt, R. S., Alexander, R. C., Egan, M. F., and Kirch, D. G. (1988). Schizophrenia, just the facts. What do we know, how well do we know it? *Schizophrenia Research, 1(1),* 3–18.

PART IV

Developmental Conceptualizations of Schizophrenia

The primary prevention of any illness requires an understanding of the nature and origins of the pathological process, so that interventions can be applied before the onset of that process. For this reason, specifying the developmental courses manifested by schizophrenic patients is of vital importance. Does vulnerability to schizophrenia involve a neuropathology that is present at birth and has a gradually increasing functional impact? Or, does the onset of the neuropathological process roughly correspond with the onset of clinical symptoms?

The latter possibility is explored by Michael Pogue-Geile in the first chapter in this section. He argues that, at least for some patients, the illness may be preceded by a developmental course that is characterized by an absence of both organic and behavioral dysfunction. He points out the lack of solid evidence for the existence of premorbid abnormalities in schizophrenia, and suggests that the disorder involves defects in genes that are "switched on (or off)" in young adulthood. In the final chapter, Elaine Walker explores a host of potential contributors to variability among patients with schizophrenia. She also describes a research program that is aimed at exploring the early developmental characteristics of patients. The eventual findings from this study and hish-risk research will play a major role in sharpening our conceptualizations of the development of schizophrenia.

SCHIZOPHRENIA
A Life-Course Developmental Perspective

275

Copyright © 1991 by Academic Press, Inc.
All rights of reproduction in any form reserved.

13

The Development of Liability to Schizophrenia: Early and Late Developmental Models

Michael F. Pogue-Geile

This chapter critically examines the widely held hypothesis that the brain abnormalities that specifically cause schizophrenic signs and symptoms develop perinatally or at a very young age. This view has become an implicit assumption of much recent research and theorizing on schizophrenia and, thus, deserves careful scrutiny. As a balance to this view, we discuss an alternative model in which these putative brain abnormalities develop much later—during adolescence and young adulthood. The different models will be described briefly first, followed by a survey of the relevant empirical findings and their discussion.

EARLY VERSUS LATE DEVELOPMENTAL MODELS OF SCHIZOPHRENIC LIABILITY

Many current models of the development of schizophrenia and much research are based on the hypothesis that the brain abnormalities that are specific causes of schizophrenic symptoms in adulthood develop perinatally (e.g., Fish, 1957; Goodman, 1988; Lewis, 1989; Lyon *et al.*, 1989; Med-

Copyright © 1991 by Academic Press, Inc.
All rights of reproduction in any form reserved.

nick *et al.*, 1989; Meehl, 1962; Murray *et al.*, 1985, 1988a,b; *Schizophrenia Bulletin*, 1987; Weinberger, 1987). The etiology of these putative early-occurring brain abnormalities has been hypothesized to be genetic, environmental, and/or some combination of the two. Obstetrical complications or *in utero* viral infections have been the most commonly hypothesized environmental contributors, and early genetic influences have been hypothesized to be due to either a single major locus or multiple loci.

The relatively late onset in young adulthood of the overt clinical signs and symptoms of schizophrenia presents a difficulty for such models and requires some hypothesized late-occurring triggering events that precipitate onset of the overt schizophrenic syndrome. Various early development models differ somewhat in the importance that they ascribe to such putative later events. Many of the diathesis–stress models (Rosenthal, 1963) of schizophrenia propose that (given brain abnormalities present at birth) experiences during childhood and adolescence may serve both to alter one's risk of eventual schizophrenia and to time the onset of clinical symptoms (Meehl, 1962; Zubin and Spring, 1977). For example, Meehl's (1962, 1989, 1990) model, which has been particularly influential, states that all persons with the hypothesized gene for schizophrenia develop presumably at birth a range of brain abnormalities (schizotaxia) that are inevitably manifested as a group of behavioral traits (schizotypy). Depending on the degree of exposure to later noxious experiences (and their own nonspecific genetic milieu), a subset of these schizotypes will develop the clinical symptoms of schizophrenia during young adulthood. In contrast, some recent early development models predict that later events serve primarily to time the onset of clinical symptoms and that they usually do not change one's lifetime risk for schizophrenia (Benes, 1989; Murray and Lewis, 1987; Randall, 1980; Weinberger, 1986, 1987). These recent early neurodevelopmental models predict that an individual's risk for eventual schizophrenia is primarily fixed at an early age and that normal developmental processes that occur during young adulthood for everyone serve only to time the onset of obvious clinical symptoms. Despite these differences in the importance ascribed to later events, the essence of all of these early development models is that they hypothesize that schizophrenia-specific brain abnormalities develop perinatally, whereas later triggering or timing influences are largely nonspecific. Therefore, the important prediction is that such schizophrenia-specific brain abnormalities can be detected, either behaviorally or biologically, from birth in individuals who will eventually be diagnosed with schizophrenia. Although this hypothesis has recently risen to the status of an implicit and often unquestioned assumption of much current research, alternative views are possible.

In contrast to this currently prominent early development view, is the possibility that brain abnormalities that are specific to schizophrenia develop much later and only precede the onset of overt clinical symptoms by months or a few years. Gottesman and Shields (1972, 1982), as early and sophisticated proponents of this viewpoint, argue that the liability to schizophrenia develops over time as disorder-specific genes are switched on and off in response to nonspecific environmental experiences. This position has been presented in detail by Feinberg (1982, 1982–1983, 1990), who hypothesized that abnormalities in genetically controlled brain development during adolescence were the specific causes of schizophrenia. Saugstad (1989a,b) and others (e.g., Hoffman and Dobscha, 1989; Woods and Wolf, 1983) have also recently proposed similar views of a late-developing liability.

Based largely on ideas proposed by Feinberg (1982–1983, 1990), we describe a version of the late development model that appears both theoretically and empirically attractive. Drawing on the emerging field of developmental behavior genetics (Plomin, 1986; Hahn et al., 1990), it is first hypothesized that the etiology of these late-developing, schizophrenia-specific brain abnormalities involve defects in some regulator gene(s) that controls brain development and is "switched on (or off)" during the post-adolescent–young adult period. Second, it is proposed that the penetrance of these abnormal developmental genes can be increased by early non-specific environmental insults, such as obstetrical complications and life experience. Although such early environmental insults may increase, via their brain sequelae, the probability that the late-onset, schizophrenia-specific developmental genetic abnormalities will produce clinical symptoms, this effect is entirely nonspecific; i.e., without the presence of the late-onset, schizophrenia-specific developmental genetic abnormalities, the early-occurring environmental insults would not increase one's risk for schizophrenia. Third, it is hypothesized that such early nonspecific environmental risk factors can also modify the eventual biological and behavioral manifestation of schizophrenia. For example, obstetrical complications may both increase the risk that abnormal developmental genes will later cause schizophrenic behavior and produce structural brain abnormalities that may give a "negative symptom" cast to the later clinical picture.

Thus, when compared with the early development models, this late development alternative reverses the relative roles of early and late events. In contrast to the early development hypothesis, here, late abnormalities are hypothesized to be schizophrenia-specific, whereas early abnormalities are nonspecific. Therefore, this model predicts that (aside from the DNA abnormalities) brain defects that are specific to schizophrenia should *not* be detected in most eventual schizophrenic patients prior to adolescence and/or clinical onset. However, early nonspecific noxious experiences and their brain sequelae may be elevated in eventual schizophrenics because they can increase the later penetrance of the abnormal developmental genes.

Before proceeding it should be noted that these two models represent extreme positions for heuristic reasons. Of course, it may be that heterogeneity exists such that both models may be valid, but for different groups of patients, as is often argued by proponents of the early development view (e.g., Murray *et al.*, 1988a). With this caveat in mind, the empirical data relevant to these two classes of models is briefly reviewed.

EARLY CHILDHOOD ABNORMALITIES AMONG PRESCHIZOPHRENIC SUBJECTS

The most basic prediction of the early development model is that some schizophrenia-specific brain abnormality exists and can be detected at an early age. This abnormality could be due to either a putative schizophrenia-specific environmental insult or an early specific genetic influence. In its strongest form, the early development model would predict that such early abnormalities are a necessary aspect of the disorder and that all eventual schizophrenic patients should show them and that they should not occur in other disorders. In contrast, the late development model predicts that schizophrenia-specific abnormalities will be absent at an early age in eventual schizophrenic patients, although it does not predict an absence of all early abnormalities. Rather, abnormalities that are not specific to schizophrenia, but that may increase the penetrance of the later hypothesized developmental gene defects, could be elevated among eventual schizophrenic patients. In contrast to the early development model predictions, these early nonspecific abnormalities should occur in only a minority of eventual schizophrenic patients and could also be increased in a range of disorders.

Because several excellent reviews of this general area are already available (Asarnow, 1988; Aylward *et al.*, 1984; Garmezy and Streitman, 1974; Offord and Cross, 1969; Neuchterlein, 1986; *Schizophrenia Bulletin*, 1987; Walker and Emory, 1983; Watt *et al.*, 1984), this survey will not duplicate them; rather, this author considers only methodologically adequate studies that have contemporaneous childhood (i.e., prior to puberty) measurements of eventual schizophrenic patients. Cross-sectional comparisons between high-risk offspring of schizophrenic and control parents will not be considered because of the uncertain relevance of such studies to the early characteristics of eventual schizophrenic patients (McNeil and Kaij,

1979). As a result, the emphasis is on retrospective studies using society's records and those few prospective high-risk studies in which subjects have entered the age of risk for schizophrenia.

Retrospective studies using contemporaneous records of preschizo-phrenics' childhood (prepubertal) social behavior that include blind ratings and control groups of some nature will be reviewed first. Studies based on retrospective recall by subjects or informants and those using only subjects who had attended child guidance clinics will not be considered because of their potential for bias. Interpretation of even these superior retrospective studies of contemporaneous records depends on several general methodological issues, with control group sampling being probably the most important. Specifically, potential index–control group differences in migratory status is an issue for those studies using both sibling and nonsibling control groups (e.g., Mednick and McNeil, 1968). Because the preschizophrenic subjects are identified based on adult records in the same geographic area as the childhood records, they are by definition nonmigratory. In contrast, generally nothing is known regarding the location in adulthood of the members of the control groups. Therefore, some proportion of the control group has probably migrated from their childhood home, and studies generally report that such out-migration is associated with higher intelligence and social class. To the extent that such factors are operating in these studies, the control group may be biased toward increased intelligence and better general adjustment due to the inclusion of subjects who will eventually migrate. In addition, in studies using nonsibling controls, the decision of whether or not to match controls with preschizophrenic subjects on parental social class may affect findings. Although not necessarily preferable (e.g., Meehl, 1971), such matching seems appropriate to the extent that the sample of preschizo-phrenic subjects may itself be unrepresentative of all schizophrenic patients. For example, several studies have identified preschizophrenic subjects from either Veterans Administration or state hospital records. To the extent that such sources are biased toward patients from lower social classes, an unmatched control group would be inappropriate.

Four such retrospective studies of childhood social behavior have been published (Warnken and Seiss, 1965; Woerner et al., 1972; Walker and Lewine, 1990; Watt, 1972, 1978). Warnken and Seiss (1965) studied teacher comments from the school records of 116 Caucasian male schizophrenic veterans and 116 control schoolmates matched on age, race, and sex (but not parental social class or eventual veteran status). They found that even during elementary school the preschizophrenic subjects were significantly more passive and had poorer achievement in school than controls. In contrast, Woerner et al. (1972) found only one significant difference on four global ratings of problem behaviors from elementary school records between 33 preschizophrenic subjects and either their well siblings or 45 prepersonality disorder subjects (who did not differ on parental social class from the preschizophrenic subjects). Similarly, in the most comprehensive such study to date, Watt (1972, 1978) found no significant differences on five behavior ratings based on elementary school records between 39 preschizophrenic subjects and control schoolmates matched on age, sex, race, and parental social class. In the most recent report of this topic, Walker and Lewine (1990) have made innovative use of the childhood home movies (prior to age 10 years) of preschizophrenic subjects, their siblings, and controls. In a preliminary report on four preschizophrenic subjects and their well siblings, untrained judges could predict at above chance levels the future status of the siblings in each family based on their home movies.

In addition to childhood social behavior, five retrospective studies of elementary school intelligence scores have also been reported (also see review by Aylward et al., 1984; Albee et al., 1964; Lane and Albee, 1965; Offord, 1974; Pollack et al., 1970; Schaffner et al., 1967; Watt and Lubensky, 1976). Lane, Albee, and colleagues compared intelligence test scores from the second and sixth grades of over 100 urban preschizophrenic subjects with both grade- and school- (but not parental social class) matched schoolmates (Albee et al., 1964) and their own siblings (Lane and Albee, 1965). In each case, the preschizophrenic subjects scored significantly below controls. Schaffner et al. (1967) reported similar differences between preschizophrenic subjects and their siblings for a middle- and upper-class suburban sample, although the preschizophrenic subjects did not differ from nonsibling grade- and school-matched controls.

Pollack et al. (1970) studied elementary school intelligence test scores for preschizophrenic subjects and their siblings and prepersonality disordered subjects from similar social class homes and their siblings. No significant differences in childhood intelligence existed between the two diagnosed groups. Importantly, both preschizophrenic and prepersonality disordered subjects scored significantly below their normal siblings, suggesting a lack of specificity to the association between low intelligence and schizophrenia.

Offord (1974) has reported results separately by gender and found that male preschizophrenic subjects showed significantly lower school intelligence scores than their siblings and age-, sex-, race-, and parental social class-matched controls, whereas female probands did not. The intelligence data are averages of test scores given in elementary and junior high school.

Watt and Lubensky (1976) also investigated gender differences but did not replicate Offord's results. Based on elementary school intelligence test scores, Watt and Lubensky found marginally significant differences between female preschizophrenic subjects and age-, sex-, race-, and parental social class-matched controls, but not between male preschizophrenic subjects and controls. In contrast to other findings, no significant difference on intelligence scores averaged across all school grades existed between preschizophrenic subjects and their siblings. Unfortunately, elementary school data were not reported separately for the comparisons of preschizophrenic subjects and their siblings.

Prospective high-risk studies are also sensitive to methodological issues that are similar to those faced by the retrospective studies. Most importantly, the preschizophrenic subjects in such studies differ from the majority of schizophrenic patients in that they have been exposed to the family disorganization that often accompanies parental psychopathology. To the extent that such family disruption affects offspring adjustment and achievement, the childhood functioning of these high-risk schizophrenic subjects will not be representative of all schizophrenic patients. Of course, there are also potential genetic differences as well between high-risk schizophrenic subjects and schizophrenic subjects in general. In addition, control group sampling may be problematic, in that control offspring of well parents, even if matched to high-risk families on parental social class, will not be exposed to parental psychopathology and its potentially nonspecific environmental effects on offspring childhood achievement and adjustment. Furthermore, because the high-risk results to date are based on subjects who are just entering the age of risk for schizophrenia, only subjects with an early age of onset can be identified thus far. To the extent that schizophrenic patients with an early age of onset show poorer adjustment than other schizophrenic patients, childhood abnormalities in schizophrenic subjects currently identified in high-risk studies may be especially elevated compared with other schizophrenic subjects.

To date, only one of the prospective high-risk studies has published results on the early childhood abnormalities of preschizophrenic subjects. Preliminary results have recently been reported from the NIMH Israeli High-Risk Study of 50 index offspring of schizophrenic parents and 50 control offspring of well parents (offspring matched on age, sex, and parental social class) comparing neurobehavioral and interpersonal characteristics at age 11 years with DSM-III diagnoses of schizophrenia and schizophrenia spectrum disorders at age 24 years (Hans and Marcus, 1987; Marcus *et al.*, 1987). Using a complex scoring scheme, Marcus *et al.* (1987) found that preschizophrenia spectrum index offspring more often scored above an apparently *post hoc* cutting score (8/9, 88%) than did nonschizophrenic index offspring (17/41, 41%) and nonschizophrenic control offspring (12/50, 24%) on items judged to be relevant to the diagnosis of attention deficit disorder at age 11 years. In addition, Hans and Marcus (1987) have reported that problems in interpersonal adjustment at age 11 years were more frequent in preschizophrenia spectrum index offspring (8/9, 88%) compared with nonschizophrenic index offspring (21/41, 51%) and nonschizophrenic control offspring (6/50, 12%). These two groups of characteristics, neurobehavioral and interpersonal adjustment at age 11 years, largely identified the same subjects as deviant. These results are still quite preliminary, as only nine high-risk subjects have been diagnosed within the schizophrenia spectrum and the average age of the offspring is still only 24 years old. Furthermore, additional details are needed to assess carefully the scaling and cut-off procedures used in the analyses.

What conclusions can be drawn from the findings reviewed above? The retrospective studies of childhood interpersonal behavior that compared preschizophrenic subjects with their siblings (Woerner et al., 1972), pre-personality disorder subjects (Woerner et al., 1972), or schoolmates matched on parental social class (Watt, 1978) were generally negative. The one exception was the early study by Warnken and Seiss (1965) of veteran patients. Because the control group in this study was not matched on parental social class with the preschizophrenic group, and the index group was drawn from Veterans Administration records, any differences may be spurious due to artifactual social class differences between the groups. In any case, although significant, the differences were not large and there was considerable overlap between the preschizophrenic and control groups. In addition, the pilot results from the home movies study by Walker and Lewine (1990) were positive, although preliminary. The interpersonal adjustment results from the NIMH Israeli High-Risk Project were also positive, although clearly preliminary and subject to the potential sampling problems described above. In summary then, currently little positive evidence indicates major deficits in social adjustment during childhood among schizophrenic patients.

The story is more complex for the case of deficits in intelligence during childhood. Although probably biased, one of two studies that employed schoolmate controls not matched on parental social class found significant childhood intellectual deficits for preschizophrenics (Albee et al., 1964; cf. Schaffner et al., 1967). Using a more appropriate design with schoolmate controls matched on parental social class, none of the three studies found significant deficits for the total preschizophrenic group (Pollack et al., 1970), although Offord (1974) found significant differences for males but not females, and Watt and Lubensky (1976) found the opposite pattern. As a more conservative test, three of the five studies that used sibling controls found overall preschizophrenic deficits (Lane and Albee, 1965; Pollack et al., 1970; Schaffner et al., 1967). However, Offord (1974) reported significant preschizophrenic/sibling differences for males but not females and Watt and Lubensky (1976) found no significant preschizophrenic/sibling differences. The latter two studies used composite intelligence scores that included both elementary and later test results. The one study that investigated the specificity of this potential association found that prepersonality disorder subjects also scored below their siblings on childhood intelligence tests (Pollack et al., 1970). Although mixed and perhaps affected by artifacts due to differences in migratory rates, these studies, especially those using sibling controls, suggest that preschizophrenic subjects may show mild deficits in tested intelligence during childhood. Even if present, it is clear, however, that such differences are generally small, with much overlap between preschizophrenic subjects and controls. Furthermore, the one available study suggests that this association is not specific to schizophrenia. This relative lack of sensitivity and specificity is consistent with the hypothesis that intelligence may be an independently determined characteristic that may affect the risk for schizophrenia (and other disorders) in a nonspecific fashion (Jones and Offord, 1975).

Overall, this review suggests little in the way of specific or frequent abnormalities during the early childhoods of schizophrenic patients-to-be. Although by no means the final word, the picture from these studies is largely of a childhood that is within the normal range for most or perhaps virtually all eventual schizophrenic patients. Of course other abnormalities may exist that were not assessed in these studies. Although having good ecological validity, elementary school teachers' comments and general intelligence tests certainly may not detect all possible abnormalities. The future results from the high-risk studies after the subjects are through the age of risk and studies such as those of Walker and Lewine (1990) will provide better tests of the hypothesis that schizophrenia-specific abnormalities will be largely absent during early childhood, but at the present time this is a reasonable conclusion.

INFERRED EARLY ABNORMALITIES AMONG PRESCHIZOPHRENIC PATIENTS

In addition to abnormalities that are actually observed during the early childhood of schizophrenic patients, investigations have also been made of abnormalities that are observed in adult patients but are inferred to have developed perinatally and to have persisted over time. These inferred abnormalities include such characteristics as minor physical abnormalities.

Minor physical abnormalities are slight morphological defects in the head, hands, and feet (Waldrop et al., 1968) that are presumed to develop during the first trimester of pregnancy and are assumed to remain unchanged after birth. Three studies of minor physical abnormalities in schizophrenia have been reported (Green *et al.*, 1989; Gualtieri *et al.*, 1982; Guy *et al.*, 1983). All of the studies found significantly increased rates of minor physical abnormalities in schizophrenic patients compared with normal control subjects (Green *et al.*, 1989; Gualtieri *et al.*, 1982) or published norms (Guy *et al.*, 1983). The major methodological issues with these studies concern the representativeness of the schizophrenic samples and potential biases due to nonblind ratings. All of the studies employed patient samples drawn from state hospitals, which may not be representative of schizophrenic patients in general and which may differ in important ways from the normal comparison groups used. In addition, all ratings were made with knowledge of group membership. In any case, not all schizophrenic patients demonstrated such abnormalities. Furthermore, minor physical abnormalities are quite nonspecific, as they have been found to be increased in autism, childhood schizophrenia, and attention deficit disorder. This lack of sensitivity and specificity is again perhaps most consistent with the hypothesis that minor physical abnormalities represent the sequelae of early environmental or genetic events that may contribute in a nonspecific fashion to risk for schizophrenia.

EARLY ENVIRONMENTAL INSULTS AMONG PRESCHIZOPHRENIC PATIENTS

Although not a necessary prediction from all early development models, many do in fact theorize that hypothesized early abnormalities are caused by perinatal environmental insults. In contrast, the late development models predict that perinatal insults may or may not be elevated among preschizophrenic patients depending on the ability of such experiences to increase in a nonspecific fashion the penetrance of the hypothesized late-occurring developmental gene defect. Two general classes of perinatal insults have been investigated: obstetrical complications and presumed viral infection during pregnancy. Although it is somewhat unclear whether obstetrical complications should best be considered as primarily environmental insults or perhaps as early manifestations of genetic abnormalities, in either case they would be predicted to be increased by early development models (e.g., Goodman, 1988, 1989; McNeil, 1988).

Because several excellent reviews of obstetrical complications among preschizophrenic patients have been published (e.g., Lewis *et al.*, 1989; McNeil, 1988; McNeil and Kaij, 1978), our survey will focus primarily on the pattern of overall findings. The same methodological issues discussed above regarding the retrospective studies of preschizophrenics' childhoods also hold for these retrospective studies of obstetrical complications in the histories of eventual schizophrenic patients. Sampling issues, such as matching on social class and mobility, remain important, as do the potential for bias in recall and the quality of contemporaneous records. The studies are briefly reviewed, organized by the nature of their control group.

Of the three retrospective studies comparing preschizophrenics with matched, nonpatient controls, two have reported significantly increased obstetrical complications among schizophrenic patients (Jacobsen and Kinney, 1980; McNeil and Kaij, 1978; McNeil, 1988; cf. Done et al., 1990). All of these studies used contemporaneous records of obstetrical complications. Although only appearing as a preliminary report to date, the one negative study by Done et al. (1990) was a large one that utilized data from a research survey of all births in the United Kingdom during 1 week in 1958, which was then crossed with a registry of all inpatient psychiatric admissions. No significant differences in obstetrical complications were found between 49 narrowly diagnosed schizophrenic patients and controls who did not appear in the psychiatric registry.

Three studies have reported results from comparisons of preschizophrenics with other psychiatric controls and two have found significant differences (Lewis and Murray, 1987; Schwartzkopf et al., 1989; cf. Woerner et al., 1971, 1973). Both positive studies used maternal reports of obstetrical complications and did not match groups on parental social class, whereas the negative study (Woerner et al., 1973) used birth records supplemented to some extent by maternal recall and groups that had similar parental social class. Two other studies have also investigated obstetrical complications in other diagnostic groups, but to date they have not reported statistical comparisons of these groups with schizophrenic patients (McNeil and Kaij, 1978; McNeil, 1988, Done et al., 1990).

Of six different samples comparing preschizophrenic patients with their siblings, four have revealed significantly increased perinatal abnormalities in eventual patients (DeLisi et al., 1987; Eagles et al., 1990; Lane and Albee, 1966; Woerner et al., 1973; cf. DeLisi et al., 1988; Pollack et al., 1966; Woerner et al., 1971). However, DeLisi et al. (1987, 1988) and Pollack et al. (1966) employed only maternal reports and Woerner et al. (1973) used them to supplement birth records. Based on the same sample, one study by Woerner et al. (1971) found no significant differences using records of birth weight and length, whereas a subsequent report by Woerner et al. (1973) showed differences in obstetrical complications when comparing schizophrenic patients with siblings who were screened to be normal. DeLisi et al. (1988) found significant differences between schizophrenic patients from families with at least two schizophrenic siblings compared with their well siblings; however, no such differences were observed in a sample of families with only one schizophrenic patient.

Only one high-risk study of offspring of schizophrenic and control parents has reported obstetrical complication information (Parnas *et al.*, 1982). Parnas *et al.* (1982) compared the retrospectively collected birth records of 12 schizophrenic, 25 borderline schizophrenic, and 39 well offspring of schizophrenic mothers. At the time of diagnosis, the offspring were only an average age of 24 years. Obstetrical data for the 90 high-risk offspring who received other nonschizophrenic diagnoses and for the offspring of the well control mothers were not reported. In this preliminary report, schizophrenic offspring demonstrated significantly increased obstetrical complications compared with only the borderline schizophrenic group. Neither the schizophrenic nor the borderline schizophrenic group differed significantly from the well offspring group. Given the young age of the group, this finding may primarily represent an association between obstetrical complications and age of onset in genetically high-risk offspring.

Several reviews of obstetrical complications in monozygotic (MZ) twin pairs discordant for schizophrenia are also available (Gottesman and Shields, 1972, 1976; McNeil and Kaij, 1978; Pollin and Stabenau, 1968; Shields and Gottesman, 1977; Torrey, 1977). Pollin and Stabenau (1968), based on both their own study at the NIMH of 15 discordant pairs and a review of 100 pairs from both published case studies and research investigations, reported that the schizophrenic twin in discordant pairs more frequently had the lower birthweight and suffered the greater obstetrical complications compared with the unaffected twin. In contrast, Gottesman and Shields (1972, 1976; Shields and Gottesman, 1977) reviewed only systematically ascertained twin series and found no association between birthweight and schizophrenia in discordant pairs (cf. Torrey, 1977). However, McNeil and Kaij (1978), reviewing these same systematic studies, found increased obstetrical complications in the schizophrenic twins. Although of great theoretical interest, these findings from discordant MZ twin pairs must be interpreted cautiously for several reasons. MZ twinning itself is an obstetrical complication and, thus, may not be representative of processes involved in singleton births. And, perhaps most importantly, all of these data relied on maternal recall to assign obstetrical complications to the appropriate member of an MZ twin pair, which is no simple task.

In summary, these findings from a range of study designs suggest a likely statistical excess of obstetrical complications in the births of eventual schizophrenic patients, although the methodological shortcomings of the studies preclude certainty at this point. Further study is clearly warranted. In any case, even the positive studies agree that only a minority of schizophrenic patients have experienced what might be conventionally considered as an obstetrical complication and that many other individuals have had obstetrical complications without schizophrenic sequelae. This relative lack of sensitivity and specificity would argue against considering obstetrical complications as a sufficient cause of schizophrenia, probably even for only a minority of cases. Furthermore, the apparent lack of association between risk for schizophrenia and social attributes that are highly correlated with rates of obstetrical complications, such as parental social class (e.g., Goldberg and Morrison, 1963) and birth in developed versus developing countries (Sartorius et al., 1986) must also suggest that obstetrical complications are probably not sufficient causal agents (DeLisi et al., 1987). Rather, these observations are more consistent with the hypothesis that obstetrical complications may play a nonspecific contributory role in the etiology of schizophrenia and, therefore, that any of their early brain sequelae do not represent a specific pathology for schizophrenia.

In addition to these studies of a broad range of obstetrical complications reviewed above, several investigations have also focused more specifically on the role of potential perinatal viral infections. These studies of potential perinatal infection have all been indirect to date; i.e., the risk for later schizophrenia has been compared between groups who differ in exposure to some more general event occurring near the time of birth that is hypothesized to be associated with perinatal viral infection. The two general events that have been most researched to date are birth during a time of viral epidemic in society at large or during the winter months. Findings from such investigations will be reviewed briefly. Studies of increased antibody titers in adult schizophrenic patients will not be considered here, because such studies do not assume perinatal infection.

Five studies have been published on the covariation between rates of schizophrenic births and the prevalence in the general population of infectious diseases (primarily influenzas) during the previous 9 months (Barr et al., 1990; Kendell and Kemp, 1989; Mednick et al., 1988, 1990a; Torrey et al., 1988; Watson et al., 1984). Although the methodological controversies surrounding these studies are both substantial and complex (cf. Bowler and Torrey, 1990; Kendell and Kemp, 1990; Mednick et al., 1990b), most have reported some evidence for a significant association (cf. Kendell and Kemp, 1989). When present, however, the strength of the association is quite weak, although such results may be underestimates because only some of the mothers in the high influenza groups presumably contracted the virus.

A larger number of studies have investigated the similar and potentially related question of an excess of winter births in schizophrenia (see review by Bradbury and Miller, 1985). Although also fraught with complex methodological controversy (e.g., M.S. Lewis, 1989), schizophrenic patients apparently have a slight, although significant, excess of winter births. Such findings are often interpreted in terms of an increased *in utero* exposure to infectious diseases during the winter months.

In summary, although by no means unanimous or without methodological weaknesses, to date these studies of obstetrical complications, risk of viral exposure, and birth during the winter months provide some evidence of an association between such presumed perinatal environmental insults and the occurrence of later schizophrenia. In all cases however, even the positive findings suggest that such experiences are only slightly increased among eventual schizophrenic patients and that most individuals who have these experiences do not develop schizophrenia. Furthermore, the existence of positive findings for several such different risk factors suggests a potential fungibility among them. How are such findings to be interpreted? Mednick *et al.* (1989), Murray *et al.* (1988a), and others have hypothesized that the timing of an insult during a critical phase of *in utero* development is particularly important, thus implying interchangeability among experiences that might occur at the same developmental period and a potential increased specificity to schizophrenia, because only a minority of all insults would occur at the crucial stage. Alternatively, such potential early environmental insults can be viewed as nonspecific stressors that may increase the risk for schizophrenia in genetically susceptible individuals to the extent that they produce relevant brain sequelae that persist until the postpubertal onset of schizophrenia (DeLisi *et al.*, 1987).

AN ALTERNATIVE HYPOTHESIS:
A LATE DEVELOPMENTAL GENETIC MODEL

In summary, the evidence in favor of a major role for early-developing abnormalities in schizophrenia is far from persuasive. Although constrained by a limited number of studies and various methodological weaknesses, currently few data suggest the presence of schizophrenia-specific abnormalities during early childhood in eventual schizophrenic patients. Furthermore, although current findings are consistent with an increased rate of a range of perinatal environmental insults in preschizophrenic patients, such events appear to be relatively infrequent, interchangeable, and associated with many conditions other than schizophrenia. If a major role for such early-appearing abnormalities currently seems implausible, what alternative hypotheses are more attractive? Based on the suggestions by Feinberg (1982–1983, 1990), Gottesman and Shields (1972), and others, we seek to increase the attention paid to the hypothesis outlined above that schizophrenia-specific abnormalities develop postpubertally due to defects in genes that control normal brain development during this period. It is further hypothesized that early environmental insults that have enduring brain sequelae may nonspecifically both influence the risk for and modify the manifestation of clinical schizophrenia in adulthood among those susceptible individuals with abnormal "postpubertal development" genes.

This hypothesis is grounded in the emerging fields concerned with the genetics of brain and behavioral development (e.g., Gottesman, 1974; Plomin, 1986; Hahn et al., 1990). The central tenet of these fields and their parent discipline of developmental genetics is that genetic influences are not constant through time and development. Although the genetic information encoded in the DNA sequence is largely identical in all cells of the body and is constant over time both within cells and across cell divisions, the genes that are actually expressed (i.e., "turned on") from this total set vary tremendously among different cells and also over time. This variation in gene expression is a basic process underlying cell differentiation and organism development. More specifically, although studies of genetic effects on late brain development are only just beginning (e.g., Benno, 1990; Chaudhari and Hahn, 1983; Wimer, 1990), an example of such phenomena is the gene that has recently been identified that controls programmed neuronal cell death late in development in the well-studied nematode *Caenorhabditis elegans* (Chalfie and Wolinsky, 1990). More examples of genetic control of late brain development are expected.

Although long acknowledged and indeed one of the central questions of modern biology, this recognition of changes in gene expression over time has been largely ignored in psychology and psychiatry. Instead, for reasons that are not readily apparent, the general belief seems to be that genetic influences are congenital, or present from birth. This misconception, along with an historical predilection for the importance for early experience and a lack of obvious specific stressors during young adulthood may explain some of the current popularity of early development theories for schizophrenia. Recognition of the possibility that some genes may only be expressed late in development reduces the necessity of postulating early-occurring neurodevelopmental abnormalities in schizophrenia.

Given that a late development model with abnormalities in genes controlling postpubertal brain development is possible in principle, why might it be preferable to early development models of schizophrenia? First, it is more parsimonious. Early development models must postulate a later triggering event to explain the onset of schizophrenia in young adulthood. Some recent early development models (Randall, 1980; Weinberger, 1987) have further hypothesized that normal developmental processes during and following puberty serve to make manifest the perinatal brain abnormalities that have been largely "silent" since birth. Rather than postulating an early abnormality, whose effects must be "unmasked" by later development, it is more parsimonious, in the absence of evidence to the contrary, to hypothesize only an abnormality in the later developmental processes themselves.

A model of schizophrenia that postulates abnormalities in genes controlling brain development during and following puberty is also plausible because this is a period of great change in normal individuals. Given such dramatic changes in normal development during this period, it is reasonable to presume that the likelihood of errors in the genetic control of these changes is also at a high point. Although still an emerging area, brain changes of several sorts have been observed during the postpubertal period. As originally pointed out by Feinberg (1982–1983, 1990), synaptic density appears to decline quite markedly during adolescence (e.g., Huttenlocher, 1979). In addition to this "synaptic pruning," increased rates of myelination have also been observed during adolescence (e.g., Benes, 1989; Goldman-Rakic et al., 1983). In short, marked changes in several brain characteristics have been observed during normal adolescent development abnormalities, which may lead to clinical schizophrenia.

A further advantage of a model of abnormalities in late development is that it does not necessarily imply progressive brain degeneration and behavioral deterioration after the clinical onset of schizophrenia. Although a point of continuing controversy, most schizophrenic patients do not seem to show a dramatic downhill course of functioning, although a minority do follow such a path (e.g., Bleuler, 1978). Similarly, although based on few studies, most patients apparently do not show substantial increases in structural brain abnormalities on CT scans after onset (e.g., Weinberger, 1984; cf. Woods and Wolf, 1983). Although this apparent lack of degeneration has been adduced as evidence in favor of early development hypotheses (e.g., Weinberger, 1987), late development models likewise do not necessarily imply a continuing pathological process.

These points, as well as the relative lack of evidence for specific early abnormalities in eventual patients and the apparent infrequent and nonspecific nature of early environmental insults reviewed above, suggest that a late developmental genetic model of schizophrenia should be given serious consideration and that early development models should not be accepted without question.

CONCLUSIONS

In summary, this chapter has critically examined the concepts and evidence concerning those early development models that have become increasingly influential in research and theory about schizophrenia. Relatively little evidence of abnormalities from retrospective and prospective studies of eventual schizophrenic patients was found, although the coming of age of the longitudinal high-risk studies and the development of innovative retrospective strategies (e.g., Walker and Lewine, 1990) may alter this conclusion. Of course, the present absence of evidence is not necessarily evidence of absence. Furthermore, findings of presumed early environmental insults, such as obstetrical complications, perinatal viral infection, and winter birth, although generally positive, appeared to be infrequent and nonspecific. Whether such early environmental insults are best considered as being sufficient causes for a small subgroup of patients or as nonspecific contributory causes for genetically susceptible individuals is difficult to resolve given the current evidence. In the face of such ambiguous evidence, a late developmental genetic model was highlighted that was initially described in general by Gottesman and Shields (1972) and others and in detail by Feinberg (1982–1983, 1990). Acknowledging that gene expression is not constant over time, this model hypothesizes that defects in genes controlling postpubertal brain development play a specific role in schizophrenia, whereas early environmental insults serve only as potential nonspecific contributing and modifying influences. The empirical and theoretical advantages of this alternative to the early development models were described. Furthermore, it is heuristically valuable and calls attention to new areas that have been largely unexplored to date. Among the most important issues for investigation from this view, are the detailed description of brain and psychological development following puberty in normal individuals, the longitudinal study of early adolescent offspring (rather than the young children) of schizophrenic parents, and the use of brain development genes as candidate markers in linkage and genetic association studies.

Although currently too few data are available to determine whether the early or the late development model is more valid (or whether both or neither are), it is also clearly too early to focus exclusively on only one possibility. It is hoped that this critical discussion will contribute to broadening constructively the current debate concerning the development of liability to schizophrenia.

ACKNOWLEDGMENT

Preparation of this chapter was supported in part by NIMH grant MH43666 to the author.

REFERENCES

Albee, G., Lane, E., and Reuter, J. (1964). Childhood intelligence of future schizophrenics and neighborhood peers. *Journal of Psychology, 58*, 141–144.

294   Michael F. Pogue-Geile

Asarnow, J. R. (1988). Children at risk for schizophrenia: Converging lines of evidence. *Schizophrenia Bulletin, 14,* 613–631.

Aylward, E., Walker, E., and Bettes, B. (1984). Intelligence in schizophrenia: Meta-analysis of the research. *Schizophrenia Bulletin, 10,* 430–459.

Barr, C. E., Mednick, S. A., and Munk-Jorgensen, P. (1990). Exposure to influenza epidemics during gestation and adult schizophrenia. *Archives of General Psychiatry, 47,* 819–874.

Benes, F. M. (1989). Myelination of cortical-hippocampal relays during late adolescence. *Schizophrenia Bulletin, 15,* 585–593.

Benno, R. H. (1990). Development of the nervous system: Genetics, epigenetics, and phylogenetics. In M. E. Hahn, J. K. Hewitt, N. D. Henderson, and R. H. Benno (Eds.), *Developmental behavior genetics: Neural, biometrical, and evolutionary approaches* (pp. 113–143). New York: Oxford.

Bleuler, M. (1978). *The schizophrenic disorders: Long-term patient and family studies.* (Translated by S. Clemens). New Haven, CT: Yale University Press. [Original work published 1972.]

Bowler, A. E., and Torrey, E. F. (1990). Influenza and schizophrenia: Helsinki vs. Edinburgh. *Archives of General Psychiatry, 47,* 876–877.

Bradbury, T. N., and Miller, G. A. (1985). Season of birth in schizophrenia: Evidence, methodology, and etiology. *Psychological Bulletin, 98,* 569–594.

Chalfie, M., and Wolinsky, E. (1990). The identification and suppression of inherited neurodegeneration in C. elegans. *Nature, 345,* 410–416.

Chaudhari, N., and Hahn, W. E. (1983). Genetic expression in the developing brain. *Science, 220,* 924–928.

DeLisi, L. E., Dauphinais, D., Goldin, L. R., and Gershon, E. S. (1988). Perinatal risk factors in familial schizophrenia. In D. L. Dunner, E. S. Gershon, and J. E. Barrett (Eds.), *Relatives at risk for mental disorder* (pp. 267–277). New York: Raven Press.

DeLisi, L. E., Goldin, L. R., Maxwell, E., Kazuba, D. M., and Gershon, E. S. (1987). Clinical features of illness in siblings with schizophrenia or schizoaffective disorder. *Archives of General Psychiatry, 44,* 891–896.

Done, J., Crow, T. J., Frith, C. D., and Johnstone, E. C. (1990). Pregnancy and birth complications as causes of psychiatric illness in adult life: A study utilizing the perinatal mortality survey (1958). *Schizophrenia Research, 3,* 91.

Eagles, J. M., Gibson, I., Bremner, M. H., Clunie, F., Ebmeier, K. P., and Smith, N. C. (1990). Obstetric complications in DSM-III schizophrenics and their siblings. *Lancet, 335,* 1139–1141.

Feinberg, I. (1982). Schizophrenia and late maturational brain changes in man. *Psychopharmacology Bulletin, 18,* 29–31.

Feinberg, I. (1982–1983). Schizophrenia: Caused by a fault in programmed synaptic elimination during adolescence? *Journal of Psychiatric Research, 17,* 319–339.

Feinberg, I. (1990). Cortical pruning and the development of schizophrenia. *Schizophrenia Bulletin, 16,* 567–568.

Fish, B. (1957). The detection of schizophrenia in infancy. *Journal of Nervous and Mental Disease, 125,* 1–24.

Garmezy, N., and Streitman, S. (1974). Children at risk: The search for the antecedents of schizophrenia. Part I. Conceptual models and research methods. *Schizophrenia Bulletin, 8,* 19–90.

Goldberg, E. M., and Morrison, S. L. (1963). Schizophrenia and social class. *British Journal of Psychiatry, 109,* 785–802.

Goldman-Rakic, P. S., Isseroff, A., Schwartz, M. L., and Bugbee, N. M. (1983). The neurobiology of cognitive development. In P. Mussen (Ed.), *Handbook of child psychology, biology, and infancy development* (pp. 282–344). New York: Wiley.

Goodman, R. (1988). Are complications of pregnancy and birth causes of schizophrenia? *Developmental Medicine and Child Neurology, 30,* 391–406.

Goodman, R. (1989). Obstetric complications and schizophrenia. *British Journal of Psychiatry, 153,* 850.

Gottesman, I. I. (1974). Developmental genetics and ontogenetic psychology: Overdue detente and propositions from a matchmaker. In A. D. Pick (Ed.), *Minnesota symposia on child psychology* (pp. 55–80). Minneapolis: University of Minnesota Press.

Gottesman, I. I., and Shields, J. (1976). A critical review of recent adoption, twin, and family studies of schizophrenia: Behavioral genetic perspectives. *Schizophrenia Bulletin, 2,* 360–398.

Gottesman, I. I., and Shields, J. (1972). *Schizophrenia and genetics: A twin study vantage point.* New York: Academic Press.

Gottesman, I. I., and Shields, J. (1982). *Schizophrenia: the epigenetic puzzle.* New York: Cambridge University Press.

Green, M. F., Satz, P., Gaier, D. J., Ganzell, S., and Kharabi, F. (1989). Minor physical abnormalities in schizophrenia. *Schizophrenia Bulletin, 15,* 91–99.

Gualtieri, C. T., Adams, A., Shen, C. D., and Loiselle, D. (1982). Minor physical abnormalities in alcoholic and schizophrenic adults and hyperactive and autistic children. *American Journal of Psychiatry, 139,* 640–643.

Guy, J. D., Majorski, L. V., Wallace, C. J., and Guy, M. P. (1983). The incidence of minor physical abnormalities in adult male schizophrenics. *Schizophrenia Bulletin, 9,* 571–582.

Hahn, M. E., Hewitt, J. K., Henderson, N. D., and Benno, R. H. (Eds.). (1990). *Developmental behavior genetics: Neural, biometrical, and evolutionary approaches.* New York: Oxford University.

Hans, S. L., and Marcus, J. (1987). A process model for the development of schizophrenia. *Psychiatry: Interpersonal and Biological Processes, 50,* 361–370.

Hoffman, R. E., and Dobscha, S. K. (1989). Cortical pruning and the development of schizophrenia: A computer model. *Schizophrenia Bulletin, 15,* 477–490.

Huttenlocher, P. R. (1979). Synaptic density in human frontal cortex—Developmental changes and effects of aging. *Brain Research, 163,* 195–205.

Jacobsen, B., and Kinney, D. K. (1980). Perinatal complications in adopted and non-adopted schizophrenics and their controls: Preliminary results. *Acta Psychiatrica Scandinavica, Supplementum, 285,* 62, 337–346.

Jones, M. B., and Offord, D. R. (1975). Independent transmission of IQ and schizophrenia. *British Journal of Psychiatry, 126,* 185–190.

Kendell, R. E., and Kemp, I. W. (1990). Influenza and schizophrenia: Helsinki vs. Edinburgh. *Archives of General Psychiatry, 47,* 877–878.

Kendell, R. E., and Kemp, I. W. (1989). Maternal influenza in the etiology of schizophrenia. *Archives of General Psychiatry, 46,* 878–882.

Lane, E. A., and Albee, G. W. (1965). Childhood intellectual differences between schizophrenic adults and their siblings. *American Journal of Orthopsychiatry, 35,* 747–753.

Lane, E. A., and Albee, G. W. (1966). Comparative birth weights of schizophrenics and their siblings. *Journal of Psychology, 64,* 227–231.

Lewis, M. S. (1989). Age incidence and schizophrenia: Part I. The season of birth controversy. *Schizophrenia Bulletin, 15,* 59–73.

Lewis, S. W. (1989). Congenital risk factors for schizophrenia. *Psychological Medicine, 19,* 5–13.

Lewis, S. W., and Murray, R. M. (1987). Obstetric complications, neurodevelopmental deviance, and risk of schizophrenia. *Journal of Psychiatric Research, 21,* 413–421.

Lewis, S. W., Owen, M. J., and Murray, R. M. (1989). Obstetric complications and schizophrenia: Methodology and mechanisms. In S. C. Schulz and C. A. Tamminga (Eds.), *Schizophrenia: Scientific progress* (pp. 56–68). New York: Oxford University.

Lyon, M., Barr, C. E., Cannon, T. D., Mednick, S. A., and Shore, D. (1989). Fetal neurodevelopment and schizophrenia. *Schizophrenia Bulletin, 15,* 149–160.

Marcus, J., Hans, S. L., Nagler, S., Auerback, J. G., Mirsky, A. F., and Aubrey, A. (1987). Review of NIMH–Israeli Kibbutz-City Study and the Jerusalem Infant Development Study. *Schizophrenia Bulletin, 13,* 425–438.

McNeil, T. F. (1988). Obstetric factors and perinatal injuries. In M. T. Tsuang and J. C. Simpson (Eds.), *Handbook of schizophrenia. Vol. 3: Nosology, epidemiology, and genetics* (pp. 319–344). New York: Elsevier.

McNeil, T. F., and Kaij, L. (1979). Etiological relevance of comparisons of high-risk and low-risk groups. *Acta Psychiatrica Scandinavica, 59,* 545–560.

McNeil, T. F., and Kaij, L. (1978). Obstetric factors in the development of schizophrenia: Complications in births of pre-schizophrenics and reproduction by schizophrenic parents. In L. C. Wynne, R. L. Cromwell, and S. Matthysse (Eds.), *The nature of schizophrenia: New approaches to research and treatment* (pp. 401–429). New York: Wiley.

Mednick, S. A., Machon, R. A., and Huttunen, M. O. (1989). Disturbances of fetal neural development and adult schizophrenia. In S. C. Schulz and C. A. Tamminga (Eds.), *Schizophrenia: Scientific progress* (pp. 69–77). New York: Oxford University.

Mednick, S. A., Machon, R. A., and Huttunen, M. O. (1990a). An update on the Helsinki influenza project. *Archives of General Psychiatry, 47,* 292.

Mednick, S. A., Machon, R. A., Huttunen, M. O., and Barr, C. E. (1990b). Influenza and schizophrenia: Helsinki vs. Edinburgh. *Archives of General Psychiatry, 47,* 875–876.

Mednick, S. A., Machon, R. A., Huttunen, M. O., and Bonett, D. (1988). Adult schizophrenia following prenatal exposure to an influenza epidemic. *Archives of General Psychiatry, 45,* 189–192.

Mednick, S. A., and McNeil, T. F. (1968). Current methodology in research on the etiology of schizophrenia. *Psychological Bulletin, 70,* 681–693.

Meehl, P. E. (1971). High school yearbooks: A reply to Schwartz. *Journal of Abnormal Psychology, 77,* 143–148.

Meehl, P. E. (1989). Schizotaxia revisited. *Archives of General Psychiatry, 46,* 935–944.

Meehl, P. E. (1962). Schizotaxia, schizotypy, schizophrenia. *American Psychologist, 17,* 827–838.

Meehl, P. E. (1990). Toward an integrated theory of schizotaxia, schizotypy, and schizophrenia. *Journal of Personality Disorders, 4,* 1–99.

Murray, R. M., and Lewis, S. W. (1987). Is schizophrenia a neurodevelopmental disorder? *British Medical Journal, 295,* 681–682.

Murray, R. M., Lewis, S. W., Owen, M. J., and Foerster, A. (1988a). The neurodevelopmental origins of dementia praecox. In P. Bebbington and P. McGuffin (Eds), *Schizophrenia: The major issues* (pp. 90–106). Oxford: Heinemann Medical Books.

Murray, R. M., Lewis, S. W., and Reveley, A. M. (1985). Towards an etiological classification of schizophrenia. *Lancet, i,* 1023–1026.

Murray, R. M., Reveley, A. M., and Lewis, S. W. (1988b). Family history, obstetric complications, and cerebral abnormality in schizophrenia. In M. Tsuang and J. C. Simpson (Eds.), *Handbook of schizophrenia. Vol. 3: Nosology, epidemiology, and genetics* (pp. 563–577). New York: Elsevier.

Nuechterlein, K. H. (1986). Childhood precursors of adult schizophrenia. *Journal of Child Psychology and Psychiatry, 27,* 133–144.

Offord, D. R. (1974). School performance of adult schizophrenics, their siblings, and agemates. *British Journal of Psychiatry, 125,* 12–19.

Offord, D. R., and Cross, L. A. (1969). Behavioral antecedents of adult schizophrenia. *Archives of General Psychiatry, 21,* 267–283.

Parnas, J., Schulsinger, F., Teasdale, T. W., Schulsinger, H., Feldman, P. M., and Mednick, S. A. (1982). Perinatal complications and clinical outcome within the schizophrenic spectrum. *British Journal of Psychiatry, 140*, 416–420.

Plomin, R. (1986). *Development, genetics, and psychology*. Hillsdale, NJ: Lawrence Erlbaum.

Pollack, M., Woerner, M. G., Goodman, W., and Greenberg, I. M. (1966). Childhood development patterns of hospitalized adult schizophrenic and nonschizophrenic patients and their siblings. *American Journal of Orthopsychiatry, 36*, 510–517.

Pollack, M., Woerner, M. G., and Klein, D. F. (1970). A comparison of childhood characteristics of schizophrenics, personality disorders, and their siblings. In M. Roff and D. Ricks (Eds.), *Life history research in psychopathology* (pp. 208–225). Minneapolis: University of Minnesota Press.

Pollin, W., and Stabenau, J. R. (1968). Biological, psychological, and historical differences in a series of monozygotic twins discordant for schizophrenia. In D. Rosenthal and S. S. Kety (Eds.), *The transmission of schizophrenia* (pp. 317–332). New York: Pergamon.

Randall, P. L. (1980). A neuroanatomical theory on the aetiology of schizophrenia. *Medical Hypotheses, 6*, 645–658.

Rosenthal, D. (1963). *The Genain quadruplets*, New York: Basic Books.

Sartorius, N., Jablensky, A., Kortey, A., Ernberg, G., Anker, M., Cooper, J. E., and Day, R. (1986). Early manifestations and first-contact incidence of schizophrenia in different cultures. *Psychological Medicine, 16*, 909–928.

Saugstad, L. F. (1989a). Age at puberty and mental illness: Towards a neurodevelopmental etiology of Kraepelin's endogenous psychoses. *British Journal of Psychiatry, 155*, 536–544.

Saugstad, L. F. (1989b). Social class, marriage, and fertility in schizophrenia. *Schizophrenia Bulletin, 15*, 9–43.

Schaffner, A., Lane, E. A., and Albee, G. W. (1967). Intellectual differences between suburban preschizophrenic children and their siblings. *Journal of Consulting and Clinical Psychology, 31*, 326–327.

Schizophrenia Bulletin (1987). Special issue on high risk studies. *Schizophrenia Bulletin, 13*, 369–526.

Schwartzkopf, S. B., Nasrallah, H. A., Olson, S. C., Coffman, J. A., and McLaughlin, J. A. (1989). Perinatal complications and genetic loading in schizophrenia: Preliminary findings. *Psychiatry Research, 27*, 233–239.

Shields, J., and Gottesman, I. I. (1977). Obstetric complications and twin studies of schizophrenia: Clarifications and confirmations. *Schizophrenia Bulletin, 3*, 351–354.

Torrey, E. F. (1977). Birthweights, perinatal insults, and HLA types: Return to the "original din". *Schizophrenia Bulletin, 3*, 347–351.

Torrey, E. F., Rawlings, R., and Waldman, I. N. (1988). Schizophrenic births and viral diseases in two states. *Schizophrenia Research, 1*, 73–77.

Waldrop, M. F., Pedersen, F. A., and Bell, R. Q. (1968). Minor physical abnormalities and behavior in preschool children. *Child Development, 39*, 391–400.

Walker, E., and Emory, E. (1983). Infants at risk for psychopathology: Offspring of schizophrenic parents. *Child Development, 54*, 1269–1285.

Walker, E., and Lewine, R. J. (1990). Prediction of adult-onset schizophrenia from childhood home movies of the patient. *American Journal of Psychiatry, 147*, 1052–1056.

Warnken, R. E., and Seiss, T. F. (1965). The use of the cumulative record in the prediction of behavior. *Personnel and Guidance Journal, 31*, 231–237.

Watson, C. G., Kucala, T., Tilleskjor, C., and Jacobs, L. (1984). Schizophrenic birth seasonality in relation to the incidence of infectious diseases and temperature extremes. *Archives of General Psychiatry, 41*, 85–90.

Watt, N., Anthony, E. J., Wynne, L., and Rolf, J. (1984). *Children at risk for schizophrenia: A longitudinal perspective*. New York: Cambridge University Press.

Watt, N. F. (1972). Longitudinal changes in the social behavior of children hospitalized for schizophrenia as adults. *Journal of Nervous and Mental Disease, 155,* 42–54.

Watt, N. F. (1978). Patterns of childhood social development in adult schizophrenics. *Archives of General Psychiatry, 35,* 160–165.

Watt, N. F., and Lubensky, A. W. (1976). Childhood roots of schizophrenia. *Journal Consulting and Clinical Psychology, 44,* 363–375.

Weinberger, D. R. (1984). Computed tomography (CT) findings in schizophrenia: Speculation on the meaning of it all. *Journal of Psychiatric Research, 18,* 477–490.

Weinberger, D. R. (1987). Implications of normal brain development for the pathogenesis of schizophrenia. *Archives of General Psychiatry, 44,* 660–664.

Weinberger, D. R. (1986). The pathogenesis of schizophrenia: A neurodevelopmental theory. In H. A. Nasrallah and D. R. Weinberger (Eds.), *Handbook of schizophrenia. Vol. 1: The neurology of schizophrenia* (pp. 397–406). New York: Elsevier.

Wimer, C. (1990). Genetic studies of brain development. In M. E. Hahn, J. K. Hewitt, N. D. Henderson, and R. H. Benno (Eds.), *Developmental behavior genetics: Neural, biometrical, and evolutionary approaches* (pp. 85–99). New York: Oxford University Press.

Woerner, M. G., Pollack, M., and Klein, D. (1971). Birthweight and length in schizophrenics, personality disorders, and their siblings. *British Journal of Psychiatry, 118,* 461–464.

Woerner, M. G., Pollack, M., and Klein, D. F. (1973). Pregnancy and birth complications in psychiatric patients: A comparison of schizophrenic and personality disorder patients with their siblings. *Acta Psychiatrica Scandinavica, 49,* 712–721.

Woerner, M. G., Pollack, M., Rogalski, C., Pollack Y., and Klein, D. F. (1972). A comparison of the school records of personality disorders, schizophrenics, and their sibs. In M. Roff, L. Robins, and M. Pollack (Eds.), *Life history research in psychopathology* (Vol. 2) (pp. 47–65). Minneapolis: University of Minnesota Press.

Woods, B. T., and Wolf, J. (1983). A reconsideration of the relation of ventricular enlargement to duration of illness in schizophrenia. *American Journal of Psychiatry, 140,* 1564–1570.

Zubin, J., and Spring, B. (1977). Vulnerability—A new view of schizophrenia. *Journal of Abnormal Psychology, 86,* 103–126.

Developmental Trajectories in Schizophrenia: Elucidating the Divergent Pathways

Elaine F. Walker
Dana M. Davis
Lisa A. Gottlieb
Jay A. Weinstein

Both divergent and convergent findings are apparent in the literature on developmental aspects of schizophrenia. In the past, many viewed the occurrence of divergent findings as problematic. Inconsistent results across studies were attributed to factors such as measurement error and method artifact; the focus was on commonalities, to the virtual exclusion of variability among patients. However, there is now increasing support among investigators for the assumption of etiologic heterogeneity in schizophrenia (Dalen and Hays, 1990). The field has witnessed a gradual trend in the direction of viewing individual differences among patients as informative, rather than representing the limitations of our methods.

The premise of this chapter is that there are multiple pathways leading to the clinical outcome labeled "schizophrenia," as well as multiple courses of the illness. These variations among patients in life-course trajectories are determined by the origins of their vulnerability and a host of moderat-

299

Copyright © 1991 by Academic Press, Inc.
All rights of reproduction in any form reserved.

ing influences. We will expand on these assumptions and discuss empirical data that support them. Another premise of this chapter is that a developmental approach to research on schizophrenia not only holds the greatest promise for elucidating the diverse trajectories leading to the disorder, but is also critical for generating plausible neurodevelopmental models of etiology. We will describe a new method—the "archival observational method"—for examining developmental precursors of clinical conditions. We will present some preliminary findings that suggest that this approach offers a unique opportunity for documenting behavioral manifestations of vulnerability to schizophrenia.

SOURCES OF VARIABILITY AMONG PATIENTS

Variability among schizophrenic patients in the phenomenology and course of their illness can be conceptualized as emanating from three sources. *First,* there is potential variability in the origins of constitutional vulnerability (Mirsky and Duncan, 1986). Some individuals may inherit the diathesis, whereas others acquire it. Furthermore, among those who inherit vulnerability, differences may exist in the genotype (Garner *et al.*, 1989). Moderating factors are a *second* source of variability. These include biological and psychosocial stressors that impinge on the vulnerable individual. The above two sources will be the chief etiologic contributors to individual differences among patients in the phenomenology and longitudinal course of their illness (i.e., between-subject variability). The *third* source of variability, developmental level, will determine changes within patients across the life span, as well as contributing to individual differences.

Heterogeneity in the Origins of Vulnerability

The findings from adoption and twin studies leave no doubt that genetic factors play an etiologic role in at least some cases of schizophrenia (Gottesman and Shields, 1982). However, at the same time, the modest concordance rates shown by monozygotic (MZ) twins demonstrate that other, nonhereditary, etiologic factors are also relevant. The results of a meta-analysis of twin studies of psychopathology indicate that the best estimate of MZ pairwise concordance for schizophrenia is between 25 and 30% (Walker *et al.*, 1991). Thus, as many as 75% of MZ pairs include only one schizophrenic member. A central question raised by the occurrence of discordant MZ twin pairs is whether or not nongenetic forms of schizophrenia exist. More generally, should our search for the determinants of heterogeneity extend to the very origins of constitutional vulnerability?

We will pay special attention to this question here because it has significant implications for research methodology and etiologic theory-building.

Before turning to a more detailed discussion of discordant MZ twins, it is important to clarify our conceptual framework and the distinctions we make among various manifest levels of pathology. The genotype for schizophrenia is presumably associated with a structural and/or biochemical abnormality of the brain. These phenotypic manifestations, at the biological level, have been referred to by Fuller and Thompson (1978) as *morphenes* (structural phenotypes) and *chemophenes* (chemical phenotypes). More generally, these authors use the term *somatophene* to refer to any biological phenotype. In the case of schizophrenia, then, the somatophene involves an organic abnormality that is associated with the behavioral phenotype labeled schizophrenia. [Following Fuller and Thompson (1978), we will refer to the behavioral phenotype as a *psychophene*.]

With respect to all genetically determined biological traits (i.e., somatophenes), we presume MZ twin-pair members to be identical. One explanation for discordance, then, is that the genotype for schizophrenia is not completely penetrant and that the level of exposure to environmental "triggers" differed for the two members of the pair. It would thus be argued that both possess the genotype and somatophene for schizophrenia, but only one was exposed to stress of sufficient magnitude to produce the schizophrenic psychophene. The nonaffected twin, therefore, possesses an unexpressed genotype. This interpretation invokes the central tenet of the diathesis–stress model of schizophrenia.

However, an alternative explanation for discordant MZ twin pairs is that neither possesses the genotype for schizophrenia, but, instead, the affected twin acquired the diathesis. The term *phenocopy* is used to refer to individuals whose manifest characteristics have been altered by the environment so that they imitate the phenotype usually associated with a particular genotype. In this case, the acquired biological abnormality would be, functionally, identical to that produced by a genotype. Or, to coin new terms, the affected twin would represent a "somatophenocopy" and "psychophenocopy."

We should note that it is also possible that the affected twin possesses a genetic liability, which is the result of a mutation not experienced by the healthy twin. In other words, the MZ twin-pair members may not be genetically identical. It is known that some MZ twin pairs are heterokaryotypic, and this is attributed to chromosomal errors in the splitting process (Porreco, 1990). If it is the case that the affected twin is expressing a mutant genotype, then the illness would *not* represent a phenocopy. Although the possibility of nonshared mutations must be acknowledged, little is known about the rate of occurrence of such mutations in MZ twin pairs (MacGillivray *et al.*, 1975; Porreco, 1990). Consequently, the present discussion will focus on phenocopies as a likely contributor to MZ discordance for schizophrenia.

The notion of schizophrenic phenocopies has been entertained by other researchers in the field. Mirsky and Duncan (1986) propose that "schizophrenic brain abnormalities" can arise from genetic (heredity or mutation) or environmental (obstetrical complications) origins. Meehl (1990) argues for a dominant gene model of schizophrenia (the "schizogene") but also assumes that certain polygenic combinations can constitute "genophenocopies," which produce a manifest syndrome that is indistinguishable from the form of schizophrenia produced by the schizogene.

It should be mentioned that, for purposes of the present discussion, we are assuming that there is a final common biological pathway in schizophrenia. In other words, that impairment in a *particular* central nervous system (CNS) structure or system is responsible for the syndrome. Although the simplifying assumption of a common organic feature or pathway may be correct, we also acknowledge the possibility that there may be more than one somatophene, and by implication more than one somotophenocopy, involved in schizophrenia.

Obstetrical Complications and Brain Abnormalities

Obstetrical complications are one obvious source of somatophenocopies. Some of the chapters in this volume offer persuasive evidence for the role of pre- and perinatal complications as contributors to vulnerability. Postnatal viral infections have also been cited as a contributory factor. Presumably, these biological insults compromise CNS development. But the primary question concerns the sufficiency of such biological stressors in producing constitutional vulnerability. In other words, are these factors sufficient for producing schizophrenia in the absence of an inherited vulnerability, or do biological stressors only serve to interact with genetic predisposition in contributing to schizophrenic outcomes? The question here may best be restated as follows: Can the genetically determined somatophene that subserves at least some cases of schizophrenia also be produced by biological insults?

In addressing this question, we might first ask whether or not any evidence indicates that affected twins in MZ pairs discordant for schizophrenia are more likely to have experienced biological insults. It has been shown that multiple births are associated with greater complications than single births, with one twin usually experiencing more difficulty than the other (MacGillivray *et al.*, 1975; Porreco, 1990). Furthermore, in early studies comparing discordant MZ twin pairs, both Pollin and Stabenau (1968) and McNeil and Kaij (1978) found that the affected twin was indeed more likely to have experienced perinatal complications. These findings are compatible with the assumption of somatophenocopies, and they raise the question of whether or not the affected twin in discordant MZ pairs is more likely to evidence CNS abnormality. The results of several investigations indicate that the answer to this question is a resounding "yes."

Findings from research on MZ twins who are discordant for schizophrenia suggest that only the affected member of these twinships possesses an organic liability. Mosher et al. (1971) found that the affected twins in discordant MZ pairs manifested a higher incidence of neurological abnormalities than their healthy cotwins. More recently, Reveley et al. (1987) examined brain density using CT and found that affected twins from discordant MZ pairs showed lower left than right hemisphere density. The reverse was found for the healthy cotwins and unrelated controls. In another recent study, Suddath et al. (1990) scanned the brains of 15 discordant MZ pairs, using magnetic resonance imaging. They found that the brains of the affected twins were characterized by larger ventricles, wider sulci, and reductions in the size of the left temporal lobe and frontal portion of the hippocampus. For 12 of the twin pairs, abnormalities were so pronounced in the ill twin that they could be visually distinguished from their healthy cotwins. Given the strength of the association between the brain abnormalities and schizophrenia demonstrated by this study, it is reasonable to conclude that the organic signs are either direct manifestations or correlates of the diathesis. It might, therefore, be argued that only the affected members of these twinships possesses the organic liability for schizophrenia and that their brain abnormalities imply a somatophenocopy.

At this point, no strong evidence supports the role of any specific brain structure or neurotransmitter abnormality in schizophrenia. However, numerous imaging and autopsy studies of the brains of schizophrenic patients have revealed structural impairments. Replicated findings include ventricular enlargement, cortical atrophy, and hippocampal cell disarray (Benes et al., 1986; Altshuler et al., 1987; Walker et al., 1990). Although the cytoarchitectonics of the hippocampus have not been extensively studied in other diagnostic populations, ventricular enlargement and cortical atrophy are known to exist in a variety of clinical conditions. Moreover, the latter two abnormalities are known to be common sequelae of perinatal complications (Kreusser and Volpe, 1984). Because ventricular and cortical abnormalities are associated with diverse disorders, they probably do not represent the specific neuropathology underlying schizophrenia. Instead, they are probably the grossest and most easily visualized manifestations of more diffuse damage that also involves the structure(s) and/or system(s) that give rise to the schizophrenic syndrome.

Given that CNS trauma can produce the same brain abnormalities that are visually apparent in some schizophrenic patients, it seems premature to rule out the possibility that nongenetic factors are sufficient for producing constitutional vulnerability to schizophrenia. With respect to the sequelae of perinatal complications, the critical factor may be the extent to which the insult produces damage in the organic substrate responsible for psychotic symptoms. To the extent that it does, it produces a somatophenocopy. However, because the CNS injuries produced by insults such as obstetrical complications and postnatal viral infections are usually nonspecific (Abel, 1989; Kubli *et al.*, 1988), cases of schizophrenia resulting from such factors would be expected to be accompanied by a variety of other functional impairments (e.g., childhood learning disabilities).

Of course, demonstrating that the affected members in discordant MZ pairs show higher rates of brain abnormalities and obstetrical complications does not rule out the possibility that the nonaffected cotwin possesses an unexpressed genotype. As Cannon, Barr, and Mednick suggest in the present volume (Chapter 2), the genetic predisposition to schizophrenia may involve an increased susceptibility to CNS insult.

The Offspring of Discordant Monozygotic Twins

To determine whether or not the nonaffected twin in discordant MZ pairs possesses an unexpressed genotype for schizophrenia, two research groups have examined the incidence of schizophrenia in the offspring of such pairs. These are extremely important studies, because if the results show comparable, high morbidity rates in offspring of affected and non-affected MZ twins, this would argue strongly *against* the existence of nongenetic sources of vulnerability. Gottesman and Bertelsen (1989) studied six discordant MZ pairs previously reported on by Fischer (1973). Out of 24 offspring of the nonaffected twins, 4 (age-corrected risk rate = 17.4%) were judged to be schizophrenic or to have schizophreniclike psychoses. Among 14 offspring of the affected twins, 1 (age-corrected risk rate = 10%) was diagnosed schizophrenic. These findings led the investigators to conclude that the nonaffected twins passed on their genetic liability to offspring. However, at the same time, Kringlen and Cramer (1989) reported results from a similar study that failed to show comparable rates of schizophrenia in the offspring of affected and nonaffected MZ twins. In this case, the rates (not age-corrected) of "schizophrenia spectrum disorder" were

17.9% (5 out of 28) for the offspring of affected twins and 4.4% (2 out of 45) for the offspring of nonaffected twins. Although the difference between these rates fell just short of the conventional 0.05 level of significance, group differences in the rate of schizotypal, paranoid, and borderline traits in offspring were statistically significant: Offspring of affected twins showed a higher rate of these disorders. These findings led the authors to suggest that the presence of psychopathology in the parent had an effect on the psychiatric outcome of offspring that was independent of genetic factors. They suggest that nonoptimal caregiving by the disturbed parent is contributing to the psychiatric morbidity in offspring. An alternative explanation that cannot be ruled out is that a mutation occurred in the affected twin that was passed on to some offspring, thus increasing their morbidity risk.

In evaluating the results of these studies of discordant MZ twins, several limitations must be taken into consideration. First, it is unavoidable that the number of subjects in both studies is small. Second, the offspring in the Gottesman and Bertelsen (1989) study were not directly assessed; information on psychiatric diagnoses was obtained from the Danish National Psychiatric Register. Third, data were not available on the psychiatric outcome of all offspring in the Gottesman and Bertelson sample; 9% were either deceased or had emigrated. However, these "missing" subjects were evidently included in the total as nonaffected offspring. (Because information on the proportions of missing offspring coming from the affected and nonaffected cotwins are not presented, the potential effects of the missing data on the findings cannot be determined.) Finally, in both studies, age differences exist between the offspring of affected and non-affected twins. In the Kringlen and Cramer study, 46% of the offspring of schizophrenic twins and 53% of those of healthy cotwins were under 40 years of age. In contrast, Gottesman and Bertelsen indicated that 32% of the schizophrenics' offspring and 4% of the healthy cotwins offspring were under 45 years. Thus, in the latter study, the normal cotwins' offspring were older and, therefore, had passed through the major risk period for schizophrenia in larger proportions. This, of course, increased the likelihood of detecting psychopathology in the nonaffected cotwins' offspring. Gottesman and Bertelsen did take the precaution of deriving age-corrected risk figures; however, there is no way of determining the effectiveness of such corrections in eliminating biases due to group differences in age. In summary, then, the findings of these studies must be interpreted with caution. At this point, the question of whether or not discordant cotwins' offspring show comparable rates of schizophrenia remains unresolved.

It is also of interest to compare the rates of psychopathology in offspring of affected twins with those of concordant and discordant pairs. As previously suggested, some or all of the affected twins from discordant MZ pairs may be phenocopies, whereas the majority of affected twins from concordant pairs presumably possess a genetic liability. Given this assumption, we would expect a higher incidence of psychopathology in the offspring of affected twins from concordant MZ pairs. This is because, as parents, they are contributing both genetic liability and environmental stress. The affected twins from discordant pairs are also contributing the latter, but they may be less likely to transmit a genetic liability. In their study, Gottesman and Bertelsen (1989) report on the psychiatric status of offspring of concordant as well as discordant MZ pairs. Examination of the data indicate that 15% (5 of 33) of the offspring of schizophrenics from concordant pairs are ill, compared with 7% (1 of 14) of those of patients from discordant pairs. The report does not provide data on the ages of offspring in these two groups, so the effects of age on these differential rates cannot be determined. However, the findings are consistent with the interpretation that a higher proportion of the affected twins from the concordant pairs possess a genetic vulnerability to schizophrenia. Equally plausible, however, is an interpretation that presumes the twins from concordant pairs possess a genetic liability that is more penetrant and thus has a greater likelihood of being expressed. Again, the results neither confirm nor disconfirm the existence of nongenetic forms of schizophrenia.

One approach that might shed light on this issue would be a comparison of the rate of obstetrical complications in concordant and discordant affected MZ twins. Demonstrating that affected twins from discordant pairs show a higher rate of complications than those from concordant pairs would be consistent with the notion that the former represent nongenetic forms of schizophrenia. Related to this, it is of interest to note that the rate of serious obstetrical complications is estimated to be 10 times higher in twin than in single births (Porreco, 1990). Consequently, if perinatal factors are the source of vulnerability for some schizophrenic patients, twins would be overrepresented in this subgroup.

Up to this point, our discussion of nongenetic sources of vulnerability has been limited to physical insults. However, some early theories presumed that psychosocial factors, particularly dysfunctional family communication, could lead to schizophrenia in the absence of pre-existing vulnerability (e.g., Bateson, 1956). But the research has yielded no convincing empirical support for these theories. As a result, psychosocial variables are no longer viewed as *likely* sources of vulnerability in contemporary models of schizophrenia, although data supporting the interactive role of psychosocial stress are accumulating. The literature on psychosocial factors as moderating variables is discussed below.

Summary

As the above discussion illustrates, garnering evidence for the existence of nongenetic sources of constitutional vulnerability is more difficult than demonstrating the effects of heredity. Behavioral genetics paradigms can offer relatively straightforward support for hereditary determinants because there is little error in the measurement of genetic relatedness. In contrast, the measurement of a variable like obstetrical complications is subject to substantial error. Retrospective parental reports and hospital records are the primary sources of data on obstetrical complications. These are likely to be subject to error due to biases, recall failure, and incomplete documentation. In addition, some complications may not be detected or may fall short of the threshold for documentation as a clinical problem (Pasamanick and Knobloch, 1966). The end results are that measures of obstetrical complications will be of low reliability, statistical power for the detection of group differences will be compromised, and the probability of type II error will be high. The same limitations apply to measures of a variety of other environmental stressors (Walker and Emory, 1985).

At this point, we can only conclude that the results of twin studies do not rule out nongenetic contributants. Until more conclusive evidence is available, we would argue in favor of a "working model," as proposed by Mirsky and Duncan (1986), which presumes that constitutional vulnerability can arise through biological insult, as well as through heredity and genetic mutation. As they, and other writers, have noted, substantial phenomenological diversity exists among schizophrenic patients. While such diversity is not, in itself, *prima facie* evidence, it is true that there are numerous disorders (i.e., psychophenes) with greater phenomenological homogeneity than schizophrenia that are known to be caused by diverse factors. For example, heredity, genetic mutations, physical insults, and sociocultural deprivation can all, independently, produce mental retardation. In commenting on the replication failures in genetic linkage studies of psychiatric disorders, Owen *et al.* (1990: 125) note that "on clinical grounds, bipolar disorder looks much more homogeneous than schizophrenia, and the demonstration that it is not makes it even more unlikely that schizophrenia will turn out to have a single cause."

The existence of nongenetic forms of schizophrenia is of critical relevance to genetic research. Phenocopies present a formidable challenge to those investigators who are concerned with modeling the familial transmission of the disorder and identifying the genotype(s); the greater the prevalence of phenocopies, the greater the difficulty in determining the mode of transmission and in isolating the relevant loci through linkage analysis (Owen *et al.*, 1990). The recent failures to replicate findings of linkage in multiplex families have been disappointing to investigators (Kennedy *et al.*, 1988; Sherrington *et al.*, 1988). These failures signal the importance of broadening our view of potential etiologic agents. We must be willing to entertain even the most complex etiologic models that presume multiple trajectories to the final common pathway(s). If researchers give consideration to nongenetic sources of vulnerability, they may increase their chances of identifying genetic determinants. Specifically, if attempts are made to identify those patients who have a history of CNS insult, more homogenous subtypes may emerge (Walker and Shaye, 1982).

In a recent paper on the heterogeneity of schizophrenia, Tsuang *et al.* (1990) refer to sources of constitutional vulnerability as "level I indicators" of etiology, and they argue forcefully for the importance of exploring a variety of such indicators, including obstetrical complications, viral infections, and family history of mental illness. They state "If progress is to be made, it is important that we continue to investigate putative causal agents, whether under the guise of discovering with factors are among the relevant 'multifactors' or investigating heterogeneity among distinct level I indicators" (Tsuang *et al.*, 1990: 25).

Heterogeneity in Moderating Factors

In the previous section, we explored the issue of etiologic heterogeneity with regard to sources of constitutional vulnerability. A second aspect of heterogeneity concerns the interaction of the diathesis with other factors. These factors might best be termed moderating variables, in that they alter the likelihood that constitutional vulnerability will be manifested in the clinical syndrome of schizophrenia. We will consider two general classes of moderator variables that are of potential relevance to the etiology of schizophrenia: environmental and genetic.

At the outset, we acknowledge that the inclusion of moderating variables, particularly genetic moderators, dramatically increases the complexity of etiologic models. As Meehl (1989: 940) notes, however, comparable or greater complexity is apparent in etiologic models of diabetes and kidney disease. He adds that "one should take it for granted that the brain is at least as complicated as the kidney."

Environmental Moderators

In addition to being a possible source of constitutional vulnerability, obstetrical complications have also been cited as one potential environmental moderator of genetically determined vulnerability (Beuhring *et al.*, 1982; Walker and Emory, 1983). Cannon, Barr, and Mednick (Chapter 2) present data linking complications with psychiatric outcome in high-risk subjects. They conclude that prenatal and perinatal stressors interact with genetic vulnerability and increase the likelihood of negative symptoms in schizophrenia.

Psychosocial stressors are another frequently discussed environmental moderator of vulnerability to schizophrenia. One source of data on the effects of psychosocial factors is the research on communication patterns in families of schizophrenic patients. In the present volume (Chapter 10), Doane discusses findings from several research groups who show that patients are more likely to relapse when, subsequent to release from the hospital, they return to families characterized by high rates of criticism and emotional lability. Although the findings suggest that these family factors are, in part, precipitating patient relapse, more definitive conclusions about causality must await further research. In particular, we cannot yet rule out the possibility that the incipient onset of symptoms that precedes relapse contributes to communication deviance in family members.

Garnering evidence that psychosocial factors are capable of precipitating first episodes of illness is even more difficult than demonstrating that such factors predict relapse. However, some evidence suggests that psychosocial stressors increase the likelihood of psychopathology in biological offspring of schizophrenic parents (Walker et al., 1981). In an adoption study, Tienari (1987) found that offspring of psychotic parents were more likely to manifest psychiatric disorder if they were reared in unstable, as compared with stable, adoptive homes. These findings indicate that psychosocial stressors may serve to trigger disorders in vulnerable individuals. It should be noted, however, that the subjects of this study are still relatively young (40% below age 25 years), so we cannot yet rule out the possibility that stressors only serve to hasten the onset of disorder, rather than increasing its likelihood.

The above findings lend support to the assumption that episodes of schizophrenia may be stress-related, but they do not indicate a *unique* susceptibility to the effects of stress on the part of vulnerable individuals. The notion that constitutional vulnerability to schizophrenia entails a heightened sensitivity to psychosocial stressors is implicit in contemporary etiologic models, such as the diathesis–stress and vulnerability models (Zubin and Spring, 1977). To demonstrate support for this assumption, it must be shown that there is a significant interactive effect of constitutional vulnerability and environmental stress on psychiatric status. A recent study by Walker et al. (1989) demonstrated such an effect; specifically, exposure to parental maltreatment was more likely to result in maladjustment in biological offspring of schizophrenics than in offspring of normal parents. Evidence suggests that genetically vulnerable individuals may also be characterized by greater sensitivity to biological stressors, such as perinatal complications (Walker and Emory, 1983).

So far, we have mentioned only the direct effects of environmental factors on the vulnerable individual. It is also important to consider mediated effects of the environment. Specifically, environmental factors may serve to alter the individual's capacity to cope with subsequent environmental stressors. Environmentally determined intellectual competencies may, for example, enhance the vulnerable individual's ability to cope with stress and/or avoid exposure to stressful events.

Genetic Moderators

Genetic factors constitute the second general class of moderator variables. At the biological level, the expression of a gene can be altered by genes at other loci (Rothwell, 1976; Weaver and Hedrick, 1989). Some genes act as *modifiers* of the expression of other genes, altering the phenotype in a measurable way. *Suppressor* genes completely prevent the expression of genes at other loci.

Interactions among genes, such as those described above, may be playing a role in the sex differences observed in schizophrenic patients. The genes that code for sex may serve to modify the expression of the schizophrenic genotype, thereby producing the sex differences in age-at-onset, symptomatology, and treatment responsiveness noted by Lewine in the present volume (Chapter 9).

Alternatively, at the level of the somatophene, the hormonal characteristics determined by genetic sex may interact with vulnerability to schizophrenia to produce sex differences in the syndrome and its course. Thus, as suggested by Lewine, the chemophene produced by the female genotype may serve to mitigate the behavioral expression of schizophrenia. Conversely, the male chemophene may exacerbate it.

At the behavioral level, one can easily imagine similar processes; independently determined, phenotypic characteristics may moderate each other. Examples of such characteristics include temperamental factors, such as arousability, and cognitive abilities. Although constitutional vulnerability for schizophrenia probably has some cognitive and temperamental components (e.g., pleiotropic effects), independently transmitted propensities in these domains undoubtedly interact with the diathesis. In the present discussion, we refer to these propensities as heritable or phenotypic moderating characteristics. Meehl (1989, 1990) evokes the same notion in his concept of "potentiators," which he defines as heritable traits that raise the probability of clinical schizophrenia in individuals with the schizogene. We use the term moderator, rather than potentiator, because we assume that the probability of clinical schizophrenia can be either *raised* or *lowered* by these factors.

The differentiation of heritable moderating characteristics from the diathesis is a formidable task because moderators will covary with the schizophrenic phenotype, due to their interaction at the behavioral level. As a case in point, it has been shown that preschizophrenic children show deficits in intellectual performance relative to their classroom peers and siblings (Aylward *et al.*, 1984; Watt and Saiz, Chapter 8, this volume). Furthermore, diagnosed schizophrenic patients manifest intellectual deficits relative to controls. Are these deficits a component of the schizophrenic phenotype, or are they independently transmitted moderators?

Another source of phenotypic covariance is assortative mating. Positive correlations between spouses have been found for many cognitive abilities and personality variables, as well as psychopathology (Plomin *et al.*, 1990). Furthermore, because assortative mating for mental status is not necessarily diagnosis-specific, the expected result is positive correlations among genetic liabilities for a variety of psychiatric disorders (Merikangas, 1982; Prilipko, 1986), as well as moderating characteristics. Although the findings of early family studies led to the conclusion that risk rates for other mental illnesses were not elevated in relatives of schizophrenic patients (Gottesman and Shields, 1982), more recent studies reveal increased rates for several psychiatric conditions in relatives of probands (Coryell and Zimmerman, 1988; Kendler, 1988; Gershon, 1988). While it is true that the linkages among genetic liabilities resulting from assortative mating are assumed to be temporary at the biological level, due to recombination, nonrandom mating occurs within each generation and, thus, reintroduces covariance among liabilities.

A Model of Etiologic Heterogeneity

The sources of etiologic heterogeneity discussed above are summarized diagrammatically in Fig. 14.1. As illustrated in the figure, it is assumed that the biological abnormality subserving schizophrenia is, depending on its origins, either a somatophene or somatophenocopy—both result in constitutional vulnerability to schizophrenia. The eventual clinical outcome (the presence or absence of schizophrenia) is, in turn, determined by a host of moderating variables. These moderators can serve to alter the probability of breakdown as well as determining the nature and course of the individual's behavioral development. Although Fig. 14.1 only depicts the impact of moderators on the developmental course preceding the clinical onset of illness, the factors are presumed to continue to influence the illness course.

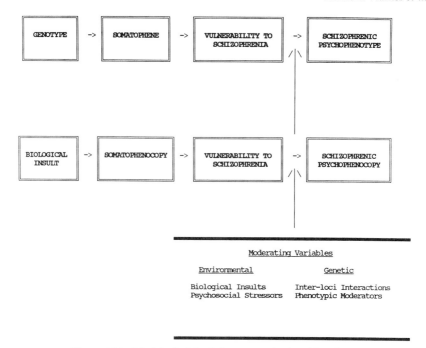

Figure 14.1   Model of etiologic heterogeneity in schizophrenia.

Figure 14.1 is, by necessity, oversimplified. There undoubtedly exist some complex interactions and bidirectional relations that are not represented in the diagram. For example, characteristics of the individual, including vulnerability, would be expected to have an impact on the psychosocial environment. It is important to keep such potential effects in mind when interpreting relations between characteristics of the individual and the environment. (For a detailed discussion of the complexities that ensue from such interactions and intercorrelations, see Walker *et al.*, 1988.)

Developmental Determinants: Longitudinal Variability

It is apparent that when a disorder is caused by multiple, interacting factors, as opposed to a singular agent, the elucidation of etiology is made more difficult. In the case of schizophrenia, there are developmental changes in symptom manifestation that contribute further to the complexity. First, the presenting clinical picture seems to vary as a function of the patient's age at onset (Asarnow *et al.*, Chapter 5, present volume; Bettes and Walker, 1987; Yassa, Chapter 11, present volume). Second, the clinical picture changes as patients age (Harding, Chapter 12, present volume). Finally, as documented by many of the chapters in this volume, there are "preclinical" manifestations of vulnerability to schizophrenia. In sum, not only does the clinical syndrome show developmental change, but the premorbid course is characterized by various, dynamic subclinical abnormalities.

It is of interest to note that some neurological disorders of known etiology also show developmental changes in clinical manifestation. In Huntington's disease, for example, the typical age at onset of the clinical syndrome is early adulthood. However, the disease has been diagnosed in children as young as 4 years, and investigators have noted symptom differences as a function of age-at-onset, such that prepubescent children show more dystonic and parkinsonian features (Shoulson, 1990).

Several mechanisms might be operative in producing developmental change in behavioral phenotypic expressions. First, the developmental changes may be directly, genetically controlled. For example, researchers have identified "regulator" or "temporal" genes that function to control the timing of developmental events in animals (for a discussion, see Plomin et al., 1990). Drawing on these findings, Pogue-Geile argues (Chapter 13 in the present volume) that the genotype for schizophrenia involves a temporal component, such that the phenotype varies with biologic development. In other words, the clinical symptoms of schizophrenia that typically arise in young adulthood may be the phenotype associated with a gene or polygenes first expressed at that point in development. Alternatively, temporal genes that are independent of the schizophrenic genotype may moderate its expression. As an illustration, the hormonal changes that mark the onset of puberty are at least partially controlled by temporal genes, and these changes may interact with a pre-existing CNS abnormality resulting from the schizophrenic genotype. Lewine (Chapter 9 in this volume) explores this possibility as it relates to sex differences in schizophrenia. Similarly, genetically determined developmental events may interact with acquired CNS abnormalities and result in a phenocopy.

Cognitive development may also play a role in determining the manifestation of symptoms. Specifically, the capacity to generate and communicate delusional and paranoid ideations may depend on the ability to engage in abstract thought processes. This assumption is consistent with findings that (1) symptoms of paranoia and delusions increase steadily with age in samples of psychiatrically disturbed children and (2) these symptoms are positively correlated with IQ (Bettes and Walker, 1987). Thus, some aspects of disordered thought may emerge in conjunction with specific cognitive abilities in vulnerable individuals.

Finally, environmental factors may contribute to developmental changes in the manifestations of vulnerability. For example, the psychosocial demands associated with adolescence may constitute a unique stressor with the capacity for triggering psychotic episodes. After the first episode, the level of interpersonal stress may determine the subsequent course of the illness (Zubin and Spring, 1977).

Summary

In the preceding sections, a variety of etiologic agents and mechanisms were discussed. At this point, there is no compelling reason for dispensing with any of them. Ultimately, we may discover that each is valid with respect to a subgroup of patients. At the present time, our longitudinal data base is insufficient; it does not lend itself to the generation of neurodevelopmental models or to the evaluation of their merits. We must, therefore, direct our efforts at eludicating the developmental pathways associated with schizophrenia. This will eventually yield a firmer data base for evaluating the relative merits of various hypotheses about etiologic processes.

NEURODEVELOPMENTAL MODELS OF SCHIZOPHRENIA

Many investigators believe that developmental changes in behavioral manifestations may hold clues to the etiologic processes underlying various forms of psychopathology. Unfortunately, data on the childhood development of schizophrenic patients have been so scarce that few writers have accepted the challenge of proposing a developmental model of the etiology of the disorder. The models that have been proposed attempt to integrate what little is currently known about the developmental course of schizophrenia with evidence from research on normal neurodevelopment. Although the models differ in the nature of the neuropathological process they describe, most share the assumption that the organic *dysfunction* subserving schizophrenia has its onset in adolescence. In other words, the somatophene or somatophenocopy does not manifest itself prior to that point.

For example, Feinberg (1982–1983) has suggested that schizophrenia may be subserved by a defect in the normative process of synaptic pruning that occurs in adolescence. He notes the changes in sleep stages, brain electrophysiology, and cognitive capacity that typically accompany adolescence and assumes, as do others, that these are linked with the demonstrated changes in synaptic density that occur at this time. He thus proposes that schizophrenia may result from an abnormality in synaptic pruning during adolescence, although he notes that there is no basis for speculating on whether the abnormality "is due to the elimination of too many or too few synapses or from the wrong ones" (Feinberg, 1982–1983: 327).

A similar approach is taken by Saugstad (1989), who proposes that sex differences in the age at onset of schizophrenia are the result of hormonal effects on synaptic elimination. Specifically, Saugstad argues that pubertal maturation coincides with the elimination of redundant synaptic connections and that individuals with a late onset of sexual maturation will be characterized by excessive elimination of synapses. Reduced density of neural synapses, particularly in the frontal lobes, is posited to be the necessary factor for schizophrenia. In addition to citing evidence for late maturation in schizophrenic patients, Saugstad suggests that the fact that males mature later than females may account for their tendency to show an earlier onset of symptoms, a more chronic course, and, possibly, a higher incidence of schizophrenia.

Weinberger (1987) proposes that a fixed lesion in the CNS, which is probably congenital, interacts with normal brain maturational events to produce schizophrenia in adulthood. He suggests that this lesion compromises the mesocortical dopamine system that projects from the midbrain to the prefrontal cortex and renders it *underactive*. This, in turn, disrupts inhibitory feedback to the mesolimbic dopamine system and renders it *overactive*. Because dopamine metabolism in the prefrontal cortex peaks in early adulthood, this developmental period is the critical one for the disruption of CNS functioning by the pre-existing lesion. Unlike Feinberg and Saugstad, who imply that the structural abnormality subserving schizophrenia is not present until late adolescence, Weinberger posits a pre-existing lesion that is essentially silent until the biological changes associated with puberty fully activate the defective system.

If it is the case that schizophrenia is due to a disruption in CNS functioning that is triggered by the biological changes accompanying adolescence, then we would expect to see a relatively unremarkable course of development up to that point. This does not, of course, preclude the existence of CNS abnormality prior to adolescence but does imply that any such abnormality is silent because it lay in a structure or system that is essentially nonfunctional prior to the onset of puberty.

In a recent paper, Taylor (in press) presents a neurodevelopmental model that does attempt to incorporate preadolescent signs of abnormality. He proposes that some cases of schizophrenia may be due to perinatal injuries to the cerebellum. He reviews the results of imaging studies, which have shown that some schizophrenic patients manifest signs of cerebellar atrophy, and postmortem studies, which have revealed cellular abnormalities in this structure. Cerebellar dysfunction would be expected to produce early signs of perceptuomotor and vestibular abnormalities. Furthermore, the human cerebellum is one of the latest maturing brain structures and does not reach full maturity until 15–20 years of age. Presumably, at that time, its structural and functional relationship with the limbic system reaches a maximum. Cerebellar dysfunction might, therefore, result in compromised modulation of the limbic system in late adolescence–early adulthood and lead to the cognitive and affective symptoms characteristic of schizophrenia.

It is reasonable to speculate that three of the above four neurodevelopmental theorists posit a functional onset of neuropathology in adolescence because the clinical and empirical evidence for behavioral dysfunction at this point in the life course of schizophrenia is well established. In contrast, as Pogue-Geile notes (Chapter 13 in this volume), although high-risk and follow-back research suggests the existence of dysfunction long before adolescence, the evidence is nonspecific. The limitations of past research methods may, therefore, be influencing the nature of our etiologic models. If, however, further research verifies the existence of neuromotor and behavioral abnormalities in preschizophrenic infants and children, it will be necessary to incorporate these findings into future neurodevelopmental models.

Clearly, our ability to generate plausible developmental models of schizophrenia hinges on knowledge of the entire premorbid life course of the disorder. Rapidly accumulating data in the fields of developmental neurobiology, psychobiology, and neuroendocrinology are illuminating the changing nature of CNS structure and function across the life span, particularly in early and middle childhood (Goldman-Rakic, 1987). However, despite rapid advances in the neurosciences, it is important to note that we still know very little about the development of the CNS in humans. Most research on neurodevelopment involves animal subjects (Goldman-Rakic, 1987; Nowakowski, 1987), so current speculations about human neurodevelopment are based on just a few postmortem investigations (e.g., Benes, 1989). There is reason, however, to expect that the revolution in technology for visualizing structural and physiological brain characteristics *in vivo* (e.g., computerized tomography, magnetic resonance imaging) will contribute to a dramatic increase in our knowledge of developmental changes in the human CNS.

AN ARCHIVAL–OBSERVATIONAL APPROACH TO RESEARCH ON THE DEVELOPMENT OF SCHIZOPHRENIA

By better documenting the ontogenesis of behavior in individuals who succumb to adult-onset psychopathology, we may be able to identify modal developmental trajectories. Moreover, by relating these trajectories to potential sources of constitutional vulnerability and moderating factors, it may be possible to identify subtypes that will inform the generation of more precise developmental models of etiology. Obtaining data on the life-span development of schizophrenic patients will be particularly important if our assumption of a final common pathway with multiple etiologic origins is correct. After the clinical onset of the disorder, we are presumably seeing the pervasive consequences and sequelae of impairment in this common pathway. The period prior to the clinical onset, however, may be the optimal one for the manifestation of signs that correspond to specific etiologic origins.

To obtain such data, we must have a research method that will yield reliable information on premorbid characteristics, preferably beginning in infancy, as well as adult psychiatric outcome. We have recently initiated a study that uses such a method. It is best described as an "archival–observational" study because the primary source of information is childhood home movies of subjects who were first diagnosed as having schizophrenia in late adolescence or early adulthood. The technology for making home movies became widely available in the 1950s, so individuals born during this decade have now passed through the major risk period for schizophrenia.

At this writing, we have collected home movies on 30 schizophrenic patients, 15 patients with affective disorder, and 20 subjects from families with no mental illness. All of the patient subjects were first referred for psychiatric treatment after the age of 16 years. Thus, none had any diagnosable behavioral problems prior to adolescence. The current mean age for the schizophrenic patients is 33 years, and for their healthy siblings the mean is 32 years. In the majority of cases, the films begin in the first few months of life and extend through adolescence. Our preliminary work with these films suggests their tremendous potential for elucidating the developmental course.

There are three characteristics of home movies that make them a useful archival source of information on behavioral development. First, they feature behavior in naturalistic settings; the modal context is the family home. Second, they are made in the absence of nonfamilial observers. This is in contrast to most observational studies of behavior, which involve either an observer in the home or a laboratory setting where behavior is filmed. Third, childhood home movies are excellent sources of information on socioemotional behavior because they feature events that are conducive to interpersonal behavior. About half of the films feature informal activities among family members in the home, and the remainder are of birthdays and holidays. These formal social events involve high expectations for interpersonal interaction and are ideal for eliciting individual differences in affective style. Finally, childhood home movies contain excellent data on neuromotor development because parents tend to film the acquisition of motor milestones such as crawling and walking.

The archival–observational method has several advantages over previous approaches to the study of childhood antecedents of schizophrenia. First, as indicated, it allows for direct observation of behavior. Researchers have demonstrated that observational procedures can be used to study a broad range of characteristics and that they can yield reliable data on microlevel behaviors (Sackett, 1978). We will, therefore, be able to study the behavior of preschizophrenic children without reliance on secondary sources (academic records or informants) that may serve to introduce biases, filter information, or provide only gross impressions. Second, the adult psychiatric outcome of the subjects is known, so we can readily ascertain the relation between antecedents and outcome. Related to this, the data were collected independent of knowledge of developmental outcome, which eliminates the problem of examiner or informant bias (Yarrow *et al.*, 1970). Third, unlike follow-up studies, the patient sample in the present study is not restricted to those with clinical conditions in childhood. And, in contrast to high-risk studies, the sample is not restricted to those with schizophrenia in a first-degree relative. Given that the overwhelming majority of schizophrenic patients (about 90%) do not have first-degree relatives with the disorder, this is a clear advantage (Gottesman and Shields, 1982). Not only is sample representativeness enhanced, but genotype–environment confounds are reduced. In sum, the sample is potentially more representative of the general population of schizophrenic patients.

As with *any* methodology, the archival–observational method also has limitations. One limitation is that the films were not made with research purposes in mind, and, consequently, do not feature standardized contexts. We must, therefore, contend with variability between subjects and families in the nature of the behavioral settings as well as the amount of "data" collected. On the other hand, as indicated previously, there is striking consistency among families in the contexts and occasions featured in the films. Another limitation of the study concerns the fact that access to the technology for making home movies is related to socioeconomic status (SES). The patients participating in this investigation are primarily from middle to upper-middle class, intact families, and in this respect they are nonrepresentative of the general population of patients. One consequence of this is that the patients were not exposed to the kinds of environmental stressors that have been shown to be associated with low SES. While it is true that the nonrepresentativeness of the sample is a limitation, it might also be argued that their high SES is an advantage with respect to the goal of identifying constitutional markers. Presumably, the higher the SES, the lower the probability that subjects were exposed to various psychogenic stressors. As a result, the sample in this study may overrepresent individuals with a strong constitutional predisposition. If this is true, we might expect the physical and behavioral manifestations of constitutional vulnerability to be more apparent.

Another potential problem concerns the possible effects of childhood abnormalities on the likelihood that parents will make home movies. Children whose behavior is problematic may be less appealing subjects and, therefore, less likely to be filmed by their parents. The end result would be that our research sample is biased in the direction of over-representing subjects with more favorable premorbid developmental courses. Obviously, this would reduce our potential for identifying developmental precursors.

The home movies will be used to study neuromotor and socioemotional development from infancy through adolescence. These areas were targeted for two reasons. First, previous findings from high-risk and follow-back research suggest that abnormalities in both neuromotor functions and social behavior may characterize preschizophrenic children (Erlenmeyer-Kimling et al., 1984; Fish, 1977; Hanson et al., 1976; Lewine, 1981; Offord and Cross, 1969; Sameroff et al., 1984; Watt, 1978; Winters et al., 1981; Watt et al., 1984). Second, with respect to neuromotor factors, it is well established that motor development is highly sensitive to CNS abnormalities (Kreusser and Volpe, 1984), and the emergence of various motor milestones is assumed to be at least partially determined by developmental changes in CNS structures (Saint-Anne Dargassies, 1986; Sarnat, 1984). Furthermore, as Meehl (1989, 1990) has noted, soft neurological signs are presumably closer, in the causal chain, to the biological substrate of schizophrenic pathology than are psychometrics, symptoms, and social behavior. In this sense, neuromotor indicators are less subject to the cumulative effects of social learning, which would be expected to contribute significantly to individual differences in cognitive functions and social behavior.

In the domain of neuromotor functions, we will study the acquisition of developmental milestones, level of motor activity, gait, and neurological soft signs. In the realm of socioemotional factors, facial expressions of emotion, social responsiveness, and the initiation of interpersonal interaction will be examined. Through microlevel observational analyses, we hope to identify the earliest point in the life span at which developmental deviations are apparent. And, for each functional domain, the developmental trajectory will be charted.

Parents are asked to provide extensive information on prenatal factors, obstetrical complications, and childhood life events, such as accidents, illnesses, and deaths of loved ones. In addition, data on family history of psychiatric disorder are collected. It will, therefore, be possible to examine the role of two potential sources of constitutional vulnerability (i.e., biological insults and hereditary factors) on the developmental characteristics of patients. Furthermore, by relating data on exogenous stressors to information on the child's developmental course, it may be possible to identify factors that alter the developmental trajectory. For example, changes in affective and interpersonal behavior may be temporally linked with stressful life events. Such a finding would lend support to the diathesis–stress model.

Extensive medical history information is also collected, and thorough assessments of the subject's current clinical status are being conducted. The latter includes neuropsychological testing and a magnetic resonance image scan of the brain. In this way, it will be possible to determine whether early developmental characteristics are linked with clinical symptoms, neuropsychological performance characteristics, or morphological abnormalities of the brain.

Through the use of three comparison groups—healthy siblings of patients, patients with affective disorders, and subjects from families with no mental illness—it will be possible to address a variety of important questions. The sibling control group is comprised of the nearest-in-age, same-sex, healthy sibling of each patient. Healthy siblings of patients appear in the same films and, consequently, the same behavioral contexts as the patients. And, of course, they are reared by the same parents. This imposes some control for environmental factors when patients are compared with siblings. On the other hand, siblings partially share the patient's genetic endowment, so, to the extent that vulnerability is genetically determined, siblings may also manifest some signs of constitutional vulnerability. The no-mental-illness comparison group has been selected to be of comparable current mean age, sex ratio, and family SES with the patient and sibling control groups. Significant differences between the sibling and no-mental-illness comparison groups would suggest a role for either family environment or genetic factors. If the differences are in the domain of early neurological soft-signs, this would argue for unexpressed constitutional vulnerability in some sibling controls. If the differences involve interpersonal behavior, either environmental or biological factors may be operative.

The patients with affective disorders have been selected so that they are comparable with the schizophrenic group on current age, age at onset of illness, and SES of the family of origin. The comparison group of patients with affective disorders will provide the opportunity to examine the diagnostic specificity of developmental precursors. If comparisons fail to reveal significant differences between the schizophrenic and affective groups, but both differ from no-mental-illness controls, this would suggest that at least some signs of vulnerability are nonspecific.

Because extensive developmental and outcome data will be collected on subjects, a broad range of questions can be addressed. Among the most important are (1) What is the relation between potential sources of vulnerability, such as obstetrical complications and family history of mental illness, and developmental factors?; (2) Do obstetrical complications, family history and/or developmental factors predict clinical outcome?; (3) What is the earliest age at which preschizophrenic children can be reliably distinguished from comparison subjects?; and (4) In what domains (i.e., neuromotor, affective expression, and interpersonal behavior) are pre-schizophrenic children distinguishable? Although some central questions will be addressed with group comparisons, the examination of individual differences among patients will be emphasized. Of critical interest are differences in the nature and timing of developmental abnormalities.

A Preliminary Study of Clinical Prediction

Prior to applying microlevel, observational coding schemes to the childhood films, we felt it was important to address the question of whether or not clinical observers would be capable of identifying the preschizophrenic children without the benefit of specific criteria. In other words, can clinicians who are blind to the psychiatric outcome of the subjects reliably distinguish the patients from their healthy siblings via unstructured observation of the early childhood films? We conducted a preliminary study, using a subset of the films, to answer this question (Walker and Lewine, 1990).

Although the patients and their siblings are the focus of the larger research program, the individuals viewing the films were the actual subjects of this preliminary study. The viewers were graduate students in psychology and experienced clinicians. The films used in the study featured five patients with DSM-III-R diagnoses of schizophrenia (four males and one female) and their healthy siblings. The siblings are all now past the age of 25 years and have no history of psychiatric disorder. The sibships were selected from a larger sample based on specific criteria involving the length and nature of the footage.

In every case, the patient was the only one in his or her nuclear family who succumbed to a psychiatric disorder. The patients were first diagnosed as schizophrenic in late adolescence or early adulthood and have been under continuous medical care since the onset of their illness (the current mean age of the patients is 29 years). None of the patients was referred for or received treatment for psychiatric problems prior to 17 years, nor were any characterized by physical illnesses or handicaps that would set them apart from their siblings.

All available 8- and 16-mm home movies of the patients and their siblings were submitted for study and transcribed to videotape. The tapes were edited to eliminate footage that did not feature one or more of the children in the sibship. Chronologically ordered segments were prepared for viewing. Because the children enter the films in order of birth, some of the initial segments did not include all children in the sibship. However, each segment included all children born prior to the date the segment ended. Also, because the siblings enter in order of birth and are subsequently featured simultaneously in the films, it was not possible to equate the subjects within sibship on the length of time featured or on the age-span covered. But, for all subjects, the films included footage in the first 17 months of life and extended to at least the fifth year.

Viewers were informed that they would be viewing videotape segments of sibships in which only one child developed schizophrenia later in life. To avoid biasing the viewers by directing their attention to particular characteristics of the subjects, *no* criteria for judging the children were provided. Viewers were instructed to use their own criteria in judging the eventual psychiatric status of the children and to note the factors that influenced their judgments on their response forms. In this way, we could determine which features of the children were most salient to the individual viewers in making their judgments. They were provided with standard forms on which to record their responses and were instructed to remain silent while viewing the videotapes and to refrain from sharing their responses with others.

Viewers were informed of the ages of the children featured in each of the chronologically ordered segments. After each segment was shown, they were asked to respond "yes" or "no" (forced choice) to the question "Is this the preschizophrenic child?", with the restriction that they respond "yes" to one and only one child from the sibship. Once they recorded their judgments, viewers were not permitted to change them; however, they were free to judge the children differently after viewing subsequent segments. In cases where the film segment included only a subset of the siblings, viewers were not required to respond "yes" to one of them. In addition to the forced-choice response, viewers were asked to indicate their confidence in their judgment of each child on a 4-point scale: 0 = no confidence, 1 = somewhat confident, 2 = confident, 3 = very confident.

Table 14.1 lists the characteristics of the sibships, the number of viewers rating the sibship, and the viewer's judgments of the children after each segment. The binomial test was used to determine the probabilities associated with the numbers of correct judgments in response to those segments that included *all* members of the sibship. The significant ($p < 0.05$, one-tailed tests) and marginally significant ($p < 0.10$) p-values associated

TABLE 14.1. Viewers' Judgments of Outcome for Children in Sibships

Sibship number	Number/sex of children in sibship[a]	Number of viewers	Age span in first segment	Viewers responding "yes"	Age span in second segment	Viewers responding "yes"	Age span in third segment	Viewers responding "yes"	Age span in fourth segment	Viewers responding "yes"
I	#1/F	12	5–11 months	7	5–5.5 years	5	5.5–6 years	2 ($p < 0.05$)	9–10 years	2 ($p < 0.05$)
	#2/M*		not present	—	1–4.5 months	7	4.5–11 months	10	4–5 years	10
II	#1/F*	12	10 months–1 year	5	1–2 years	6	2–3 years	6	4–7 years	9 ($p = 0.10$)
	#2/F		not present	—	1–4 months	6	4–14 months	6	3–5 years	3
III	#1/M*	8	1–6 months	7	1–2 years	6 ($p < 0.10$)	3–4 years	5	4–6 years	6 ($p = 0.10$)
	#2/M		not present	—	1–10 months	2	1–2 years	3	2–5 years	2
IV	#1/F	7	1–4 years	5	6–10 years	0				
	#2/M*		3 months–1 year	2	3–7 years	5 ($p < 0.05$)				
V	#3/F		not present	—	1–5 years	2				
	#1/M		1 month–4 years	0	4–7 years	0	7–17 years	1	17–18 years	1
	#2/M*		1 month–1 year	5	1–4 years	6	4–14 years	6 ($p < 0.05$)	14–15 years	5 ($p < 0.05$)
	#3/M		not present	—	1 month–2 years	1	2–12 years	0	12–13 years	1
	#4/M		not present	—	not present	—	1 month–9 years	0	9–10 years	0
	#5/F		not present	—	not present	—	1–2 years	0	2–3 years	0

[a] * Indicates the preschizophrenic child.

with these judgments for each sibship are listed in Table 14.1. In two cases, the p-values are less than or equal to 0.10 at the final judgment and in three cases less than 0.05. For sibship I, the p-value is less than 0.05 following the 3rd viewing segment—the point at which the preschizophrenic child was less than 1 year of age. When the results from the three sibships containing two children are combined, the total correct judgment is 25 out of 32, with $p < 0.05$. (Data from the larger sibships cannot be included in the combined analysis because the chance probability for correct judgment is greater than 0.05.)

There was no significant relation between accuracy of judgment and confidence ratings or clinical experience of the viewers. However, most viewers commented on interpersonal and/or motor characteristics of the children, and several noticed the same "abnormalities" in the preschizophrenic children. Recorded observations about the preschizophrenic children included less "responsiveness," eye contact, positive affect, and poorer fine and gross motor coordination.

This investigation is the first to provide evidence that, through behavioral observation, individuals who succumb to schizophrenia in early adulthood can be differentiated from their healthy siblings prior to the age of 8 years. These findings are noteworthy for several reasons. First they lend support to the notion that the diathesis presumed to underlie schizophrenia is present long before the onset of psychotic symptoms. Second, the fact that viewers identified the preschizophrenic children at above-chance levels, without being instructed to use specific criteria, suggests that the distinguishing characteristics of these children are apparent at a gross level of analysis. Third, the results indicate that the archival–observational approach to the study of developmental precursors holds promise for illuminating the trajectories leading to schizophrenia.

The present findings should not be taken to imply that all individuals who eventually develop schizophrenia can be distinguished from their siblings in childhood. It should also be noted that the characteristics of the preschizophrenic children that determined the viewers' judgments may not be direct manifestations of the schizophrenic diathesis but, rather, nonspecific signs of vulnerability that are associated with increased risk for a variety of disorders. We will attempt to address these issues in future studies that will compare various diagnostic groups and subgroups.

Identifying Developmental Subtypes

As indicated, one of the chief aims of our research program is to identify subtypes of patients based on their developmental course. Ultimately, data derived from the observational coding of the videotapes will be of central importance in defining these subtypes. In the interim, we conducted a preliminary analyses of this nature using information provided by parents. Specifically, data on obstetrical complications, family history of psychopathology, academic performance through high school, socioemotional adjustment in childhood, age at onset of disorder, and clinical symptom characteristics were entered into a cluster analysis. The above variables were selected with the goal of including potential sources of constitutional vulnerability and indicators of pre-and postmorbid course. The aim was to determine whether or not theoretically meaningful subtypes emerge and, if so, whether or not these subtypes are subsequently validated in analyses using the observational data.

In this analysis, subjects were 29 schizophrenic patients (25 males and 4 females). All had DSM-III-R diagnoses of schizophrenia, as determined by the administration of a structured diagnostic interview (Schedule for the Assessment of Affective Disorders and Schizophrenia). The current mean age of the patients is 33 years (SD = 6.28), and the mean age at first diagnosis is 21 years (SD = 4.33). With the exception of one male, all patients are on medication. Three are currently hospitalized and the remainder are either living with their parents or in structured independent living situations. None are married and only one was previously married. Mean years of education is 13.5 (SD = 3.38).

The total number of pre-and perinatal complications was taken from a 36-item checklist completed by the mother of each patient. Both parents provided data on the presence of psychotic disorders in first- and second-degree relatives, and the subject was assigned a score that was the total number of affected relatives. Academic performance in each grade (Kindergarten through twelfth) was rated below average (1), average (2), or above average (3), and these ratings were summed to yield an index of academic performance. Childhood socioemotional adjustment was rated on a 7-point scale, with "0" indicating no problems and "7" indicating the most extensive problems. Separate ratings were made for the early childhood (up to age 6 years) and middle childhood (ages 6–15 years) years. Age at first diagnoses was used as the measure of age at onset of disorder. Finally, for each subject, a positive and negative symptom score was derived from a symptom checklist completed by parents.

Cluster analysis was conducted using the eight variables described above. Applying Ward's method, the optimal number of clusters was four. The four clusters were then compared, using one-way analysis of variance (ANOVA), on the variables used to derive them. The means and standard deviations of the variables, by cluster, are presented in Table 14.2. Also presented are the results of the group comparisons.

ANOVAs revealed that the clusters were significantly different on the majority of the defining variables. Cluster A (n = 5) is characterized by a significantly higher incidence of obstetrical complications than the other

TABLE 14.2. Means and Standard Deviation for Patient Clusters

	Cluster							
	A (n = 5)		B (n = 6)		C (n = 5)		D (n = 13)	
	x	SD	x	SD	x	SD	x	SD
Familial schizophrenia (F = 1.08, p = 0.30)	0.60	(0.67)	1.67	(1.00)	0.90	(0.83)	1.07	(1.00)
PCs[1a] (F = 5.84, p = 0.01) (A > B & D)	9.80	(2.77)	3.50	(1.97)	5.40	(1.14)	4.53	(3.25)
Academic performance[2b] (F = 11.47, p < .001) (D > A, B, & C; B > C; A > C)	20.20	(3.76)	22.83	(2.71)	13.40	(3.13)	34.23	(2.74)
Early childhood social adjustment[3c] (F = 11.47, p < .001) (C > A, B & D)	1.00	(1.00)	1.83	(1.72)	7.20	(1.30)	1.69	(2.42)
Middle childhood social adjustment[3c] (F= 3.40, p = 0.03) (C > D)	3.40	(2.51)	2.66	(2.87)	4.80	(2.58)	1.31	(1.49)
Age at first diagnosis (F = 1.78, p = 0.17)	21.20	(1.72)	21.00	(1.90)	17.00	(2.12)	21.85	(5.46)
Positive symptom score (F = 7.38, p = 0.001) (B > A & D)	7.00	(4.24)	14.83	(1.47)	13.40	(4.82)	8.00	(3. 61)
Negative symptom score F = 3.02, p = 0.05	4.20	(1.48)	4.83	(3.31)	8.40	(3.57)	7.23	(2. 45)

[a]Pre-, peri-, and neonatal complications.
[b]Higher scores indicate better performance.
[c]Higher scores indicate poorer adjustment.

three groups, and the lowest levels of familial mental illness, early childhood maladjustment, and positive and negative symptoms. Cluster B (n = 6), in contrast, shows the highest rate of familial mental illness, the lowest rate of obstetrical complications, and the greatest positive symptomatology. For Cluster B, scores on the remaining variables fall in the middle range. Cluster C (n = 5) is distinguished by the lowest levels of social and academic functioning in childhood, the greatest negative symptoms, and the earliest age at onset (x = 17 years; SD = 2.12). Rates of familial mental illness and obstetrical complications fall in the middle range for Cluster C. The patients in Cluster D (n = 13) show the *highest* levels of childhood social and academic functioning but are unremarkable with respect to the other variables. Finally, it is of interest to note that there was no link between sex of subject and cluster assignment; one of the four females appeared in each cluster.

Due to the small sample and the retrospective nature of much of the data, our interpretive comments about these clusters must be considered tentative. However, several aspects of the findings are noteworthy. First, there is substantial variability among the patients in their premorbid histories. Some show above-average academic abilities and, according to parent's reports, good social adjustment; others are below average academically and are perceived by parents as having social adjustment problems in early childhood. (It is important to emphasize, however, that none of the subjects were diagnosed as having any neurological or psychiatric disorder in childhood.) Again, it is the premise of this chapter that this variability in course holds important information about etiologic origins. Second, it is of interest that the two etiologic variables, obstetrical complications and family history of psychopathology, occur at their highest rates in two different clusters. This is the pattern that would be predicted if these two variables represented independent and sufficient etiologic agents. In a recent study by O'Callaghan et al. (1990), a similar dissociation between the presence of obstetric complications and family history of psychiatric disorder was found.

CONCLUSIONS

There is every indication that we are entering a new era in research on schizophrenia, but it is unlikely to be one that is marked by watershed discoveries that launch revolutions in treatment or prevention. Advances in molecular genetics and the neurosciences are offering us exciting new techniques and conceptual frameworks for exploring the nature and origins of psychopathology. However, the application of each new technique yields findings that suggest greater complexity, rather than providing specific answers. Clearly, the scientific study of schizophrenia is not a field that is well suited to those who have a low tolerance for ambiguity.

The human tendency to favor simplifying assumptions must give way to an appreciation for the complexity of schizophrenia and for the rudimentary nature of our knowledge of it. As currently defined by DSM-III-R, schizophrenia is, at best, a loose syndrome; there is not one required or core symptom. Furthermore, our criteria for differential diagnosis of schizophrenia and major affective disorder are, in large part, arbitrary. Given the current state of our knowledge, we must assume that we have yet to identify the symptom distinctions that are valid with respect to etiology.

Building a valid and reliable taxonomy of schizophrenia is a task that still lays ahead.

Moreover, even when a valid taxonomy of schizophrenic syndromes emerges, it is not likely to bear a one-to-one correspondence with categories of etiologic factors. In other words, although some subtypes of schizophrenia may be the consequence of a single etiologic agent (e.g., a completely penetrant genotype), others are likely to be the end product of multiple, interacting factors.

Staking out the boundaries of valid diagnostic types or subtypes will require more than cross-sectional studies of patients. Subtypes that are homogeneous with respect to phenomenology, cognitive profiles, neurochemistry, brain morphology, and/or treatment responsivity will not necessarily be homogeneous in etiology. The identification of etiologically valid subtypes is more likely to be achieved by employing a longitudinal approach that encompasses the patient's life course.

REFERENCES

Abel, E. L. (1989). *Behavioral teratogenesis, behavioral mutagenesis: A primer of abnormal development.* New York: Plenum.

Altshuler, L. L., Conrad, A., Konelman, J. A., and Scheibel, A. (1987). Hippocampal pyramidal cell orientation in schizophrenia. *Archives of General Psychiatry, 44*, 1094–1099.

Aylward, E., Walker, E., and Bettes, B. (1984). Intelligence in schizophrenia: A review and meta-analysis of the literature. *Schizophrenia Bulletin, 10*, 430–459.

Bateson, G. (1956). Toward a theory of schizophrenia. *Behavioral Science, 1*, 251–264.

Benes, F. M. (1989). Myelination of cortical-hippocampal relays during late adolescence. *Schizophrenia Bulletin, 15*, 585–594.

Benes, F. M., Davidson, J., and Bird, E. D. (1986). Quantitative cytoarchitectural studies of the cerebral cortex of schizophrenics. *Archives of General Psychiatry, 43*, 31–35.

Bettes, B., and Walker, E. (1987). Positive and negative symptoms in psychotic and other disturbed children. *Journal of Child Psychiatry and Psychology, 28*, 555–568.

Beuhring, J., Cudeck, R., Mednick, S. A., Walker, E. F., and Schulsinger, F. (1982). Susceptibility to environmental stress: High-risk research on the development of schizophrenia. In R. W. Neufeld (Ed.), *Psychological stress and psychopathology* (pp. 67–90). New York: McGraw-Hill.

Coryell, W., and Zimmerman, M. (1988). The heritability of schizophrenia and schizoaffective disorder. *Archives of General Psychiatry, 45*, 323–327.

Dalen, P., and Hays, P. (1990). Aetiological heterogeneity of schizophrenia: The problem and evidence. *British Journal of Psychiatry, 157*, 119–122.

Erlenmeyer-Kimling, L., Kestenbaum, C., Bird, H., and Hilldoff, U. (1984). Assessment of the New York High-Risk Project subjects in sample A who are now clinically deviant. In N. Watt, E. J. Anthony, L. Wynne, and J. Rolf (Eds.), *Children at risk for schizophrenia* (pp. 227–240). New York: Cambridge University Press.

Feinberg, I. (1982–1983). Schizophrenia: Caused by a fault in programmed synaptic elimination during adolescence. *Journal of Psychiatric Research, 17*, 319–334.

Fischer, M. (1971). Psychosis in the offspring of schizophrenic monozygotic twins and their normal co-twins. *British Journal of Psychiatry, 118*, 43–52.

Fischer, M. (1973). Genetic and environmental factors in schizophrenia. *Acta Psychiatrica Scandinavica, 238,* 1–158.

Fish, B. (1977). Neurologic antecedents of schizophrenia in children: Evidence for an inherited, congenital neurointegrative deficit. *Archives of General Psychiatry, 34,* 1297–1313.

Fuller, J. L., and Thompson, W. R. (1978). *Foundations of behavior genetics.* St. Louis, MO: C. V. Mosby.

Garner, D. L., Reich, T., Isenberg, K. E., and Cloninger, C. R. (1989). Schizophrenia and the question of genetic heterogeneity. *Schizophrenia Bulletin, 15,* 421–439.

Gershon, E. S. (1988). A controlled family study of chronic psychosis. *Archives of General Psychiatry, 45,* 337–388.

Goldman-Rakic, P. S. (1987). Development of cortical circuitry and cognitive function. *Child Development, 58,* 601–622.

Gottesman, I. I., and Bertelsen, A. (1989). Confirming unexpressed genotypes for schizophrenia. *Archives of General Psychiatry, 46,* 867–872.

Gottesman, I., and Shields, P. (1982). *Schizophrenia: The epigenetic puzzle.* New York: Cambridge University Press.

Hanson, D., Gottesman, I., and Heston, L. (1976). Some possible childhood indicators of adult schizophrenia inferred from children of schizophrenics. *British Journal of Psychiatry, 129,* 142–154.

Kendler, K. S. (1988). Familial aggregation of schizophrenia and schizophrenia spectrum disorders. *Archives of General Psychiatry, 45,* 377–386.

Kennedy, J. L., Guiffra, L. A., Moises, H. W., Canelli-Sforza, L. L., Pakstis, A. J., Kidd, J. R., Castiglione, C. M., Sjogren, B., Wetterberg, L., and Kidd, K. K. (1988). Evidence against linkage of schizophrenia to markers on chromosome 5 in a northern Swedish pedigree. *Nature, 336,* 167–170.

Kreusser, K. L., and Volpe, J. J. (1984). The neurological outcome of perinatal asphyxia. In C. R. Almli and S. Finger (Eds.), *Early brain damage.* New York: Academic Press.

Kringlen, E., and Cramer, G. (1989). Offspring of monozygotic twins discordant for schizophrenia. *Archives of General Psychiatry, 46,* 873–877.

Kubli, F., Patel, N., Schmidt, W., and Linderkamp, O. (Eds.). (1988). *Perinatal events and brain damage in surviving children.* New York: Springer-Verlag.

Lewine, R. (1981). Sex differences in schizophrenia: Timing or subtypes. *Psychological Bulletin, 90,* 432–444.

MacGillivray, L., Nylander, P. S., and Corney, G. (1975). *Human multiple reproduction.* London: Saunders.

McNeil, T. F., and Kaij, L. (1978). Obstetric factors in the development of schizophrenia: Complications in births of preschizophrenics and reproduction by schizophrenic parents. In L. C. Wynne, R. L. Cromwell, and S. Matthysse (Eds.), *The nature of schizophrenia: New approaches to research and treatment* (pp. 401–429). New York: John Wiley.

Meehl, P. (1989). Schizotaxia revisited. *Archives of General Psychiatry, 46,* 935–944.

Meehl, P. (1990). Toward an integrated theory of schizotaxia, schizotypy and schizophrenia. *Journal of Personality Disorders, 4,* 1–99.

Merikangas, K. R. (1982). Assortative mating for psychiatric disorders and psychological traits. *Archives of General Psychiatry, 39,* 1173–1180.

Mirsky, A., and Duncan, C. (1986). Etiology and expression of schizophrenia: Neurobiological and psychosocial factors. *Annual Review of Psychology, 37,* 291–319.

Mosher, L., Pollin, W., and Stabeneau, J. R. (1971). Identical twins discordant for schizophrenia; Neurological findings. *Archives of General Psychiatry, 24,* 422–430.

Nowakowski, R. S. (1987). Basic concepts of CNS development. *Child Development, 58,* 568–595.

O'Callaghan, E., Larkin, C., Kinsella, A., and Waddington, J. L. (1990). Obstetric complications, the putative familial-sporadic distinction and tardive dyskinesia in schizophrenia. *British Journal of Psychiatry, 157*, 578–584.

Offord, D., and Cross, L. (1969). Behavioral antecedents of adult schizophrenia. *Archives of General Psychiatry, 21*, 267–283.

Owen, M., Craufurd, D., and St. Clair, D. (1990). Localization of a susceptibility locus for schizophrenia on chromosome 5. *British Journal of Psychiatry, 157*, 123–127.

Pasamanick, B., and Knobloch, H. (1966). Retrospective studies on the epidemiology of reproductive casuality: Old and new. *Merrill-Palmer Quarterly, 12*, 7–26.

Plomin, R., Defries, J. C., and McClearn, G. E. (1990). *Behavioral genetics.* New York: W. H. Freeman and Company.

Pollin, W., and Stabenau, J. (1968). Biological, psychological and historical differences in a series of monozygotic twins discordant for schizophrenia. In D. Rosenthal and S. Kety (Eds.), *The transmission of schizophrenia.* Oxford: Pergamon.

Porreco, R. P. (1990). Twin gestation. *Clinical Obstetrics and Gynecology, 33.*

Prilipko, L. L. (1986). Biological studies of schizophrenia in Europe. *Schizophrenia Bulletin, 12*, 83–100.

Reveley, M. A., Reveley, A. M., and Baldy, R. (1987). Left cerebral hemisphere hypodensity in discordant schizophrenic twins. *Archives of General Psychiatry, 44*, 625–633.

Rothwell, N. V. (1976). *Understanding genetics.* Baltimore, MD: Wilkins & Wilkins.

Sackett, E. (1978). *Observing behavior: Volume II: Data collection and analysis of methods.* Baltimore, MD: University Park Press.

Saint-Anne Dargassies, S. (1986). *The neuro-motor and psycho-affective development of the infant.* New York: Elsevier.

Sameroff, A., Barocas, R., and Seifer, R. (1984). The early development of children born to mentally ill women. In N. Watt, E. J. Anthony, L. Wynne, and J. Rolf (Eds.), *Children at risk for schizophrenia* (pp. 482–514). New York: Cambridge.

Sarnat, H. B. (1984). Anatomic and physiologic correlates of neurologic development in prematurity. In H. B. Sarnat (Ed.), *Topics in neonatal neurology.* New York: Grune & Stratton.

Saugstad, L. (1989). Social class, marriage and fertility in schizophrenia. *Schizophrenia Bulletin, 15*, 9–44.

Sherrington, R., Brynjolfsson, J., Petursson, H., Potter, M., Dudleston, K., Barraclough, B., Wasmuth, J., Dobbs, M., and Gurling, H. (1988). Localization of a susceptibility locus for schizophrenia on chromosome 5. *Nature, 336*, 164–167.

Shoulson, I. (1990). Huntingtons disease: Cognitive and psychiatric features. *Neuropsychiatry, Neuropsychology and Behavioral Neurology, 3*, 15–22.

Suddath, R. L., Christison, G. W., Torrey, F., Casanova, M. F., and Weinberger, D. (1990). Anatomical abnormalities in the brains of monozygotic twins discordant for schizophrenia. *The New England Journal of Medicine, 322*, 789–794.

Taylor, M. A. (in press). The role of the cerebellum in the pathogenesis of schizophrenia. *Neuropsychiatry, Neuropsychology, and Behavioral Neurology.*

Tienari, O. (1987). Genetics and psychosocial factors in schizophrenia: The Finnish Adoptive Study. *Schizophrenia Bulletin, 13*, 477–484.

Tsuang, M. T., Lyons, M. J., and Faraone, S. V. (1990). Heterogeneity of schizophrenia conceptual models and analytic strategies. *British Journal of Psychiatry, 156*, 17–26.

Walker, E., Cudeck, R., Mednick, S. A., and Schulsinger, F. (1981). The effects of parental absence and institutionalization on the development of clinical symptoms in high-risk children. *Acta Psychiatrica Scandinavica, 63*, 95–109.

Walker, E., Downey, G., and Bergman, A. (1989). The effects of parental psychopathology and maltreatment on child behavior: A test of the diathesis–stress model. *Child Development, 60*, 313–321.

Walker, E., Downey, G., and Caspi, A. (1991). Twin studies of psychopathology. *Schizophrenia Research, 4*, 1–11.

Walker, E., Downey, G., and Nightingale, N. (1988). The nonorthogonal nature of risk factors: Implications for research on the causes of maladjustment. *Journal of Primary Prevention, 9*, 143–163.

Walker, E., and Emory, E. (1983). Infants at risk for schizophrenia: Offspring of schizophrenic parents. *Child Development, 54*, 1269–1285.

Walker, E., and Emory, E. (1985). Interpretational bias in behavior genetics research. *Child Development, 56*, 665–669.

Walker, E., and Lewine, R. (1990). Prediction of Adult-onset Schizophrenia From Childhood Home Movies of the Patients. *American Journal of Psychiatry, 147*, 1052–1056.

Walker, E., Lewine, R., and Lucas, M. (1990). Neuropsychological aspects of schizophrenia. In T. Puente and B. McCaffrey (Eds.), *Psychobiological factors in clinical neuropsychological assessment*. New York: Plenum.

Walker, E., and Shaye, J. (1982). Familial schizophrenia: A predictor of neuromotor and attentional dysfunction in schizophrenia. *Archives of General Psychiatry, 39*, 1153–1160. [Also in *Digest of Neurology and Psychiatry*, January 1983.]

Watt, N. (1978). Patterns of childhood social development in adult schizophrenics. *Archives of General Psychiatry, 35*, 160–165.

Watt, N., Anthony, E. J., Wynne, L., and Rolf, R. (Eds.). (1984). *Children at risk for schizophrenia*. New York: Cambridge University Press.

Weaver, R. F., and Hedrick, P. W. (1989). *Genetics*. Dubuque, IA: W. C. Brown Publishers.

Weinberger, D. R. (1987). Implications of normal brain development for the pathogenesis of schizophrenia. *Archives of General Psychiatry, 44*, 660–670.

Winters, K. C., Stone, A. A., Weintraub, S., and Neale, J. M. (1981). Cognitive and attentional deficits in children vulnerable to psychopathology. *Journal of Abnormal Child Psychology, 9*, 435–453.

Yarrow, M. R., Campbell, J. D., and Burton, R. V. (1970). Recollections of childhood: A study of the retrospective method. *Monographs of the Society for Research in Child Development, 35*, no. 5.

Zubin, J., and Spring, B. (1977). Vulnerability: A new view of schizophrenia. *Journal of Abnormal Psychology, 49*, 313–320.

Index

List of Previous Volumes

*Titles initiated during the series editorship of Brendan Maher.